YOUNG OFFENDERS LAW

Other books in *Essentials of Canadian Law* Series

Criminal Law

The Law of Evidence

Statutory Interpretation

Media Law

The Law of Trusts

Intellectual Property Law

Income Tax Law

The Law of Partnerships and Corporations

Constitutional Law

Immigration Law

Environmental Law

ESSENTIALS OF
CANADIAN LAW

YOUNG
OFFENDERS
LAW

NICHOLAS BALA

IRWIN
LAW

YOUNG OFFENDERS LAW

Published in 1997 by
Irwin Law
1800 Steeles Avenue West
Concord, Ontario
L4K 2P3

ISBN: 1-55221-025-1

Canadian Cataloguing in Publication Data

Bala, Nicholas, 1952–
 Young offenders law

(Essentials of Canadian law)
Includes bibliographical references and index.
ISBN 1-55221-025-1

1. Juvenile justice, Administration of – Canada.
2. Juvenile courts – Canada.   I. Title.   II. Series.

KE9445.B35 1997   345.71'08   C97-931540-9
KF9779.B35 1997

Printed and bound in Canada.

1   2   3   4   5   00   99   98   97

SUMMARY
TABLE OF CONTENTS

DETAILED
TABLE OF CONTENTS

FOREWORD

This book provides a unique and valuable contribution to understanding the law as it applies to youthful offenders in Canada. In a logical and coherent manner, it explains the *Young Offenders Act* from a legal perspective as well as offering a social and historical context. Key points are illustrated by reference to recent court cases, relevant articles, and comparative information from other jurisdictions. It also provides critical commentary, identifies current issues, and provokes the reader to consider solutions, both legal and social.

One would not expect less, since Professor Bala is by reputation an outstanding scholar and one of Canada's foremost experts in the area of youth justice. A prolific writer, he has also appeared before Senate and House of Commons committees dealing with youth justice issues, and he is frequently asked by the media to comment on issues related to family and children's law.

Professor Bala's experience and communication skills are well demonstrated in this book. As result, it will be a valuable teaching tool for students in a variety of disciplines in addition to law, including social work, corrections, and criminology. But it is also a "must read" for every professional involved in the youth justice system, including judges.

Judge Heino Lilles
Yukon Territorial Court

PREFACE

This book is intended to give law students, lawyers, and judges an introduction to an important, controversial area of Canadian law. The way in which we respond to young persons who violate the criminal law is profoundly significant, not only for those who are directly involved in the process, but also for society as a whole. While the primary focus of this work is on the *Young Offenders Act* and the functioning of the youth justice system, an understanding of legal issues, especially those that affect families and youth, requires some discussion of broader social and political issues. As well, this book explores some of the ethical and practical issues that confront lawyers and other professionals working in the youth justice system.

This work should also be a useful text for probation officers, social workers, and mental-health professionals who work with young offenders, as well as for university and college students with an interest in youth justice issues. The book, however, focuses on matters that make the youth justice system distinctive from the adult system, and readers will have to look elsewhere in the *Essentials of Canadian Law* series or other sources for a detailed introduction to the elements of substantive, procedural, and evidentiary law that are applicable to both adult and youth proceedings.

Chapter 1 provides an introduction to the youth justice system offering the rationale and history of the system and a description of the problem of youth crime in Canada. Chapter 2 discusses the principles that guide responses to youth crime; the primary focus is on the explicit Declaration of Principle found in Canada's *Young Offenders Act*, but some consideration is given to the principles that apply in other countries so that readers can appreciate the choices that have been made in this country. Chapter 3 explains the jurisdiction of the youth courts, including the controversial issues related to age jurisdiction.

Chapters 4 to 9 provide a more detailed discussion of the salient issues that can arise in a youth court case. Chapter 4 considers the issues related to the apprehension of a young person and first appearance in court, including arrest, police questioning, and pre-trial detention. Chapter 5 describes the efforts that are being made to divert young persons, especially those facing less serious charges, from the youth court before any formal hearing into various forms of alternative programs. Chapter 6 deals with access of young persons to legal services and the controversies around the role of lawyers in the youth justice system. Chapter 7 discusses youth court trials, including issues of confidentiality, publicity, and records. Chapter 8 deals with the sentencing of young offenders, including issues related to custodial placements and the judicial review of dispositions. Chapter 9 discusses transfer to adult court, an option that arises only in the most serious cases.

While law reform is not a major theme of this book, an effort is made to offer some suggestions on how to improve Canada's responses to youth crime, in particular in Chapter 10, in the context of a discussion that recognizes the limits of the law as a "solution" to the universal human problem of adolescent deviance and delinquency.

This book provides an introduction to a set of complex, interdisciplinary topics that can be the subject of lifelong study. While there are references to jurisprudence and literature, it is not my intention to offer a comprehensive legal research tool. Those with a special interest in legal issues, including law students and lawyers, will want to consult the case law and specialized legal texts. Non-lawyers with specific legal problems should get appropriate legal advice. Readers are also encouraged to study the growing body of non-legal literature that deals with youth crime. Some of the significant literature is written by criminologists and psychologists; there is also an increasing amount of research by scholars and practitioners taking a "critical" perspective, including works by feminists, Aboriginal writers, and those who have had personal experiences with the youth justice system.

Readers are also cautioned that the law is a dynamic field: case law and legislation are always subject to change. While the principles and fundamental issues related to responding to youth crime in Canada are unlikely to change dramatically, those with specific legal problems should check for recent legal developments.

I wish to thank Catherine Lawrence (Queen's Law '97), a student hired under the student summer program of Osler, Hoskin & Harcourt, for her research assistance, and also to acknowledge the support of the Dean, library, and secretarial staff at the faculty of law at Queen's University, in particular Ms. Vyvien Vella and Ms. Nancy Leake. I acknowledge as well the advice of my colleagues at Queen's, especially Donald Stuart, and David Paciocco at the University of Ottawa. I am also grateful to Judge Heino Lilles for his support and for writing the Foreword, to Curtis Fahey and Rebecca Thompson for their painstaking editorial work, and to Bill Kaplan of Irwin Law for his encouragement.

Nicholas Bala
October 1997

CHAPTER 1

THE PROBLEM OF YOUTH CRIME IN CANADA

A. ADOLESCENCE AND THE RATIONALE FOR A YOUTH JUSTICE SYSTEM

Every legal system recognizes that youths are different from adults, and should not be held accountable for violations of the criminal law in the same fashion as adults, though there are substantial differences among countries in how this principle is given effect and in how the concept of "youth" is defined. The nature and extent of special legal treatment for youth has evolved over the course of Canadian history and remains controversial today, but there is widespread appreciation that children and adolescents have special needs and limited capacities, and hence require distinctive, or at least separate, treatment from adults.

When children are born, they have no physical, moral, or social capacities. Although newborn infants have legal rights (for example, to inherit property) and are entitled to the protection of the law, these legal rights can be exercised only through a legal guardian or other adult. As they mature, children gradually gain in physical strength, intellectual judgment, and social maturity and can begin to exercise legal rights and assume legal obligations on their own. By the time adulthood is reached (currently at the age of eighteen or nineteen in Canada), a person generally has a full range of legal rights and obligations.

By the beginning of adolescence, about the age of twelve, youths display a growing sexual, social, and moral awareness, as well as increasing physical size and strength, though most continue to mature

1

physically and socially until adulthood. Indeed, attitudes, values, and behaviour change over the course of adult life as well.

Adolescence is a time of great change and development for most youth, as parents, teachers, and adolescents themselves know. Sometimes adolescents seem quite childish, but at other times they act like adults or at least want to be treated like adults. Adolescence is a period of growing self-awareness and increasing autonomy, as well as a time of challenging authority figures and testing limits. While adolescents have a growing knowledge of the world around them, they often lack judgment and maturity. Frequently, they feel as though they are "invulnerable" and act in an irresponsible fashion. In far greater numbers than adults, they engage in high-risk activities, such as unsafe sex, drunken driving, and substance abuse. There are enormous differences between countries in types and levels of crime and deviant behaviour, but in all modern societies the rates of delinquent and antisocial behaviour peak between the ages of sixteen and twenty, in late adolescence and early adulthood, reflecting the immaturity and lack of judgment of this period of life as well as its energy and search for excitement.

The present Canadian legal regime recognizes three distinct stages of criminal accountability. Childhood, lasting to the age of twelve, is without criminal liability. Youth, from twelve through seventeen years of age, a period corresponding roughly to adolescence, is a stage of life with limited accountability under the *Young Offenders Act*[1] (YOA). Adulthood, starting at eighteen, provides full legal accountability as well as a full set of adult rights. The rationale for this distinctive age-based treatment can be found in the basic premises of criminal law. The fundamental criminal law concept of moral accountability and the policy objective of social protection through deterrence of crime and rehabilitation apply differently to children and youth than to adults, because youths are different from adults.

A central premise of criminal law is that individuals are held accountable for their acts only if they have a requisite degree of moral culpability or responsibility, often known as the *mens rea* or guilty mind. Thus, a person who kills another by accident, such as the driver of a car who runs over a child who darted in front of the vehicle, may have no criminal accountability. A person who commits a criminal offence while sleepwalking, even a very serious offence like killing another person,[2] must be acquitted because of lack of intent. Those who

---

1   R.S.C. 1985, c. Y-1 [*YOA*].
2   *R. v. Parks*, [1992] 2 S.C.R. 871.

commit criminal acts while suffering from a mental disorder that renders them "incapable of appreciating the nature and quality" of their acts are not subject to conviction, though they may be confined to protect the public or themselves.[3] Because of the lack of capacity at the time of the offence, they are not accountable; if they later recover their mental capacity, they must be released, even if they have committed very serious acts.

Similarly, the *YOA* is premised on a recognition that to be a youth is to be in a state of "diminished responsibility" in a moral and intellectual sense. Adolescents, and even more so children, lack a fully developed adult sense of moral judgment. Adolescents also lack the intellectual and emotional capacity to appreciate fully the consequences of their acts. In many contexts youth will act without foresight or self-awareness. When youths are apprehended and asked why they committed a crime, the most common response is: "I don't know." Because of their lack of judgment and foresight, youths tend to be poor criminals as well, and, at least in comparison to adults, are relatively easy to apprehend. Often youths who commit horrible murders will boast of their deeds to their friends, or even take their friends to see the body of the victim, making their arrest inevitable. This is not to argue that adolescent offenders should not be morally or legally accountable for their criminal acts, but only that their accountability should, in general, be more limited than is the case for adults.

An important function of the criminal justice system is the protection of society through deterrence of potential offenders. People may resist the impulse to commit crimes for fear of being caught and punished. However, because youth, especially those who are prone to committing offences, generally have little foresight or judgment, the deterrent effect to the youth justice system is much weaker than that of the criminal justice system for adults. Although improved policing — increasing the chances of getting caught — can have some deterrent effect on youth crime, increasing the severity of sanctions — that is, increasing the consequences of getting caught has no apparent impact on youth crime.[4] This is to suggest, not that there should be no consequences for youths who commit criminal offences, but that one should not expect that social protection can be increased by imposing more severe punishments on young offenders.

---

3   *Criminal Code*, R.S.C. 1985, c. C–46 [*Code*].

4   See, e.g., A.N. Doob, V. Marinos, & K.N. Varma, *Youth Crime and the Youth Justice System in Canada: A Research Perspective* (Toronto: Centre of Criminology, University of Toronto, 1995) at 56–71.

Historically, the prime rationale for establishing a youth justice system that is separate from the adult system is the belief that youths are more amenable to rehabilitation than adults and that long-term social protection can be achieved by concentrating resources on them. At the very least, there are concerns about the corruption or abuse of children and youth if they are placed in correctional facilities with adult offenders. However, concerns about the special needs and rehabilitation of youth do not necessarily translate into "more lenient" treatment and in some circumstances actually may form the basis for an argument for a more intrusive approach or a longer period in a custody facility, albeit one that is distinct from that used for adults and has the potential for significant rehabilitation.

B. HISTORY OF THE YOUTH JUSTICE SYSTEM AND THE JUVENILE DELINQUENTS ACT

Prior to the nineteenth century there was little social or legal recognition of the special needs of children and youth. Children were subjected to harsh discipline. Except among the upper classes, from about the age of seven children were expected to work along with adults on farms and in shops, mines, and factories. Only upper-class children would receive any schooling, with the emphasis on the education of boys. While youths had few civil or property rights until the age of twenty-one, criminal liability started at the age of seven, and children convicted of criminal offences were subjected to the same punishments as adults, including hanging for such offences as theft. Children under seven were considered to be "under the age of discretion" and were not criminally accountable at common law.[5] Children between the ages of seven and fourteen could sometimes raise a *doli incapax* ("incapacity to do wrong") defence, if it was not proven that they had the capacity to "understand the nature and consequences of their acts."

The nineteenth century was a period of growing understanding of the nature and importance of childhood, with the beginnings of the modern disciplines of psychology and psychiatry. There was a growing social-reform effort aimed at improving the lives of children which was loosely linked to the movements to end slavery and later to gain the vote for women. Legislation was enacted to prohibit child labour, publicly funded education was introduced, and child-protection agencies were

---

5   *Marsh v. Loader* (1863), 14 C.B. (N.S.) 535, 143 E.R. 555 (C.P.)

established to care for homeless and orphaned children. In the latter part of the nineteenth century the "positivist" approach to criminology came into prominence, premised on a belief that children and adolescents engage in criminal behaviour as a result of external influences, such as poverty, family breakdown, and lack of education, and that with appropriate social intervention these youthful offenders could be "saved" from a life of crime. In 1857 the first Canadian legislation was enacted to separate child and adolescent offenders from adults, placing them in "training schools" or "reformatories" rather than adult penitentiaries. There were also the beginnings of community-based alternatives to juvenile incarceration, and the first juvenile probation officers began to work with youth.

In 1899 the first juvenile court was established in Chicago to deal with youthful offenders in a special judicial setting. In Canada reformers persuaded Parliament to enact the *Juvenile Delinquents Act* (*JDA*) in 1908,[6] creating a juvenile justice and corrections system with a distinct *parens patriae* ("father of the country") or welfare-oriented philosophy that was premised on positivist criminology. This approach reflected the belief that there was little need to distinguish between juveniles who were offenders and those who were abandoned or neglected by parents. W.L. Scott, one of the principal drafters of the *JDA*, explained the philosophy of the Act:

> There should be no hard and fast distinction between neglected and delinquent children. All should be recognized as in the same class and should be dealt with a view to serving the best interests of the child. . . . The spirit of the court is always that of a wise and kind, though firm and stern, father. The question is not "What has this child done?" but "How can this child be saved?"[7]

Under the *JDA* children could be subjected to "delinquency proceedings" for any violation of any federal, provincial, or municipal law or for the status offence of "sexual immorality or any similar form of vice." Although this latter "status offence" was not an offence for adults, it was felt that the welfare of children who engaged in this type of behaviour could be promoted if they were subjected to juvenile court jurisdiction and thereby obtained appropriate "treatment."

---

6   Enacted as S.C. 1908, c. 40; subject to minor amendments over the years, finally as *Juvenile Delinquents Act*, R.S.C. 1970, c. J–3 [*J.D.A.*].

7   Quoted in O. Archambault, "Young Offenders Act: Philosophy and Principles" (1983) 7:2 Prov. Judges J. 1 at 2–3.

The welfare-oriented philosophy was reflected in provisions of the *JDA* and provincial child-welfare laws that dealt in similar ways with delinquents and children in need of protection, generally processing them through the same courts and often placing them in the same facilities. Most provinces allowed children to be committed to training school for truancy and such vague "offences" as "unmanageability." The original juvenile courts were informal; most of the judges had no legal training and lawyers appeared rarely. This was intended to ensure that "unnecessary technicalities" would not interfere with or delay the treatment considered to be in the child's best interests. Indeed, the *JDA* specified that no action of a juvenile court was to be set aside because of any "informality or irregularity where it . . . [appeared] that the disposition of the case was in the best interests of the child," and it also restricted rights of appeal to courts presided over by legally trained judges.[8]

The *JDA* required judges to treat a delinquent "as far as practicable . . . not as criminal, but as a misdirected and misguided child . . . needing aid, encouragement, help and assistance."[9] This philosophy was reflected in indeterminate custodial sentencing; if a juvenile court judge ordered a delinquent to reside in a training school, the youth would be released only when juvenile correctional officials determined that this was consistent with the "best interests" of the youth, and there were broad powers to return a youth to training school until the juvenile became an adult at the age of twenty-one.

The *JDA* and the juvenile justice system that it created were an enormous improvement over the harsh treatment previously inflicted on children and adolescents, and even today the Act's child-oriented philosophy has appealing aspects. Yet it must also be recognized that the *JDA* was often applied in an arbitrary or discriminatory fashion. Youths from "good families" who committed quite serious offences might be returned to the care of their middle-class parents, while children from lower-income, Aboriginal, and immigrant families could serve long periods in training school because this was considered to be in their "best interests." Female adolescents were often sent to training school for the vaguely worded status offence of "sexual immorality," which in practice was used almost exclusively against girls, typically those from socially disadvantaged backgrounds.[10]

---

8   *JDA*, above note 6, ss. 17 & 37.
9   *Ibid.*, s. 38.
10   S. Barnhorst, "Female Delinquency and the Role of Women" (1978) 1 Can J. Fam. L. 254.

While "training schools" in theory promoted the "best interests" of their residents, their often harsh environments subjected many youths to physical and sexual exploitation by staff.[11] Tragically, the stories of the abuse of youths in juvenile facilities did not begin to become publicly known until the 1980s when the former residents, many of them emotionally scarred adults, came forward to disclose the horrors that they experienced decades earlier as juveniles in the care of the state. Although abuse in youth corrections facilities continues to be a concern, it would seem that increased government supervision and improved access to the courts for young inmates have resulted in less abuse by correctional staff.

By the 1960s the *JDA* was coming under growing scrutiny and attack. There were more legally trained judges and an increasing number of lawyers were appearing in juvenile court; the informality and lack of legal rights for youths were being challenged, especially since the *JDA* created a highly discretionary regime which gave judges, police, and juvenile correctional officials broad powers to deal with individual juveniles in accordance with the "best interests of the child." Too often, and perhaps inevitably, the discretionary "best interests" standard seemed to reflect the values and biases of individual decision makers.

There was also a concern that the *JDA* allowed for substantial interprovincial variation in how juveniles were treated. This was most obvious in regard to age jurisdiction, with the minimum age of juvenile court jurisdiction varying by province from the age of seven to fourteen, and the maximum age ranging from the sixteen to eighteen. There were also substantial disparities in access to legal services and respect for legal rights, use of diversion from juvenile court, and use of custodial sentences for juveniles.

Questions were being raised, too, about the fundamental child-oriented philosophy of the *JDA*. While there was acceptance of the importance of promoting the welfare of juveniles, there was a growing controversy about whether this should be the *only* principle guiding the societal response to juvenile offenders. A number of critics challenged the rehabilitative ideal, pointing out that many delinquents were not being rehabilitated by the juvenile justice system. Not only were there

---

11   There have been public inquiries, as well as civil suits and criminal prosecutions, against staff at many of the juvenile institutions as a result of abuse in the period from 1940 to 1980; see, e.g., "Reform school compared with Bastille," Southam News, 4 Nov. 1996; "Lay order's assets short of compensation claims," Canadian Press, 30 Oct. 1996; and *R. (G.B.) v. Hollett* (1996), 30 C.C.L.T. (2d) 215 (N.S.C.A.) [*Hollett*].

problems of abuse by staff in some juvenile correctional institutions, but even in well-run facilities many juveniles who were incarcerated under the *JDA* were not being rehabilitated and reoffended after their release.[12] The protection of the public and the accountability of offenders, critics of the *JDA* argued, were as important as rehabilitation.

Indeed, it was apparent that, even under the *JDA* as it stood, judges were not in practice focusing exclusively on the interests of children. Concerns about social protection and accountability were reflected in sentencing decisions under the *JDA*, but were most apparent in decisions about transfer to adult court, which, under the terms of the Act, was to occur only if both the "*good of the child* and the interest of the community *demand* it."[13] On its face, this standard for transfer would seem to be a high one, especially in murder cases where a juvenile might face capital punishment after transfer. Judges nevertheless regularly persuaded themselves that the "good of the child . . . [demanded]" the possibility of facing hanging rather than the much more lenient juvenile sentence.[14] While these transfer decisions may have been socially justifiable, it was appropriate to rewrite the law to acknowledge frankly that the interests of the child are not the only factor that affect decision making about transfer.

Though the deficiencies in the *JDA* were obvious, reform of the Act was not a priority of the federal government, especially in the face of controversy among different provincial governments and various advocacy groups about the best solution. The 1965 release of the federally commissioned report *Juvenile Delinquency in Canada*[15] began a lengthy period of debate and gradual reform. While some provinces, most notably Quebec, took steps to change their juvenile justice system by, for example, ensuring that youths had access to lawyers and by establishing a system of diversion of some cases from the juvenile courts, other provinces continued to maintain informal juvenile courts with little recognition of legal rights. On a federal level, discussion papers and

---

12   See, e.g., S. Shamsie, "Anti-Social Adolescents: Our Treatments Do Not Work —
      Where Do We Go From Here?" (1981) 26 Can. J. Psychiatry 357.
13   J.D.A., above note 6, s. 9(1) [Emphasis added].
14   See, e.g., *R. v. Truscott*, [1959] O.W.N. 320 at 321 (H.C.J.): ". . . [I]t would be for
      the good of the child to have his position in respect of such a serious charge
      established by a jury which would remove any possible criticism of having such
      a serious matter determined by a single [Juvenile Court] judge in *in camera*
      proceedings."
15   Canada, Department of Justice, Committee on Juvenile Delinquency, *Report:
      Juvenile Delinquency in Canada* (Ottawa: Queen's Printer, 1965).

draft legislation were released and commented upon, but it was only in February 1981 that the bill which would finally be enacted as the *Young Offenders Act* was tabled in Parliament.

The constitutional entrenchment of the *Canadian Charter of Rights and Freedoms*[16] in 1982 provided a strong impetus to federal action. The informality and lack of legal rights for juveniles in the *JDA* were inconsistent with the legal protections recognized in the *Charter,* while the interprovincial variation allowed by the *JDA* appeared inconsistent with the equal protection of the law guaranteed by section 15 of the *Charter,*[17] a provision that came into effect in 1985. The *Young Offenders Act* was enacted with the support of all members of Parliament in 1982 and came into force on 1 April 1984.

The *YOA* provided much more recognition of legal rights than the *JDA* as well as establishing a uniform national age jurisdiction from twelve to eighteen, consistent with the emphasis in the *Charter* on due process of law and equal treatment under the law. The *YOA* balances a concern for the special needs of youth with the importance of protection of the public; in particular, with regard to sentencing issues, it provides for determinate (fixed) custodial dispositions, subject to early judicially controlled release. The *YOA* regulates every stage of the youth justice process, including arrest and police questioning, alternatives to court, access to legal counsel, disclosure of information, and the sentencing process, as well as the possibility of transfer to adult court for those youth charged with the most serious offences. The *YOA* moved away from a welfare-oriented philosophy, abolishing the vague status offence of "sexual immorality" and focusing on federal criminal offences. At the same time as the *YOA* came into force, most provinces transferred some or all of the responsibility for young offenders from the social services ministry to the adult corrections ministry, though this was not required by the *YOA* and Quebec maintains a youth justice and corrections system that is closely linked to the child-welfare system.

In 1986 several minor amendments were made to respond to some of the concerns raised by police and provincial governments about difficulties with implementing the *YOA,* regulating such matters as record

---

16 Enacted as Part I of the *Constitution Act, 1982,* being Schedule B to the *Canada Act 1982* (U.K.), 1982, c. 11 [*Charter*].

17 *Ibid.* Policy makers in 1982 *feared* that the differences in age jurisdiction under the *JDA,* above note 6, would violate s. 15 of the *Charter* and acted to prevent a court challenge. No court ever ruled on this issue, and there is an argument that such variations might be constitutionally justifiable in a federal state; see *R. v. S.(S)* [1990] 2 S.C.R. 254, [*S. (S.)*].

keeping, breach of probation orders, and publication of identifying information about dangerous young persons.[18]

By the late 1980s the *YOA* was becoming the subject of growing public criticism, in particular about the perceived inadequacy of the maximum three-year sentence for dealing with violent young offenders, especially those convicted of murder, and of the difficulty in transferring youths to the adult court, where they would face much longer sentences. The Progressive Conservative government responded by enacting amendments that came into force in 1992, lengthening the maximum sentence for murder in youth court to five years less a day, and amending the transfer provisions to stipulate that the "protection of the public" was to be the "paramount" consideration.[19]

In 1995 the Liberal government enacted another set of amendments, primarily intended to demonstrate a "get tough" approach to the public, in particular for the most violent offenders. These amendments lengthened the maximum youth court sentence for murder to ten years, facilitated transfer of youths charged with the most serious offences to adult court where longer sentences could be imposed, and promoted information sharing with professionals in the community, such as teachers.[20] At the same time, amendments were introduced to emphasize the rehabilitative themes of the *YOA* and to attempt to increase the use of community-based dispositions for youths who do not pose a risk of serious harm to the community.

C. CANADIAN POLITICS AND YOUTH CRIME

It is ironic that the *YOA*, which was supported by all federal political parties when enacted by Parliament in 1982 and was hailed as ushering in a "new era" in juvenile justice, has become the focus of public controversy and is attacked by federal and provincial politicians across a broad political spectrum for being too lenient with young offenders and

---

18   *An Act to amend the Young Offenders Act, the Criminal Code, the Penitentiary Act and the Prisons and Reformatories Act,* R.S.C. 1985 (2d Supp.), c. 24, in force 1 September 1986 and 1 November 1986.

19   *An Act to amend the Young Offenders Act and the Criminal Code,* S.C. 1992, c. 11. See N. Bala, "Dealing with Violent Young Offenders: Transfer to Adult Court and Bill C-58" (1990) 9 Can. J. Fam. L. 11; see also ch. 9.

20   *An Act to amend the Young Offenders Act and the Criminal Code,* S.C. 1995, c. 19 [*YOA*]. See N. Bala, "The 1995 *Young Offenders Act* Amendments: Compromise or Confusion?" (1994) 26 Ottawa L. Rev. 643 ["Amendments"]; see also ch. 9.

failing to protect society adequately. In 1993, for the first time in Canadian history, politicians made young offenders an election "issue," with all parties taking a "stand" on (or more typically against) the YOA. In the 1993 election the four "national" parties played to growing public fears of youth crime and pledged to "toughen" the YOA, though the Bloc Québécois was prepared to "speak out against law and order rhetoric" and supported the YOA, taking an approach consistent with the more child-welfare-oriented policies of the province of Quebec.[21] These attacks on the YOA continued in the 1997 election campaign.

While there has been an increase in police reports of youth crime in Canada in recent years, there is debate about whether this is largely a reflection of changes to reporting practices — for example, by school officials who are now required by "zero tolerance" policies to report minor assaults that in the past would have been informally resolved[22] — or whether there has actually been an increase in levels of youth crime in Canada since the YOA came into force in 1984. Certain key indicators of serious youthful criminality, like the youth homicide rate, have remained relatively constant. However, media reports of youth violence and public anxiety about the problem have escalated dramatically in Canada[23]; there is now a widespread view that the JDA afforded the public much greater protection than the YOA, even though there have been substantial increases under the YOA in rates of use of custody for young offenders. The media, by focusing on relatively rare instances of serious youth violence, may distort public perceptions. Fears about youth crime may also be fuelled by the aging make-up of the population and by the insecurity felt by many in the face of accelerating social and economic change. Some of the fear may also have unarticulated elements of racism, as reflected in certain expressions of concern about crimes committed by immigrant or visible-minority youth.

There may also be an element of "anti-youth" sentiment in criticism of the YOA. While the social and economic prospects of young people today are worse than those a generation ago, it is also true that the dress, language, and appearance of many adolescents are less respectful of adults than in the past. Adolescent attitudes of today reflect a culture

---

21   The Liberals, Reform, Progressive Conservatives, and even the "leftist" New Democratic Party. See Bala, "Amendents," ibid. at 652.

22   Contrast P.J. Carrington, "Has Violent Youth Crime Increased? Comment on Corrado and Markwart" (1995) 37 Can. J. Crim. 61; and A. Markwart & R.R. Corrado, "A Response to Carrington" (1995) 37 Can. J. Crim. 74.

23   J.B. Sprott, "Understanding Public Views of Youth Crime and the Youth Justice System" (1996) 38 Can J. Crim. 271.

that is more individualistic and less respectful of authority. Does some of the political rhetoric about the *YOA* reflect adult fears that young people seem increasingly "out of control" and perhaps less likely than the youth of earlier generations to assume future roles as productive tax-paying citizens?

An important element of the political and administrative concerns about youth justice issues relates to the division of responsibilities between the federal and provincial governments[24] in this sphere. The federal government has jurisdiction under the *Constitution Act, 1867,* section 91(27), over "Criminal Law . . . [and] procedure," while the provinces have jurisdiction under section 92(14) for the "Administration of Justice" as well as responsibility for such related matters as education, child welfare, and health. The federal legislative power in this area has been interpreted by the courts "in its widest sense" to permit the federal Parliament to enact laws "intended to prevent . . . juveniles [from becoming] prospective criminals and to assist them to be law-abiding citizens."[25] The courts have consistently rejected challenges under section 92 of the *Constitution Act* to the scope of the *JDA*[26] and the *YOA*. They have also rejected *Charter* challenges to the *YOA*, accepting that some restrictions on the rights of young persons are justifiable in light of the more limited sanctions that they face.[27]

While the federal government has a broad power to enact legislation dealing with young offenders, and may deal with such issues as protection of the privacy of proceedings[28] and the establishment of non-court alternative measures,[29] it is the provincial governments which are obliged to implement these laws, including paying for all of the legal, judicial, correctional, and social services required for youths. The federal government has paid some of the increased expenses

---

24   Territorial governments have the same responsibilities as provincial governments, but for the sake of simplicity most references in this text are to only provincial governments.

25   *British Columbia (A.G.) v. S.,* [1967] S.C.R. 702 at 710.

26   Some of the provisions of the *JDA,* above note 6, which failed to adequately recognize legal rights were successfully challenged in the period after the *Charter* came into effect in 1982 and before the *YOA,* above note 1, came into force in 1984. See N. Bala "Constitutional Challenges Mark Demise of Juvenile Delinquents Act" (1983) 30 C.R. (3d) 245.

27   See, e.g., *R. v. L.(R.)* (1986), above note 16, 52 C.R. (3d) 209 (Ont. C.A.), upholding denial of right to a jury trial.

28   *Southam Inc. v. R.* (1984), 48 O.R. (2d) 678 (H.C.J.), aff'd. (1986), 53 O.R. (2d) 663 (C.A.).

29   *S.(S.),* above note 17.

caused by the enactment of the *YOA*, such as part of the increased costs for legal services for youths, but over the years different provincial governments have disagreed with various provisions of the *YOA* for both financial and philosophical reasons. For example, when the *YOA* was enacted, provinces like Ontario, which had a maximum age of sixteen under the *JDA*, opposed establishing eighteen as the minimum age of adult jurisdiction; however, Quebec, which already used eighteen under the *JDA*, supported this age. The opposition of Ontario reflected concerns about the cost of an increase in their youth-court age jurisdiction, as well as belief that sixteen- and seventeen- year-olds are mature enough to be treated like adults.

In a federal system, it is understandable that provincial politicians will criticize federal politicians for imposing costs and obligations on provincial governments. Although the federal government consults with provincial governments about changes to the *YOA*, the provinces do not always agree among themselves, and consensus with the federal government may not be achieved. The federal government has provided some financial support for young offenders services, but the amounts are diminishing while federal conditions for providing funds are increasing. This is bound to cause political tension and to be reflected in the statements of politicians about the *YOA*.

There is another dimension to some of the provincial critiques of the *YOA*. With growing public concern over youth crime, the Act is an easy target for provincial politicians who are responsible for many of the expensive services that actually affect public safety, such as policing, social services, and welfare. It may be easier for provincial politicians to attack the *YOA* for not being "tough enough" than to take responsibility for improving police services to increase community protection or to make the changes to the health, education, and social service systems that will in the long term produce a less violent society.

The political demands for "getting tough" have included calls to amend the *YOA* to have longer sentences and more transfers to adult court, public disclosure of names of young offenders, lowering of the maximum and minimum ages, and parental financial liability for the crimes committed by their children. There have even been demands for the *YOA's* repeal, though even the advocates of this position foresee having separate correctional facilities for youths and perhaps special treatment for less serious adolescent offenders.[30] The demands to "get

---

30 See, e.g., R. Howard, "Reform's grassroots dig in on tough ground: Party would scrap Young Offenders Act, new gun-control law," [Toronto] *Globe and Mail* (8 June 1996) A4.

tough" are an important, and at times dominant, theme of the present political discourse about the problem of youth crime, but most politicians also appear to appreciate the limitations of this approach.

At the same time as making demands for "getting tough" with youth crime, politicians are increasingly aware of the costs of an approach to youth crime that emphasizes use of expensive custody facilities. While the numbers of youth in custody has risen sharply since the YOA came into force, more than three-quarters of youth receiving custodial dispositions have not committed violent offences. One of the less publicized themes of the 1995 YOA reforms has been a direction to the judiciary to increase use of community-based sentences for youths not committing offences involving serious personal injury. There was also a specific addition to the Act's Declaration of Principle recognizing that crime prevention and the protection of society are best achieved by addressing the causes of crime and rehabilitating youth.[31] Although less publicized than the demands to toughen the YOA, there are many examples of Canadian politicians recognizing the need to address the root causes of youthful criminality. In introducing the 1995 YOA amendments that increased youth sentences for murder, the then justice minister, Allan Rock, observed: "If the answer to crime was simply harsher laws, longer penalties and bigger prisons, then the United States would be nirvana today. . . . We are only going to be able to have long term and effective results if we create a society in which we minimize the conditions which breed crime."[32]

Even Ontario's Progressive Conservatives, who campaigned on a law-and-order platform and a promise of "boot camps" for young offenders, recognized once in office that there is no "quick fix" for youth crime. The government's "strict discipline" custody pilot program emphasizes competent staffing, counselling, education, and employment skills, while accepting that "discipline" as a punishment will not prevent youths from reoffending but must be part of a program to change the attitudes and values of young offenders and instil self-discipline. Following

---

31   YOA 1995, above note 20, s. 15(i) (enacting YOA, above note 1, s. 24 (1.1). YOA 1995, ibid., s. 1 (enacting YOA, ibid., s. 3(i)(a) and (c.1)). See ch. 8. Even the Reform Party, which is seeking to "replace the Young Offenders Act with measures that hold young criminals accountable for their actions," also pledges to "[p]ursue crime prevention through social policies that strengthen families and communities." "Pledges run from jobs to criminal justice changes" [Toronto] Globe and Mail (18 October 1996) A4. Also Reform Party of Canada, A Fresh Start for Canadians (1997 election platform), ch. 4.

32   R. Howard, "Longer terms for young killers expected in legislation today," [Toronto] Globe and Mail (2 June 1994) A6.

a period in a secure-custody setting, the new program has a significant community-placement component which involves families and, where appropriate, helps the youth secure employment.[33]

Between 1995 and the spring of 1997 a House of Commons committee held hearings across Canada to review responses to youth crime and propose amendments. The final report of the committee[34] reflected the political tensions over youth justice issues. The Liberal majority wrote a report that tried to place greater emphasis on crime prevention and rehabilitation while at the same time "toughening" the YOA. The report, for example, recommended increased federal spending on crime prevention and greater use of alternatives to the youth court such as family-group conferencing. It advocated explicit recognition of the principle that the protection of society is the main goal of criminal law but that, for young offenders, protection of society, crime prevention, and rehabilitation are mutually reinforcing strategies. However, the report also recommended lowering the minimum age of youth court jurisdiction to ten years for serious offences, publication of the names of young offenders who are believed to pose a risk of serious harm to the community after their release, and the enactment of provisions to facilitate the admission of statements made by youths to the police.

The Bloc Québécois members of the committee criticized the majority report for its lack of understanding of the problem of youth crime and opposed any amendments to the Young Offenders Act. The Bloc also opposed any efforts by the federal government to change provincial spending priorities in the youth justice field, arguing that provincial jurisdiction must be respected. The Reform Party likewise criticized the Liberal majority for its recommendations about spending in the crime prevention field, since this is primarily an area of provincial jurisidiction. It advocated sweeping changes to the YOA, including lowering the age jurisidiction to ten through fifteen years of age, providing automatic transfer to adult court for fourteen- and fifteen- year-olds charged with violent offences, imposing longer sentences in youth court, and increasing the publication of identifying information about young offenders.

---

33   Ontario, Solicitor General & Minister of Correctional Services, *Recommendations from Task Force on Strict Discipline for Young Offenders* (Toronto: Queen's Printer, 1996); see also Canada, House of Commons. *Twelfth Report of the Standing Committee on Justice and the Solicitor General: Crime Prevention in Canada: Toward a National Strategy* (Ottawa: Supply and Services, 1993) (Chair: Bob Horner).

34   Canada, House of Commons *Thirteenth Report of the Standing Committee on Justice and Legal Affairs: Renewing Youth Justice* (Ottawa: Supply & Services, 1997).

The present justice minister, Anne McLellan, has recognized the lack of public confidence in the youth justice system and appears determined to respond to the growing public fears about violent crime.[35] She has indicated that the federal government will be providing financial support for various crime-prevention initiatives but will also amend the *YOA* to deal more severely with the most violent of youths. This might involve lowering the age of youth court jurisdiction to ten, at least for the most serious cases, and a further round of amendments to the transfer provisions to provide longer sentences in adult facilities for the most serious offenders. While these measures may appease some of the critics of the Act, given the level of public anger and the fact that the youth crime is not likely to be significantly affected by these legislative measures, demands for further "toughening" of the *YOA* are unlikely to be silenced soon.

D. THE NATURE AND CAUSES OF YOUTH CRIME

While a detailed discussion of the nature and causes of youth crime is beyond the scope of this work, one must have an appreciation of these issues in order to understand the youth justice system, and professionals must have sensitivity to the complexities and variation in youth crime to work effectively in that system.

In 1994–95 almost 110,000 criminal cases involving young persons were heard by youth courts, representing about 18 percent of all criminal cases in Canada, even though youths aged twelve to seventeen represent only about 8 percent of the population.[36] Since some youths were charged on more than one occasion, these cases involved about 67,000 youths, roughly 3 percent of the population aged twelve through seventeen. Charge rates are low for twelve-year-olds but increase rapidly each year until sixteen, when they start to level off; over half of all charges under the *YOA* involve sixteen- and seventeen-year-olds.

Males represent just over 80 percent of youths charged, though the proportion of female adolescents charged has been slowly increasing in recent years. The majority of youths are charged with property-related offences like break and enter or theft. Over one-fifth of all charges against young persons arise out of breach of probation terms, or a failure to

35   "McLellan targets youth crime," [Toronto] *Globe and Mail*, 25 Aug. 1997, A1.
36   Statistics Canada, Canadian Centre for Justice Statistics, *Youth Court Statistics 1994–95* (Ottawa: Statistics Canada, 1996) [Statistics].

attend court or to obey a court order; in other words, a substantial number of youths are involved in the youth justice system, not because of any immediate danger to the public, but because of their failure to respond appropriately to earlier judicial intervention concerning another offence.

About one-fifth of charges involve violence, with minor assaults being by far the most common offence. While the media focuses on youth homicide (murder, manslaughter, and infanticide), these represent a tiny fraction of all charges, with under 100 youth homicide charges a year. The youth-homicide rate in Canada has remained relatively constant over the past few decades at about 2 per 100,000 youths. Although Canada's youth-homicide rate is less than one-sixth of that of the United States, it is the second-highest in the industrial world.[37]

The number of charges under the YOA has increased dramatically over the past decade, but it now appears to be levelling off, at least in regard to property offences, though youth court charges for some categories of violent offences continue to increase. Official youth court statistics, however, only tell part of the story, and there is a serious debate among criminologists about whether or not the level of youth crime in Canada is increasing.[38] Most offences involving youth are not reported to the police or other authorities, and, even for those cases reported to the police, there is significant discretion about whether to lay a charge and take a youth to court or deal with the matter informally (for example, by warning the youth and speaking to the parents). Some criminologists argue that the increase in youth crime statistics is due to increased reporting to the police: for instance, by school officials with a "zero tolerance" policy that requires reporting to the police of minor assaults which in the past might have been dealt with by the schools. Other criminologists, and many of those who work with youth, in schools as well as other places, recognize that some of the increase in youth court cases reflects changes in reporting practices, but they also believe that changes in the family, social, and cultural structure of Canadian society are producing youth who are more prone to violence and offending.

We now live in a society where mass culture, in particular movies and music but also computer games and television, sometimes seems to glorify violence. Family structures and behaviour are changing, with divorce and single-parent families increasingly common; even in two-parent families, both parents may be working long hours, leaving less

---

37   W. Meloff & R.A. Silverman, "Canadian Kids Who Kill" (1992) 34 Can. J. Crim. 15; T. Harper, "The truth is, kids aren't getting away with murder," *Toronto Star* (7 September 1996) C1.

38   Contrast Carrington, above note 22, and Markwart and Corrado, above note 20.

time and energy for involvement with their children. We are also living at a time when youth unemployment is at an historic high and the economic future for many youths seems uncertain. All of these factors may be affecting youth crime rates in Canada. Ultimately, it is not possible to establish with certainty the extent to which the increase in reported youth crime reflects actual changes in behaviour as opposed to changes in reporting. Probably both factors play a role.

Even if the level of youthful offending is not increasing, considering the extent of underreporting, youth violence is a serious social problem. In particular, it is apparent that the most frequent victims of youth crime are other adolescents, and there is significant evidence that many Canadian youth are afraid of acts of violence and extortion perpetrated by other youths in their schools and elsewhere.[39]

Studies based on interviews and anonymous surveys of adolescents indicate that almost all youth commit some offences, primarily property-related or involving drugs or alcohol, but that most of these offences are not reported. Indeed, widespread adolescent offending occurs in all societies, though its nature and extent vary. Typically, youths commit relatively few, minor offences and may not be apprehended, or, if arrested and sent to youth court, do not reoffend. Other adolescents, however, have a more serious history of illegal behaviour; they commit a greater number and broader range of offences, and, if apprehended, may reoffend, despite a custodial sentence. A relatively small portion of all adolescents are within the latter group of more serious, repeat offenders, but they are responsible for a disproportionately large amount of violent offences and cause the youth justice system the greatest difficulty. A Montreal study, for example, found that 6 percent of youths account for 20 percent of those brought before the youth courts and for 50 percent of the charges.[40]

There is no single theory or explanation for why adolescents commit crimes, or why some youths commit more violent offences or repeatedly offend. There is no model that can predict with certainty whether a particular youth will or will not offend, or, whether if apprehended and sent to youth court, will reoffend despite intervention by the youth justice system. There are cases of youths who are seemingly normal and from advantaged backgrounds without any prior history of

---

39 See, e.g., C. Ryan, F. Matthews, & J. Banner, *Student Perceptions of Violence* (Toronto: Central Toronto Youth Services, 1993); and S. Trevethan, "Teenage Victims of Violence" (1992) 12:6 Juristat 1. Also: "Shakedowns in the schoolyard," [Toronto] *Globe and Mail*, 4 Oct. 1997, A1.

40 National Crime Prevention Council, *Offender Profiles* (Ottawa: The Council, 1995), at 5.

offending and who commit the most brutal crimes, with no apparent explanation, but these cases where offending behaviour appears inexplicable are relatively rare. More commonly, there are social and personal "risk factors" that are strongly predictive of adolescents who are likely to be involved in the youth justice system on a recurrent basis. The American Psychological Association observes:

> Although no definitive answer yet exists that would make it possible to predict exactly which individuals will become violent, many factors have been identified as contributing to a child's risk profile. Biological factors, child rearing conditions, ineffective parenting, emotional or cognitive development, gender differences, sex role socialization, relation to peers, cultural milieu, social factors such as economic inequality and lack of opportunity, and media influences among others, all are thought to be factors that contribute to violent behaviour. Psychologists continue to search for a unified theoretical model that can account for these factors and assign them appropriate weight as risk factors for a child's or adolescent's involvement as a perpetrator, victim, bystander or witness.[41]

Among the factors that are associated with a high risk of serious or repeat offending are

- poor parenting behaviour, which includes abuse, poor supervision or neglect, and erratic or excessive discipline;
- high levels of parental conflict and living in a family where there is spousal abuse or battering (even without direct abuse of the children);
- parental drug addiction, alcoholism, violence, lack of maturity, or a parental record of criminal activity;
- school difficulties, which may be due to learning disabilities[42] or a condition like fetal alcohol syndrome;
- economic deprivation, especially when associated with parental unemployment or receipt of social assistance (poverty often exacerbates other risk factors but in itself does not significantly correlate with delinquency); and
- drug or alcohol abuse.

---

41 American Psychological Association, Commission on Youth Violence, *Violence and Youth: Psychology's Response* (Washington, D.C.: American Psychological Association, 1993) at 17.

42 Research indicates that as many as three-quarters of young offenders in custody have some form of learning disability; assessment and treatment of young offenders should take this into account. See Learning Disabilities Association of Canada, *Position Paper on the Proposed Amendments to the Young Offenders Act* (Ottawa: The Association, 1996).

While most serious or repeat offenders have at least one of these risk factors, and often more than one, not all of them do and many youths from "deprived" backgrounds do not have difficulties with the justice system. The lack of a clear explanation for youthful criminality suggests that this is a social problem that can never be totally "solved." The fact that virtually all youths engage in some criminal activity also indicates that at least some level of youthful offending should probably be viewed as "normal." Although social and legal policies may reduce (or increase) levels of offending behaviour, they cannot eliminate all youth crime. This does not mean that youth crime should not be the subject of legal response, but it is important to view the issue in context.

E. GROUP AND GANG OFFENCES

One of the realities of youth crime is that most offences involve more than one adolescent perpetrator. In many cases, a few youths form an informal group of friends who become involved in committing criminal acts, perhaps with one or more youths taking a ringleader role and others feeling in some way pressured to participate. Adolescents who are generally law-abiding may become involved in criminal activities when they are with a group of peers. This has, for example, resulted in incidents of "swarming," where large groups of middle-class adolescents become involved in robberies or acts of violence, sometimes against lone individuals.

The term "gang" does not have a precise legal or sociological definition, but it is generally used to describe a group of adolescents and young adults who regularly engage in joint criminal activity. There is great diversity in the composition and activities of youth gangs. Some gangs are essentially a loose group of friends who only occasionally engage in criminal acts, usually without much planning. Other gangs can have a quite stable membership and leadership structure, perhaps with some form of a code of behaviour or dress. Some of these criminally oriented gangs form along ethnic lines, though they may also be ethnically mixed; these gangs may engage in criminal acts with more deliberation and a clearer monetary objective, for example, engaging in drug dealing and extortion. Violence between and within such criminal gangs, as well as against innocent victims, may be common.[43]

---

43   See, e.g., R. Weiler, T. Caputo, & K. Kelly, *Youth Violence and Youth Gangs: Responding to Community Concerns* (Ottawa: Solicitor General Canada, 1994); I.A. Spergel, *The Youth Gang Problem: A Community Approach* (New York: Oxford University Press, 1995).

Participation in group or gang activity may be legally significant in that youths may be charged as "parties" to an offence pursuant to section 21 of the *Criminal Code* if they form a common intention to commit a criminal act and provide assistance in doing the act. A "party" to an offence is technically equally guilty to the principal perpetrator. However, youth courts tend to be more lenient in transfer to adult court and sentencing decisions when dealing with a youth whose role in the offence was that of a relatively minor party as opposed to a principal perpetrator. In particular, if a situation involves a very serious offence, like homicide or a sexual assault, the court will assess the violence and character of each youth before passing sentence or deciding whether to transfer the youth to adult court. As observed by one judge in a transfer case: "[It] is self-evident that a young person who delivers the death blows to a victim is more likely to be a threat to the safety of the public than one who is an aider or abetter, and perhaps a somewhat reluctant one, to a murder."[44]

Sometimes a youth court will feel that a particularly severe response to an offence is necessary because it involved a gang member and a "message" must be sent to other gang members in the community — that is, a sentencing or transfer decision may be intended to have a deterrent effect. In upholding a sentence of twenty-four months' service custody for a seventeen-year-old member of a "street gang" who injured another youth while the gang was stealing skateboards, the Manitoba Court of Appeal stated:

> Although deterrence to others is less of a goal in the case of a young offender, it remains a factor in a group crime such as this. Extremely violent behaviour by groups of youth simply cannot be tolerated. A lengthy term of secure custody is therefore in order.[45]

---

44 *R. v. S.(G.)* (1991), 5 O.R. (3d) 97 at 108 (C.A.), Goodman J.A.

45 *R. v. E.(R.K.)* (1996), 107 Man. R. (2d) 200 at 204 (C.A.), Twaddle J.A. Amendments to the *Code*, above note 3, enacted by *An Act to amend the Criminal Code (Criminal Organizations) and to amend other Acts in consequence*, S.C. 1997, c. 23, also create a specific offence for a person who "participates in or substantially contributes to the activities of a criminal organization . . . and . . . is a party to the commission of an indictable offence . . . in association with the criminal organization" (s. 467.1). Sentencing of a young person convicted under this provision is under the *YOA*, above note 1; unlike for adults, under the *YOA* there is no automatic penalty for a violation of s. 467.1.

F. VISIBLE MINORITY AND ABORIGINAL OFFENDERS

While youths from all economic and racial backgrounds commit offences, there are special issues related to visible-minority and Aboriginal youth in Canada and indeed in other countries as well. There is no nationwide Canadian data on the race of young offenders, other than Aboriginal status, since this type of information can be difficult to obtain reliably and governments have been reluctant to collect it for fear that it may be misused. A number of studies have been done, however, and some police forces and corrections departments have race-based information. It is clear from the available data that a majority of young offenders are Caucasian, but youths from certain racial and national backgrounds, including Black, Aboriginal, and East Asian youth, are over-represented in the youth justice system.[46]

Although there is debate about the causes for the higher representation of youths from certain racial backgrounds in the justice system, there are two basic explanations. First, the social and economic conditions faced by youths with certain racial and ethnic backgrounds affect relative rates of offending behaviour. Secondly, racism and discriminatory behaviour on the part of police, justice, and corrections officials affect how youths of different races are dealt with by the justice system. While some try to argue that differences in reported offence rates are exclusively a product of racism, or exclusively a reflection of the differential offending patterns which in turn are a product of social and economic conditions,[47] it is apparent that both are operative concerns.[48] It is also

---

46 See, e.g., Ontario, *Report of the Commission on Systemic Racism in the Ontario Criminal Justice System* (Toronto: Queen's Printer, 1995) at 85 [*Systemic Racism*]; and L.D. Bertrand *et al.*, *The Experiences of Minority Youth in the Canadian Justice System* (Calgary: Canadian Research Institute for Law and the Family, 1996).

47 There are also a few "biological determinists," like psychologist Philippe Rushton of the University of Western Ontario, who seek genetic explanations for differential rates of criminal behaviour, though there is no evidence from biologists or geneticists to support these extreme views.

48 Since Canadian researchers are only starting to address this type of issue, it is difficult to draw conclusions about the weighting of the factors. An American scholar writing about his assessment of the experience in the United States concluded: "Racial disparities, especially affecting Blacks, have long bedeviled the criminal justice system. . . . Racial bias and stereotyping no doubt play some role, but they are not the major cause. In the longer term, disparities in jail . . . are mainly the result of racial differences in offending patterns." M. Tonry, "Racial Politics, Racial Disparities, and the War on Crime" (1994) 40 Crime & Delinquency 475 at 479–80.

apparent that, in some of the incidents of race-related violence in high schools, visible-minority youth are as likely to be victims as perpetrators.

From all that is known about the causes of delinquent behaviour, one would expect that youths who are members of minority groups that are socially and economically disadvantaged would have higher youth crime rates. While media reports express concerns about Aboriginal and immigrant youth gangs and violence in urban Canada, more in-depth news reports also acknowledge that "[p]olice, sociologists and outreach workers agree the street-gang phenomenon is the consequence of an endemic and unrelenting cycle of poverty, racism, family breakdown and unemployment."[49]

Children from some disadvantaged immigrant groups have higher youth crime rates: the relative poverty, social dislocation, family stresses, and cultural upheaval often associated with immigration all play a role. Children who have grown up in brutal war-torn environments or refugee camps and then move to Canada may face special risks.[50]

Aboriginal youth on reserves and in cities also face enormous challenges. They often grow up in communities that are culturally and economically marginalized by the dominant society and where parenting skills have been damaged by intergenerational cycles of abuse and violence; patterns of abuse can often be traced back to the victimization that was experienced in residential schools.[51] Unemployment and a host of social problems also affect Aboriginal communities and have an impact on the criminal behaviour of adolescents.

Studies have long documented the problem of racism in the American justice system.[52] There is now a growing body of evidence that racism affects how Canadian youth are dealt with by the justice system, including police arrest practices, as well as decisions in the courts by judges, lawyers, and probation officers and the actions of corrections officials.[53] While many of those who work in the youth justice system in Canada are sensitive to issues of racism, and are trying to ensure that their decisions and actions are not tainted, there continues to be concerns, for

---

49   D. Roberts, "The street gangs of Winnipeg," *[Toronto] Globe and Mail* (18 May 1996) D5.

50   See, e.g., T. Appleby, "Battle-scarring tied to violence" *The [Toronto] Globe and Mail* (13 June 1990) A8; and M. Valpy, "When Jamaican children come to Canada" *[Toronto] Globe and Mail* (5 March 1996) A17.

51   See, e.g., R. Ross, *Returning to the Teachings: Exploring Aboriginal Justice* (Toronto: Penguin, 1996) [*Returning*].

52   See, e.g., L. LeFlore, "Minority Youth in the Juvenile Justice System: A Judicial Response" (1990) 41 Juv. & Fam. Ct. J. 1.

53   See, e.g., *Systemic Racism*, above note 46 at 85; and Bertrand *et al.*, above note 46.

example, about the high incidence of police shooting of visible-minority youths and young adults.

In recent years, incidents of overt racism have been relatively rare, at least in the courts, since professionals are more cautious about what they say, though outside the courtroom there are many documented cases of police and correctional workers using racial epithets and stereotyping, and some lawyers and judges may do so as well. In some cases in the courtroom, judicial bias is barely disguised, as in a 1990 Toronto case where the sentencing judge stated:

> [s]ometimes I send young men from Vietnam to jail rather severely. They've been in Canada a short time . . . and I have to work out a sentence that appears to have no bias. We're supposed to treat everyone in front of us the same way . . . but often I have to lay out sentences to make it clear that in the circumstances of recent immigrants' arrival into Canada. . . . I lay out some severe sentences that perhaps wouldn't apply in the same set of facts with someone who'd been in Canada [longer].[54]

This judge, while alluding to the need to treat everyone fairly, is stating that recent immigrants from Vietnam should be punished more severely. Surely this is a discriminatory practice.

Beyond the more obvious discriminatory attitudes and acts, there is a concern that race may have a subtle, often unconscious cumulative effect over a range of decisions, including those involving charging and arrest, failure to use non-court diversion, pre-trial detention, adjudication and sentencing, and access to programs and release from custody.[55] Important decisions about a youth and assessments of credibility may be affected by the "attitude" and demeanour of the youth or parents, but decision makers may be unaware that these may be influenced by cultural factors or communication difficulties.

The complexity of the task of identifying and responding to racism is illustrated by R. v. S.(R.D.), a youth court case from Nova Scotia. A fifteen-year-old black youth was charged with interfering with an arrest and with assault on a police officer arising out of an incident that occurred when a white police officer was arresting the youth's cousin. The officer alleged that the youth came onto the scene, yelled at the officer, and that the youth then pushed into him.

---

54   R. v. *Butcher* (4 September 1990), (Ont. Prov. Div.) [unreported].

55   See, e.g., P. J. Carrington, S. Moyer, & F. Kopelman, "Factors Affecting Pre-Dispositional Detention and Release in Canadian Juvenile Courts (1988) 16 J. Crim. Just. 463.

The youth acknowledged that he was at the scene of the arrest but said that he was only speaking to his cousin, who was already in the police car, to ask if the cousin's mother should be called. The youth denied that he pushed into the officer but testified that the officer told him "Shut up, shut up, or you'll be under arrest too," and that when he kept talking to his cousin the officer put him in a choke hold and arrested him.

The case was tried before the only black female judge in Nova Scotia, Judge Sparks. She concluded:

> The Crown says, well, why would the officer say that events occurred in the way in which he has repaled them to the Court this morning. I am not saying that the Constable has misled the court, although police officers have been known to do that in the past. I am not saying that the officer overreacted, but certainly police officers do overreact, particularly when they are dealing with non-white groups. That to me indicates a state of mind right there that is questionable. I believe that probably the situation in this particular case is the case of a young police officer who overreacted. I do accept the evidence of [R.D.S.] that he was told to shut up or he would be under arrest. It seems to be in keeping with the prevalent attitude of the day.
>
> At any rate, based upon my comments and based upon all the evidence before the court, I have no other choice but to acquit.

The Crown appealed the acquittal, arguing that there was a reasonable apprehension that the judge was biased against the Caucasian police officer. The Supreme Court of Canada was badly split on how to deal with the case, though the majority upheld the acquittal.[56]

In writing the decisive opinion, Justice Cory acknowledged the problem of racism in the Canadian justice system.

> [T]here is a realistic possibility that the actions taken by the police in their relations with visible minorities demonstrate both prejudice and discrimination . . . racial tension exists at least to some degree between police officers and visible minorities. Further, in some cases, racism may have been exhibited by police officers in arresting young black males.[57]

But Justice Cory went on to suggest that the Judge Sparks's comments were troubling since "there was no evidence . . . that would suggest that anti-black bias influenced this particular police officer's reactions." Justice Cory concluded that considering the judge's reasons in their

---

56   [1997] S.C.J. No. 84 (QL).
57   Para. 149

entirety, the Crown had not demonstrated that there was a reasonable apprehension of bias, though the remarks were "close to the line."

Justices L'Heureux-Dubé and McLachlin agreed in the result, but went farther than Cory J., arguing that Judge Sparks was "alive to the well known racial dynamics that may exist in interactions between police officers and visible minorities." They concluded that her

> oral reasons show that she approached the case with an open mind, used her experience and knowledge of the community to achieve an understanding of the reality of the case, and applied the fundamental principle of proof beyond a reasonable doubt. . . . In alerting herself to the racial dynamic in the case, she was simply engaging in the process of contextualized judging which, in our view, was entirely proper and conducive to a fair and just resolution of the case before her.[58]

In a dissenting judgment, Major J. argued that, in absence of evidence of racist attitudes or behaviour by this particular officer, the trial judge herself was displaying bias:

> It can hardly be seen as progress to stereotype police officer witnesses as likely to lie when dealing with non-whites. This would return us to a time in the history of the Canadian justice system that many thought had passed. This reasoning, with respect to police officers, is no more legitimate than the stereotyping of women, children or minorities.[59]

Although the Supreme Court was split on the question of how trial judges should take account of the possibility that racist attitudes have affected the conduct or testimony of police officers in a particular case, they all recognized that racism is a serious concern in the administration of justice in Canada, including the youth justice system.

While it may never be possible to determine fully the effects of racism on the administration of youth justice in Canada, it is clear that many members of Aboriginal and visible-minority communities believe that there is bias in the justice system. All of those who work in the justice system need to be aware of problems of subtle racism and cultural bias. Lawyers in particular need sensitivity and training for representing youths from different backgrounds. Programs for young offenders need to take account of the needs of youths from a range of cultural and racial backgrounds, and there should be appropriate mechanisms for dealing with complaints about bias.

---

58   Para. 59
59   Para. 18

There are special concerns relating to Aboriginal youth that reflect both the unique constitutional and political position of Canada's First Nations and the relatively large numbers and concentration of Aboriginal offenders in certain youth courts and custodial facilities in Canada. In some parts of the country, Aboriginal youths form a majority of the population in custody, and in some youth courts, especially those sitting in Aboriginal communities, all of those who appear are Aboriginal youth.

Aboriginal communities are anxious about youth crime issues because members of their communities are the most frequent victims of the offending and bear the immediate costs of it. There is also profound worry that these communities will suffer long-term consequences if its young members grow into adult offenders rather than productive, contributing members of their society. The treatment of Aboriginal people in Canada's justice system is a long and well-documented story of at best insensitivity and at worst blatant racism.[60] Problems in the courts may be compounded by cultural and language difficulties. Some aboriginal youth may be pleading guilty in circumstances where other youth might plead not guilty because of a lack of comprehension of legal concepts like "not guilty," or because their cultural background makes them reluctant to engage in an adversarial trial process.[61]

While there are significant variations between Aboriginal communities, Aboriginal peoples often have different traditions and philosophies for dealing with offending behaviour from those found in the Canadian justice system. As stated by the Oji-Cree Sandy Lake First Nation in Ontario: "Probably one of the most serious gaps . . . is the different perceptions of wrongdoing and how to best treat it. In the non-Indian community, committing a crime seems to mean that the individual is a bad person and therefore must be punished . . . the Indian communities view a wrongdoing as a misbehaviour which requires teaching or an illness that requires healing."[62]

---

60 See, e.g., Manitoba, *Report of the Aboriginal Justice Inquiry of Manitoba* (Winnipeg: Queen's Printer, 1991), ch. 15; Canada, Royal Commission on Aboriginal Peoples, *Bridging the Divide: A Report on Aboriginal People and Criminal Justice in Canada* (Ottawa: Supply & Services, 1996); R. Ross, *Dancing with a Ghost: Exploring Indian Reality* (Markham: Octopus, 1992); and D. Bercuson & B. Cooper, "Justice system is no friend to Indians," *[Toronto] Globe and Mail* (8 February 1997) D2.

61 See, e.g., T.T. Daley, "Where Cultures Clash: Native Peoples and a Fair Trial" (1992) 8 Can. Fam. L.Q. 301; C.C. Brant, "Native Ethics and Rules of Behaviour" (1990) 35 Can. J. Psychiatry 534.

62 From the Justice proposal made to the Ontario government, quoted from Ross, *Returning*, above note 51 at 123.

Although the philosophy of the *YOA* may be closer to the traditional Aboriginal philosophies than those principles used for dealing with adult offenders, the challenges of dealing effectively with Aboriginal youth with offending behaviours does not have an easy solution. Some Aboriginal communities are working towards establishing Aboriginal control over police forces and justice programs, with a special emphasis on dealing with young persons. The alternative measures provisions of the *YOA* (s. 4) are being increasingly used to give Aboriginal communities some control over their youthful offenders, involving community members and elders to make decisions that invoke Aboriginal concepts of restorative justice.

The Canadian justice system is also being modified for dealing with Aboriginal offenders, with judges using "sentencing circles" composed of community members, the victim, and the offender, as well as the police, prosecutor, and defence counsel, to try to reach a consensus about an appropriate disposition. Some Aboriginal communities are also establishing special treatment programs for Aboriginal young offenders, often involving community elders as well as Aboriginal philosophy and healing principles. These innovations are being used both on reserves and in urban settings where there are significant Aboriginal populations, especially in northern and western Canada. A long-term objective of many Aboriginal groups is the establishment of autonomous Aboriginal justice systems, and some projects have been established to deal with certain less serious offences in some Aboriginal communities. There are, however, many political, practical, and philosophical questions to be addressed in undertaking this type of project,[63] to ensure that adequate attention is paid to the interests of the offender, the victim, the Aboriginal community, and Canadian society.

G. FEMALE YOUNG OFFENDERS

Although more than four-fifths of charges under the *YOA* involve males, there are special concerns about how female young offenders are treated.

Under the *JDA* there were relatively few charges against females, but girls were far more frequently charged with the status offences of "sexual immorality" and "unmanageability" than boys. Some girls were charged with these "delinquent acts" for prostitution-related activities, and it was quite common for parents to have charges brought when their daughters were perceived as being "out of control" or merely sex-

---

63 C. LaPrairie, "Community Justice or Just Communities? Aboriginal Communities in Search of Justice" (1995) 37 Can. J. Crim. 521. For a good discussion about the idea of Aboriginal justice, see Ross, *Returning, ibid.*

ually active. Girls charged with "sexual immorality" or considered unmanageable could serve long periods in training schools, where we now know there was often sexual exploitation by the staff, inevitably exacerbating the condition of the girls sent there.[64] The *YOA*, with its offence-oriented focus, reduced the possibility of the juvenile justice system being used in this highly discriminatory and destructive fashion, though it has not eliminated concerns related to gender bias.

In 1994–95 about 19 percent of charges were against females, a rate that had increased slowly over the decade that the Act was in force.[65] Charge rates and the opinions of professionals in the field indicate that female adolescents are becoming more violent, though they are clearly not as violent as males.[66] While female adolescents rarely commit the most serious offences involving homicide or sexual assault, they are charged with a greater proportion of ordinary assaults (about 30 percent) than property offences (about 20 percent). Female adolescents are much more likely than males to be charged with prostitution-related offences.

It is apparent that courts are more "lenient" with female young offenders than with males; a female is less likely to receive a custodial sentence for any given offence than a male, even taking account of prior record.[67] While this "lenient" treatment may seem to be advantageous to females, and may reflect judicial biases about females, it may also result in females being more likely to be left in dysfunctional family settings. Further, because females constitute a relatively small proportion of the custodial population, they have difficulty getting access to appropriate programming and services. In particular, a disproportionate number of female offenders have been victims of physical and sexual abuse but do not have access to adequate treatment in custody for the emotional and behavioural problems that often result from such abuse. Though many open-custody facilities have both males and females, programming tends to be geared to the males who are the majority of residents. While some secure-custody facilities are co-educational, there is a tendency to segregate older and more serious offenders by sex, resulting in fewer facilities for the relatively

---

64   See, e.g., *Hollett*, above note 11.
65   *Statistics*, above note 36; "Female Young Offenders, 1990–91" (1992) 12: 11 Juristat 1.
66   See, e.g., I. Vincent, "Girl-gang violence alarms experts," *[Toronto] Globe and Mail* (12 Sept. 1995) A10.
67   See, e.g., M. Reitsma-Street, "A Review of Female Delinquency" in A.W. Leschied, P.G. Jaffe, & W. Willis, eds., *The Young Offenders Act: A Revolution in Canadian Juvenile Justice* (Toronto: University of Toronto Press, 1992) 248; and P. Pearson, *When She Was Bad: Violent Women and the Myth of Innocence* (Toronto: Random House Canada, 1997).

small number of female offenders and a greater likelihood that they will be sent farther away from home or even placed in adult facilities. Such women often have difficulty reintegrating into their communities and families.

Available Canadian research indicates that females have substantially lower recidivism rates following probation or a custodial sentence than male young offenders.[68] Research also shows that male offending increases with age throughout adolescence and peaks between the ages of eighteen and twenty-one, while female offending peaks at the age of fifteen, and declines in the sixteen- and seventeen- year-old population.[69]

H. OVERVIEW OF THE YOUTH COURT PROCESS

Before beginning a detailed study of the principles and provisions of the *YOA*, it is useful to have an overview of the youth court process and the issues that typically arise in these cases. (See Figure 1.)

A significant number of offences committed by youths, especially minor ones, are resolved informally by victims or are not detected. Many offences, however, are reported by witnesses or victims to the police. If the police are not able to discover who committed an offence, they can take no further action. The police investigation will involve the questioning of the victim and any witnesses, and possibly some forensic work such as the taking of fingerprints from a crime scene, or, in a sexual assault case, having a medical exam performed on the victim. The police will usually attempt to interview the suspected perpetrator of the offence; the *YOA* requires that the police must take special measures to protect the rights of young persons who are being questioned by police about offences that they are suspected of having committed. In some cases involving less serious offences and no prior record of offending, the police may decide not to take any official action against a youth whom they believe committed an offence; they may talk to the youth about not committing any further offences, perhaps speaking to the parents as well. The youth, and possibly the parents, may also be referred to a social agency or some other source for assistance on a voluntary basis.

---

68   S. Moyer, *A Profile of the Juvenile Justice System in Canada* (Ottawa: Federal-Provincial-Territorial Task Force on Youth Justice, 1996), at 182.

69   P.J. Carrington, *Age and Youth Crime in Canada* (Ottawa: Department of Justice, 1995).

Figure 1

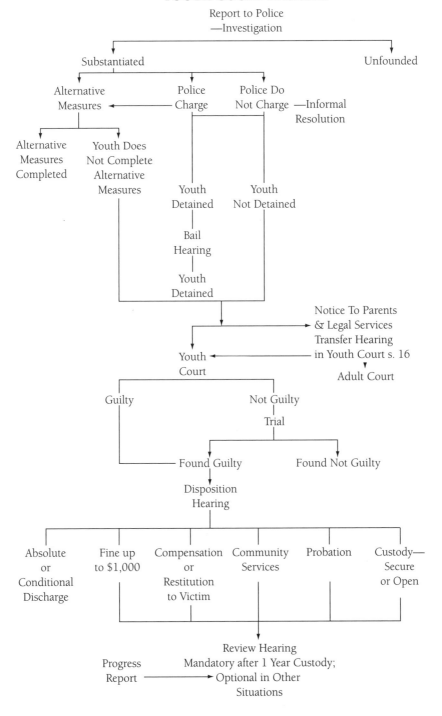

YOUTH COURT PROCESS

If the police have reasonable grounds to believe that a youth has committed an offence, the police may lay charges and commence the youth court process. Before or after a charge is laid, a youth may be referred to an alternative measures or diversion program; these programs are intended to provide a relatively expeditious, informal resolution for less serious cases and may, for example, involve restitution or an apology to a victim. In more serious cases, the Crown prosecutor, in consultation with the police, may decide to seek detention of the youth in a custody facility pending trial. The decision about whether to detain a youth is made by a judge at a pre-trial detention (bail) hearing; the judge may decide not to detain the youth but nevertheless impose conditions on the release.

As soon as a youth is arrested, the police must inform the youth of the right to consult a lawyer. In proceedings under the *YOA*, if a youth wants to have legal assistance and is unable to afford a lawyer, there is a right to have a government-paid lawyer. The lawyer may provide assistance at the time of pre-trial questioning by the police at a pre-trial bail hearing, at trial, and at a sentencing or review hearing.

After an initial appearance before a judge, a youth, generally acting with the advice of a lawyer, will decide whether to plead guilty or to plead not guilty and have a trial. In practice, most youths decide to plead guilty, sometimes in the context of a plea bargain with the Crown prosecutor. Except for murder cases, trials in youth court are resolved by a judge sitting without a jury, with special rules to limit the public disclosure of information about the youth before the court. After a trial, a youth may be found not guilty (acquitted) or guilty of the offence. If there is a finding of guilt, the youth court judge will impose a disposition (sentence the youth). In some cases, a disposition will be imposed immediately after the finding of guilt. In more serious situations, the case is likely to be adjourned so that a pre-disposition report may be prepared, or a medical or psychological assessment may be carried out for the disposition (sentencing) hearing.

The *YOA* gives judges a range of dispositional alternatives, from an absolute discharge to three years in youth custody; for youths convicted of murder in youth court, the maximum sentence is ten years. There is no parole for young offenders, but the youth court retains jurisdiction to review dispositions. For example, a young offender may be released from custody by a youth court judge at a review hearing if there has been sufficient progress towards rehabilitation. Unless a youth is in breach of a term of an original order, a more severe disposition cannot be imposed as part of the review process. The most serious cases may be transferred to adult court for trial and, if a conviction occurs, for sentencing in that court. A transfer can occur only before a plea is entered in youth court, and it generally requires a transfer hearing before a youth court judge.

The principal purpose of the transfer process is to allow adult court to impose a much longer sentence on a convicted young offender, up to life imprisonment, that will often be served in the adult correctional system.

FURTHER READINGS

BALA, N. *et al.*, *State Responses to Youth Crime: A Consideration of Principles* (Ottawa: Canadian Research Institute for Law and the Family, 1993)

CANADA, FEDERAL-PROVINCIAL-TERRITORIAL TASK FORCE ON YOUTH JUSTICE, *A Review of the Young Offenders Act and the Youth Justice System in Canada* (Ottawa: Supply & Services, 1996) chs. 2 and 12

CANADA, HOUSE OF COMMONS, *Thirteenth Report of the Standing Committee on Justice and Legal Affairs: Renewing Youth Justice* (Ottawa, Supply & Services, 1997)

CORRADO, R. *et al.*, eds., *Juvenile Justice in Canada: A Theoretical and Analytical Assessment* (Toronto: Butterworths, 1992)

DOOB, A.N., V. MARINOS, & K.N. VARMA, *Youth Crime and the Youth Justice System in Canada: A Research Perspective* (Toronto: Centre of Criminology, University of Toronto, 1995)

GRISSO, T., "Society's Retributive Response to Juvenile Violence: A Developmental Perspective" (1996) 20 Law & Human Behaviour 229

HUDSON, J., J.P. HORNICK, and B.A. BURROWS, eds., *Justice and the Young Offender in Canada* (Toronto: Wall & Thompson, 1988)

LESCHIED, A.W., P.G. JAFFE, and W. WILLIS, eds., *The Young Offenders Act: A Revolution in Canadian Juvenile Justice* (Toronto: University of Toronto Press, 1991)

PLATT, P., *Young Offenders Law In Canada,* 2d ed. (Toronto: Butterworths, 1995), ch. 1

ROSS, R., *Returning to the Teachings: Exploring Aboriginal Justice* (Toronto: Penguin, 1996)

WEST, W.G., *Young Offenders and the State: A Canadian Perspective on Delinquency* (Toronto: Butterworths, 1984)

CHAPTER 2

PRINCIPLES FOR RESPONDING TO YOUTH CRIME

The *Juvenile Delinquents Act, 1908* articulated a *parens patriae* or welfare-oriented philosophy, stating that a delinquent was not to be treated "as criminal, but as a misdirected and misguided child, and one needing aid, encouragement, help and assistance."[1] This philosophy was reflected in the informality of the *JDA*, with its status offences and overlap with child-welfare laws and the indeterminate length of committals to training school. The *Young Offenders Act*, which came into force in 1984, represented a sharp change in philosophy.

The *YOA* is clearly criminal law, not child-welfare legislation. The justification for state intervention in the life of a youth is the violation of criminal legislation, and this violation must be established by due process of law; indeed the *YOA* includes special protections for the legal rights of youth. However, once it is established that a criminal offence has occurred, rehabilitative concerns and the special needs of the adolescents may affect the way a youth is dealt with.

The *YOA* establishes a youth justice system for adolescents twelve through seventeen which is separate from the adult criminal justice system and distinctive in several critical respects. First, while the Act recognizes that young persons must be held accountable for criminal acts, they generally will not be held accountable in the same manner or to the same extent as adults. Secondly, in recognition of their vulnerability,

---

1   S.C. 1908, c. 40, s. 31 [later *Juvenile Delinquents Act*, R.S.C. 1970, c. J-3, s. 38].

the *YOA* extends legal protections to youth which are more extensive than those afforded adults. Perhaps most important, the Act recognizes that youth, because of their immaturity, have special needs and circumstances which require special treatment.

When considering the adequacy of the principles that are articulated in the *YOA*, one must be aware of international standards for dealing with youth, in particular those in the *United Nations Convention on the Rights of the Child* which establishes some important principles for dealing with children and adolescents. It is also necessary to understand how different countries are responding to youth crime.

Most of this chapter is devoted to a consideration of the Declaration of Principle found in section 3 of the *YOA*. The chapter concludes with a discussion that situates the Canadian approaches to youth crime in an international context. Much of the rest of this book discusses how the principles of section 3 are reflected in the substantive provisions of the Act, and how Canadian courts have applied and interpreted these principles in different contexts.

A. THE DECLARATION OF PRINCIPLE OF THE *YOA*

When Parliament enacted the *YOA*, section 3 was included as an explicit Declaration of Principle that was intended to reflect the philosophy of the drafters and give direction to the judges, police, prosecutors, and youth correctional staff who are responsible for the implementation and interpretation of the Act. The Declaration was amended in 1995,[2] with the addition of what are now sections 3(1)(a) and 3(1)(c. 1), to emphasize the Liberal government's view of the importance of crime prevention and rehabilitation. The Declaration of Principle now reads:

3.(1) It is hereby recognized and declared that

(a) crime prevention is essential to the long-term protection of society and requires addressing the underlying causes of crime by young persons and developing multi-disciplinary approaches to identifying and effectively responding to children and young persons at risk of committing offending behaviour in the future;

---

2   *An Act to amend the Young Offenders Act and the Criminal Code*, S.C. 1995, c. 19, s. 1 [*YOA 1995*].

(*a.1*) while young persons should not in all instances be held accountable in the same manner or suffer the same consequences for
their behaviour as adults, young persons who commit offences
should nonetheless bear responsibility for their contraventions;

(*b*)   society must, although it has the responsibility to take reasonable measures to prevent criminal conduct by young persons, be
afforded the necessary protection from illegal behaviour;

(*c*)   young persons who commit offences require supervision, discipline and control, but, because of their state of dependency and
level of development and maturity, they also have special needs
and require guidance and assistance;

(*c.1*) the protection of society, which is a primary objective of the
criminal law applicable to youth, is best served by rehabilitation,
wherever possible, of young persons who commit offences, and
rehabilitation is best achieved by addressing the needs and circumstances of a young person that are relevant to the young person's offending behaviour;

(*d*)   where it is not inconsistent with the protection of society, taking
no measures or taking measures other than judicial proceedings
under this Act should be considered for dealing with young persons who have committed offences;

(*e*)   young persons have rights and freedoms in their own right,
including those stated in the *Canadian Charter of Rights and
Freedoms* or in the *Canadian Bill of Rights*, and in particular a
right to be heard in the course of, and to participate in, the processes that lead to decisions that affect them, and young persons
should have special guarantees of their rights and freedoms;

(*f*)   in the application of this Act, the rights and freedoms of young persons include a right to the least possible interference with freedom
that is consistent with the protection of society, having regard to
the needs of young persons and the interests of their families;

(*g*)   young persons have the right, in every instance where they have
rights or freedoms that may be affected by this Act, to be
informed as to what those rights and freedoms are; and

(*h*)   parents have responsibility for the care and supervision of their
children, and, for that reason, young persons should be removed
from parental supervision either partly or entirely only when
measures that provide for continuing parental supervision are
inappropriate.

Subsection 3(2) directs that the *YOA* should "be liberally construed
to the end that young persons will be dealt with in accordance with the

principles" set out in section 3(1). The Supreme Court of Canada has recognized that section 3 "should not be considered as merely a preamble. Rather it should be given the force normally attributed to substantive provisions."[3]

The Supreme Court has emphasized the importance of the principles set out above, indicating that they should be utilized by the decision makers for such purposes as determining whether to refer a youth to alternative measures and making disposition and transfer decisions. However, the application of section 3 is often far from straightforward. Most of the principles articulated in section 3(1) are broad and there are some seeming inconsistencies or at least tensions between them. It has been suggested by some critics that, in the absence of any statutory priorization, section 3 does little to direct decision makers but rather leaves them a wide personal discretion to select and apply the principles as they see fit. However, it can also be argued that it is possible to reconcile and balance the principles of section 3 to derive a coherent message.

B. CRIME PREVENTION: SECTION 3(1)(a)

Growing public concerns have made crime prevention an important political issue in the 1990s, and in 1995 the Liberal government amended the Declaration of Principle of the *YOA* to acknowledge its importance. The federal government established the twenty-five member National Crime Prevention Council in 1994, composed of volunteers serving essentially advocacy and advisory functions. The Council recognizes that the concept of "crime prevention" has several distinct meanings:

- measures designed to reduce an individual's inclination to commit crimes, either though intervention after an offence has been committed — rehabilitation — or through intervention in the lives of children and adolescents at high risk of offending ("crime prevention through social development");
- measures taken to reduce the opportunity to commit crimes, such as increased policing, neighbourhood crime-watch programs, and enhanced security and lighting as well as programs that assist the vulnerable and reduce the likelihood of individual victimization ("situational" or "opportunity reduction crime prevention"); and
- measures aimed at the apprehension and punishment of individual offenders, the goal being to prevent future crime either by deterring

---

3   *R. v. M.(J.J.)*, [1993] 2 S.C.R. 421 at 428, Cory J. [*M.(J.J.)*].

people from committing offences or if incarceration results, by "inca-pacitation" of likely offenders.[4]

The Council notes that traditional crime-prevention efforts in Canada have focused on the second and third types of measures, though their effectiveness is limited. Situational crime-control efforts can reduce total levels of offending, though not infrequently these efforts simply protect certain "targets" and "shift" crime to other locales. Longer cus-todial sentences have had little or no impact on rates of youth offending, and the Council has endorsed placing a priority on "crime prevention through social development" as the most effective long-term method of reducing levels of crime in Canada.

The different meanings of the term "crime prevention" are reflected in the "politics of crime control." For those on the right of the political spectrum, crime prevention often means taking a "law and order" approach, with increased efforts at law enforcement and tougher sanc-tions for offenders. For those on the political left, "solving" the "crime problem" (or, more accurately, reducing levels of criminality) is more likely to involve attempts to address the causes of crime, both in terms of early intervention in the lives of children at risk and by responding in a rehabilitative fashion to young persons who commit offences.

The Liberal government tried to appeal to the different views about crime control. A significant number of legislative and administrative reforms were intended to take a law and order approach to "combat crime," including those provisions in the 1995 YOA reforms that facili-tate the transfer of youths charged with serious offences to adult court and provide longer sentences for youths who commit murder.[5] However, recognizing the views of the Council on Crime Prevention and the weight of research which strongly supports approaches to crime preven-tion that address the causes of crime,[6] the Liberal government also added provisions to the YOA in 1995 to reflect at least a symbolic commitment to an approach to crime prevention based on the Council's concept of

---

4   National Crime Prevention Council, *Money Well Spent: Investing in Preventing Crime* (Ottawa: The Council, 1996) at 27.

5   This emphasis on both amending the *YOA*, R.S.C. 1985, c. Y-1, [*YOA*] to "get tough" with offenders, especially violent offenders, and increase efforts at crime prevention through social development is also apparent in the *Report* of Canada, House of Commons, *Thirteenth Report of the Standing Committee on Justice and Legal Affairs: Renewing Youth Justice* (Ottawa: Supply & Services, 1997).

6   See, e.g., House of Commons, *Twelfth Report of the Standing Committee on Justice and the Solicitor General: Crime Prevention in Canada: Toward a National Strategy* (Ottawa: Supply & Services, 1993).

"social development," namely section 3(1)(a), on prevention through early intervention, and section 3(1)(c), on protection of society through rehabilitation. Both of the principles added in 1995 recognize the limited role that the youth justice system can have in protecting society, and in particular section 3(1)(a) emphasizes the value of "multi-disciplinary approaches" to crime prevention.

Putting crime prevention as the first of the principles in section 3 was intended to be a symbolic statement, though the ordering of the paragraphs in that section has no legal significance. While the message of section 3(1)(a) is socially important and doubtless reflects sound social policy, it may have a somewhat hollow ring. The federal government, and most of those working with the *YOA* in the youth justice system, have little direct responsibility over the type of crime-prevention measures in section 3(1)(a), those aimed at children and adolescents who are at risk of becoming future offenders. It is the provincial governments and those who work in the health, education, and social-service fields who have the primary responsibility for children and adolescents at risk. The federal role is largely limited to providing funding, but in recent years the federal government has been reducing its financial support to the provinces for the health, education, and welfare programs that tend to prevent crime. Despite its location in the Act, section 3(1)(a) should be seen as serving only a symbolic role, with little direct applicability to those who work in the youth justice system. It is to be hoped, however, that this section will serve to help politicians and policy makers in making decisions and developing programs that affect youth crime.

C. ACCOUNTABILITY: SECTION 3(1)(a. 1)

The principle of accountability is premised on the assumption that adolescents are capable of independent thought and judgment and hence should be morally and legally accountable for their acts. Accordingly, if a young person is guilty of an offence, the youth is to be held accountable to society generally and, where appropriate, to the victim. Accountability may involve some form of restitution to a victim. Accountability of offenders may also involve "retribution," that is, the "imposition of a just and appropriate punishment." Retribution is not, however, equivalent to "vengeance." As Chief Justice Lamer stated:

> Vengeance [is] . . . motivated by emotion and anger, as a reprisal for harm inflicted. . . . Retribution . . . by contrast, represents an objective, reasoned and measured determination of an appropriate punish-

ment which reflects the *moral culpability* of the offender, having regard to the intentional risk-taking of the offender, the consequential harm caused by the offender, and the normative character of the offender's conduct.[7]

The application of notions of retribution requires that adolescents should, in general, receive a lesser sanction than an adult for any given offence. Because of their limited intellectual, moral, and psychological development, it is inappropriate to hold adolescents accountable in the same manner and to the same extent as adults. The immaturity and lack of judgment of youth is a reason for denying rights and privileges, such as those involving voting or driving, and also a reason for limiting accountability. Thus, the maximum disposition under the YOA is three years in a youth custody facility (or ten years for murder) compared to the life imprisonment in penitentiary which an adult may face. The principle of limited accountability is especially important when sentencing youth or when deciding whether to divert a young person from the formal youth justice system to an alternative measures program.

Even those youth who commit the most serious offences and are transferred into the adult courts may have more limited accountability than adults; youths sentenced for murder in adult court after transfer will face the possibility of life in prison, but they are eligible for parole earlier than adults.[8]

Consistent with the notion that criminal liability is normally imposed only if there is the requisite intent to commit a criminal act, an exception to a person being held accountable for illegal acts arises if, pursuant to section 16 of the *Criminal Code,* that person is found to be exempt from criminal responsibility by reason of a mental disorder that rendered him or her "incapable of appreciating the nature and quality" of their acts or of "knowing that it was wrong." If a youth is found to be not criminally responsible on account of a mental disorder, he or she may be committed to a mental-health facility until it is determined that the illness has been cured or release is required by law.

---

7   *R. v. M.(C.A.),* [1996] 1 S.C.R. 500 at 557–58. [Emphasis in original].

8   *Criminal Code,* R.S.C. 1985, c. C–46, s. 743.1, enacted by *An Act to amend the Young Offenders Act and the Criminal Code,* S.C. 1992, c. 11, s. 16 [*YOA 1992*], discussed in ch. 9.

D. PROTECTION OF SOCIETY: SECTION 3(1)(b)

Another central principle of the *YOA* is that society must be afforded necessary protection from the illegal behaviour of young persons. In section 3(1)(a) there is a recognition that a fundamental strategy for increasing the long-term protection of society is preventive intervention with children and adolescents at high risk of offending, while section 3(1)(c.1) recognizes the importance of rehabilitation of young offenders as a way of protecting society. The principle of protection of society in section 3(1)(b) includes prevention and rehabilitation, but it also encompasses the responsibility of Canada's youth justice system to provide more immediate protection through the incarceration of offenders who pose a significant risk to the community, as well as through the imposition of sentences that may serve a deterrent function to the offender before the court (specific or individual deterrence) and other potential offenders (general deterrence). The principle of protection of society is especially important when decisions are being made about sentencing and transfer to adult court, but it may also be relevant for decisions about pre-trial detention and use of alternative measures.

Youth court judges take account of deterrence when dealing with young offenders; however, Canadian case law clearly indicates that, considering all of the provisions of section 3, deterrence should not be as much of a factor for young persons as for adults.[9] Further, when considering whether the protection of society is achieved by court-imposed punishments that are intended to deter young offenders, one would do well to keep in mind the conclusion of Anthony Doob, a leading Canadian criminologist, and some of his colleagues:

> [t]he likelihood of apprehension — or more importantly, the *perceived personal likelihood* of apprehension can be important for some offences in determining whether or not a young person will commit offences. However, a review of the literature on size of sanction suggests that this [length of sentence or even transfer to adult court] is likely to be irrelevant to whether or not a young person commits an offence . . . changing levels of punishment will not change youth crime.[10]

---

9   See, e.g., *M. (J.J.)*, above note 3, and *R. v. E. (R.K.)* (1996), 107 Man. R. (2d) 200 (C.A.).

10   A.N. Doob, V. Marinos, & K.N. Varma, *Youth Crime and the Youth Justice System in Canada: A Research Perspective* (Toronto: Centre of Criminology, University of Toronto, 1995) at 81. [Emphasis in original].

E. REHABILITATION AND THE SPECIAL NEEDS OF YOUTH — SECTIONS 3(1)(c) AND (c.1)

Although the *YOA* is clearly criminal legislation, it is also distinct from the law applicable to adults in its recognition that adolescents have special needs, and that those who commit offences are impressionable and amenable to rehabilitation. Section 3(1)(c) of the Declaration of Principle requires that the limited maturity and dependency of youth be taken into account and that decisions made about youth reflect their "special needs," while section 3(1)(c.1), added in 1995, articulates the related principle that the protection of society is "best served" by addressing the "needs and circumstances" of the youth that are related to the offending behaviour.

The Supreme Court of Canada has accepted that the *YOA* has a rehabilitative emphasis, with Chief Justice Lamer writing in *Reference Re Young Offenders Act (Prince Edward Island)*:

> It is clear . . . that the *Young Offenders Act* does not generally recognize any proportionality between the gravity of the offence and the range of sanctions. It rather recognizes the special situation and the special needs of young offenders and gives to the judges different sentencing options that are not available for adults. It is still primarily oriented towards rehabilitation rather than punishment or neutralization.[11]

In the case of many adolescents involved in the youth justice system, criminal behaviour constitutes an isolated and often not very serious act. For these youth, various provisions in the *YOA* — alternative measures, the involvement of parents, the ban on the publication of identifying information, and restrictions on use of records — may be adequate to meet their special needs. Such provisions recognize the immaturity and vulnerability of adolescents.

For some youth, however, criminal behaviour is part of a pattern of more serious difficulties. It is essential to try to understand the special needs of these youths if their interests and the long-term interests of society are to be met. In particular, for purposes of making a sentencing or transfer decision, a youth court judge may order a pre-disposition report or a medical or psychological assessment to learn more about the needs and circumstances of a youth before the court.

Many troubled, offending youths have ongoing needs that cannot all be met by the criminal justice system. There are cases where the

---

11   [1991] 1 S.C.R. 252 at 271.

needs of a young person who has committed an offence can best be met in the provincial child-protection, education, or mental-health systems, either concurrently with a youth-justice response or instead of it.

Making various decisions about young persons, especially concerning sentencing, requires a careful balancing of the principles of accountability, protection of society, and recognition of special needs. In some cases decisions are relatively easy, and it is possible to impose a sentence which recognizes "treatment" needs. For example, for some offences related to drug use, the best response for the youth, family, and society may be to have a probation term imposed, with a condition that the youth attend substance-abuse counselling. In some situations, a residential or custodial disposition may be made which also involves the provision of rehabilitative or treatment services.

Other decisions are more difficult. Some youth commit very serious or repeat offences, and a judge may decide that the need to protect society — through giving effect to the principles of accountability, deterrence, or incapacitation — requires a disposition that does not meet the needs of the youth. Perhaps the clearest choice between accountability and the protection of society on the one hand, and the needs of a youth on the other, is when a decision is being made to transfer to adult court pursuant to section 16 of the *YOA*, since the prospects for addressing rehabilitative needs are more limited in the adult system but there is the possibility of a much longer incapacitating sentence.[12] Section 16(1.1) requires the court to attempt to reconcile the protection of the public and the rehabilitation of the youth, but it specifies that if these two objectives cannot be reconciled, the protection of the public is paramount and the youth shall be transferred.

While section 3(1)(c.1) recognizes the value of rehabilitation, it also has a realistic qualifier: "wherever possible." Although many offending youths can be "rehabilitated," it is also clear that not all young offenders can be. Some youths lack the motivation, at least at some points in their lives, to engage in rehabilitative efforts. Treatment professionals can try to engage a youth, but a resistant offender cannot be rehabilitated. Further, no program or facility can rehabilitate all young offenders; some youths will reoffend despite their participation in any

---

12   The alternatives were especially stark before 1992 when the effect of a transfer decision was automatically to place an adolescent in an adult facility on a pre-trial basis, as well as for any sentence; since the 1992 *YOA* amendments (see *YOA 1992*, above note 8), ss. 16.1 and 16.2 allow courts to make a transfer order but keep a youth out of adult correctional facilities pending adjudication and even after sentencing in adult court.

rehabilitative regime,[13] even after they have completed their disposition, let alone at the time that the court is deciding what disposition to impose. It may not be possible to identify which youths are not amenable to rehabilitation.

For those who work in the youth justice system in Canada, there is also the stark reality that the appropriate rehabilitative resources are often not available. While there are some excellent programs and facilities with good records for rehabilitating young offenders, in many places justice system professionals are often faced with cases where there is a lack of real options: perhaps little or no appropriate treatment is available in the youth's community, the only custody facilities offering little more than security, accommodation, and access to some educational services.[14]

In a 1996 Alberta case a judge decided to invoke section 3(c.1) of the YOA as the basis for an order requiring the provincial government to pay for treatment services needed by a youth. The youth was convicted of property offences related to painting graffiti on buildings or "tagging." He spent two months in detention pending adjudication and then pled guilty. A custodial sentence was clearly not warranted, especially since the youth had already been in detention for a significant period of time, but defence counsel requested probation with the requirement that the youth receive treatment at a drug-addiction program, with a court direction that the provincial Ministry of Justice should pay the costs not otherwise covered. The Crown prosecutor argued that there was no authority in the YOA for a judge to order a government to pay for needed services. The Crown and judge accepted that drug addiction was the root cause of the youth's problems. While acknowledging that there was no specific statutory power to allow a judge to direct that a government provide or pay for services, Judge Cook-Stanhope noted the 1995 amendments to section 3 and concluded that they create

> a positive duty on this youth court to assess and then to address, appropriately, the needs and circumstances of every individual young person . . . with a view to ameliorating those risks which are likely to

---

13   A.W. Leschied, P.G. Jaffe, D. Andrews, & P. Gendreau, leading Canadian proponents of rehabilitation for young offenders, write : "[I]t is now clear that the average effect of 'treatment' is the reduction of recidivism, *to at least a mild degree*." (A.W. Leschied *et al.*, " Treatment Issues and Young Offenders: An Empirically Derived Vision of Juvenile Justice Policy" in R.R. Corrado *et al.*, eds., *Juvenile Justice in Canada* (Toronto: Butterworths, 1992) 347 at 360.

14   See, e.g., "Myths, Facts and the Potential of the Treatment Option" in Ontario Social Development Council, *Youth Justice in Crisis* (Toronto: The Council, 1994) 114.

cause the individual to continue to exhibit offending behaviours. . . .
If the principles enunciated in s. 3 are to be more than just hollow-
sounding rhetoric, youth courts must be equipped with the authority
to ensure that their orders will take effect. Failing that, this statute will
not operate effectively as a special code for young persons. . . . If the
youth courts are not possessed of such powers to attend to the rehabilitative requirements of young persons, public clamour for more and
harsher punitive measures instead of more effective rehabilitative ones
will continue to build and eventually completely overtake other
informed debate concerning appropriate . . . measures to deal with our
young people who come into conflict with the law.[15]

As a matter of law there may be some doubt as to whether a judge has the
authority to order the government to pay for or provide particular services
in the absence of a clear statutory power or a *Charter* violation; for a judge
to assume such authority is inconsistent with the generally accepted judicial role in Canada.[16] However, one can appreciate the judge's frustration
in the face of provincial unwillingness to provide appropriate rehabilitative services. It is also easy to sympathize with the judicial desire to prevent the words of section 3 from having a "hollow" ring, especially in
regard to the provision of preventive and rehabilitative services.

F. ALTERNATIVE MEASURES AND NO MEASURES — SECTION 3(1)(d)

Section 3(1)(d) encourages youth justice professionals to respond to
youth offending outside the formal youth court process. Section 4 of the
YOA specifically allows for young persons to be referred to "alternative
measure" programs instead of the youth court. Use of such programs is
generally restricted to relatively minor, first offences, though some repeat
and more serious offenders may also be sent to an alternative measures
program. These programs have the advantage of being expeditious and
informal, and they tend to minimize the stigmatizing effects of an appearance in youth court. Many of the programs also have greater possibilities

---

15   *R. v. A.(L.)*, [1996] A.J. No. 957 (Prov. Ct.) (QL). The decision was not appealed.
16   See, e.g., *Peel (Regional Municipality) v. MacKenzie*, [1992] 2 S.C.R. 9 [no
     jurisdiction under *JDA*, above note 1, for court to order municipality to pay for
     services]; *R. v. B.(K.)* (5 November 1992), (Alta. Q.B.) [unreported], Deyell J. [no
     jurisdiction to order government to pay for *YOA*, above note 5, s. 22 treatment
     order — provision now repealed].

than the courts for involving victims, parents of the offender, and members of the community, a fact that makes such programs especially well suited to the initiatives being taken by Aboriginal peoples to deal with their youth in ways that are more consistent with concepts of restorative justice.

Section 3(1)(d) is also intended to provide guidance to police and Crown attorneys who are considering whether to lay charges. It indicates that, in the case of less serious offences, there may be situations where it is appropriate to take "no measures," that is, to lay no charges. This serves as a formal endorsement of the traditionally exercised police discretion to caution informally the youth and parents rather than commence criminal proceedings.

In R. v. T.(V.)[17] a fourteen-year-old girl who was living in a group home had been charged with offences relating to verbal abuse and the throwing of things at a staff member in the course of an argument about house rules. The British Columbia Court of Appeal observed that, under section 3(1)(d) of the YOA, the prosecuting authorities are required to exercise discretion in deciding whether to lay charges, but, if they have failed to do so, a youth court judge has "ultimate responsibility" for a case and can dismiss the charges. The Court ruled that a judge could dismiss a charge for a relatively minor offence if it involved a person in a "parent-like role" (that is, a group-home staff member) making use of the court system for "minor disciplinary infractions" for which a "real parent" would not ordinarily resort to the courts for dealing with the youth. However, the Supreme Court of Canada reversed the decision of the Court of Appeal and ruled that, except in cases of a clear "abuse of process," a judge has no discretion as to whether charges should be laid.[18] The Supreme Court held that police, Crown prosecutors, and youth workers are the appropriate officials to exercise authority under section 3(1)(d) of the YOA. Any judicial discretion should be exercised at the sentencing stage, where an absolute discharge might be an appropriate disposition if a judge felt that charges should not have been laid.

Section 3(1)(d), therefore, gives no power to judges but is aimed primarily at police, prosecutors, and youth court workers. It is also directed towards the provincial officials who are responsible for funding and establishing alternative measures programs, though it is clear that they too have a discretion as to whether these programs should be established, and if so under what guidelines.[19] While all Canadian jurisdictions now have alternative measures programs, there are substantial

---

17   (1991), 64 C.C.C. (3d) 40 (B.C.C.A.).
18   [1992] 1 S.C.R. 749 [T.(V.)].
19   R. v. S.(S.), [1990] 2 S.C.R. 254.

variations in what types of cases are referred. Available data reveal that less than one-fifth of youth cases in which police are involved are being diverted and Canada appears to be making less use of informal youth-justice responses than other countries.[20]

G. RIGHTS OF YOUNG PERSONS — SECTIONS 3(1)(e) AND (g)

Sections 3(1)(e) and (g) of the Declaration of Principle recognize that young persons have the same "rights and freedoms" as adults, and additionally, because they often lack knowledge and have difficulty in exercising their rights, they "should have special guarantees of their rights and freedoms" and should be "informed" of same. This means that youths have all of the protections afforded adults under the *Charter of Rights* at the time of arrest and in the criminal process. One of the special rights of young persons under the *YOA* is the opportunity to have a lawyer paid by the state if they are unable to obtain or afford a lawyer. Adults only have "the right . . . to retain . . . counsel" under the *Charter*, and, if they cannot afford to pay a lawyer, they are generally forced to rely on the discretion of the legal aid authorities, who are increasingly reluctant to provide counsel for less serious cases.[21]

Another important special protection for youths is found in section 56 of the *YOA*, which excludes from a trial any statement made by a young person to the police unless special cautions are provided the youth before a statement is made, most notably a warning of the right to remain silent and of the right to consult with a parent or lawyer and to have them present when a statement is made to the police. The special cautions required by section 56 reflect section 3(1)(g), which provides that young persons must be advised of their rights.

---

20 J.P. Hornick & S. Rodal, *The Use of Alternatives to Traditional Youth Court: An International Comparison* (Calgary: Canadian Research Institute for Law and the Family, 1995).

21 See *R. v. Prosper*, [1994] 3 S.C.R. 236 ruling that there is no obligation on the state to provide counsel for adult accused persons, though some judges are prepared to invoke s. 7 of the *Canadian Charter of Rights and Freedoms*, Part I of the *Constitution Act, 1982*, being Schedule B to the *Canada Act 1982* (U.K.), 1982, c. 11 [*Charter*] to order that proceedings are stayed (suspended) unless the state ensures that counsel is provided for an adult accused without the resources to retain counsel privately. This discretionary authority is exercised only in complex, serious cases and is clearly narrower than the statutory authority under the *YOA*, above note 5, s. 11.

It was felt by Parliament that these types of special protections are essential because young persons generally do not fully understand their rights and are not able to exercise them fully without assistance. There is also a concern that without these protections adolescents could be pressured by the police into making false statements. The Supreme Court of Canada has taken a protective stance towards youths who are being interrogated by the police, excluding evidence if there has been even a minor, technical violation of section 56 of the YOA or any other indication that the statement has not been made voluntarily.[22] The Supreme Court is giving police a clear message that, if the rights of young persons are not respected, these youths may be found not guilty of charges of which they are in fact guilty.

The granting of these special rights to young persons has been questioned by those who believe that allowing youths to be acquitted on "technicalities" is inconsistent with the principles of protection of the public and accountability for criminal behaviour. This is a familiar debate in the criminal justice field and certainly is not restricted to juvenile justice. However, in the context of youth court proceedings, the debate has an added poignancy since it can be argued that the exercise of legal rights may serve to defeat the needs of a young person. This type of concern is expressed, not only by victims, police, and Crown prosecutors, but sometimes also by parents of young persons charged under the YOA, who expect their children to be held accountable for their wrongs and hope that they may receive needed help from the youth justice system. Parents may feel undermined in their efforts to raise their children to be honest and law-abiding if there are acquittals on the basis of "technicalities," such as the failure of the police to caution a youth adequately before a statement is made.

The prominent Canadian defence lawyer Edward Greenspan has acknowledged this "dilemma of due process":

> Due process is a costly, time consuming process and the procedural safeguards which make up "due process" are not always self-evident. . . .
> In ordinary circumstances, the child is urged to tell the truth and confess; under due process, the young person may be acquitted even though he has acknowledged responsibility to his lawyer. The dilemma of due process results in "some young people receiving the wrong message as to the appropriateness of their behaviour and the values underlying our system of justice."

---

22   See *R. v. J.(J.T.)*, [1990] 2 S.C.R. 755 [*J.(J.T.)*]; and *R. v. I.(L.R.)*, [1993] 4 S.C.R. 504, discussed in ch. 4.

Due process has undoubted benefits for the child, who is now "entitled to protection from arbitrary or well meaning but mistaken government." The young person can no longer be removed from his/her home unless there has been "a scrupulous determination of the facts."[23]

Despite concerns about the financial and social costs of affording due process to young persons, Canada has clearly become a "rights-based society," a fact that was both reflected by and reinforced through the introduction of the *Canadian Charter of Rights and Freedoms* in 1982, the same year that the YOA was enacted. While the granting of rights always involves some costs, it also has benefits for the individuals affected and for society as a whole. Women, employees, tenants, consumers, Aboriginal peoples, the disabled, and others have increasingly asserted legal rights and have seen those rights recognized in the courts. It would be anomalous and surprising to find that, while everyone else in society was receiving more legal protection, young persons were receiving less. In the present social climate, those who work with children and adolescents will have to accept that there is unlikely to be any significant retrenchment of due process rights, though the controversy about due process for young offenders will continue. It is clear, for example, that the views of defence lawyers vary about how aggressively to defend the strict legal rights of adolescents, and that judges also have differing views about how strictly to respect those rights.[24]

H. MINIMAL INTERFERENCE: SECTION 3(1)(f)

The principle of "least possible interference" has its origins in the concept of "non-intervention."[25] This theory holds that the best response to youthful crime is often the least intrusive one, not only because an intrusive response violates the freedom of a youth, but also because official intervention has the potential to be disruptive or even harmful to a youth's development. The offending youth who becomes more deeply involved in the youth justice system may be subject to negative social stereotyping, as well as to the negative influence of other, more serious, offenders.

---

23   Quoted in Ontario Social Development Council, *Young Offenders Act Dispositions: Challenges and Choices* (Toronto: The Council, 1988) at 14.

24   Contrast the views of Cory J. and L'Heureux-Dubé J. in *J.(J.T.)*, above note 22. See ch. 6.

25   E. Schur, *Radical Non-intervention: Rethinking the Delinquency Problem* (Englewood Cliffs, N.J.: Prentice Hall, 1973).

The principle of least possible interference requires that decision makers take the least intrusive measures when dealing with a young person, such as favouring alternative measures over court or a community-based disposition over custody. The principle may also be relevant to pre-trial detention decisions. However, the notion of least possible interference in section 3(1)(f) is considerably qualified by the stipulation that any desire not to interfere must be consistent with "the protection of society," as well as having regard to the "needs of young persons and the interests of their families."

The difficulty in applying section 3(1)(f) is illustrated by the 1993 case of *R. v. M.(J.J.)* where the Supreme Court of Canada upheld a sentence of two years in open custody for a youth convicted of several property-related offences, rejecting the argument that this was an excessive response to the offence. The Court held that "proportionality" between the offence and the sentence is of greater significance for adult offenders than for youths. In this case the Aboriginal youth came from abusive and "depressing home conditions" and had unsuccessfully tried to get himself help from the child-welfare authorities before the offences were committed. The Supreme Court felt that a long period of residence in an open-custody facility, with its rehabilitative services, would best meet the needs of the youth. Justice Cory wrote:

> In the long run, society is best protected by the reformation and rehabilitation of a young offender. In turn, the young offenders are best served when they are provided with the necessary guidance and assistance to enable them to learn the skills required to become fully integrated, useful members of society.[26]

While the approach of *R. v. M.(J.J.)* was consistent with sections 3(1)(c) and (c. 1), it gave very heavy weight to the qualifiers to least possible interference in section 3(1)(f), namely the needs of the young person and the protection of society. A better social response in a case like *R. v. M. (J.J.)* would have been to involve the child-welfare authorities; if this had been done, the need to have an intrusive youth-justice response to promote the interests of the youth would have been minimized. A child-welfare approach, by concentrating on therapeutic goals and avoiding the stigmatization associated with a criminal record, constitutes a less intrusive response to a youth's problems than resorting to the youth justice system, but a judge acting under the *YOA* has no authority to order the state to take such a route.

---

26 M.(J.J.), above note 3 at 433.

In 1995 the *YOA* was amended to specify that in section 24(1.1) "custody shall not be used as a substitute for appropriate child protection, health and other social measures" and that custody "shall only be imposed when all available alternatives to custody that are reasonable in the circumstances have been considered."[27] This amendment suggests that the approach of *R. v. M.(J.J.)* may need to be reconsidered, and that the principle of "least possible interference" and section 24(1.1) require that at the sentencing stage the *YOA* should not be used as a vehicle for imposing a disposition on a youth which is more severe than warranted by the offence but which can be justifiable on the grounds of treatment. Crown prosecutors, defence counsel, and child-protection staff may have to be more active in trying to improve linkages between the youth justice and child-welfare systems to give effect to this principle.

I. PARENTAL INVOLVEMENT: SECTION 3(1)(h)

Often the effect of an adolescent's involvement in the youth justice system is to weaken the role of parents in their children's lives by substituting the state in the role of disciplinarian. The *YOA* attempts to address this concern; it recognizes that parents have an important responsibility for their children and that adolescents can often be best helped in a familial context. The problems that lie at the root of criminal behaviour by young persons are generally most likely to be effectively addressed if parents are involved in any treatment or dispositional plan. Most young offenders will remain with or return to their families after their involvement with the justice system is completed.

It is important, however, not to "romanticize" the role of parents in the lives of their children, especially those youths who are serious or repeat offenders. Often involvement in the youth justice system reflects problems with the parent-child relationship or a lack of appropriate parenting. Some young offenders have been victims of physical, emotional, or sexual abuse at the hands of their parents, and some have ceased to have meaningful relationships with their parents before they are involved in the youth court system. Further, the fact that a youth is charged with a criminal offence frequently strains the relationship with parents, and those involved in dealing with young offenders should be realistic about the role that parents are likely to play in their children's lives.

---

27   *YOA*, above note 5, s. 24(1.1), enacted by *YOA 1995*, above note 2.

In some cases the parents are the victims of a young person's offence, for example, a theft or an assault; indeed, a significant proportion of youth homicides involves cases in which adolescents have killed their parents.[28] Sometimes the police are called only because the parents feel that they cannot "control" their child and are looking to the youth justice system to "help."

Section 3(1)(h) requires that decisions about such issues as pre-trial detention and sentencing take into consideration the desirability of parental supervision. The *YOA* provides that parents are to be notified of the arrest of their child and of youth court proceedings. In certain cases, parents may be ordered to attend court. Further, they are normally interviewed in connection with the preparation of a pre-disposition report. Parents also have the right to make submissions to the court prior to a decision being made about a sentence or transfer, though often they may feel intimidated and reluctant to speak in a relatively formal setting like a youth court.

It is important to appreciate that, while parents are encouraged to be involved, they are not parties to a youth court proceeding. It is only the youth who can retain and instruct counsel; parents are sometimes confused about this matter and want to be involved in directing a case. Indeed, some defence lawyers, rather than taking directions from their young clients, may be influenced by parental views about their child's "best interests," though this is contrary to the ordinary professional conduct rules about following a client's instructions. There is a particular concern about parental influences on counsel if they are paying the bills; section 11(8) requires a judge to order that a young person have "independent" representation if parents have retained a lawyer for their child but their interests conflict.

An important provision of the *YOA* requires police to advise young persons who are being questioned in connection with a suspected offence of the right to see their parents before making a statement, as well as of the right to consult a lawyer. As stated by Justice Kerans of the Alberta Court of Appeal: "[S]ometimes at least, the young person needs to speak to somebody other than a lawyer. Affection, empathy, love, and comfort do not fall within the scope of traditional legal services."[29]

There is, however, real ambiguity about the role that parents should play when meeting with a child who has been arrested by police and faces questioning. While a lawyer is clearly going to focus on the youth's legal rights, and is very likely to advise the youth to remain silent at the

---

28   W. Meloff & R.A. Silverman, "Canadian Kids Who Kill" (1992) 34 Can. J. Crim. 15.

29   *R. v. S. (J.L.)* (1995), 162 A.R. 388 at 391 (C.A.).

investigative stage, parents may encourage their children to "do the right thing" and make a confession, a strategy that can entail very serious consequences. For example, in an Ontario case a mother who met with her son before police questioning in connection with a sexual assault charge advised him to tell the police everything that he knew, believing that he had done nothing wrong and that the police would release her son as soon as a statement was made. The youth gave a statement, but he was not released; the statement was later used to help secure a conviction against him in court.[30] It is clear with hindsight that the mother's advice caused her son legal difficulties.

The old *Juvenile Delinquents Act* provided that parents could be fined if they did any act "contributing" to their children becoming delinquent, or "knowingly" neglected doing something that would have tended to prevent their child from committing a delinquent act.[31] The *YOA* eliminated parental liability, requiring that young persons alone should be responsible for their illegal acts, though recognizing that parents may have an important role in their children's rehabilitation. The rationale for eliminating parental liability in the *YOA* was that efforts to "punish the parent" under the *JDA* often had negative effects on rehabilitation and resulted in manipulative behaviour by some adolescents. This was recognized by a 1965 federal government report on the *JDA* which commented on the provision of that Act which allowed the juvenile court to fine parents of delinquents:

> [t]he effect is to aggravate still further an already disturbed family relationship. The parent tends to respond to punishment by increasing . . . hostility to, and rejection of, the child. The child in turn reacts to the parent's anger by getting into further trouble. Moreover, such a law places a tremendous weapon in the hands of an angry child.[32]

While youthful offending can often be related to some form of parental neglect or inadequacies, this is clearly not always the case. Some parents may try hard to prevent their children from offending, but biological factors or the influence of peers or the community may overwhelm parental efforts. Sometimes the offending behaviour may appear to be "inexplicable." Imposing liability on parents is also inconsistent with the premise of the *YOA* that young persons are accountable for their acts.

---

30 *R. v. M.(S.)* (1996), 28 O.R. (3d) 776 (C.A.).
31 *JDA*, above note 1, s. 33. See, e.g., *Re S.(A.C.)* (1969), 7 C.R.N.S. 42 (Que. S.C.).
32 Canada, *Juvenile Delinquency in Canada: The Report of the Department of Justice Committee on Juvenile Delinquency* (Ottawa: Queen's Printer, 1965) at 203.

By the mid 1990s, however, there were moves to reimpose parental liability, at least to provide compensation to victims of their children's offences. Some Canadian stores began to send letters to parents of youthful shoplifters seeking "restitution." In a 1996 Manitoba case a youth was caught stealing about $60 worth of merchandise and sent to alternative measures by the police. Although the goods were recovered, the store demanded $225 from his mother to compensate for the "incremental" costs associated with shoplifting, such as employing security staff and surveillance equipment. A court ruled that at common law[33] a parent has no liability for the acts of a child unless it is proven that the parent was directing the act or was in some way negligent (for example, by leaving easy access to a firearm that was used in a shooting).[34]

There are demands from the Reform Party and others to amend the *YOA* to hold parents liable to victims,[35] though one can question whether the federal criminal law jurisdiction under the *Constitution Act*, section 91(27), extends so far as to allow Parliament to impose potentially substantial civil liability on parents who have violated no criminal laws; the *JDA* only provided for the fining of parents, with the fines payable to the state.

Led by Manitoba, some of the provinces, looking to laws in many American states as models, are enacting legislation that imposes civil liability to victims by parents of young offenders.[36] Under the Manitoba law parents are liable to a victim for up to $5000 for deliberate property damage caused by their child unless they can show that they "exercised reasonable supervision over the child" and made "reasonable efforts in good faith to prevent or discourage the child from engaging in the kind of activity that resulted in the property loss." This type of legislation is intended both to compensate victims and to encourage parents to take

---

33   Under Quebec's *Civil Code* (Art. 1459 C.C.Q.) parents are in theory liable for the delicts (wrongful acts) of their children unless the parents can show an absence of fault in their supervision, though in practice there does not seem to be any effort in Quebec to use that provision to pursue the parents of youths committing criminal offences. In some provinces there is legislation imposing liability on parents for damages caused by their children to school property; e.g., British Columbia *School Act*, S.B.C. 1989, c. 61, s. 10, interpreted narrowly so as to exclude parental liability in *Central Okanagan School District No. 23 v. Brazeau* (19 January 1996), (B.C. Prov. Ct.) [unreported] [summarized] (1996), 7 E.L.J. 308].

34   *D.B.C. v. Zellers* (1996), 111 Man. R. (2d) 198 (Q.B.).

35   S. Fine, "Let parents pay for crimes by children, Manning urges: Reform supporters applaud liability proposal," *[Toronto] Globe and Mail* (6 August 1993) A1.

36   *Parental Responsibility Act*, S.M. 1996, c. 61. C. Harper, "Manitoba Bill puts parents on the hook for damage caused by kids" *Lawyers Weekly* (28 June 1996) 3. Ontario is considering enacting similar legislation, but at the time of writing it has not done so.

their parental responsibilities more seriously, though there is considerable doubt that it will have any effects on reducing criminal behaviour. Indeed, this type of law may exacerbate some family situations and then lead to situations where further criminal acts are committed.

J. THE PRINCIPLES OF THE *YOA*: AN ASSESSMENT

Some commentators have argued that the different principles set out in section 3 are inconsistent with one another and hence offer no real guidance for the implementation of the *YOA*.[37] Others have been critical of the lack of legislative prioritization among the principles articulated, arguing that this gives judges and other decision makers applying the Act a broad discretion that may be influenced by personal values and biases. In a 1987 transfer case, Laycraft J.A. of the Alberta Court of Appeal complained about the lack of parliamentary direction: "Section 3 contains some statements which directly conflict with other declarations of principle in the same section. The balance between these conflicting principles is, in the individual case, not easy."[38]

However, the Supreme Court of Canada has been more supportive of section 3, recognizing the tensions within the Declaration but not regarding the principles articulated there as contradictory. In the Supreme Court decision of *R. v. T.(V.)*, L'Heureux-Dubé J. quoted with approval from an earlier work co-authored by this writer:

> . . . [W]hile I am not unmindful of the apparent inconsistencies of the stated goals of the Act as contained in section 3(1), in my opinion the better view is that advocated by Bala and Kirvan in . . . *The Young Offenders Act: A Revolution in Canadian Juvenile Justice* (1991) . . . :
>
> > It is apparent that there is a level of societal ambivalence in Canada about the appropriate response to young offenders. On the one hand, there is a feeling that adolescents who violate the criminal law need help to enable them to grow into productive,

---

37 See P. Platt, *Young Offenders Law in Canada* (Toronto: Butterworths, 1989) at 2–6: "The difficulty is that they are not coherent and, in some cases, are positively inconsistent." In the second edition (P. Platt, *Young Offenders Law in Canada*, 2d ed. (Toronto: Butterworths, 1995)) [*Young Offenders*], this more trenchant critique is dropped, but Platt still observes that the section "will remain a fertile ground for searching out Parliament's legislative intention" (at 34).

38 *R. v. M.(S.H.)* (1987), 78 A.R. 309 at 315 (C.A.).

law-abiding citizens; this view is frequently reflected in media stories about inadequate facilities for rehabilitating young offenders. On the other hand, there is a widespread public concern about the need to control youthful criminality and protect society. This view is reflected in media stories and editorials commenting on the perceived inadequacy of the three-year maximum disposition that can be applied to young offenders, a particular public concern in regard to those youths who commit very serious, violent offences.

While it may not be inaccurate to suggest that the Declaration of Principle reflects a certain societal ambivalence about young offenders, it is also important to appreciate that it represents an honest attempt to achieve an appropriate balance for dealing with a very complex social problem. The YOA does not have a single, simple underlying philosophy, for there is no single, simple philosophy that can deal with all situations in which young persons violate the criminal law. While the Declaration as a whole defines the parameters for juvenile justice in Canada, each principle is not necessarily relevant to every situation. The weight to be attached to a particular principle will be determined in large measure by the nature of the decision being made and the specific provisions of the YOA that govern the situation. There are situations in which there is a need to balance competing principles, but this is a challenge in cases in the adult as well as the juvenile system.[39]

In R. v. M.(J.J.) Justice Cory of the Supreme Court of Canada agreed with the need for a balancing of principles:

A quick reading of that section [section 3] indicates that there is a marked ambivalence in its approach to the sentencing of young offenders. Yet that ambivalence should not be surprising when it is remembered that the Act reflects a courageous attempt to balance concepts and interests that are frequently conflicting.[40]

As the Supreme Court has recognized, the philosophical tensions in section 3 of the YOA reflect the complex nature of youthful criminality and the inadequacy of a single-minded approach in dealing with young offenders. Further, it is not accurate to say that the YOA gives no signals about prioritization of principles. While there is a tension in the YOA between such competing ideals as due process for youths and securing access to treatment, in almost all situations the Act gives precedence to

39   Above note 18 at 765–66.
40   Above note 3 at 426.

due process, consistent with the *Charter of Rights*.[41] Accountability and the protection of society are important, and in some situations dominant considerations; however, the 1995 amendments to section 3, with their emphasis on prevention and rehabilitation as the best routes to achieving societal protection, indicate that, broadly speaking, the rehabilitation of the young person should take precedence in any dispositional decision. The Declaration of Principle can therefore be seen as providing real, albeit general, guidance to those who must implement the Act, but it must be appreciated that section 3 also gives individual decision makers substantial discretion to emphasize the principles they consider most important in any individual situation. Inevitably, different professionals exercise their discretion in different ways, and there is substantial variation in how the *YOA* is interpreted and applied,[42] which may contribute to Canada having high rates of youth custody.[43]

K. THE UNITED NATIONS CONVENTION ON THE RIGHTS OF THE CHILD

In 1991 Canada ratified the *United Nations Convention on the Rights of the Child*,[44] joining over one hundred other countries in pledging to

---

41   There is only one provision of the *YOA*, above note 5, which clearly gives precedence to needs over due process. S. 13(7) allows a judge to withhold all or part of a medical or psychological report from a young person if the judge is satisfied that "disclosure . . . would seriously impair the treatment or recovery of the young person. . . ." The lawyer for the youth must always receive the full report.

42   See, e.g., A.N. Doob & L.A. Beaulieu, "Variation in the Exercise of Judicial Discretion with Young Offenders" (1992) 34 Can. J. Crim. 35, commenting on the effect of the lack of prioritization of principles in s. 3 on the wide variations in dispositional practices of judges under the *YOA, ibid.*

43   Judge Heino Lilles of the Yukon Territorial Court, writing before the enactment of the 1995 amendments to *YOA*, s. 3, concluded: "In the absence of a clear philosophy towards young offenders, judges have been free to emphasize those principles which correspond most closely to their value systems. . . . In my view, the absence of a clear direction . . . has contributed significantly to the high rates of custody imposed . . . and the wide variations in the use of custody." H. Lilles, "Canada's Young Offenders Act: Some International Perspectives for Reform" (1995) 5 J. Law & Social Work 41.

44   20 November 1989, 28 I.L.M. 1448 [*Convention*]. Another document that Canada has adopted is also relevant for determining international standards, the 1959 *United Nations Standard Minimum Rules for the Administration of Juvenile Justice* (known as the *Beijing Rules*) (New York: Department of Public Information, 1986) adopted by General Assembly Resolution 40/33 (29 November 1985).

adhere to certain internationally accepted principles and minimum standards for government treatment of children in a whole range of matters including health, education, welfare, and juvenile justice. The *Convention,* which was the product of a decade of debate and compromise at the United Nations, applies to "children" up to the age of eighteen, setting out the general principle that in "all actions concerning children . . . the best interests of the child shall be *a* primary consideration."[45] Notice the tiny but crucial qualifying term to the use of "best interests" — this factor shall be "*a*" primary consideration. Other considerations may also apply.

Of particular relevance is Article 40 on the Administration of Juvenile Justice:

> 1. State Parties recognize the right of every child alleged as, accused of, or recognized as having infringed the penal law to be treated in a manner consistent with the promotion of the child's sense of dignity and worth, which reinforces the child's respect for the human rights of and fundamental freedoms of others and which takes into account the child's age and the desirability of promoting the child's reintegration and the child's assuming a constructive role in society.

Article 40(2)–(4) sets out a number of specific rights that should be afforded children, including

- [t]o have the matter determined without delay by a competent, independent and impartial authority or judicial body . . . in the presence of legal or other appropriate assistance [2(iii)];
- [n]ot to be compelled to give testimony or to confess guilt [2(iv)];
- [t]o have his or her privacy fully respected at all stages of the proceedings [2(vii)].

Governments are expected to have special laws and institutions for dealing with children separate from adults. Among other things, there should be

- a minimum age below which children shall be presumed not to have the capacity to infringe the penal law [3(a)];
- [w]henever appropriate and desirable, measures for dealing with such children without resorting to judicial proceedings, providing that human rights and legal safeguards are fully respected [3(b)]; [and]
- [a] variety of dispositions . . . to ensure that children are dealt with in a manner appropriate to their well-being and proportionate both to their circumstances and the offence [4].

---

45   *Convention, ibid.,* art. 3(1). [Emphasis added].

Although Canada has ratified the *Convention,* it does not have the same legal status as a Canadian statute, let alone a constitutional instrument like the *Charter of Rights.* While the *Convention* can be used in the case of ambiguity as an aid to the interpretation of the *YOA* or the *Charter of Rights,* it does not have the force of law in Canada.[46]

Canada's federal government, however, appears to take the *Convention* seriously. When ratifying the *Convention,* Canada specifically made a "reservation" with respect to Article 37(c), which requires that children who are deprived of their liberty "shall be separated from adults unless it is considered in the child's best interest not to do so . . . save in exceptional circumstances." The fact that Canada filed a reservation, accepting the principle of Article 37(c) but "reserving" the right to detain youths with adults when separate detention is not "appropriate or feasible,"[47] indicates that in general the federal government intends to adhere to the *Convention.* Any failure to comply may be reported at the United Nations through the *Convention's* monitoring process and could be a source of international embarrassment and political criticism. Accordingly, advocates for youth may view the *Convention* as a political tool that can be used to influence how Canada's youth justice policy evolves. Indeed, during the parliamentary hearings on the 1995 *YOA* amendments, there was criticism of the transfer provisions based on the violation of Article 37(c) of the *Convention,* even though Canada had reserved on that provision.[48]

Not surprisingly, a document like the *Convention,* which is intended to have broad application in many different countries, is frequently vague and provides only general guidance. One might, for example, question whether some of the 1995 *YOA* amendments allowing limited release under specified circumstances of a young offender's identity to neighbours of the youth[49] violate the privacy-protection stipulation in Article 40(2)(vii), but it is difficult to be certain on this point since that article of the *Convention* is not specific about what the "respect of privacy" entails.

On the whole, the principles and provisions of the *YOA* seem broadly consistent with the *Convention.* Both documents require a balancing of

---

46   On the limited effect of the *Convention, ibid.* in Canada, see. A.F. Bayefsky, *International Human Rights Law: Use in Canadian Charter of Rights and Freedoms Litigation* (Toronto: Butterworths, 1992), at 94–103. For a young offenders case where the *Convention* was cited by the court but not ultimately used, see *R. v. H. (A.B.)* (1993), 12 O.R. (3d) 634 (C.A.).

47   See *YOA,* above note 5, ss. 7(2), 16.1 and 16.2 for provisions allowing detention with adults.

48   See, e.g., Testimony of R.W. Hatton, *Minutes of Proceedings and Evidence of the Standing Committee on Justice and Legal Affairs* (3 April 1995).

49   *YOA,* above note 5, s. 38(1.5), enacted by *YOA 1995,* above note 2, s. 27(2).

interests, including a recognition of the importance of accountability, while in general placing rehabilitation in *a* primary position. However, in practice Canada's rate of formal youth-court response to adolescent crime and of custody for adolescents is among the highest in the world. This raises serious concerns about the application of the diversionary and rehabilitative ideals reflected in these documents. Further, if some of the more radical proposals for the "reform" of the *YOA* were accepted — for example, to lower the minimum age of adult court jurisdiction to sixteen, or to publicize the names of all young offenders — there would clearly be violations of the *Convention*.

L. THE INTERNATIONAL CONTEXT

One can gain a better understanding of the choices that have been made in Canada about how to respond to youth crime by considering some of the approaches that are being used in other countries. In making an international comparison, it is apparent that Canada makes more use of a formal youth-court response and less use of diversion into informal programs for handling adolescent offenders than other countries. The rate of use of incarceration for adult offenders in Canada is among the highest in the world but still only about one-third the adult rate in the United States. However, Canada's rate of custody use for adolescent offenders is substantially higher than the rate in the United States.

1) *The United States*[50]

While the rates of youth crime for property offences are roughly comparable in Canada and the United States, the American rates of youth violence, and in particular youth homicide, are much higher. Some of the differences in violent crime are probably attributable to a range of social and cultural factors, but differences in access to firearms also play an important role. Although most American states have enacted laws to prevent adolescents from having firearms, they still have relatively easy access to guns. Angry and immature adolescents with access to firearms are especially dangerous.

---

50   J.P. Hornick & S. Rodal, *The Use of Alternatives to Traditional Youth Court: An International Comparison* (Calgary: Canadian Research Institute for Law and the Family, 1995); and J.P. Hornick, N. Bala, and J. Hudson, *The Response to Juvenile Crime in the United States: A Canadian Perspective* (Calgary: Canadian Research Institute for Law and the Family, 1995).

Criminal law is largely a matter of state responsibility, and there is substantial variation across the United States. Most states rely on the common law to set the minimum age of juvenile court responsibility at seven years, while legislation specifies that adult jurisdiction starts at sixteen to nineteen years of age. The American Supreme Court has held that juveniles have a right to "due process" and to state-provided lawyers if they are unable to afford to retain counsel,[51] but in practice many judges and parents discourage juveniles from having a lawyer unless the charges are very serious.

With rising rates of juvenile crime,[52] crime has become a major political issue in the United States and various efforts have been made to "get tough" on juvenile offenders. While originally the statutory statements of principle for dealing with juvenile offenders focused exclusively on the welfare of juveniles, since 1980 many states have added clauses to their statements of principle that have emphasized the protection of the public and the accountability of juvenile offenders. Most states have moved away from indeterminate sentences to determinate juvenile sentencing; a number have adopted specific sentencing "grids," which take account of the nature of the offence and prior record to guide juvenile court judges in their sentencing decisions. American states and cities are increasing their range of legal responses to youth crime, including the introduction of juvenile curfews, parental responsibility laws, and automatic school suspensions for students found in possession of weapons.

All states have provision for juvenile transfer (or "waiver") into adult court. In many states transfer is automatic for certain serious offences or is a matter for prosecutorial discretion, while other states have a judicial transfer model (similar to that in Canada). Most states and the federal government have taken steps to increase the numbers of youths dealt with in the adult courts, and the country as a whole has a much higher rate of juvenile incarceration in adult prisons than Canada. In a number of states there is the possibility of capital punishment for juveniles sixteen or older at the time of commission of a murder.[53] This is contrary to

---

51 *Re Gault*, 387 U.S. 1 (1967).

52 There is evidence that juvenile crime in the U.S.A. may have begun to fall in the mid 1990s. Although the causes for the decline, or at least plateauing, are not certain, many experts believe that improved policing may be playing a role, while doubting that "tougher" laws have had any impact. F. Butterfield, "After a decade, juvenile crime begins to drop," *New York Times* (9 August 1996) A1.

53 In 1993 twelve states expressly allowed capital punishment for those under eighteen. Challenges to the constitutionality of capital punishment for juveniles based on the argument that it is "cruel and unusual punishment" have failed; *Stanford* v. *Kentucky*, 492 U.S. 361 (1989), *Arizona* v. *Jackson*, 216 Ariz. Adv. R. 9 (1996).

Article 37(a) of the *United Nations Convention on the Rights of the Child,* but the United States is not a signatory to that document.

While there is an emphasis on more punitive and interventionist responses to violent youth crime in the United States, there is actually substantially more use of informal diversion programs for property offences and for less serious offenders than in Canada. There are also innovative programs in a number of localities that attempt to respond to youth crime by dealing with the underlying problems that youth face, generally involving family members and community-based dispositions.

2) England[54]

England has three categories of youthful offenders who can be dealt with under criminal law. Children are those ten to thirteen years of age; they are presumed to be incapable of committing an offence but may be dealt with by the courts if the presumption is rebutted; children aged ten and over charged with homicide are dealt with in adult court. Young persons are those aged fourteen to seventeen; they are dealt with by youth court except for the most serious offences. Young adults are eighteen to twenty inclusive; they are dealt with in adult court but with special provisions for sentencing.

English policies towards youthful offenders have been in a state of considerable flux. By the 1980s extensive use was being made of informal police cautioning for dealing with youthful offenders outside the courts, but there was still concern about the excessive number of custodial dispositions for young persons under the welfare-oriented legislation. This led to the enactment of the *Criminal Justice Act, 1991,* which contained provisions intended to limit use of custody. However, with growing anxiety about juvenile crime, some of the key provisions of the 1991 Act were amended in 1993 and 1994 to permit more use of custodial dispositions, especially for fourteen- to seventeen- year-olds.

3) New Zealand[55]

Since the 1980s there has been dramatic political and economic changes in New Zealand, with major emphasis being placed on a more market-

---

54 Hornick & Rodal, above note 50; Platt, *Young Offenders,* above note 37 at 577.
55 Hornick & Rodal, *ibid.*; Lilles, above note 43; Platt, *Young Offenders, ibid.*, ch. 23; B.J. Brown & F.W.M. McElrea, *The Youth Court in New Zealand: A New Model of Justice* (Auckland: New Zealand Legal Research Foundation, 1993).

oriented economy and a smaller government and debt. At the same time, the country has moved to adopt new approaches to juvenile justice, enacting the *Children, Young Persons, and Their Families Act 1989* for those ten through sixteen years of age. The Act encourages resolution of youth crime problems outside the formal court system, having the following as its first guiding principle: ". . . [u]nless the public interest requires otherwise, criminal proceedings should not be instituted against a child or young person if there is an alternative means of dealing with the matter."[56]

The New Zealand statute makes specific reference to a process of police "street cautioning" of youths for minor offences, as well as more elaborate warnings provided to youths and their parents at police stations by members of the specialist Youth Aid Section. The legislation also provides for family-group conferences, based loosely on the aboriginal Maori methods of responding to offending behaviour. At these conferences a youth and family members, the victim, and a support person, a police representative, and possibly a social worker or probation officer can meet with a youth justice coordinator to discuss the offence and arrange an appropriate (non-custodial) resolution that takes account of the concerns of the victim and the needs of the youth and family, as well as the interests of society. The youth is encouraged to be actively involved in this process and take responsibility for his or her acts. Research indicates a substantial degree of victim satisfaction with the outcomes of such conferences, though some victims continue to feel excluded or disappointed with the process.[57] The introduction of these reforms in New Zealand has resulted in a substantial reduction in the use of custody and the closing of a number of custodial facilities. There is also an indication that offending rates among young adults are falling, leading one New Zealand judge to "suggest that the new youth court is producing adults who are less likely to be prosecuted in the adult courts."[58]

Only about 10 percent of the youth cases that police are involved with in New Zealand come to the youth court, a fraction of the rate of court use in Canada. There are some cases involving violent or recurrent offending, or deeply disturbed families, where court is the only appropriate response and a custodial disposition or residential treatment is necessary, but the rate of custody use is substantially lower than in Canada. For the most serious cases, transfer to adult court is possible, and it is automatic for murder and manslaughter charges.

---

56 *Children, Young Persons, and Their Families Act 1989* (New Zealand), 1989, No. 24 s. 208.
57 Hornick & Rodal, above note 50 at 37.
58 F.W.M. McElrea, "Restorative Justice: The New Zealand Youth Court — A Model for Developments in Other Courts?" (1994) 4 J. Judicial Admin. 36 at 53.

4) *Sweden*[59]

Like several other European countries, Sweden has a relatively high minimum criminal responsibility age, fifteen, and a rehabilitation-oriented system for those aged fifteen to twenty, which includes young adults. Youths less than fifteen are dealt with exclusively by the child welfare authorities. Youths up to eighteen may be referred by the prosecutor to the child-welfare authorities, provided that they confess guilt; if they deny guilt, a criminal trial is held. Only about 15 percent of youth cases are sent to court by prosecutors.

Youth cases are dealt with by the same judges as adult prosecutions, though youths sent to custody are placed in separate correctional facilities. Judges may also order a youth to be placed in the care of welfare authorities instead of imposing a custodial sentence. The minimum penalties that apply to some adult offences do not apply to youths. In law, youths face the same maximum penalties for most offences as adults, with a maximum sentence of sixteen years' imprisonment, but in practice judges are far more lenient in dealing with youths and custodial sentences are relatively rare.

M. CONCLUSION

There are real limits to the effects of criminal laws and the juvenile justice system on youth crime. Public policies related to health, education, child welfare, law enforcement, and gun control, as well as a range of subtle cultural and social factors, are much more important for determining a country's youth crime rate than its youth justice regime. It is clear from the American experience that merely enacting "get tough" laws is not a solution to the youth crime problem, and that a rethinking of Canadian approaches may be appropriate. Judge Lilles of the Yukon Territorial Court has observed:

> Canada appears to be at a crossroad, at the same decision point where the United States was in the in the early 1980s. Will it take the same path, by passing more punitive laws, building more jails and by enlarging the existing criminal justice industry, with commensurate cuts in social programs? Or will Canada take the other path, the one modelled by New Zealand. . . ? We have the distinct advantage of seeing where both roads lead.[60]

---

59   Platt, *Young Offenders*, above note 37 at 590–91.
60   Lilles, above note 43.

FURTHER READINGS

BALA, N. *et al.*, *State Responses to Youth Crime: A Consideration of Principles* (Calgary: Canadian Research Institute for Law and the Family, 1993)

BALA, N. & H. LILLES, eds., *Young Offenders Service* (Toronto: Butterworths, 1984) (looseleaf), ss. 3:2:1 to 3:4:12

CANADA, FEDERAL-PROVINCIAL-TERRITORIAL TASK FORCE ON YOUTH JUSTICE, *A Review of the Young Offenders Act and the Youth Justice System in Canada* (Ottawa: Supply & Services, 1996), chs. 1 and 2

CANADA, HOUSE OF COMMONS, *Thirteenth Report of the Standing Committee on Justice and Legal Affairs: Renewing Youth Justice* (Ottawa: Supply & Services, 1997)

CANADIAN COALITION ON THE RIGHTS OF THE CHILD. *Canada and the UN Convention on the Rights of the Child: Developing a Monitoring Framework* (Ottawa, 1997)

HARRIS, P.J., ed., *Young Offenders Act Manual* (Aurora: Canada Law Book, 1984) (looseleaf), 3.1–3.54

HORNICK, J.P., N. BALA, & J. HUDSON, *The Response to Juvenile Crime in the United States: A Canadian Perspective* (Calgary: Canadian Research Institute for Law and the Family, 1995)

HORNICK, J.P. & S. RODAL, *The Use of Alternatives to Traditional Youth Court: An International Comparison* (Calgary: Canadian Research Institute for Law & the Family, 1995)

LILLES, H., "Canada's Young Offenders Act: Some International Perspectives for Reform" (1995) 5 J. Law and Social Work 41

PLATT, P., *Young Offenders Law in Canada*, 2d ed. (Toronto: Butterworths, 1995), chs. 2 & 23

CHAPTER 3

YOUTH COURT JURISDICTION

A. YOUTH COURTS IN CANADA

Under section 2 of the *YOA* each province and territory has the responsibility to designate a court as its "youth court." One might expect that this should be a "special" court with judges who have experience or educational qualifications to equip them for dealing with troubled youth, or a distinctive philosophy, or at least a physical locale that is separate from the adult courts. In some places in Canada (and elsewhere in the world) the courts that deal with adolescent offenders have these special characteristics, but the provinces and territories have a great deal of discretion about the designation, staffing, and resources of youth courts, and there is substantial variation in how these courts operate across the country.

Quebec established a specialized youth court, which has provincially appointed judges with jurisdiction over *YOA* proceedings, child protection, and adoption[1] and generally sits in special courthouses separate from where adults appear. These judges usually have interpreted the *YOA* in a manner that has emphasized the limited accountability and rehabilitation of young persons and that has resulted in lower rates of custody use and transfer to adult court than elsewhere in Canada. This

---

1   Known technically as the Youth Division of the Court of Québec, and commonly as the Youth Court (Tribunal de la Jeunesse) *Courts of Justice Act*, R.S.Q. c. T–16, s. 83.

is consistent with the general approach to young offenders in Quebec, which has a youth justice system that is closely linked to the child-welfare system. Quebec has a broad range of social policies that are among the most supportive of children and youth in Canada.

In most provinces and territories, jurisdiction for YOA cases is given to the judges of the provincial or territorial court who generally deal with less serious adult criminal cases. These judges are appointees of the provincial or territorial government, and all recent appointees have had legal training. In some provinces, like Ontario, legislation requires a minimum of ten years' experience as a lawyer before being eligible for appointment to the provincial court. While judges with a responsibility for adult criminal cases will be familiar with the substantive and evidentiary issues that arise in YOA cases, there may be a concern that some of these judges may not take a different approach with youths than with adult offenders, though adult and youth cases will generally be scheduled for hearing at different times.

In some places, such as Manitoba, responsibility for YOA cases is given to judges with a jurisdiction over a range of family and domestic matters, such as child protection and spousal support. The rationale for this approach is that these judges may be more understanding of the family problems faced by many young offenders and more familiar with the types of community resources that are available to assist them. In New Brunswick, jurisdiction for YOA cases is given to the federally appointed judges of the Family Division of the Court of Queen's Bench, who have a broad jurisdiction over all family law issues, including divorce and child protection.

Ontario and Nova Scotia adopted a "two tier" youth court model when the YOA came into force in 1984. As was the practice under the *Juvenile Delinquents Act*, twelve- to fifteen- year-olds continued to be dealt with in Family Court, while sixteen- and seventeen- year-olds appeared in the adult Criminal Division of the Provincial Court, albeit with adult criminal court judges nominally sitting as youth court judges. Critics argued that, by maintaining the court jurisdiction in effect under the JDA, Ontario and Nova Scotia simply acted in an expedient fashion and failed to implement the spirit of the YOA.[2] It has also been argued that the older youths may be subjected to harsher treatment by the judges with adult criminal law experience and that they may have less access to certain kinds of rehabilitative services than the younger age group.[3]

---

2   D. Stuart, "Annotation to R. v. C.(R.)" (1987), 56 C.R. (3d) 185.

3   Ontario Social Development Council, *Young Offenders Act Dispositions: Challenges and Choices* (Toronto: The Council, 1988) at 99.

The Ontario Court of Appeal, however, ruled that the two-tier implementation model is permitted under the *YOA* and does not violate the
Canadian Charter of Rights and Freedoms, since the judges in both courts

> all . . . have the same powers and duties, but for administrative pur-
> poses some sit in the Criminal Division, some sit in the Family Divi-
> sion, and some in both. All of these judges are qualified to sit as judges
> in the youth court. . . .[4]

In 1990 the Ontario government began a process of court restructuring and in theory merged the Family and Criminal Divisions into the
Ontario Court of Justice (Provincial Division), while slowly extending
the Unified Family Courts,[5] with plans at that time eventually to transfer
responsibility for all young offenders cases to judges with a family-law
focus. This restructuring process proceeded slowly, and in many localities in Ontario older youths continue to appear before judges who generally deal with adult offenders, while twelve- to fifteen- year-olds are
the responsibility of judges with a primarily family focus. The gradual
transfer of responsibility to the family-law judges was part of a plan for
restructuring the Ontario judicial system and a response to the problem
of overcrowding in the criminal courts. However, more recently there
have been indicators that the Progressive Conservative government of
Ontario may give the adult criminal court judges responsibility for all
youth cases, as part of a "get tough" approach to youth crime. Ontario
has also maintained a division of ministerial responsibility in the provision of alternative measures, probation, and correctional services for
young offenders. Twelve- to fifteen- year-olds (known as "Phase 1" youths)

---

4   *R. v. C.(R.)* (1987), 56 C.R. (3d) 185 at 187 (Ont. C.A.). See, however, *R. v. B.(R.)*
     (18 September 1986), (Ont. Prov. Ct.) [unreported] [summarized (1986), 17
     W.C.B. 217] which invoked s. 15 of the *Canadian Charter of Rights and Freedoms*,
     Part I of the *Constitution Act, 1982*, being Schedule B to the *Canada Act 1982*
     (U.K.), 1982, c. 11 [*Charter*] to place a sixteen-year-old youth in a local open-
     custody facility designated for twelve- to fifteen- year-olds. The failure to have an
     open-custody facility near the youth's home was held to violate the *Charter*. It may
     well be that individual youths who can clearly establish detrimental treatment
     because of the two tiers can invoke the *Charter*.
5   Under s. 96 of the *Constitution Act, 1867* (U.K.), 30 & 31 Vict. c. 3 [*CA 1867*]
     courts with provincially appointed judges only have a limited jurisdiction over
     family matters such as child support, child protection, and adoption as well as
     Young Offenders Act, R.S.C. 1985, c. Y-1 [*YOA*] cases. However, federally appointed
     judges, such as those in Ontario's Unified Family Court or the New Brunswick
     Court of Queen's Bench (Family Division), can have jurisdiction over a full range
     of family matters, including divorce and property division as well as support, child
     protection, and *YOA* cases.

are to be dealt with by the Ministry of Community and Social Services, which also has responsibility for child protection and other children's services, while sixteen- and seventeen- year-olds ("Phase 2" youths) receive services from the Ministry of Correctional Services, a ministry with responsibility for adult offenders and a reputation for placing less emphasis on treatment and rehabilitation than Community and Social Services. As with court jurisdiction, there are indications that the Ontario government may consolidate all responsibility for young offenders in the corrections ministry.

In most places in Canada, the judges who sit in youth court are appointed by the provincial or territorial government. This was challenged on the ground that it violates the *Constitution Act, 1867,* section 96, which provides that only the federal government can appoint judges to sit in the "Superior" courts (like the Court of Queen's Bench and the Unified Family Court). It was argued that the youth courts were in effect exercising the jurisdiction of superior courts and hence should have federally appointed judges. This argument was rejected by the Supreme Court of Canada in *Reference Re Young Offenders Act (Prince Edward Island).*[6] The Supreme Court held that the YOA creates "a complete and comprehensive scheme" for dealing with young offenders, "designed to respond to what was a novel [i.e. post-1867] concern of society," and hence does not interfere with the jurisdiction that was historically exercised by superior courts. The Supreme Court also accepted that, while the provinces could appoint youth court judges, this did not preclude provincial governments from designating federally appointed "superior" court judges as youth court judges, thus validating the scheme of provinces such as New Brunswick where the federally appointed Family Division of the Court of Queen's Bench is the youth court.[7]

The process for appointment of judges to the youth court varies between jurisdictions. Youth court judges who are members of the Unified Family Court or Court of Queen's Bench, such as in New Brunswick, are appointed by the federal government. Provincial Court judges who sit in youth court are appointed by the provincial government. Each jurisdiction has a somewhat different method of screening and making judicial appointments. While historically judges were appointed at the

---

6   [1991] 1 S.C.R. 252.

7   A superior court judge in New Brunswick had earlier ruled that giving his court jurisdiction for youth court cases was inconsistent with the "accepted . . . role and status of Superior Courts" and hence contrary to s. 96 of the *CA 1867*, above note 5, but the Supreme Court rejected this argument; see *R. v. D.(Y.)* (1985), 67 N.B.R. (2d) 269 (Q.B.).

discretion of the government, and appointment decisions could be affected by patronage or political influence, in recent years there has been an effort to reduce political pressures in the appointment process and screen out unsuitable candidates, though some appointments may still be politically influenced.[8] There is no requirement that judges appointed to the youth court have any particular background or training. Once appointed, judges are encouraged to attend various judicial-education programs, which are generally organized by judges' organizations or the National Judicial Institute, but there is no requirement to do so.

B. JUSTICES OF THE PEACE

The lowest level of judicial officer in Canada is the justice of the peace (often known as the JP) who is appointed by provincial governments. Most justices of the peace are lay persons and receive some training and supervision from Provincial Court judges. Justices of the peace generally deal with procedural aspects of cases within the jurisdiction of the Provincial Court; some of them also have functions as court clerks and may, for example, adjourn cases in the absence of a judge. Under the *Criminal Code,* justices of the peace usually have responsibility for a range of procedural issues, such as pre-trial detention (bail) hearings and issuing summons to witnesses as well as commencing proceedings by issuing summons or warrants for the accused. Although their responsibilities vary from one province to another, justices of the peace generally also have authority to accept pleas and to sentence adults for a range of less serious (or summary) offences under the *Criminal Code,* as well as to conduct trials under such provincial legislation as highway traffic laws.

The *Young Offenders Act,* section 6 provides that justices of the peace have the same procedural jurisdiction in youth court proceedings as they do in adult court. However, section 6, specifies that a justice of the peace cannot accept a plea, preside over a trial, or sentence a young person. This restriction reflects the view that youth cases are more sensitive than those involving adults and hence should be presided over by more qualified judicial officers. Only a youth court judge can satisfy the requirements of section 12(3) of the *YOA* — to ensure that an unrepresented youth understands the charges and is given an explanation of the option to plead guilty or not guilty. Also, section 19 requires that, before accepting a youth's guilty plea,

---

8   See, e.g., G.L. Gall, *The Canadian Legal System,* 4th ed. (Toronto: Carswell, 1995) at 263–79.

the judge must be satisfied that "the facts support" this plea. The intent of these provisions (which have no statutory equivalents in adult proceedings) is that a youth court judge, who generally has legal training, can provide at least some protection for the rights of a young person.

The *YOA* originally provided that, because of their sensitive nature, pre-trial detention hearings had to be conducted by youth court judges, but amendments were passed in 1986 to ease the burden on judges and facilitate administration of the Act in locales where judges were not readily accessible.[9] Justices of the peace may now conduct detention hearings for youths (as well as adults), but section 8(2) of the *YOA* gives a young person who has been detained before trial by a justice of the peace the right to have a rehearing by a youth court judge. In practice it seems that justices of the peace still more commonly deal with pre-trial detention of adults than young persons.

The Yukon has a special program to give some of its justices of the peace a relatively broad authority in youth court proceedings to accept pleas and conduct trials, in order both to provide better access to courts in remote locales and to allow Aboriginal justices to have more responsibility for their communities. The more serious youth cases must be dealt with by the legally trained judges of the Court, who reside in Whitehorse and travel to the remote localities as needed. In *R. v. G. (A.P.)* the Yukon Territory Court of Appeal upheld the validity of legislation which deems all justices of the peace of the Yukon Territorial Court to also be judges of the Yukon Youth Court, with jurisdiction to accept pleas, conduct trials, and impose sentences in less serious youth cases.[10] The Appeal Court concluded that section 6 of the *YOA* applies only to justices of the peace who are not also appointed to be youth court judges, and it noted that there is technically no requirement in the *YOA* for youth court judges to have legal training.

C. OFFENCE JURISDICTION

Under the old *Juvenile Delinquents Act* juvenile courts had a broad offence jurisdiction. Any violation of any federal, provincial, or municipal law, or "sexual immorality or any similar form of vice," constituted the offence

---

9   *An Act to amend the Young Offenders Act, the Criminal Code, the Penitentiary Act and the Prisons and Reformatories Act*, R.S.C. 1985 (2d Supp.) c. 24, s.4.
10 (1990), 57 C.C.C. (3d) 496 (Y.C.A.), leave to appeal refused (1991), 61 C.C.C. (3d) vi (note) (S.C.C.). The Yukon Court of Appeal actually is composed of judges from the British Columbia Court of Appeal.

of "delinquency" and gave the juvenile court the authority to impose any disposition under the *JDA*.[11] The vaguely worded "sexual immorality and any similar form of vice" were "status offences," that is, offences that only those with the status (age) of a juvenile could commit. Status offences were intended to give juvenile courts a protective mandate, though in practice the provisions were often applied in a discriminatory fashion.

Subject to a few exceptions, section 5 of the *YOA* gives the youth court exclusive jurisdiction over alleged violations by young persons of the federal criminal law, which includes the *Criminal Code* and a number of other statutes, principally related to drug offences. Consistent with the due process and accountability orientation of the *YOA*, the concept of "status offences" was abolished under federal law.[12] Young persons are charged with "offences" under the relevant legislation, such as the *Criminal Code*, and it is not technically necessary for court documents (like the information that commences the prosecution) to state that a young person is involved, though this is usually done.[13]

Violations of provincial or territorial laws, like the highway traffic code, municipal bylaws, or measures for the regulation of noise, are technically not dealt with under the *YOA*. Each jurisdiction except for Manitoba, the Yukon, and the Northwest Territories has enacted legislation that

---

11   *Juvenile Delinquents Act*, R.S.C. 1970, c. J–3, ss. 2(1) and 3 [*JDA*].

12   There is one remaining "status offence" under provincial law — truancy, the wilful failure to attend school for those under sixteen years of age. Under the *JDA*, *ibid* it was quite common for children to be prosecuted for truancy and even to be sent to training school for failing to attend school. In a number of provinces, like Quebec, legislation now specifies that only parents are liable to prosecution if their child fails to attend school or otherwise receive an appropriate education (for example, by parental instruction at home). In some provinces a youth may still be prosecuted under legislation like Ontario's *Education Act*, R.S.O. 1990, c. E.2, s. 30 for a wilful failure to attend school or otherwise receive an education, but in practice in recent years some judges have shown reluctance to impose even probationary sentences on youths who violate school attendance laws, preferring to view this as strictly an educational issue and unsuitable for resolution in the court system; *R. v. R.(B.)*, [1996] O.J. No. 980 (Gen. Div.) (QL). Other judges will, however, still place a youth who fails to attend school on probation; the failure to attend school then becomes a breach of probation for which the youth may receive a custodial sentence.

It is not uncommon for a judge acting under the *YOA*, above note 5, to make school attendance a condition of probation for a youth who commits a criminal offence if it is felt that the offence occurred because the youth "had too much time on his hands." Many youths who commit offences have school attendance problems, and may find it difficult to comply with this type of probationary term, resulting in further "offending" behaviour, this time a breach of probation charge.

13   *R. v. C.(P.)* (27 November 1984), (Ont. Prov. Ct.) [unreported] [summarized (1984), 13 W.C.B. 227].

governs the procedure and sentencing for those between the ages of twelve and seventeen who are charged with violations of municipal bylaws and provincial or territorial law. In general, these statutes are intended to afford young persons charged the same protection as those in the *YOA* and give the youth court jurisdiction to deal with these less serious offences, though there are some differences. In Ontario, Nova Scotia, and Saskatchewan, the provisions of the *YOA* apply only to those aged twelve through fifteen, and so, for example, sixteen- and seventeen- year-olds who violate the highway traffic law in these provinces are treated like adults and parents do not receive notice of the charges. Most provinces do not give youths charged under provincial laws the same access to a government paid lawyer as is provided under section 11 of the *YOA*. In Manitoba, the Yukon, and the Northwest Territories, youths who are charged with violating provincial, territorial, or municipal laws are dealt with in the same way as adults.

D. EXCEPTIONS TO THE OFFENCE JURISDICTION OF THE YOUTH COURT

There are a limited number of exceptions to the exclusive jurisdiction of the youth court to deal with a criminal charge against a young person. The most important is when a case has been transferred to adult court pursuant to section 16 of the *YOA*, generally because the sentencing options under the *YOA* are considered inadequate. Transfer is more fully discussed in chapter 9.

Section 5(1) of the *YOA* also specifies that the Act does not apply for discipline or court martial proceedings under the *National Defence Act* against a member of the armed forces who is under eighteen. A seventeen-year-old can join the armed forces with parental consent, though in recent years it has been rare for such youths to be accepted in the forces. The rationale for this exception to youth court jurisdiction is that those in the forces undergo a change of legal status, and if considered mature enough to join the forces they should be subject to its discipline. The armed forces would be reluctant to have members who are not subject to its discipline code and procedures. However, youths who join the cadets (who are twelve to nineteen years of age) are not subject to military discipline. Similarly, youths who commit offences on military premises, such as children of armed forces personnel, may be charged with offences under the *National Defence Act* (for example, for destruction of base property) but are dealt with under the *YOA*.

Section 47(1) of the *YOA* provides that in general a young person who is "cited" (charged by a judge) with contempt of court — on grounds, for example, of disrupting a judicial proceeding or refusing to testify — *may* be dealt with by a youth court even if the contempt occurs in regard to conduct related to another court. Under section 47(2) an act of contempt "in the face of the court" other than a youth court may be dealt with either by the other court or by a youth court.

In one legally significant contempt case that ended in the Supreme Court of Canada, a youth who was already in custody was called by the Crown as a witness to testify at a preliminary inquiry in the Provincial Court against two adults charged with attempted murder. In the witness box, the youth threw the Bible on the floor, crossed his arms, put his foot on the railing of the witness box, and told the clerk of the court that he would not testify. The following exchange took place:

> B.K.[the youth]: Fuck it, man, I ain't testifying.
>
> Court: I'm sorry, I didn't hear you.
>
> B.K.: I ain't testifying, man. Fucking charge me. Whatever you fucking want, man. I ain't testifying.
>
> Court: I find you guilty of contempt in the face of this Court.
>
> B.K.: Up yours, you dick.
>
> Court: And I sentence you to a period of six months consecutive to any —
>
> B.K.: Fuck you, you goof.
>
> Court: . . . time now being served.
>
> B.K.: Goof.
>
> Court: Get him out of here.
>
> B.K.: Fucking goof.[14]

After the youth left the witness box the Crown indicated that it had no other witnesses to call, and the two men accused of attempted murder were immediately discharged. The youth appealed the conviction and sentence for the contempt charge. The Supreme Court of Canada ruled that the trial judge was "amply justified" in "citing" the youth for this contempt in the face of the Court. However, even in such an obvious case, the rules of "natural justice" require that a person should be given notice that he is being "cited" for contempt of court for his behaviour, and given the opportunity to consult counsel and make submissions before a ruling is made and sentence is imposed.[15] Under section 47(2)

---

14   *R. v. K.(B.)*, [1995] 4 S.C.R. 186 at 190–91.
15   *Ibid.* at 197–98.

of the *YOA* a charge for contempt in the face of the court can be dealt with by the court where it occurs or referred to a youth court.

While section 47(2) creates a concurrent jurisdiction for "contempt . . . in the face" of the court (that is, conduct in a courtroom) between the court where the contempt occurs and the youth court, it states that the youth court shall have exclusive jurisdiction for contempt against any court that occurs outside the face of the court (*ex facie curia*). Contempt outside the face of a court occurs when an order of the court that affects behaviour in the community is disobeyed.

In *Macmillan Bloedel Ltd.* v. *Simpson*[16] an order was made by the British Columbia Supreme Court to prohibit the protest activities of environmentalists which interfered with logging in Clayoquot Sound. A seventeen-year-old youth was charged in the Supreme Court of British Columbia along with other adult protesters for being in contempt of the court order. As a young person, he applied to have his case dealt with in youth court pursuant to section 47(2) of the *YOA*, presumably hoping for more lenient and sensitive treatment in youth court. The adult court trial judge refused the application, found him guilty, and sentenced him to forty-five days' imprisonment and a $1000 fine. The youth appealed; the fine was removed but the jail sentence affirmed. The youth appealed again to the Supreme Court of Canada on the jurisdictional issue. The dissent of L'Heureux-Dubé J. would have applied section 47(2) and allowed the youth court, with its expertise and experience, to have exclusive jurisdiction to deal with the defiant young person. The majority of the Supreme Court, however, ruled that section 47(2) of the *YOA* violated section 96 of the *Constitution Act, 1867*, to the extent that it gave *exclusive* jurisdiction over contempt of a "superior" court order to an "inferior" court,[17] like the youth court. However, the Supreme Court accepted that the validity of

---

16   [1996] 2 S.C.R. 1048.

17   The term "superior court" refers to a court with a federally appointed judge under s. 96 of *CA 1867*, above note 5, who exercises the inherent general jurisdiction that judges of the superior courts had in 1867. "Inferior courts" have provincially appointed judges with a jurisdiction that is defined by statute. Although the terms "superior" and "inferior" have historical roots and are intended to be "technical," they obviously have certain connotations, and "inferior" court judges, who deal with most cases involving children, youth, and the poor, are paid less money and given less respect by the legal profession than the "superior court" judges, who deal with cases involving large sums of money as well as the most serious adult criminal charges. However, the Supreme Court of Canada has affirmed that provincially appointed "inferior court" judges have the same constitutionally guaranteed judicial independence as federally appointed judges: *Reference Re Remuneration of Judges of the Provincial Court of Prince Edward Island* [1997] S.C.J. No. 75 (QL).

a concurrent jurisdiction so that the *ex facie curia* contempt of an order of a superior court may be dealt with by that court, if the judge of that court wishes to exercise jurisdiction, or may be referred to a youth court.

E. JURISDICTION OVER *YOA* OFFENCES

Although most of the cases dealt with in youth court involve charges under the *Criminal Code* or federal drug legislation, the *YOA* itself creates certain offences related to the administration of the Act. By far the most frequently used offence provision in the Act is section 26, which creates an offence for a youth who wilfully fails to comply with a youth court sentence (for example, by breaching a probation order). Youth courts have exclusive jurisdiction over section 26 charges, even if the person has become an adult by the time of the breach. This provision is considered in chapter 8, in the context of a discussion of review of *YOA* dispositions.

The *YOA* has some less frequently used offence provisions that regulate the conduct of police and other adults responsible for the administration of the Act, in particular section 46, which creates an offence for unauthorized disclosure of information about young persons being dealt with by the youth courts. Section 38(2) creates an offence for any person or organization that publishes information that identifies a young person involved in the youth justice system.

There are also offences under the *YOA* that may be committed by parents or other adults who are responsible for the care of young persons. Section 7.2 makes it an offence for persons to fail wilfully to comply with an undertaking to supervise a youth released pending trial. Section 10(3) of the *YOA* creates an offence of contempt of court for a parent to disobey a judge's order to attend youth court; the youth court has exclusive jurisdiction over this type of contempt. Section 50 creates an offence for any person who wilfully interferes with a sentence imposed on a young offender, including inducing or assisting a youth to escape from a custody facility; under section 50(2) a charge under this provision is within the exclusive jurisdiction of a provincial court judge. In practice, charges against police, parents, or other adults under these provisions are rare and usually dealt with by a youth court judge, pursuant to section 5(4) of the *YOA*, which gives a youth court judge all the powers of a provincial court judge.

F. AGE JURISDICTION

Youth courts generally have jurisdiction over a criminal offence committed by a "young person," defined in section 2(1) as a person starting from their twelfth birthday and ending at their eighteenth, a period roughly corresponding to the stage of human development known as adolescence. From the perspective of criminal law and section 2(1) of the *YOA*, a "young person" is between the stage of being a "child" — a person under the age of twelve and without criminal liability — and being an "adult" — a person with full legal accountability.

The date for determining *YOA* jurisdiction is the date of the alleged offence, so that a person who is seventeen at the time of the alleged offence will be dealt with under the *YOA* even if he or she is over seventeen when charged or brought to court. There have been some cases, especially involving sexual offences if victims have delayed reporting their allegations to the police because of fear or embarrassment, where alleged perpetrators have been in their twenties and still dealt with under the *YOA* since the allegations related to a time when they were "young persons."[18] These "young persons" are entitled to most of the protections of the Act, such as the ban on publication of identifying information. However, the fact that the "young person" is already an adult may be an important factor, under section 16 of the *YOA*, in having the case transferred to adult court for trial and, in the event of a conviction, sentencing. There is also provision in section 24.5 of the *YOA* for allowing a youth court to direct that a custodial sentence imposed on a "young person" who has become an adult may be served in an adult correctional facility, so that this person will not disrupt the environment or exploit the more lenient conditions of a youth facility. In such a case, maximum sentence length and sentence review are still governed by the *YOA*.

In *R. v. A.(E.A.)* an accused was convicted in youth court of the sexual assault of a young child whom he was babysitting. While the child could testify about the alleged assault, the precise time it occurred could not be established because the victim was too young to have a sense of time. But it was sometime between 9 p.m. and 1 a.m.; at midnight the accused began his eighteenth birthday. The Ontario Court of Appeal upheld the jurisdiction of the youth court to deal with the case:

---

18   See, e.g., *R. v. Daniels*, [1995] S.J. No. 577 (Q.B.) (QL) where the complainant was nine years old at the time of the alleged sexual abuse and did not report it until she was nineteen, by which time the accused was twenty-six years of age. The youth court had jurisdiction.

Under such circumstances, it would be most favourable to [him] . . . to conclude that the time of the commission of the offence was when he was a young person since the disposition. . . . available under the *Young Offenders Act* [is] . . . more favourable to the appellant than if he were tried in an adult court.[19]

Section 2(1) specifies that a "young person" . . . includes any person who is charged . . . with having committed an offence while he was a young person, but the application of the *YOA* to "young persons" who have become adults is qualified by the statement that this meaning applies only "where the context requires." In *R. v. Z.(D.A.)* the accused was seventeen when he allegedly committed a theft, but he was not arrested by the police until he was eighteen. After his arrest, the police wanted to question him. The police complied fully with the *Charter of Rights* but did not give the accused the more extensive rights afforded by section 56 of the *YOA*, such as affording him the opportunity to consult a parent before questioning. The police questioned him, and his written statement admitting guilt was a key part of the Crown's case against him. The trial judge ruled that the failure of the police to comply with section 56 of the *YOA* rendered the statement inadmissible, and acquitted the accused. On appeal, the Supreme Court of Canada ruled that, since the accused was an adult at the time of police questioning, the "context" referred to in section 2(1) did not require treating him as a young person and giving him special legal protections in regard to police questioning. Writing for a majority of the Court, Lamer C.J.C. observed: "Persons over the age of 18 have long been deemed to possess sufficient maturity and control over the situation they may find themselves in to no longer require the watchful eye of a parent. . . ."[20]

While *R. v. Z.(D.A.)* indicates that in some contexts a "young person" over eighteen will not be afforded all the protections of the *YOA* in general the *YOA* continues to apply to those who were under eighteen when the offence is alleged to have occurred even if they are eighteen or older by the time they are in youth court. This is to prevent any unfairness that could arise to youths if their cases are not resolved until after the eighteenth birthday has passed, and it also gives individuals the benefit of more lenient treatment for the "mistakes of their youth."

Section 2(1) specifies that a young person is one "who is or, in the absence of evidence to the contrary, appears to be" between the ages of twelve and eighteen. Generally, the police will establish age by asking a

19   (1987), 22 O.A.C. 83 at 84 (C.A.).
20   *R. v. Z.(D.A.)*, [1992] 2 S.C.R. 1025 at 1053.

person who appears to be a youth their age, and then confirming age by checking with a parent[21] or by examining a birth certificate or other record. It is not necessary for the Crown to establish the age of the accused as part of its case or to gain jurisdiction. Unless the accused raises the question and introduces some evidence to rebut the inference of age based on appearance, a youth court does not need to address the issue of age to deal with a case.[22]

Occasionally, young persons who are arrested by the police will lie about their age, perhaps to avoid having their parents notified or as part of a ruse to deceive the police about their true identity. In this situation, the police may fail to afford the youth the protections of section 56 of the YOA in regard to questioning. The YOA was amended to deal with this problem in 1995; section 56(5.1) now provides that a statement by a youth to the police will be admissible even if the latter have failed to comply with section 56, provided that the youth held out himself or herself as being eighteen years of age or older and there were reasonable grounds to believe that this was true. The case must be dealt with in youth court, however, once the correct age has been established.

G. MAXIMUM AGE — THE POLICY DECISION

Under the JDA the provinces had significant flexibility in the establishing of minimum and maximum ages, with the minimums varying from seven to fourteen and the maximum from the sixteenth to the eighteenth birthday. The YOA established a uniform national age jurisdiction, a measure that was widely considered to be required by the "equality under the law" provision of section 15 of the Charter of Rights, which came into effect in April 1985. Establishing uniformity required every province and territory to make some changes. Given the practical and

---

21 At common law, only a mother or a father who was present at a child's birth could establish age, since other evidence was "hearsay," including testimony from an individual about their own birthday. In a technical sense, a person does not have first-hand knowledge of their birth date but can only relate the evidence of another person: R. v. Hicks (1968), [1969] 4 C.C.C. 203 (B.C.S.C.). Section 57 of the YOA, above note 5, provides that, if the issue of age arises, it can be established by the testimony of a parent, by a birth certificate, or by any other information . . . that it [the court] considers reliable."

22 See, e.g., R. v. H.(D.W.) (1986) 62, Nfld. & P.E.I.R. 55 (Nfld. S.C.T.D.). Under the JDA, above note 11, proof of age was an "essential element" of the Crown's case, and if the Crown failed to prove age a juvenile's age, a juvenile was entitled to an acquittal; R. v. Crossley (1950), 10 C.R. 348 (B.C.S.C.).

philosophical effects of such a change, it is not surprising that age-juris-diction issues remain the subject of intense political controversy.

The most widely debated issue among politicians at the time of enact-ment of the *YOA* in 1982 concerned the maximum age for youth court jurisdiction. Under the *JDA* only Manitoba and Quebec had eighteen years of age as the start of adult jurisdiction, and most of the provinces had sixteen years as the beginning of adult responsibility. Those prov-inces that were required to raise their age jurisdiction as a result of enact-ment of the *YOA* faced the costs and administrative difficulties associated with this change. There was also a widespread view that sixteen- and sev-enteen- year-olds should be held more fully accountable than younger adolescents and hence should be dealt with in the adult system. This view is still expressed by some critics of the *YOA* who continue to advocate lowering the minimum age of adult responsibility back to sixteen.[23]

Because of the controversy and costs surrounding the implementa-tion of the higher age limit, when the *YOA* came into force on 1 April 1984 the proclamation of the Act's uniform maximum-age provision was delayed until 1 April 1985 in order to allow all jurisdictions suffi-cient time to adapt.[24] As noted earlier, Ontario and Nova Scotia, which had to raise the minimum adult age level from sixteen to eighteen, adopted "two tier" implementation, with twelve- to fifteen- year-olds dealt with, as under the *JDA*, in the Family Court and by the ministry responsible for child welfare and social services, while sixteen- and sev-enteen- year-olds remained the responsibility of the adult criminal court and the adult corrections ministries.

Any maximum (or minimum) age level that is chosen for youth court jurisdiction will have arbitrary aspects, with some whose chrono-logical age is above the line seeming less mature than some below the line. Having a clear line, especially for the maximum level, is generally preferable to having individualized assessments since it is much easier to administer, though the transfer provisions offer some individual flex-ibility for treating older youths who are charged with the most serious offences in a fashion similar to adults.

---

23 The Reform Party favours lowering the start of adult jurisdiction to eighteen; for example, see Canada, House of Commons, Standing Committee on Justice and Legal Affairs, *The Reform Party Report on Amending the Young Offenders Act* (Ottawa: Supply & Services, 1997).

24 This was also consistent with the *Charter*, above note 4, which came into force in 1982, except for s. 15, the Equality Rights provision, which came into force on 15 April 1985 to give governments time to comply. Until April 1985, there was no constitutional impetus for uniformity of age.

Eighteen was chosen at least in part because, for most civil and international purposes, adulthood starts at that age. For many individuals, the eighteenth birthday roughly marks the end of their physical maturation and growth process, as well as the start of adulthood in a social sense with the end of high school. Society considers seventeen-year-olds too young to vote; why should they be considered old enough to be as fully accountable as adults? The *United Nations Convention on the Rights of the Child* also sets eighteen years of age as the start of adulthood, and many countries have rehabilitation-oriented youth justice and correction systems for youths up to that age or even older.

While there are good reasons for having chosen eighteen as the start of adult criminal responsibility, the issue has remained controversial and the 1995 *YOA* amendments created a presumption that sixteen- and seventeen- year-olds who are charged with the most serious offences should be dealt with in adult court.[25] This presumption, which is discussed in chapter 9, can be seen as a recognition of the political force of the argument in favour of lowering the age level of *YOA* jurisdiction.

H. THE MINIMUM AGE OF TWELVE: HISTORY AND POLICY

The English common law set seven as the minimum age of criminal responsibility. Children between seven and thirteen could also rely on the *doli incapax*[26] defence and were only to be convicted if the prosecution could prove beyond a reasonable doubt that the child had sufficient mental capacity to be held criminally accountable.

The common law presumption of incapacity was incorporated into Canada's *Criminal Code* in 1892[27] and thus was applicable under the *JDA*. Until the *YOA* came into force in 1984, it was theoretically necessary for the prosecution to prove that a child between seven and fourteen years of age was "competent to know the nature and consequences of his conduct, and to appreciate that it was wrong." In practice, the issue of incapacity was infrequently raised in juvenile court proceedings, and judges tended to assume that children had the capacity to appreciate the nature and consequences of their acts, especially as they approached the age of

25 *YOA*, above note 5, s. 16(1.01), enacted by *An Act to amend the Young Offenders Act and the Criminal Code*, S.C. 1995, c. 19, s. 8(1).
26 Latin for "incapacity to do wrong."
27 *The Criminal Code, 1892*, S.C. 1892, c. 29, ss. 9 and 10; later *Criminal Code*, R.S.C. 1970, c. C–34, ss. 12 and 13.

fourteen.[28] There were, it is true, cases in which this defence was successfully raised; for example, in *R. v. C.(B.)*, a twelve-year-old boy charged with the murder of his stepmother was acquitted on the basis of the *doli incapax*[29] defence. However, relatively few young children were being brought before the juvenile courts, and, as the process of reform of the *JDA* began, it was widely felt that the minimum age of seven was too low. Bringing younger children into a process that was more criminally and due-process oriented than the informal welfare-oriented model of the *JDA* was increasingly seen as inappropriate.

The 1965 Department of Justice Committee report, *Juvenile Delinquency in Canada*, recommended a minimum age of ten, or at most twelve. In 1975 a report of the Solicitor General's Committee, "Young Persons in Conflict with the Law," recommended fourteen as a minimum age. Although Quebec supported this proposal, there was considerable concern expressed in other provinces about such a high minimum age.

In 1977 the federal Department of the Solicitor General recommended twelve as a minimum age, and this was reflected in the *YOA* as enacted in 1982. While the selection of twelve was in part a political compromise, for most youths the ages of twelve through seventeen correspond roughly with the period of maturation known as "adolescence," the twelfth birthday marking the approximate beginning of puberty and its concomitant changes in physical, psychological, and sexual development. For many children, twelve also marks the approximate age of leaving primary or elementary school and the beginning of an intermediate or senior elementary school program, reflecting the different social and intellectual needs of children and adolescents.[30]

---

28   See J.L. McLeod, "Doli Incapax: The Forgotten Presumption in Juvenile Court Trials" (1980) 3 Can. J. Fam. L. 251.

29   (1977), 39 C.C.C. (2d) 469 (Ont. Prov. Ct.). The boy had "abnormal psychiatric features" and the judge observed (at 475): "The evidence of the doctors indicates that the accused may not realize that his stepmother is dead; that he had no concept that what he allegedly did was morally wrong; that he did not appreciate what kill means. Such evidence leaves doubts regarding the competency of the accused and his ability to appreciate when an act is wrong." The judge concluded his decision by recommending that the boy should receive "immediate and appropriate treatment," presumably under provincial mental-health legislation, though the judge had no jurisdiction to make a direct order of this kind.

30   Any community or residential program intended to respond to children under twelve involved in offending behaviour must recognize their distinctive needs and abilities. Pre-adolescent children are in crucial respects different from adolescents and require separate and distinctive treatment.

At the time that the *YOA* was enacted, the minimum-age issue received much less attention than the change in maximum age, and only British Columbia advocated a lower minimum age. However, since the Act came into force there has been growing criticism of the designation of twelve as the minimum age of criminal responsibility. The *YOA* is premised on the assumption that children under twelve who commit criminal offences will be dealt with by their parents or, if state intervention is needed, by the child-welfare or mental-health authorities.

A common theme of media reports about the *YOA* has been a concern that the legal system cannot deal adequately with offending behaviour by children under twelve, and as a result this type of criminal conduct has been increasing.[31] Public anxiety was heightened in 1993 by the brutal slaying of a toddler in England by two ten-year-old boys, especially when it became apparent that Canadian law might not deal adequately with such a situation in this country. This was chillingly emphasized by a highly publicized 1996 Toronto rape perpetrated by an eleven-year-old boy against a thirteen-year-old girl. The boy reportedly knew that he could not be charged, telling police: "You got me. So what are you going to do?"[32]

Some of the media reports may have exaggerated the problem, for children under twelve commit a relatively small proportion of all offences. For example, in 1983, the last full year that the *JDA* was in force, less than 2 percent of all juvenile charges were laid against children under twelve; seven- to eleven- year-olds had a charge rate of 1.3 per 1,000, while twelve-year-olds had a charge rate of 12.9 per 1000 and seventeen-year-olds a rate of 103 per 1000.[33]

A 1992 Statistics Canada study of police records indicates that children under twelve committed about 1.2 percent of all crimes, compared to 20.8 percent for young offenders (twelve to seventeen) and 78 percent for adults; if all children under twelve were charged, this would represent about 5 percent of youth crime. While some of the reports of offending behaviour involve children as young as four or five, the police reports indicate that almost two-thirds of the offences by children under

---

31   See, e.g., "Law courts spawn fagans, officials fear," *[Toronto] Globe and Mail* (9 November 1985).

32   See, e.g., H. Hess, "Police can't charge 11-year-old accused of rape," *[Toronto] Globe and Mail* (18 May 1996) A12. This boy was in fact placed in a group home under child-welfare legislation as part of a "best interests" response, but this did little to reduce public anger at the inadequacy of the legal response.

33   Statistics Canada, Canadian Centre for Justice Statistics, *Juvenile Court Statistics 1983* (Ottawa: Statistics Canada, 1984).

twelve involved ten- and eleven- year-olds; males accounted for 89 percent of the children involved. Although most of the crimes committed by children under twelve were property related (especially mischief, theft, and break and enter), one offence of serious concern was arson; about 13 percent of all arson cases involved children under twelve. About 6 percent of the offences by children under twelve involved violence.[34]

A 1994 Canadian study raised some disturbing questions about sexual offending by children under the age of twelve.[35] Based on police records, about 20 percent of all sex offences were committed by youths under eighteen: of these, about 10 percent (2 percent of all sexual offences) were committed by children under the age of twelve. Many of the acts committed by this youngest age group were such intrusive acts as oral sex and vaginal penetration, and typically involved younger victims. Those sexual offenders under twelve were more likely to act with co-perpetrators, while older sexual offenders are more likely to act alone.

At least part of the rationale for choosing twelve as the minimum age of criminal responsibility was that it marked the approximate beginning of adolesence. Further, there were concerns that younger children might not appreciate the consequences of their acts, or at least would have difficulty in comprehending the nature of the criminal process. In fact, there is controversy among psychologists about how age affects the ability to understand crime or the court process, and little *empirical* work justifies the choice of any particular age. Dr Michele Peterson-Badali, a Toronto psychologist, has observed:

> One of the most interesting and important, and yet unstudied, areas of developmental psychology involves the cognitive capacities and development of children as they relate to public policy, which in its ultimate form is often embodied in law. . . . no study has systematically examined the relevance of the ages set out in our juvenile legislation to the issues in development as they have been studied by psychologists.[36]

---

34   While not conclusive, this type of information should tend to dispel the perception created by some media stories that children under twelve are commonly being exploited by adults for such purposes as drug dealing. However, such cases have occurred in Canada. See, above note 31.

35   J.P. Hornick, F.H. Bolitho, & D. LeClaire, *Young Offenders and the Sexual Abuse of Children* (Ottawa: Department of Justice, 1994) at 47, 67.

36   M. Peterson, "Children's Understanding of the Juvenile Justice System: A Cognitive-Developmental Perspective" (1988) 30 Can. J. Crim. 381 at 382–83.

Peterson-Badali concludes that twelve years of age appears to be a "reasonable minimum" for the application of formal criminal sanctions, though she notes that many children in the twelve- to fourteen- age group lack a "more refined understanding" of such matters as the relativistic nature of liability or knowledge of the age boundaries of youth court jurisdiction. However, in a more recent, focused experimental study of competency to make plea decisions, Peterson-Badali and Abramovitch conclude that

> a majority of even the 10 year old subjects used legal rather than moral criteria in making their plea decisions [for hypothetical scenarios]. The actions of these children clearly indicate their ability to distinguish a legal domain, with its own set of rules and principles, from the domain of morality.[37]

This type of research suggests that, to the extent that the establishment of a minimum age in the *YOA* is based on assessments about capacity of children to participate meaningfully in legal processes that affect them and to understand the criminal justice system, consideration should be given to lowering the minimum age of criminal responsibility from twelve years.

I. OFFENDERS UNDER TWELVE: CHILD-WELFARE RESPONSES

The most common police response to offending behaviour by a child under twelve is to take the child home and discuss the situation with the parents. The police may caution the child directly, and, if the behaviour is more serious or repetitive, they may make a referral to an appropriate agency or service for voluntary assistance. If the police are aware of a program that deals specifically with offending behaviour by children under twelve, a referral may be made to such a program; there are a few of these programs in major urban centres in Canada.[38]

Only if the behaviour is very serious or if the police have other protection concerns, such as apparent parental abuse or neglect, is a referral

---

37 M. Peterson-Badali & R. Abramovitch, "Grade Related Changes in Young People's Reasoning about Plea Decisions" (1993) 17 Law & Human Behaviour 537 at 548. See also J.T. Dalby, "Criminal Liability in Children" (1985) 27 Can. J. Crim. 137.

38 S. Moyer, *Summary Report of Survey of Legislation, Procedures and Services in Six Jurisdictions* (Ottawa: Department of Justice, 1990), reports on a few such programs in British Columbia and Ontario.

likely to be made to child-welfare authorities. When a child-welfare agency receives reports of offending behaviour, which may come from police or other sources, the agency will investigate whether there are abuse or neglect concerns that would in themselves merit intervention, with the offending behaviour being considered primarily as the child's response to an unsatisfactory home situation. If parental abuse or neglect concerns are present, the agency will intervene. If abuse or neglect is not evident but offending behaviour is a serious concern, the response of child-welfare agencies will vary. Some agencies appear quite willing to respond to the offending behaviour by children under twelve years of age, at least by meeting with parents and perhaps making a voluntary referral to another agency, but in many child-welfare agencies these cases have a low priority for overburdened staff. Police officers are often aware of agency priorities and are reluctant to make a referral if they expect that the agency will not take action.

In every Canadian jurisdiction there is in theory some possibility of a child-welfare or mental-health response in the case of serious offending behaviour by a child under the age of twelve. However, there are real limitations to these responses.

In every province the primary legal basis for response to offending by children under twelve is child-welfare law. When parents[39] are considered unwilling or unable to care adequately for their children, child-welfare legislation authorizes involuntary intervention by a state-sponsored child-welfare agency.[40] The agency can become involved in a broad range of circumstances, including physical, emotional, or sexual abuse, physical or emotional neglect, parental death, a parental desire to have a child placed for adoption, and other situations where parents are unwilling or unable to care for their children, such as when an adolescent is "out of control." Under the legislation, child-welfare workers, and in some jurisdictions police officers, have the authority to "apprehend" a child believed to be in need of protection. A child who is appre-

---

39   The concept of "parent" is broadly defined in child-welfare legislation and generally includes biological parents, legal guardians, and other persons like grandparents if they have had responsibility for the care of the child.

40   Child-welfare agencies in Canada are all under provincial government control and receive all, or almost all, their funding from government. In most provinces, the agency operates as part of a government department, and the staff are civil servants. In some provinces, like Ontario, there are semi-autonomous Children's Aid Societies, which have local boards but still operate under government control and regulation. Increasingly, Aboriginal child-welfare agencies are being established in various parts of Canada to work with Aboriginal children and families, within the legal framework of provincial child-welfare legislation.

hended is removed from parental care and usually placed in a foster home or a temporary care facility. If a child is apprehended from parental care, there must be an interim-care hearing in Family Court within a relatively short period to review the apprehension and either return the child to parental care, perhaps under agency supervision, or confirm the removal pending trial. While legislation varies from one jurisdiction to another, there is always an onus upon the agency to justify an apprehension as necessary to protect a child from harm, since apprehension represents a great intrusion into family life.

Although not a perfect analogy, the power to apprehend under child-welfare legislation can be viewed as similar to the authority of police to arrest and detain a person charged with a criminal offence, especially in the context of offending behaviour by children under twelve. In child-welfare proceedings, however, the sole focus in justifying such an apprehension at an interim-care hearing must always be on protecting the child from harm or promoting the interests of the child, and not with protecting society or possible victims.

When a case comes before the court for a full child-welfare hearing, the judge has essentially four options:

- dismiss the application;
- return the child to parental care, but subject to some form of supervision by the agency;
- place the child in the temporary care of the agency, with the child being placed by the agency with a relative of the child under agency supervision, in a foster home or group home, or in a treatment facility (in some provinces, there are provisions to restrict the placement of children by agencies in secure treatment facilities and mental-health facilities); and
- make the child a permanent ward of the agency. (This may result in a termination of visitation and other parental rights, with the possibility of adoption by another family. Alternatively, parental visitation may be continued and some form of long-term non-parental child care arrangements made.)

While each child-welfare statute has its own criteria for decision making, in a broad sense the decision about what type of order to make rests on an assessment of the best interests of the child. In several Canadian provinces, there are provisions for children to have their own legal representation in child-welfare proceedings.[41] Other jurisdictions, however, give only parents the formal right to be involved in such proceedings, an approach premised on the view that the adults involved (the parents and the agency) can fully represent the *interests of the child.*

A child-welfare proceeding can be highly adversarial and involve a lengthy contested trial. It is, however, quite common for these cases to be resolved on a "consent basis," with the parents and agency, and where legally required the child, agreeing to a particular disposition. Such a non-adversarial resolution may be by means of a "consent order," formally made by a judge with the approval of all parties, or it may be the result of a voluntary agreement not brought before the court.

While each Canadian jurisdiction has its own unique child-welfare legislation, it is possible to classify the statutes according to the degree of specificity for dealing with offending behaviour by children under twelve:

- offending behaviour by a child under twelve is itself a ground for intervention — Newfoundland, New Brunswick, Yukon, and Northwest Territories;
- offending behaviour *combined* with parental inability to act is ground for intervention — Nova Scotia, Ontario, and Saskatchewan;
- offending behaviour is not mentioned in definition of "child in need of protection," but special provisions are included for police reporting or apprehension in the event of offending behaviour — Alberta, British Columbia, and Prince Edward Island; and
- offending behaviour is not specifically referred to, but child-welfare legislation may in more serious situations be invoked under more general criteria, such as on the basis of being a child "beyond the control of the person caring for him" — Manitoba and Quebec.

In all jurisdictions, the sole focus of a child-welfare response is the "best interests" of the child, and in some situations it may be argued that this does not adequately take account of interests of social protection and accountability.

---

41   Ontario and Quebec have the most extensive programs for child representation for children. In most other jurisdictions, such representation occurs only on an exceptional basis. In Manitoba, *The Child and Family Services Act*, R.S.M. 1987, c. C80, s. 34(2) provides that only a child twelve years of age or older can *instruct* counsel. Similarly, under Nova Scotia's *Children and Family Services Act*, S.N.S. 1990, c. 5, s. 37(2), legal representation is provided only to a child twelve or older. See S.G. Himel, "Representing Children" in N. Bala, J. Hornick, & R. Vogl, eds., *Canadian Child Welfare Law* (Toronto: Thompson Educational Publishing, 1990) at 196–205.

J. THE POSSIBILITY OF A MENTAL-HEALTH RESPONSE FOR UNDER-TWELVES

In some cases, offending behaviour is a manifestation of a mental disorder and the child may pose a serious threat to his or her own safety or the safety of others. Sometimes, mental-health professionals provide services for such children (and families), either on a voluntary basis or as part of a child-welfare order involving supervision in the community. In cases involving more severe or disruptive behaviour, consideration may be given to having the child placed in some type of mental-health facility for treatment of a behavioural or emotional problem, though this is less common than involving a child-welfare agency. Mental-health facilities generally have some degree of security and can provide a degree of social protection as well as treatment. Although mental-health legislation will allow for apprehension and confinement of the child for an indefinite period, it can provide only a limited response to cases of offending behaviour by the most seriously disturbed children since it focuses exclusively on treatment and mental health.

The legal issues surrounding use of mental-health facilities for young children are complex, and there is little legal literature available in Canada on the subject.[42] In some provinces there are overlapping services and legislative regimes, with some facilities governed by mental-health legislation and others by child-welfare legislation. As with other types of children's services, in many localities there are resource and other restrictions on access to children's mental-health services and facilities. Many children's mental facilities in Canada have significant waiting lists, though cases involving very disruptive or disturbed behaviour may receive priority for admission.

Facilities also have policies that restrict admission. In one of the few reported cases involving a legal response to offending behaviour by a child under twelve, the Nova Scotia Hospital refused admission to a ten-year-old boy with a severe conduct disorder who had been engaging in behaviour that was dangerous to himself and others. The boy's parents were not willing to consent to his admission, and the hospital's treatment program for pre-adolescents restricted admission to children whose parents were willing to consent and to be active participants in the treatment process. The child-welfare authorities, who had legal

---

42 See, e.g., G.B. Robertson, *Mental Disability and the Law in Canada*, 2d ed. (Toronto: Carswell, 1994) at 374–77 [*Mental Disability*]; and B.M. Knoppers, ed., *Canadian Child Health Law* (Toronto: Thompson Educational Publishing, 1992) at 171–75.

guardianship of the boy under the provincial *Children's Services Act,* believed that the hospital nevertheless had the only suitable program in the province and applied for a court order requiring his admission. Judge Niedermayer of the Nova Scotia Family Court recognized that there was no express statutory basis for making such an order, but he ruled that the general statements in the provincial child-welfare legislation about court action being guided by "the principle that the welfare of the child is the paramount consideration" gave him the authority to order the hospital to admit the boy.[43] While the decision is legally questionable, one can sympathize with the judge's decision to resolve a dispute between two government-funded agencies in a manner that appeared to promote both the child's best interests and the protection of society. This case illustrates the complexity of the interrelationship of different public agencies serving children.

As a result of the general common law rules about parental consent for the provision of medical services and the silence of the bulk of mental-health legislation on this subject, in most Canadian provinces only a parent's or guardian's consent is legally required for a child under twelve to be admitted to a mental-health facility, though legislation or hospital policies also require that the medical staff must be satisfied that the child has an emotional or mental disorder that justifies such confinement.[44] Children who are admitted in this way must be released if a parent or guardian withdraws consent; however, in this situation attending medical staff may seek involuntary admission if they believe that the child poses a significant danger to self or others. In some provinces, like Ontario, legislation requires court review of parental decisions placing children in mental-health facilities.[45]

All Canadian jurisdictions have civil-commitment legislation that allows a person who is considered dangerous to be placed "involuntarily" in a mental-health facility, which for children means placement without the consent of a parent or guardian; except in Ontario, the same

---

43 *Nova Scotia (Minister of Community Services)* v. *P.(K.)* (1991), 101 N.S.R. (2d) 405 (Fam. Ct.) [*P.(K.)*]. See also M. Boyle, "Children's Mental Health Issues: Prevention and Treatment" in L.C. Johnson & R. Barnhorst, eds., *Children, Families and Public Policy in the 90's* (Toronto: Thompson Educational Publishing, 1991) 73–104; and S. Moyer, *Summary Report of Survey of Legislation, Procedures and Services in Six Jurisdictions* (Ottawa: Department of Justice, 1990) at 12.

44 In Saskatchewan, the *Mental Health Services Act,* S.S. 1984–85–86, c. M–13.1, s. 17 permits a voluntary admission only at a person's "own request." This suggests that parents cannot request their child's "voluntary admission" in Saskatchewan. See Robertson, *Mental Disability,* above note 42 at 375.

45 See, e.g., Ontario, *Child and Family Services Act,* R.S.O. 1990, c. C.11, s. 124.

legislation governs involuntary commitment for both children and adults. While a detailed consideration of such legislation is beyond the scope of this book, the basic scheme involves an initial assessment of dangerousness and committal by a doctor, and possibility of review of that decision by a court or review board.

The exact criteria for commitment vary from jurisdiction to jurisdiction, depending on the relevant legislation, though there are also broad similarities in that individuals are only subject to continuing committal if they:

(1) are suffering from a "mental disorder"; and
(2) pose a significant risk to themselves or others.

It should be appreciated that most offending behaviour by children under twelve is *not* the result of a "mental disorder," and a response involving confinement under mental-health legislation is generally not appropriate, though the provision of mental-health services in the community is sometimes an appropriate part of the response to such behaviour. There are only a relatively small number of cases involving significant violence which can be dealt with under existing mental-health legislation, and then only if there are facilities with resources to deal with the specific needs of the child. In most provinces the admission to such a facility may be made by a parent or guardian, or, if necessary, on an involuntary basis by court order.

Any involuntary use of mental-health facilities is subject to the child being released when treatment personnel, or a review body, are no longer satisfied that the child presents a sufficient, immediate risk to the community or to himself or herself. In practice, the criteria for involuntary committal are interpreted in a fairly narrow way, since this involves a great incursion in personal liberty and may result in invasive treatment, such as the use of psychotropic drugs.

There are complex challenges in diagnosing and treating children under the age of twelve for mental-health problems; most standardized clinical tests to determine psychological status are not reliable with this age group, and traditional therapeutic interventions, which are based on verbal communication, can be difficult to implement with young children. Given the limited mental-health facilities suitable for children, and the intrusive nature of placement in such facilities, confinement there is only rarely a response to offending by children under twelve.

K. OFFENDING BEHAVIOUR BY UNDER - TWELVES: IS LAW REFORM DESIRABLE?

It is apparent that offending behaviour by children under twelve is a significant social problem that is not satisfactorily addressed by existing programs and legislation. At present, the most common police response to such behaviour is to contact parents, discuss the situation with them, and perhaps make a referral to an agency or program for voluntary assistance. While some large communities have special programs to which police can make such voluntary referrals, in many localities there are no such programs and only a general voluntary referral can be made, such as to a family doctor. More serious cases, either in terms of frequency of offending behaviour or the nature of the behaviour, or because of a parental unwillingness to take appropriate measures to deal with their child's behaviour, may be referred to child-welfare authorities, and under some circumstances the most severe cases may be considered for placement in a mental-health facility. While all jurisdictions have child-welfare and mental-health legislation that has potential applicability to at least some situations involving offending behaviour by children under twelve, there are also problems with the statutory regimes.

Many cases of offending behaviour by children under twelve are being dealt with adequately at present. Yet there are significant problems with the existing responses. A fundamental one is that offending behaviour is often not a priority for child-welfare agencies, unless there is other evidence of abuse or neglect. The institutional priorities of child-welfare agencies and the professional orientation of their staffs tend to restrict the ability of these agencies to respond to offending behaviour. The result is that too often victims, police, and citizens may feel that little or nothing is being done in these cases, though the more serious the offending behaviour the more likely child-welfare authorities are to respond. In at least some of the cases where child-welfare agencies are not becoming involved, because of either legal or resource constraints, an opportunity for earlier and potentially more effective intervention is being lost and the child must pass his or her twelfth birthday before there is a societal response. While for some families and children a voluntary referral may result in the provision of appropriate services for a child, there are also parents who are unwilling or unable to follow up on a voluntary recommendation that assistance is needed. There are a few good programs in Canada for children under the age of twelve who have behavioural problems, but these largely operate on a voluntary basis and there is a concern that some of the children most in need of help are not receiving it.

Although most children under twelve who commit offences should be dealt with informally, or under child-welfare or mental-health legislation, there is a strong argument that it is wrong to adopt an approach that focuses solely on the "best interests" of the child and gives no weight to accountability or the protection of society. It can be argued that the present legal regime fails to deter child offenders and hence fails to protect society adequately. While there is substantial evidence that longer sentences do not deter youths from committing offences,[46] it may well be that the complete absence of *any* criminal response and a perception[47] that "nothing can happen" leads some relatively sophisticated children under the age of twelve to engage in offending behaviour. There is anecdotal evidence that this may be occurring in Canada.[48]

Further, the criminal law has an important symbolic value for society in general and victims of crime in particular. The public's sense of injustice at the lack of accountability of offenders under twelve may have negative implications for the entire justice system and certainly frustrates victims, the police, and in some cases the parents of child offenders as well.

It is for these reasons that the 1997 report of the House of Commons Justice Committee recommended lowering the age of criminal responsibility to ten, with restrictions to ensure that a criminal response is used in an appropriate, restrained fashion.[49]

If the age of criminal responsibility is lowered, measures should be introduced so that pre-adolescent children are rarely, if ever, placed in the same residential setting as older adolescents. As Nova Scotia Family Court Judge Niedermayer observed in a case involving a ten-year-old boy with a severe conduct disorder:

---

46 At least in part this may relate to the ignorance of children and adolescents about the actual consequences of legal involvement, but more fundamentally it reflects the lack of judgment and consideration by youths. See, e.g., M. Lipsey, *Juvenile Delinquency Treatment: A Meta-Analytic Inquiry into Variability of Effects* (Beverley Hills, Calif.: Russell Sage Foundation, 1990); and A.W. Leschied *et al.*, "Treatment Issues and Young Offenders: An Empirically Derived Vision of Juvenile Justice Policy" in R.R. Corrado *et al.*, eds., *Juvenile Justice in Canada* (Toronto: Butterworths, 1992) 347 at 354–56.

47 The existence of a more effective and consistent child-welfare response combined with greater professional and public awareness of its existence could also serve to alter this perception.

48 See, e.g., Moyer, above note 43 at 24.

49 Canada, House of Commons, *Thirteenth Report of the Standing Committee on Justice and Legal Affairs: Renewing Youth Justice* (Ottawa: Supply & Services, 1997) at 59–61.

It is well-recognized in medical/social work literature and thought that it is inappropriate to mix pre-adolescents with adolescents; these two separate types of individuals who require different programs. The personnel who are clinically involved with these groups require a different type of training.[50]

It should be appreciated that merely changing the law will likely have little effect in terms of reducing criminal behaviour of children in this age group unless steps are also taken to ensure that appropriate services are available, services that recognize that children under twelve have different needs and capabilities than older youths and must be treated distinctly. In most cases, the most appropriate response will involve parents in both treatment and social control. It must also be recognized that, even if the *YOA* is amended, there will continue to be an important role for child-welfare agencies and the mental-health system for dealing with offending behaviour by children, both as a result of referrals from the police and youth justice system, and in regard to children under ten. Early identification and treatment of children at risk of future criminal behaviour is probably one of the most effective means of ensuring the long-term protection of society, and there is growing evidence that by the age of six or younger children can be identified who require intervention by suitably trained professionals.[51] Justice system personnel, including police, judges, and lawyers, will need special sensitivity and skill to communicate and work effectively with this younger population.

L. YOUTH JUSTICE AND OTHER CHILDREN'S SERVICES

Invoking the jurisdiction of the youth justice system is only one possible response to the problems of a youth who is committing offences. As recognized in the Declaration of Principle of the *YOA* section 3(1)(d): "[W]here it is not inconsistent with the protection of society, taking . . . measures other than . . . proceedings" under the Act "should be considered for dealing with young persons who have committed offences." As the preceding discussion reveals, these non-*YOA* responses are espe-

---

50   *P.(K.)*, above note 43 at 406–7.
51   See, e.g., D. Day & A. Hunt, *Predictive Validity of a Risk Model with Under 12 Offenders* (Toronto: Earlscourt Child and Family Service Centre, 1993). These researchers conclude that aggressiveness and variety of antisocial behaviour were the best predictors of future delinquent behaviour, and that these were highly correlated with the early-age onset of problem behaviour.

cially important for children under twelve who are committing offences, but there are also cases of young persons over twelve where responses involving the child-welfare, mental-health, or education systems are more appropriate than a youth justice proceeding.

Under the *JDA* juvenile court judges had substantial legal authority to shape dispositions that met the needs of delinquents; for example, they could place a delinquent youth in the care of child-welfare authorities.[52] Under the *YOA* a youth court judge has a narrower set of powers. Though there are cases in which youth court judges have successfully "urged" the child-welfare authorities to become involved with a young person and then taken the agency intervention into account in making a decision about pre-trial detention[53] or sentencing,[54] a youth court judge lacks the legal authority to stop a prosecution because the judge thinks some other response is more appropriate or the charge is not serious.[55]

While the promotion of the welfare of a young offender is an important factor in the youth court process, appeal courts have indicated that it is wrong to impose sentence merely to meet a youth's needs. At least in theory, a youth court sentence should not be more severe than is necessary to hold an offender accountable. For example, in a 1985 decision reducing a long custody sentence that a youth court judge had imposed, Thorson J.A. of the Ontario Court of Appeal stated:

> The fact that this young offender may require some long-term form of social or institutional care or guidance if there is to be any real prospect of his rehabilitation does not mean that the vehicle of the Young Offenders Act can be employed for that purpose. Here, as under the Criminal Code, it is a cardinal principle of our law that . . . the punishment should fit the crime but should not be stretched so that it exceeds it, even where that might be thought desirable by some in the interest of providing some extra protection for the public.[56]

---

52 Above note 11, s. 20(1)(h).
53 *R.* v. *T.(B.)* (12 April 1984), (B.C. Prov. Ct.) [unreported] [summarized Y.O.S. 84–001]. See also *R.* v. *H.(R.)* (26 November 1984), (Alta. Prov. Ct.) [unreported] [summarized (1984), 13 W.C.B. 170] one of the few reported cases where a judge made an order under s. 10 of the *YOA*, above note 5, to compel the attendance of a "parent." The case involved a youth who was the ward of the child-welfare authorities (his lawful "parent"), who appeared to be abandoning their ward to the youth justice system.
54 *R.* v. *M.(J.)* (1986), 44 Man. R. (2d) 25 (C.A.); *R.* v. *L.(T.)* (13 June 1984), (Alta. Prov. Ct. (Youth Div.) [unreported] [summarized Y.O.S. 84–016].
55 *R.* v. *T.(V.)*, [1992] 1 S.C.R. 749.
56 *R.* v. *I.(R.)* (1985), 44 C.R. (3d) 168 at 178 (Ont. C.A.). See also *R.* v. *B.(M.)* (1987), 36 C.C.C. (3d) 573 (Ont. C.A.).

This approach, which restricts the use of the youth justice system as a basis for intervention in a youth's life, was reinforced by the enactment of section 24(1.1)(a) of the YOA in 1995, providing that an "order of custody shall not be used as a substitute for appropriate child protection, health and other social measures."

Yet it must be acknowledged that, despite these abstract pronouncements, some youth court judges take account of social circumstances when dealing with detention or sentencing issues; for instance, they may place a youth who is "living on the street" in custody when this is not warranted by the circumstances of the offence. There may also be a tendency for child-welfare and mental-health agencies to try to "dump" clients who face charges under the YOA in the belief that "this kid is no longer our problem."[57]

Those who work in the youth justice system, whether as police, prosecutors, probation officers, or defence counsel, need to be familiar with the resources available outside the youth justice system, in particular in the child-welfare, mental-health, and education systems, and should try to communicate effectively to ensure that there is an appropriate response to each youth. Sometimes a youth who has committed an offence may be dealt with outside the youth justice system *instead* of being prosecuted; in other cases different external resources may be used *as part of* a youth justice response, for example, a term of probation.

Lawyers for youths can play an important part in obtaining appropriate assistance, and they must be familiar with the resources in the youth justice system and elsewhere that are available to assist their clients and be prepared to explore various options. Defence counsel may also have an important informal advocacy role, communicating and working with different agencies and with parents to develop a suitable plan, provided always that the lawyer is acting on the client's instructions and respecting any confidential information that may have been received. Some youths, even after careful explanation, would rather be dealt with by the youth justice system than some other agency, and a lawyer for that young client must respect this decision.

---

57   See, e.g., J. Gandy, *Judicial Interim Release (Bail) Hearings* (Toronto: Policy Research Centre on Children, Youth & Families, 1992). Also the tragic case of James Lonee, the first youth murdered by another youth in an Ontario custody facility who was "devastated" when the child-welfare agency terminated his long-term wardship once he was in custody under the YOA, since the agency was concerned about "double-resourcing"; this ended his involvement with the agency social worker, who had the longest, most committed relationship he experienced in his sad, short life. K. Toughill, "A life in pain," *Toronto Star* (22 September 1996).

Other professionals in the youth justice system, however, are not so constrained and may work towards the youth's "best interests" regardless of his or her express wishes. While a treatment plan that is truly imposed on a hostile adolescent may have limited chances of success, youths are sometimes ambivalent about their situation and may come to cooperate in plans that they initially appear to reject. Although a youth court should not impose a disposition that is inappropriately onerous given the circumstances of the offence and the record of the offender, an appropriate judicial response will consider both rehabilitation and accountability and in doing so may well serve to promote the welfare of a youth.

FURTHER READINGS

BALA, N., J. HORNICK, & R. VOGL, *Canadian Child Welfare Law* (Toronto: Thompson Educational Publishing, 1990)

BALA, N. & H. LILLES, eds., *Young Offenders Service* (Toronto: Butterworths, 1984) (looseleaf)

DALBY, J.T., "Criminal Liability in Children" (1985) 27 Can. J. Crim. 137

CANADA, FEDERAL-PROVINCIAL-TERRITORIAL TASK FORCE ON YOUTH JUSTICE, *A Review of the Young Offenders Act and the Youth Justice System in Canada* (Ottawa: Supply & Services, 1996), ch. 3

GALL, G.L. *The Canadian Legal System,* 4th ed. (Toronto: Carswell, 1995)

HARRIS, P.J., ed., *Young Offenders Act Manual* (Aurora: Canada Law Book, 1984) (looseleaf)

LESCHIED, A.D.W. & S.K. WILSON, "Criminal Liability of Children Under Twelve: A Problem for Child Welfare, Juvenile Justice or Both?" (1988) 30 Can. J. Crim. 17

PLATT, P., *Young Offenders Law in Canada,* 2d ed. (Toronto: Butterworths, 1995), chs.4, 5, 6, 9 and 18

WILSON, L.C., "Changes to Federal Jurisdiction Over Young Offenders: The Provincial Response" (1990) 8 Can. J. Fam. L. 303

CHAPTER 4

ARREST, POLICE QUESTIONING, AND PRE-TRIAL DETENTION

The police may become involved in responding to the suspected criminal behaviour of a young person either as a result of direct observation of an ongoing offence — for example, by observing an assault or by stopping the driver of a car who appears to be impaired — or because of to a report from a member of the community, such as the victim, a witness, or some other person who knows about the offence, like a schoolteacher. The police will generally respond initially by providing immediate assistance to anyone who has been injured and beginning an investigation. The nature and sophistication of the investigation will depend on the seriousness and circumstances of the offence.

As a broad generalization, adolescents tend to be less "careful" criminals than adults, and the crimes they commit are usually less difficult for police to "solve" than those perpetrated by adults. Adolescent offenders are less likely to take steps to hide their identity and are more likely to inform friends of their involvement in a crime. Police investigations of crimes often focus on interviewing the victim and witnesses, though some cases involve sophisticated forensic investigative techniques, including fingerprinting, DNA analysis,[1] and electronic surveillance such as wiretapping.

If the police have reasonable grounds to believe that a person has committed a criminal offence, they are in a position to commence a criminal proceeding. This may be done by arresting that person or by issuing him or her with a document requiring their appearance in court. After the youth is arrested, the police may interview the suspect. The arrest, questioning, and any detention of a suspected offender are governed by the *Canadian Charter of Rights and Freedoms*, the *Criminal Code,* and the *Young Offenders Act.* At this initial stage of the court process, the *YOA* provides that young persons have special rights that are intended both to afford them special protection and to involve their parents in the process. This chapter will focus on the legal issues that arise at the beginning of the youth court process as the police move from an investigation towards possible arrest and detention. It pays particular attention to the special rights of youths that arise under the *YOA*.[2]

In less serious cases, especially those involving first offenders, the police may decide to respond to a case outside the formal youth court process, either by informally discussing the situation with the youth and warning against the commission of further offences, or by referring the youth to an alternative measures program. These options are discussed in chapter 5.

A. POLICE ARREST POWERS AND THE *CHARTER*

In addition to those rights guaranteed to all of those who are arrested under the *Criminal Code* and the *Charter of Rights*, the *YOA* affords special rights and protections to youths who are arrested. Some of these provisions are premised on the recognition that adolescents generally lack the maturity and sophistication to appreciate fully their situation and hence require special legal rights; other provisions are intended to involve parents in the process, both to protect the rights of their children and to recognize the supportive role that parents may play.

---

1   DNA analysis refers to a comparison of human tissues, such as blood, semen, or hair samples, left at a crime scene, with those tissue samples of a suspected offender. Under s. 487.05 to 487.09 of the *Criminal Code*, R.S.C. 1985, c. C-46 [*Code*], the police can obtain a warrant from a provincial court judge to take tissue samples from a person suspected of committing certain listed, serious offences; this may require a small amount of hair, blood, or saliva from a suspect. The term DNA, short for deoxyribonucleic acid, refers to the substance that forms the basis of human cells and is distinctive for almost every person; some individuals, such as identical twins, may share the same DNA. See L. Papoff, "DNA evidence can be devastating to defence" *Lawyers Weekly* (1 November 1996) 12.

2   The general law applicable to the arrest, questioning, and detention of accused persons, both adults and youths, is complex and will only be summarized here. For a more detailed consideration, see, e.g., R. Delisle & D. Stuart, *Learning Canadian Criminal Procedure*, 4th ed. (Toronto: Carswell, 1996), ch. 2.

Under section 495(1) of the *Criminal Code,* police officers can arrest without a warrant a person whom they reasonably believe has committed an indictable or hybrid[3] offence or whom they find committing any offence. The police can search any person who has been arrested in order to preserve evidence that might otherwise be lost[4] and to ensure the safety of the officer (for example, to ascertain if the person has a weapon). The officer does not have to have reason to believe that anything will be discovered in order to carry out a search following arrest. As long as the arrest was lawful, anything that is discovered in the subsequent search can generally be used against the individual.[5]

If an officer arrests a person for a summary or hybrid offence, like theft under $5000, pursuant to section 495(2) the officer should release the person with a notice to appear in court unless the officer believes that detention is necessary: to establish the identity of the person; to secure or preserve evidence; to prevent the commission of another

---

3   In the *Code,* above note 1, offences are categorized as: indictable, summary, and hybrid. Indictable offences are the more serious offences, like robbery and homicide, for which longer sentences may be imposed; adults charged with indictable offences generally have the right to a preliminary inquiry and a jury trial. A relatively small category of the least serious offences are summary offences, and adults charged with these offences must be tried by a "summary" process without a jury. Many offences, like sexual assault and theft, are hybrid, with the Crown having an "election" (or choice) to proceed summarily or by indictment; for adults, if the Crown elects to proceed summarily, the maximum penalty is a shorter jail term, but the accused loses the opportunity to have a jury trial. By virtue of s. 52 of the *Young Offenders Act,* R.S.C. 1985, c. Y-1 [*YOA*], all proceedings (except murder) against young persons in youth court have a summary process (no jury or preliminary inquiry), though the offences retain their character as summary, hybrid, or indictable for such purposes as police arrest powers. At the time of arrest, a hybrid offence, even for a young person, is regarded as indictable; *Interpretation Act* R.S.C. 1985, c. I-21, s. 34(1)(a). Thus police have fairly wide powers of arrest since most offences are hybrid or indictable.

4   *R. v. Stillman,* [1997] S.C.J. No. 34 (QL) [*Stillman*] deals with the scope of police authority to search an accused after arrest. The accused was a seventeen- year-old youth charged with sexual assault and murder and transferred to adult court. The Supreme Court ruled that hair samples, buccal swabs (throat swabs), and dental impressions taken from the youth after his arrest without his consent violated his rights under the *Canadian Charter of Rights and Freedoms,* Part I of the *Constitution Act, 1982,* being Schedule B to the *Canada Act 1982* (U.K.), 1982, c. 11 [*Charter*], and were inadmissible. The Court held that the relatively intrusive methods needed to take this evidence were not part of a lawful arrest. The arrest in *Stillman* occurred in 1991; since 1995 the *Code, ibid.,* s. 487.05 can be used to obtain a warrant to take hair samples and buccal swabs for purposes of DNA analysis and comparison to tissue (semen or blood) samples found on the body of a victim.

5   See, *e.g., R. v. Morrison* (1987), 58 C.R. (3d) 63 (Ont. C.A.).

offence; or to ensure the attendance of the person in court. Unless police officers observe a person committing a summary offence, they must go before a justice of the peace to get a warrant to arrest a person believed to have committed a purely summary offence. Ordinarily the police commence a proceeding for summary offences without making an arrest and issue a summons or notice to appear in court.

Section 494 of the *Code* provides that individuals who are not police officers can make a "citizen's arrest," in particular if they find an individual committing any indictable offence; an arrest can also be made of a person committing any offence in relation to property by the owner of that property or any person authorized by the owner. This arrest power is typically exercised by private security guards or store personnel, who may use "reasonable force" to effect an arrest; however, individuals are obliged to contact the police as soon as they make a citizen's arrest.

The *Charter of Rights* protects the rights of individuals who have been detained or arrested, providing:

8. Everyone has the right to be secure against unreasonable search or seizure.

9. Everyone has the right not to be arbitrarily detained or imprisoned.

10. Everyone has the right on arrest or detention

    (*a*) to be informed promptly of the reasons therefor;
    (*b*) to retain and instruct counsel without delay and to be informed of that right; and
    (*c*) to have the validity of the detention determined . . . and to be released if the detention is not lawful.

The section 10(b) *Charter* right to consult a lawyer upon arrest and have a lawyer present during police questioning is in addition to the *YOA* statutory rights, such as the right to consult a parent.[6] If the police violate the *Charter* — for example, by carrying out an illegal search in which they discover incriminating evidence — this does not result in an automatic exclusion of the evidence in later court proceedings. Rather, a judge must apply section 24(2) of the *Charter* and determine whether "having regard to all the circumstances, the admission of it in the proceedings would bring the administration of justice into disrepute," which requires an assessment of the seriousness of the *Charter* breach as well as consideration of whether the police were acting in "good faith" (that is, not knowingly violating the rights of the accused) and

---

6   *R.* v. *I.(L.R.)*, [1993] 4 S.C.R. 504 [*I.(L.R.)*].

whether the evidence was likely to have been obtained even without the right's violation.[7]

The rights that are guaranteed to all under the *Charter* are possibly of special significance to young persons, since they may be particularly vulnerable to police supervision or deprivations of their rights by "well intentioned" adults.

In *R. v. V. (I. C.)* a police officer observed a fifteen-year-old girl chatting quietly on a street corner in a place known by the officer to have an "almost magnetic appeal for children who have run from home, some of whom have become the so-called 'street kids,' and acts as a focal point for many persons involved in prostitution and drug trafficking."[8] The officer believed that she was either "loitering" (an offence removed from the *Code* before the case arose) or was "possibly a runaway," and he purported to arrest her under provincial child-welfare legislation. A struggle ensued and the girl was charged with assaulting the police officer. In acquitting the girl of this charge, the judge observed:

> [T]he evidence presented . . . is more than sufficient to find that Christina V.'s rights were infringed under ss . . . 8 and 9 of the *Charter*. . . . she was deprived of her liberty, the security of her person was invaded, her property was unjustly seized and searched and she was arbitrarily detained and imprisoned. These gross violations of her fundamental rights were totally out of proportion with the situation and prescribed nowhere by law. Even if the law had provided for such interference, it would be unreasonable to find that such was demonstrably justified in a free and democratic society. . . . The phenomenon of the runaway

---

7   See *Stillman*, above note 4, for the proper interpretation of s. 24(2) of the *Charter*.

8   (25 September 1985), (Ont. Prov. Ct.) [unreported] [summarized 15 W.C.B. 31], Main Prov. J. The location was the Yonge and Dundas St corner of the Eaton Centre in Toronto.

Under Ontario's child-welfare legislation, *Child and Family Services Act*, R.S.O. 1990, c. C.11, s. 41(4) [*CFSA*], a peace officer may apprehend a child under sixteen without a warrant if there are reasonable grounds to believe that the child has left the lawful care of a Children's Aid Society and there is a "substantial risk" to a child's health or safety. Under s. 40(8) a child-welfare worker may apprehend a child without a warrant, if there is a "substantial risk to the child's health or safety"; a peace officer may *assist* in such an apprehension. Under s. 43 of the *CFSA* parents may obtain a warrant from a justice of the peace to have a child under sixteen apprehended by police if the child has left parental care and it is believed that a child's health or safety are at risk.

Of course, with the consent of a youth, an officer who considers the youth to be in an "undesirable" location may take the child from that place to his or her home or some other safe place.

child is, in the first instance, a social problem. Left unaddressed, it too often escalates into a legal issue involving either or both child welfare authorities and law enforcement officers. The magnitude of the problem as it relates to downtown Toronto . . . requires an urgent response. Undoubtedly, as a result of pressure from concerned parents, politicians and business people in the area, the . . . Police Department has felt obliged to provide that response. Unfortunately, the standard law enforcement approach to the problem is woefully inadequate as well as improper.

As was exhibited in this case, good faith and a sense of duty on the part of the police falls far short of adequately addressing the situation. The runaway child who has been reported missing but has not committed any criminal offence, *may* indeed be a child at risk. That is the issue which must be addressed first and it can only be accomplished in a competent and caring fashion by trained child care workers.

In *R. v. W.(J.P.)* a police officer obtained some information that suggested that a particular youth might be in possession of stolen property, but the officer did not have sufficient evidence to obtain a search warrant, let alone charge the youth.[9] The officer went to the youth's home, but he was not there. The officer obtained the permission of the father to search the youth's room, where he discovered some stolen items. While the search was in progress, the youth returned home and was arrested; his permission for the search was not sought. The judge ruled that the father could not waive his son's "reasonable expectation of privacy" and his rights under section 8 of the *Charter*. The evidence was excluded, and the youth acquitted. The judge observed:

> Young persons, like adults, are fully entitled to the rights secured by the Charter. . . . What more private place could teenagers have than their bedroom. . . . The risk that a parent might [lawfully] enter a teenager's bedroom does not destroy the right that a young person has against unlawful and unreasonable intrusion by the agents of the state.

This decision, and many others, illustrate that the courts will protect the rights of accused young persons and encourage police compliance with the law even if this means that youths who are "in fact guilty" are acquitted.

---

9   [1993] B.C.J. No. 2891 (Youth Ct.) (QL). But see *R. v. T.(F.)* (21 November 1995), (B.C. Prov. Ct.) [unreported] [summarized [1996] W.D.F.L. 257] (police search of youth's room at request of mother and seizure of firearms did not violate s. 8 of *Charter*, above note 4).

In some cases, the youthful victims of an improper police arrest may obtain monetary compensation for false arrest and imprisonment, as occurred in *Walkley* v. *Canada (A.G.)*.[10] A storekeeper in a small British Columbia town noticed that a teddy bear was missing immediately after three girls left the store, but she had not seen them take anything. A person outside the store reported to the storekeeper that through the window he had seen one of the girls take the teddy bear. The police were immediately notified and two officers soon located the girls, two of whom were twelve, and the other eleven. The officer questioned the girls, who denied taking the teddy bear. They had been Christmas shopping and produced receipts for all the goods in their possession; at an officer's request they opened their jackets and emptied their pockets, but no bear was discovered. The officers nevertheless concluded that the girls committed the theft and told one of them that she was a "liar and a thief." She was arrested, handcuffed, and taken to the police station, and the other girls were also accused of lying and taken to the station. Upset and crying, the girls were questioned by the police; eventually, they were placed in a holding cell. Shortly after the arrest, a parent of one of the girls was located but was told by the police that it would be "a good lesson for the girls" to leave them longer at the police station; the girls were not picked up for more than two hours. No teddy bear was ever recovered and the girls were not charged.

The girls, acting through their parents as litigation guardians, sued the police officers and government, and each girl was awarded $10,000 for what the court characterized as "an extremely traumatic experience . . . which was entirely unnecessary." The judge accepted that the initial questioning of the girls was reasonable and lawful, but thereafter the conduct of the police was unacceptable since the circumstances and nature of the alleged offence did not justify the arrest and imprisonment of the girls:

> [L]iberty is a hallmark of our society . . . [and] children in our society ought to be the constant object of our nurturing and support. In cases such as this where people and property are not at risk, where there is no violence, where the demeanour of the children is normal, where there is no attempt to be evasive and where time and distance allow a quick check on identification, there can be no justification for the arrest and imprisonment of 11 and 12 year old children.

This case illustrates that police cannot take "the law into their own hands" and seek to punish youths in order to "teach them a lesson."

---

10   [1997] B.C.J. No. 599 (S.C.) (QL).

B. POLICE QUESTIONING :
YOA, SECTION 56(2) AND (4)

In addition to the general protections afforded to all persons at the time of arrest under the *Charter of Rights*, special provisions in section 56 of the *YOA* are intended to ensure that there is no improper questioning of young persons by police or other persons in authority. But, despite these protections, most youths who are questioned by the police will make a statement that implicates them in the offence. The taking of a statement from a youth is often an important part of a police investigation, and later of the Crown's case in court against the youth. In practice most cases are ultimately resolved by a guilty plea, but if there is a trial one of the issues most likely to be litigated is the admissibility of the youth's statement to the police. So the taking of statements is an important issue for police officers who work on young offenders cases, as well as for judges and lawyers in youth court.

The statutory provision that now governs the admissibility of statements made by young persons, and accordingly regulates police practice, is section 56(2) of the *YOA*:

> 56. (2) No oral or written statement given by a young person to a peace officer or to any other person who is, in law, a person in authority on the arrest or detention of the young person or in circumstances where the peace officer or other person has reasonable grounds for believing that the young person has committed an offence is admissible against the young person unless
>
> (*a*) the statement was voluntary;
>
> (*b*) the person to whom the statement was given has, before the statement was made, clearly explained to the young person, in language appropriate to his age and understanding, that
>
>> (i) the young person is under no obligation to give a statement,
>>
>> (ii) any statement given by him may be used as evidence in proceedings against him,
>>
>> (iii) the young person has the right to consult counsel and a parent or other person in accordance with paragraph (*c*), and
>>
>> (iv) any statement made by the young person is required to be made in the presence of counsel and any other person consulted in accordance with paragraph (*c*), if any, unless the young person desires otherwise;

(c) the young person has, before the statement was made, been given a reasonable opportunity to consult

  (i) with counsel, and

  (ii) a parent, or in the absence of a parent, an adult relative, or in the absence of a parent and an adult relative, any other appropriate adult chosen by the young person; and

(d) where the young person consults any person pursuant to paragraph (c), the young person has been given a reasonable opportunity to make the statement in the presence of that person.[11]

Section 56(2)(a) provides that a youth's statement must be "voluntary," and so the established jurisprudence on the general concept of "voluntariness" applies to the statements of youths. A statement is "voluntary" only if it is made without "fear of prejudice or hope of advantage exercised or held out by a person in authority."[12] A statement in response to police threats of violence is involuntary and hence inadmissible. If the police tell a youth: "You might as well tell us the whole truth instead of getting yourself into more trouble," this may also be regarded as a threat rendering a statement involuntary and inadmissible.[13] A youth's statement made after police tell him that if he cooperates with them and makes a statement, they will help him secure a lesser sentence, will be viewed a "promise of advantage" that will render a statement involuntary.[14] A statement is "voluntary" only if it is the product of an "operating mind," and statements have been ruled inadmissible because of impairment by drugs or alcohol[15]; this can apply to those adolescents who are in an impaired physical or emotional state when being questioned by the police.[16]

Section 56(2) requires the police to fully inform youths of their rights prior to a statement being made. The warning is substantially broader than that given an adult under the *Charter*. An adult only has to be informed of the reason for arrest and of the right to retain counsel. An adult in law has

---

11   As discussed below, there were some amendments to s. 56 in *An Act to amend the Young Offenders Act and the Criminal Code*, S.C. 1995, c. 19, s. 35(2) [*YOA 1995*] that are reflected in the provision quoted here.

12   *Ibrahim v. R.*, [1914] A.C. 599 at 609 (P.C.).

13   *R. v. C.(D.E.)* (11 August 1986), (Ont. Prov. Ct. (Fam. Div.)) [unreported] [summarized [1986] W.D.F.L. 2047] [*C.(D.E.)*], Morrison Prov. J.

14   *R. v. C.(D.J.)* (1993), 124 N.S.R. (2d) 371 (C.A.).

15   *R. v. Clarkson*, [1986] 1 S.C.R. 383.

16   See, e.g., *R. v. R.(No.1)* (1972), 9 C.C.C. 274 (Ont. Prov. Ct. (Fam. Div.)).

no obligation to answer police questions, but in Canada the police have no obligation to advise an adult of the right to silence. As well, police may question an adult who has retained counsel in the absence of that legal adviser, unless the accused asks for counsel to be present.[17]

Under section 56(2)(b) a youth must be advised of the right to silence and warned of the potential use of any statement against him or her, as well as of the right under section 56(2)(c) to consult with counsel *and* a parent, and under (2)(d) to have those persons present while a statement is being made. While these rights may be waived by the youth, under section 56(4) any such waiver must "be videotaped or . . . in writing, and where it is in writing it shall contain a statement signed by the young person that the young person has been apprised of the right being waived." By way of contrast, an adult may give an oral waiver of the *Charter*-based right to counsel, and, provided that there was an adequate warning of the right, may be deemed to have waived the right to counsel by answering police questions.

Section 56 is premised on the recognition that young persons may lack the sophistication and maturity to appreciate fully their legal rights or the consequences of making a statement and so require special protections when being questioned by police. There is a significant body of social-science research that indicates that adolescents do not have the same understanding of legal concepts as adults and are less likely to appreciate the consequences of making a statement confessing guilt or waiving the right to consult a lawyer.[18] They may, for example, only think that it is useful to contact a lawyer if they are truly "innocent," that is, unjustifiably charged. As a result, even after being cautioned the majority of youths who are questioned by police waive their rights to consult a lawyer and make an inculpatory statement confessing guilt.

While the majority of these confessions are reasonably accurate, youths may be intimidated by adult authority figures and tend to make statements which they believe those authority figures want to hear, whether such statements are true or not.[19] In enacting section 56, Parliament felt

---

17   *R. v. Hebert*, [1990] 2 S.C.R. 151 [*Hebert*].

18   See, e.g., R. Abramovitch, M. Peterson-Badali, & M. Rohan, "Young People's Understanding and Assertion of their Rights to Silence and Legal Counsel"(1995) 37 Can. J. Crim. 1; R. Abramovitch, K. L. Higgins-Biss, & S. R. Biss, "Young Persons' Comprehension of Waivers in Criminal Proceedings" (1993) 35 Can. J. Crim. 309.

19   There are cases in Canada of adolescents feeling coerced by aggressive police questioning into making statements that they knew to be false. Perhaps the best-documented and most infamous case arose out of the Donald Marshall murder trial in Nova Scotia; see Nova Scotia, *Report of the Royal Commission on the Donald Marshall, Jr., Prosecution*, vol. 1 (Halifax: Queen's Printer, 1989) at 63.

that consultation with a parent or lawyer should protect the legal rights of young persons and prevent the making of false statements.

Some advocates for youths argue that section 56 does not go far enough to protect youths, and that the law should at a minimum require consultation with a lawyer before a statement can be made. In advancing this position, a Toronto legal aid clinic that specializes in representing adolescents graphically described some of its concerns:

> We are frequently faced with youth who advise us that they are frightened and intimidated at the police station. Youth are often told of their right to counsel but then that right is not translated into action, that is, they are not given a telephone, or they are left to wait for some considerable time. Often, there are youth who sign the waivers and don't know why they are doing so or can't recall whether or not they have signed anything. Many youth have a vague recollection of being told their rights but do not truly understand what their rights entail. Youth are often left in the interrogation room for long periods of time and are separated from other youth that they are charged with. We are also aware of youth left in the interrogation room without any clothes on. Many of our clients . . . were advised of their right to counsel and . . . did sign a waiver . . . however, when asked [by us] to articulate what the waiver meant they are unable to do so. . . .
>
> In our experience, fear, apprehension and the belief that the police will "give them a break," encourage young persons to make statements that they may not otherwise have made. At the time of arrest and detention, young persons are in an extremely vulnerable position. Often they are afraid of the police and the reaction of their parents. Thus it is not surprising that few youth want to talk to their parents or have their parents present when making a statement. Yet youth are not encouraged to speak to counsel. . . . on numerous occasions we have heard from youth: "Well I thought of calling a lawyer but I didn't know one.". . . Despite the fact that police are obliged to tell young persons about duty counsel, the concept of contacting a lawyer (usually a stranger) is itself intimidating for a youth.[20]

While many youths will waive their rights and make a statement to the police without fully appreciating the consequences, such a statement will be inadmissible if the police did not fully comply with section 56 of the *YOA*. Unlike a *Charter of Rights* violation, which still gives a judge a discre-

---

20   Justice for Children & Youth, *Submission of the Canadian Foundation for Children, Youth and the Law on the Importance of Statement Protections Under the Young Offenders Act Section 56* (Toronto, 1995).

tion to admit evidence if satisfied that doing so would not bring "the administration of justice into disrepute" (section 24(2)), a violation of section 56 of the *YOA* creates an automatic bar to the admission of a statement.

The importance of full compliance with section 56 was emphasized in the 1990 decision of the Supreme Court of Canada in R. v. J.(J.T.), where the confession of a seventeen-year-old youth to the brutal sexual assault and murder of a three-year-old child was excluded, with the Court ruling that under the circumstances the remaining admissible evidence would permit him only to be tried for manslaughter and not murder.[21]

In R. v. J.(J.T.) the police invited the youth to come to the police station for questioning, without charging him. At that time the police suspected that the youth had killed the girl but lacked the evidence to lay charges. After several hours of questioning, the youth made a statement in which he implicated himself. The police then charged him and advised him of his rights under the *Charter* as well as of his right under the *YOA* to consult an adult relative and a lawyer. The youth met in private with an adult relative and then with a lawyer. After the lawyer left, the police again asked the youth whether he wanted to make a statement, to which he responded: "No. She [the lawyer] told me not to." The police told the youth about some of the evidence that they had obtained which appeared to implicate him and then asked further questions, which the youth answered. However, prior to resumption of questioning, the police failed to advise the youth again of his right to consult and have present an adult and a lawyer during questioning. After the youth made a statement confessing guilt, he refused to sign a written waiver of his right of consultation as required by section 56(4) of the *YOA*.

The Supreme Court of Canada ruled all three of the statements inadmissible, with Cory J. stating:

> By its enactment of s. 56, Parliament has recognized the problems and difficulties that beset young people when confronted with authority. It may seem unnecessary and frustrating to the police and society that a worldly wise, smug 17-year-old with apparent anti-social tendencies should receive the benefit of this section. Yet it must be remembered that the section is to protect *all* young people of 17 years or less. A young person is usually far more easily impressed and influenced by authoritarian figures. No matter what the bravado and braggadocio that young people may display, it is unlikely that they will appreciate their legal rights in a general sense or the consequences of oral statements

---

21   The youth was ultimately tried as an adult, convicted of manslaughter, and sentenced to life imprisonment: R. v. J.(J.T.) (1991), 73 Man. R. (2d) 103 (C.A.).

made to persons in authority; certainly they would not appreciate the nature of their rights to the same extent as would most adults. Teenagers may also be more susceptible to subtle threats arising from their surroundings and the presence of persons in authority. A young person may be more inclined to make a statement, even though it is false, in order to please an authoritarian figure. It was no doubt in recognition of the additional pressures and problems faced by young people that led Parliament to enact this code of procedure. . . .

Section 56 itself exists to protect all young people, particularly the shy and the frightened, the nervous and the naive. Yet justice demands that the law be applied uniformly in all cases. The requirements of s. 56 must be complied with whether the authorities are dealing with the nervous and naive or the street-smart and worldly-wise. The statutory pre-conditions for the admission of a statement made by a young person cannot be bent or relaxed because the authorities are convinced, on the basis of what they believe to be cogent evidence, of the guilt of the suspect. As soon as the requirements are relaxed because of a belief in the almost certain guilt of a young person, they will next be relaxed in the case of those whom the authorities believe are probably guilty, and thereafter in the case of a suspect who might possibly be guilty but whose past conduct, in the opinion of those in authority, is such that he or she should be found guilty of something for the general protection of society. Principles of fairness require that the section be applied uniformly to all without regard to the characteristics of the particular young person.[22]

Although not explicitly discussed by the Supreme Court in R. v. J.(J.T.), it is apparent from the decision that the YOA cannot be invoked to exclude physical evidence obtained by the police as a result of information in a statement that is inadmissible because of the failure to comply with section 56. In R. v. J.(J.T.) the youth took the police to the scene of the crime and showed them a concrete block; the concrete block was admissible as physical evidence, but the statement that the youth made at the scene was not admissible because section 56 was violated.

Similarly, in R. v. C.(S.A.)[23] the Alberta Court of Appeal held that a knife and clothing used in a robbery and discovered by police as a result of statements of a young person were admissible in evidence, despite the inadmissibility of the statement because of the failure of the police to

---

22   R. v. J.(J.T.), [1990] 2 S.C.R. 755 at 766–68.
23   (1989), 92 A.R. 237 (C.A.). S. 56 does not, however, apply to a breathalyzer test; R. v. L.(D.J.), (1995), 139 Sask. R. 47 (Q.B.).

comply with section 56. The Court observed that the words of section 56 applied only to "oral or written statements." At common law, courts have always displayed a greater concern with excluding improperly obtained statements, which are the product of self-incrimination and have the potential to be false, than in excluding physical evidence which may have been illegally obtained by the police. However, if physical evidence is obtained in violation of a young person's rights under the *Charter*, it may still be excluded if "the admission of it . . . would bring the administration of justice into disrepute."[24]

One controversial issue that the Supreme Court of Canada decision in *R. v. J.(J.T.)* did not fully resolve is whether a statement made to the police by a youth who is not charged with an offence at the time that the statement is made has to satisfy section 56 of the *YOA*. In *R. v. J.(J.)* a fourteen-year-old girl reported to a social worker and a police officer that she had been sexually abused. She was warned about the seriousness of her allegation but not advised of her rights under section 56 of the *YOA*, which was not surprising since she was viewed as a victim at that time. It was later discovered that the girl had deliberately made a false accusation and she was charged with mischief. At her trial on the mischief charge the statement was held admissible by the Ontario Court of Appeal, with Cory J.A. concluding that section 56(2) "must refer to young persons *accused* of committing offences"[25] and not to statements of young persons not charged with an offence.

The 1995 amendments to the *YOA* make clear that the caution requirements of section 56(2) apply whenever the police have "reasonable grounds for believing that the young person has committed an offence," even if the youth has not been formally charged. Thus, when the police are questioning the youth as a potential witness or victim, as in the case of *R. v. J.(J.)*, section 56 will have no application.

The test of "reasonable grounds for believing" that the young person has committed an offence in the amended section 56(2) is the same as that used in the *Criminal Code* as being necessary for the laying of

---

24   *Charter*, above note 4, s. 24(2); see *R. v. Collins*, [1987] 1 S.C.R. 265. See also *R. v. D.(C.M.)*, [1996] B.C.J. No. 2649 (C.A.) (QL) where a statement was ruled inadmissible because of a violation of *YOA*, above note 3, s. 56, and, without any discussion of the rationale, the Court also ruled inadmissible a weapon that the youth had led the police to after making the statement. See also *R. v. Stillman*, above note 4.

25   (1988), 65 C.R. (3d) 371 at 383 (Ont. C.A.). [Emphasis added]. See also accompanying "Annotation" at (1988) 65 C.R. (3d) 372–76 by N. Bala, which compares the Ontario and Manitoba judgments.

charges, and it would appear to mean that section 56 does not apply when police are asking a "potential suspect" questions based on a mere "hunch" or "police intuition." This was illustrated by the decision of the Ontario Court of Appeal in R. v. W.(J.), a case decided before the 1995 amendments. Two police officers were patrolling in an industrial neighbourhood at 2 a.m. when they observed two youths leaving the parking lot of a business, with one carrying a knapsack. The officers approached the youths and asked what they were up to. One youth responded: "We're going over to a friend's place." The police asked to look in the knapsack that the other youth was carrying and he said "sure." As the knapsack was being searched, the first youth said: "There's a . . . crowbar in there which belongs to my friend. . . . It's my buddy's, and I was just borrowing it to take a dent out of my mom's car." At this point the officers had grounds to suspect that the youths had been trying to break into the business premises, a suspicion subsequently confirmed when the police found fresh footprints in the snow leading from one window to another. The youths were then arrested and advised of their rights.

At issue was the admissibility of the first youth's statements to the police on a charge of being in possession of a burglary tool contrary to section 351 of the *Criminal Code*. Without those statements, the Crown could not link him to the tools, since the other youth had physical possession. The Ontario Court of Appeal ruled the statements inadmissible since section 56 was not satisfied, stating that section 56 in its original form applied to any statement made by a youth to a police officer except in a situation like R. v. J.(J.) where the statement forms the "*actus reus* of the crime."[26] Justice McKinlay contrasted the law applicable to R. v. W.(J.) with the 1995 amendment:

> The amended version of s. 56(2), which came into force in December of 1995 [S.C. 1995, c. 19, s. 35], makes it clear that the protection of the section now applies only to young persons arrested or detained, or where the peace officer involved has reasonable grounds for believing that the young person has committed an offence. . . . in this case . . . [the] statements were made by the appellant at a time when he was neither detained by the police nor suspected of any crime.[27]

In a strict technical sense the youths were not being legally "detained" or "reasonably" suspected of any offence when being questioned by the police; in theory the youths could have kept walking and refused to

---

26   *Actus reus* is a Latin expression for the "guilty act," as distinguished from the *mens rea*, or "guilty mind."

27   (1996), 30 O.R. (3d) 342 at 349 (C.A.) [W.(J.)].

answer any questions, though they undoubtedly felt obliged to answer the questions posed by the police. The police may not have had "reasonable grounds" to believe that the youths had committed an offence and so could not legally arrest the youth before the first statement was made, though they undoubtedly had some suspicions of wrongdoing.

The judgment of McKinlay J.A. in *R. v. W.(J.)* suggests that as a result of the 1995 amendments the courts should take a broader view of the circumstances in which youths "voluntarily" answer police questions. This approach would afford police a little more latitude to ask questions of a youth without giving a caution than they were allowed by the Supreme Court in *R. v. J.(J.T.)* in 1990; a mere police "hunch" or "suspicions *without reasonable* foundation" would not require cautioning before questioning. It should, however, be appreciated that the remarks of McKinlay J.A. about the 1995 amendments are only *obiter dicta* and may not be followed by other judges. There are other cases that suggest that a youth who is answering police questions under a feeling of "psychological compulsion," but without having been legally arrested, may be entitled to the cautions required by the *Charter* and the *YOA*.[28] The argument for applying section 56 in such situations seems strong, since youths lack knowledge of their legal rights and generally feel compelled to answer a police officer's questions. Such an interpretation would encourage police officers to respect the rights of adolescents and would be consistent with section 3(1)(g) of the *YOA* which requires "young persons . . . to be informed as to what [their] . . . rights and freedoms are."

C. AN EXPLANATION "APPROPRIATE TO HIS AGE AND UNDERSTANDING": SECTION 56(2)(b)

Section 56 has been frequently invoked by the courts to exclude statements made by young persons because the police have not provided the youth with an explanation that is "appropriate to his age and understanding." With an adult, a statement will generally be admissible if the police advise accused persons of their rights using the language of the *Charter*, and the police have printed "caution cards" to assist them in doing this. The *YOA* presents police who are questioning a youth with a greater challenge. A simple "reading of rights" will not suffice; rather,

---

28   See, e.g., *R. v. Hawkins* (1992), 102 Nfld. & P.E.I.R. 91 (Nfld. C.A.).

there must be an explanation that is appropriate, having regard to the youth's language skills and developmental stage. Providing an appropriate caution for a youth takes longer than for an adult, and police should have specific training about the requirements of the *YOA*.

In *R. v. M.(M.A.)*, a sixteen-year-old youth with a learning disability was charged with gross indecency. The police officer who arrested the youth purported to inform him of his rights by reading from a form which recited the words used in section 56(2) of the *YOA*. The young person then signed a statement in which he waived his right to have a lawyer or parent present, in accordance with section 56(4). In upholding the ruling of the trial judge that the statements were inadmissible, Hinkson J.A. of the British Columbia Court of Appeal wrote:

> . . . [I]t appears . . . that the learned trial judge was confronted with the requirements of s. 56 and concluded that having the contents of the two forms read to him, the young person did not know what to do in the circumstances and did not know why a lawyer would be necessary.
>
> . . . In my opinion, the course followed by the police officer in the present case did not meet the requirements of s. 56 of the *Young Offenders Act*. The forms themselves appear to be clear, but Parliament indicated the requirement that before the statement was made there must be a clear explanation to the young person. I am not persuaded that reading the contents of those two forms met the requirements imposed by Parliament before the statement could be taken from the young person. . . .
>
> Parliament has paid special attention to the needs of young people for protective advice and has called on the police to provide it. There should be a genuine endeavour by the person in authority to describe the function of the lawyer and the benefits to the young person of having a lawyer, or parents, or relatives, or an adult friend present. That endeavour should be designed to lead to an appreciation on the part of the young person of the consequences of the choices that he makes.
>
> Even had this young person been a person without any learning disability, the mere reading over of these two statements and then asking the young person to sign them, without any explanation to him whatsoever, would not, in my opinion, have been compliance with . . . s. 56 of the *Young Offenders Act*.[29]

Strictly speaking, s. 56(4) does not require that the youth actually understand the advice provided (that is, the test for the adequacy of a

---

29   (1986), 32 C.C.C. (3d) 567 at 571 & 573 (B.C.C.A.).

caution is not subjective), but only that the explanation must be in "language appropriate" to the youth's "age and understanding" (meaning, the test is objective but nonetheless takes into account the age and capacities of the particular youth being questioned). However, in practice, police should try to ensure that the particular youth being questioned actually understands the caution being given. Generally, this requires a caution that avoids or explains such technical terms as "counsel" and "retain." A useful practice is for the police to test the youth's understanding by asking the youth to state in his or her own words the meaning of the caution that was provided. Some police forces have begun to audio- or video- tape the section 56(2) and *Charter* police cautions to demonstrate that appropriate care was taken. Another alternative is to have the youth write out, preferably in his or her own words, the cautions that have been given.

The case law indicates that, when advising a youth of the right to consult with a lawyer prior to making a statement and to have a lawyer present when a statement is made, the police should specifically mention that if a youth is unable to afford a lawyer, one can be obtained without charge through legal aid or by order of a court. The police should also indicate the means (telephone number) by which a legal aid lawyer can be contacted for advice prior to police questioning; if a youth expresses the desire to consult with a lawyer, there is an obligation on the police to facilitate this contact and allow for a private consultation.[30] While most provinces have programs in place for consultation twenty-four hours a day, often by means of a toll-free consultation with a lawyer (generally known as "duty counsel"), there is no legal obligation on the government to provide this type of service. If a lawyer is not available and the youth wishes to consult one, the police should not question the youth.

A 1993 decision of the Supreme Court of Canada, *R. v. I.(L.R.)*, dealt with the admissibility of statements made by a sixteen-year-old youth charged with second degree murder.[31] The Supreme Court emphasized that a youth must be advised of the right to consult and have present both a lawyer *and* a parent (or other adult if a parent is not available). The parent and lawyer have different roles and the youth should understand that both may be consulted and present during a

---

30 See *R. v. Brydges*, [1990] 1 S.C.R. 190; and *Re C.(V.K.)*, [1991] A.J. No. 382 (Prov. Ct. (Youth Div.)) (QL); *R. v. Bartle*, [1994] 3 S.C.R. 173.

31 *I.(L.R.)*, above note 6. In 1995 s. 56(2)(b) was amended to reflect this Supreme Court decision; the original wording of s. 56(2) was less clear than the present wording about whether a youth could consult either a parent or a lawyer, or both a parent *and* a lawyer. See *YOA 1995*, above note 11.

police interview.[32] The youth is not expected to choose between consulting a lawyer *or* a parent.

The Supreme Court also ruled that, if a youth makes a statement that is inadmissible because of an inadequate police caution, a subsequent statement made after a proper caution may be "tainted" and ruled inadmissible unless precautions are taken by the police. Sopinka J. wrote:

> [T]he admissibility of a confession . . . which has been preceded by an involuntary [inadmissible] confession . . . [involves] a factual determination based on factors designed to ascertain the degree of connection between the two statements. These . . . include . . . the time span between the two statements, advertence to the previous statement during questioning, the discovery of additional incriminating evidence subsequent to the first statement, the presence of the same police officers at both interrogations and other similarities between the two circumstances. . . . An explanation of one's rights either by a police officer or counsel may not avail in the face of a strong urge to explain away incriminating matters in a prior statement.[33]

As *R. v. I.(L.R.)* indicates, it may not be sufficient for the police merely to advise a youth of legal rights in accordance with section 56 and the *Charter* if a prior inadmissible statement has been made. It may be necessary to tell the youth specifically that the earlier statement may be inadmissible and the youth should feel no compulsion to explain the earlier statement.[34]

Another issue raised in *R. v. I.(L.R.)* was whether police must ensure that the youth has an awareness of "the extent of his or her jeopardy" when making a statement. In particular, if the offence is serious and the youth is fourteen or older, are the police required to advise the youth of the *possibility* of transfer of the case to adult court, where much more serious sanctions may be imposed? The Supreme Court acknowledged that there is no express requirement in section 56(2) that a youth must be warned of the possibility of transfer, but it pointed out that the pre-*YOA* cases on the voluntariness of statements of adolescents suggested that it was a good practice for police to include such information in their cautions.[35] The Supreme Court ruled that

---

32   Similarly, even if a parent is actually consulted, a youth must still waive in writing or on videotape the right to consult counsel and have counsel present. *R. v. D. (M.)*, [1996] O.J. No. 1162 (Prov. Div.) (QL).

33   *I.(L.R.)*, above note 6 at 526–27.

34   *R. v. H.(C.G.)*, [1996] M.J. No. 628 (Prov. Ct.) (QL).

35   See, e.g., *R. v. Yensen*, [1961], O.R. 703 (H.C.J.).

a warning that a young person may be raised to adult court should not be interpreted as an absolute requirement. . . . [but it] is one factor to be considered in determining voluntariness, the importance of which will vary depending on the other facts of the case, including the age, level of understanding and sophistication of the young person and whether or not the young person has consulted with counsel.[36]

Justice Sopinka clearly indicated that it would "be preferable" for a warning of the possibility of transfer to be given, even if before the statement was given the youth had consulted with counsel who would be expected to provide such advice . However, ultimately the Court did not rule whether the failure to give this warning was fatal to the admissibility of the statement in this case.

The 1996 Ontario Court of Appeal decision in *R. v. M.(S.)* upheld the admissibility of a statement made by a seventeen-year-old youth in connection with a sexual assault, despite the failure to warn of the possibility of transfer to adult court.[37] The Court of Appeal noted that *R. v. I.(L.R.)* did not set out a "mandatory requirement" for such a caution. The Court stated that in murder cases like *R. v. I.(L.R.)*, a warning of the possibility of transfer may be most appropriate since the difference between adult court and youth court sanctions is greatest in this context.[38]

Though not expressly mentioned by the Supreme Court in *R. v. I. (L.R.)*, the warning concerning the possibility of transfer will be more appropriate if the charge is very serious, making the likelihood of transfer greater. In *R. v. I.(L.R.)* the youth was not actually transferred, though the Crown had made an unsuccessful transfer application. If a youth has been transferred, the failure of the police to have warned of this possibility is likely to be viewed negatively by the adult court when deciding whether to admit the statement. Conversely, if, as in *R. v. M. (S.)*, no attempt is made to transfer the youth, the absence of this warning may be less significant.

Another aspect of understanding the "extent of one's jeopardy" is that the youth must know the charges that are being investigated. It is a requirement of section 10(a) of the *Charter of Rights* that the police inform individuals at the time of arrest of the reasons for their arrest, that is, individuals must be informed of the charges they face. Concerns

---

36 *I.(L.R.)*, above note 6 at 524, Sopinka J.
37 (1996), 28 O.R. (3d) 776 (C.A.).
38 For murder, the maximum sentence in youth court is ten years, whereas in adult court the automatic sentence is life imprisonment, though transferred youth are eligible for parole in five to ten years. Transfer is discussed in ch. 9.

arise when a youth is arrested for one offence and, during the course of making a statement to the police, begins to confess to other, unrelated crimes. The courts have articulated a general principle in interpreting the right to counsel, guaranteed by section 10 of the *Charter*, namely, that

> the police must restate the accused's right to counsel when there is a fundamental and discrete change in the purpose of the investigation, one involving a different and unrelated offence or a significantly more serious offence than that contemplated at the time of the warning.[39]

There is a similar duty for the police to recaution an accused youth of rights under the *YOA* if questioning is "redirected to a new topic" so that the youth can appreciate the consequences of making the statement. In *R. v. Z.(C.)*[40] the police arrested three youths in connection with a convenience store robbery, and, after an appropriate caution and waiver, questioned each of the youths individually. After one of the youths made a confession to the robbery, the officer then began to ask questions about the robbery of another store the day before, believing that the three youths had also been responsible for that offence, but without recautioning the youth. The judge ruled that the statement was not admissible in regard to a charge for the robbery of the second store because of the failure of the police officer to charge the youth with that offence and again satisfy section 56(2):

> Although these offences are of the same delict, they are sufficiently distinguishable in time and place and participation of all involved so as to give rise to different possibilities for a defence to any or all of the perpetrators.

A 1997 British Columbia case raised the issue of whether section 56 applies to statements overheard by an undercover police officer while a youth is in custody. For adults, the Supreme Court of Canada has held that, as long as an undercover officer makes no attempt to elicit a statement, there is no need for the Crown to prove voluntariness or comply with the *Charter*.[41] However, in *Re G.(D.B.)*, it was held that different rules apply to youths.[42]

In that case two youths were arrested in connection with a serious fire that they were believed to have started. They refused to make a statement and at 4 a.m. were placed in separate cells in the police sta-

---

39   *R. v. Evans*, [1991] 1 S.C.R. 869 at 893.

40   [1995] O.J. No. 4010 (Prov. Div.) (QL).

41   *Hebert*, above note 17.

42   [1997] B.C.J. No. 1203 (Prov. Ct.) (QL).

tion, with the intent to take them to a youth facility in the morning. An undercover police officer was placed in an adjacent cell, where he pretended to be a prisoner, sleepy and disinterested. During the next few hours, the youths conversed and made several incriminating statements that the officer overheard. Judge Ehrcke ruled the statements inadmissible since the officer had not satisfied section 56 of the *YOA*. She wrote:

> The youths were not aware they were making statements to a peace officer. . . . Freedom of choice for a youth who is detained requires that the youth is cognizant of the fact that he is speaking to or in the presence of a police officer, at least where an interested police tactic is invoked. . . . It may be that in other circumstances, where an officer unintentionally overhears something, a youth can be taken to have accepted the risk.

In reaching this decision, the judge cited *I.(L.R.)*. While a statement made by an adult in similar circumstances would be admissible, "the special situation of youths" demanded protection of "their vulnerability."

D. WHO IS A "PERSON IN AUTHORITY"?

Section 56(2) requires a "peace officer *or* other person who is, in law, a person in authority" to advise youths of their rights in order for a statement (or "confession") to be admissible [emphasis added]. The requirement for providing cautions under section 56 and the *Charter* applies only to "persons in authority," since only these individuals are considered to be in a position to coerce a youth into making a statement. Otherwise, a statement from any party to litigation to someone who is not a person in authority is an "admission" (as opposed to a "confession"[43]) and will generally be received in evidence against that person without any concern about whether it was "voluntary" or whether the person who made it was cautioned.

---

43   Some legal authorities distinguish between a "confession" and an "admission." A "confession" is generally defined as an inculpatory statement made by an accused person to a police officer or other person in authority; at common law it is admissible in evidence only if it is voluntary. An "admission" is any statement accepting responsibility by a party to litigation (such as an accused) that is not covered by the "confession rule." Admissions do not need to be proven to be "voluntary" to be received in evidence. Neither type of statement needs to be a full admission of guilt to be admissible against the accused.

A difficult question is the extent to which individuals such as school-teachers, probation officers, social workers, and even parents may be regarded as "persons in authority." In practice, individuals other than police officers lack the training and knowledge to provide an appropriate caution or otherwise respect the rights of a youth. If they are considered to be "persons in authority" or "agents of the state," a statement made to them by a youth will inevitably be excluded for a failure to comply with the requirements of the *Charter of Rights* and section 56 of the *YOA*. In a real sense a youth is likely to view adults like social workers, teachers, and parents to be just as much "persons in authority" as police officers and may feel pressured by them into answering questions. However, section 56 of the *YOA* refers to an individual who, *in law*, is a "person in authority" and the legal definition is relatively narrow.

In *R. v. B.(A.)* a youth was charged with having committed sexual offences against his two young half-sisters. An important piece of evidence against the youth was a statement he made to his mother admitting that he had abused the girls, after she promised to "get some help" for him if he told her the truth about what happened; also important were similar statements he made to two physicians who later treated him. The Ontario Court of Appeal ruled that neither the mother nor the physicians were "persons in authority" and there was no need for the Crown to establish the "voluntariness" of the statements or prove that section 56(2) was satisfied. Justice Cory wrote:

> As a general rule, a person in authority is someone engaged in the arrest, detention, examination or prosecution of the accused. When the word "examination" is used . . . it refers to interrogation by police officers, detention or security guards and members of the Crown attorney's office. . . . Certainly, in the ordinary sense of the term, A.B.'s mother was a person in authority. To a boy of 13, his mother must be an authoritative figure. . . . most particularly in a position of authority in light of her maternal desire to protect her young daughters.[44]

However, the judge concluded that the mother was not a person in authority, emphasizing that when she asked her son about his acts, she had no intention of calling the police or instituting court proceedings but rather wanted to find out what had happened so that she could get him psychiatric help. While recognizing that there might be circumstances in which a parent could become a "person in authority," Cory J.A. concluded: "Only the most serious continued and flagrant miscon-

---

44   (1986), 50 C.R. (3d) 247 at 256–57 (Ont. C.A.) [*B.(A.)*].

duct could ever be expected to lead parents to call the authorities about their own child. Until that time, parents would not, in law, be persons in authority."[45]

In *R. v. H.*[46] a thirteen-year-old student was charged with the theft of money in a school, and the prosecutor wanted the court to hear about statements made by the youth admitting guilt to his teacher and the school principal. Prior to the statements being made, the teacher promised that if the money was returned, nothing further would happen. Not surprisingly, neither the teacher nor the principal had complied with the *Charter* or section 56 of the *YOA*, since they had no training in the taking of legally admissible statements. Judge Russell of the Alberta Youth Court ruled that the youth's statements to the teacher and principal were inadmissible because of the violation of the *YOA* and section 10 of the *Charter of Rights*. *R. v. H.* does not require school personnel to advise adolescent students of all their legal rights, such as the right to counsel, in all situations where disciplinary action is being taken, but it does indicate that if these rights are not afforded a youth prior to questioning, statements which are made may later be ruled inadmissible in youth court proceedings.

A somewhat different approach was taken in *R. v. G. (J.M.)*,[47] where a fourteen-year-old boy was charged with possession of a small amount of marijuana. His school principal learned that the youth might have placed drugs in his socks, and he called the youth to his office. Asking the youth to remove his shoes and socks, the principal discovered a marijuana cigarette. The police were called, and the youth was arrested and advised of his rights. The Ontario Court of Appeal recognized that, for some purposes at least, a school principal is an agent of the state and must act in accordance with the *Charter of Rights*. A similar search by a police officer, without a lawful arrest being made and without any advice about the right to counsel, would have violated sections 8 and 10 of the *Charter of Rights*. However, the Court accepted that the principal's

---

45   *Ibid.* at 259.
46   (1985), 43 Alta. L. R. (2d) 250 (Prov. Ct. (Youth Div.)), Russell Prov. J. To a similar effect, see *R. v. R.(F.)* (10 November 1988), (Man. Prov. Ct. (Fam. Div.)) [unreported] [summarized [1988] W.D.F.L. 2561].
47   (1986), 56 O.R. (2d) 705 (C.A.). The same outcome occurred in the similar case of *R. v. M.(M. R.)*, [1997] N.S.J. No. 144 (C.A.) (QL) where the court noted that in "order to determine the reasonableness of the search, it is essential to consider the nature and manner in which the search is conducted. The age and sex of the student may also . . . be a significant factor . . . This was not a highly invasive search as compared with a strip and body cavity search, nor was it conducted, for example, by a male teacher of a young female student which could, in certain circumstances, amount to a violation under s. 8 [of the *Charter*, above note 4]."

search was carried out in the context of his normal duties of maintaining discipline in the school and hence was "reasonable" and not in violation of section 8 of the *Charter*; accordingly, the marijuana was admissible in evidence. Further, the Court accepted that the principal had no obligation to advise the student of his right to counsel before undertaking a search, since it was a "reasonable disciplinary or investigative procedure" of the school.

The Court recognized, however, that while the relationship between student and principal was not like that of policeman and citizen, there may be circumstances when "such [significant legal] consequences are inevitable and the principal becomes an agent of the police in detecting crime," for example, in an investigation into a serious crime, like a sexual assault or a homicide. In such a situation the failure to respect legal rights and properly caution a youth might result in evidence obtained being ruled inadmissible.

These cases illustrate that the courts will closely scrutinize each situation to determine the extent to which a principal or other person should be treated as an agent of the state. It may also be significant that *R. v. G.(J.M.)* involved the seizure of physical evidence, which was clearly and independently probative of the fact that the crime in question had been committed and would probably have been discovered in the course of a legal search that a police officer could have carried out. On the other hand, *R. v. H.* involved only an incriminating statement that might not have been made if the youth's rights had been respected, and the *YOA* has special provisions precluding the admission of such statements if rights have been violated.

As established in *R. v. B.(A.)*, a doctor or psychiatrist will generally not be regarded as a "person in authority," even if the physician is carrying out an assessment pursuant to a court order. As a result, lawyers will sometimes instruct their young clients not to discuss anything related to the offence with any treatment or assessment personnel prior to the conclusion of court proceedings, or at least until an adjudication of guilt or innocence has been made, though there are cases where the lawyer will want the client to reveal "his side of the story" to a medical assessor.

A probation officer will generally be viewed as a person in authority, that is, one who can effect or control a prosecution against the youth. As a result, unless the probation officer specifically cautions the youth, an unlikely event, statements made by a youth are not admissible, even for the purpose of establishing a breach of probation.[48] On the other

---

48   *R. v. H.(C.)*, [1995] O.J. No. 932 (Prov. Div.) (QL), Lenz Prov. J.

hand, when a youth has made a statement to a staff person in a group home, there is a tendency not to view the staff as "persons in authority," presumably because they have no direct role in the administration of justice or prosecution of offences.[49]

E. WHO IS A "YOUNG PERSON" AND SECTION 56(5.1)

For the purposes of section 56 of the *YOA*, a "young person" is someone between the ages of twelve and eighteen, as of the date of questioning by police. In *R. v. Z.(D.A.)* the Supreme Court of Canada held that the police do not need to comply with section 56 of the *YOA* for a statement to be admitted in evidence if a youth who was seventeen at the time of the alleged offence but had passed his eighteenth birthday at the time of police questioning. While, for purposes of jurisdiction and disposition he was a "young person" to be dealt with under the *YOA* in youth court, he did not have to be given the special protections of section 56. Writing for a majority of the Supreme Court, Lamer C.J.C. commented: "Persons over the age of 18 have long been deemed to possess sufficient maturity and control over the situation they may find themselves in to no longer require the watchful eye of a parent. . . ."[50]

Sometimes youths who are arrested by the police lie about their age,[51] perhaps to avoid having their parents notified, or in order to be kept in detention with older friends, or as part of a ruse to deceive the police about their true identity. If this happens, the police may fail to comply with section 56 of the *YOA* in regard to questioning. The *YOA* was amended in 1995 to deal with this type of situation; Section 56(5.1) now gives a youth court judge the discretion to admit a statement made by a young person to the police even if they have failed to comply with section 56, provided that the youth held out himself or herself as being eighteen years of age or older, and there were reasonable grounds to believe that this was true. The case must be dealt with in youth court, however, once the correct age has been established.

---

49   *R. v. B.(L.J.)* (16 January 1986), (Man. Prov. Ct. (Fam. Div.)) [unreported] [summarized [1986] W.D.F.L. 550].

50   *R. v. Z.(D.A.)*, [1992] 2 S.C.R. 1025 at 1053.

51   See, e.g., *R. v. H.(K.J.)* (27 October 1984), (Ont. Prov. Div.) [unreported] [summarized [1995] W.D.F.L. 83] [*H.(K.J.)*].

F. SPONTANEOUS STATEMENTS: SECTION 56(3)

Section 56(3) of the *YOA* provides that the requirements of section 56(2)(b) do not apply in respect of "oral statements . . . made spontaneously" by a youth before the police have a "reasonable opportunity" to comply with the cautioning requirements of section 56(2). This provision recognizes that there are situations in which a youth "spontaneously" makes a statement, and since in such cases the police cannot reasonably have been expected to comply with section 56(2), the use of the statement is not an infringement of the rights of the youth. Further, the circumstances in which these statements are made often provides some assurance that they are not the product of coercion. To ensure that the police do not exploit section 56(3), the courts have generally interpreted this provision narrowly, indicating that "any doubt as to whether the statement is spontaneous should be resolved in favour of the young person."[52]

In a Quebec case the police arrested a youth for a sexual assault and gave him a caution satisfying the *Charter,* though not section 56(2) of the *YOA.*[53] The alleged victim's father was making threatening gestures towards the youth and the police quickly put the youth in a patrol car and drove him to the police station, a few minutes away. On the way, he made two statements. The court refused to invoke section 56(3) and excluded the statement. While there was not enough time for the police to allow the youth to consult with parents or counsel before the statements were made, the police had sufficient opportunity to give him at least the rudiments of the more elaborate caution to be given to youths under section 56(2), in particular to advise him of the right to silence and of the right to consult with a parent and counsel before making a statement.

Section 56(3) has been invoked by courts to admit statements that youths have made just as they are being arrested, for example, as a gratuitous response to being informed of the reason for the arrest as required by the *Charter of Rights.*[54] It has also been used to admit statements made to an officer who was speaking to a youth, without suspecting that this individual had committed an offence, when the youth blurted out a confession.

An interesting example is provided by *R. v. H. (K. J.),*[55] where a youth was apprehended at a store for shoplifting and gave the police officer

---

52   *W.(J.),* above note 27 at 346.
53   *R. v. L.(M.),* [1987] R.J.Q 709 (Youth Ct.).
54   *R. v. M.(C.J.) (No. 2)* (1986), 43 Man. R. (2d) 138 (Q.B.).
55   Above note 51.

who came to the store a false name and birth date, one which indicated that he was an adult. The officer was suspicious of the youth's identity and took him to the police station, telling the youth that if his identity were not established, the police would bring him before a justice of the peace to seek to have him detained. At that point, the police had no intention of taking a statement. The youth told the officer: "I will tell you who I am if you give me a cigarette." The officer nodded acquiescence and said : "Who are you?" The youth replied: "Kevin H. I tried to kill Gavin N. two days before my birthday September 17." The officer then asked further questions, without cautioning the youth. On charges related to the attempted homicide, Judge Hardman ruled that the first statement admitting the killing was spontaneous and admissible under section 56(3), though the later responses to the questions were not admissible since the officer had an opportunity to warn the youth that serious charges might be laid and to caution about his rights.

The courts have held that, when a police officer is questioning a youth who is suspected of committing an offence but has not been arrested, section 56(3) does not apply since the statement should be viewed not as "spontaneous" but rather as a response to a police question.[56] Since the enactment of the 1995 amendments to the *YOA*, which specify that section 56(2) applies when there are "*reasonable grounds for believing that the* young person" [emphasis added] has committed an offence, it might not be necessary to satisfy section 56(2) or rely on section 56(3) if the police are questioning a youth based on a mere "hunch," that is, questioning based on a suspicion without "*reasonable grounds.*" Under this amendment, there will probably be cases in which the Crown will seek to have admitted in evidence a statement that a youth made to police without any caution: specifically, in circumstances where the police stop a youth and ask for a "volunteered" response but do not have "reasonable grounds" for a belief that the youth has committed an offence (in such circumstances, the police cannot detain the youth if the latter decides to refuse to answer questions). As discussed above, there is an argument that section 56(2) should be broadly interpreted to exclude statements made to police in any situation where a youth feels "psychologically compelled" to answer questions, but it remains to be seen how the courts will interpret this part of the *YOA*.

---

56   W.(J.), above note 27.

G. THE ROLE OF COUNSEL AT POLICE STATIONS

Section 56(2) of the *YOA* and section 10 of the *Charter* provide a right for youths to consult a lawyer upon arrest and before making a statement. This is reinforced by section 11(2) of the *YOA,* which requires that upon arrest the police "shall, forthwith" advise the youth of his or her right to be represented by counsel and the youth "shall be given an opportunity to obtain counsel." Many adolescents, relying on images from television and the movies, naively believe that lawyers only have a role in helping the innocent, and most waive their right to consult with a lawyer after arrest and before making a statement to the police. However, some youths, especially those who are more familiar with the youth justice system or who are more sophisticated, exercise their right to consult a lawyer.

If the youth expresses a desire to consult with a lawyer, whether by phone or in person, the youth has a right to a private consultation with the lawyer. To satisfy section 11(2) of the *YOA* and the *Charter,* police should ordinarily offer a youth access to a phone and a list of lawyers who will, without charge to callers, provide summary advice to youths detained by the police.

If contacted by a youth in this situation, it is generally premature for the lawyer to discuss the offence with the youth in the emotionally stressful state immediately after arrest, even if there is a time and place to do so. A lawyer should, especially at this stage, take care to communicate in clear and comprehensible language with the youth. Some of the things that the lawyer will want to do at this initial contact include:

- advise the youth that whatever is told the lawyer is confidential and cannot be shared with others without the client's permission, but that the youth's conversations with others, including parents or cellmates, may later be used against him or her;
- advise the youth that there is no obligation to give police any information other than name, age, and parents' identity (Lawyers will invariably strongly urge a client at this stage not to make a statement, show the police evidence, or otherwise cooperate with the police investigation. There will be ample time to offer an explanation or plead guilty at a later point, when there has been an opportunity for reflection and the lawyer has had disclosure of the Crown's case.);
- caution the youth that the police may use different techniques to try to induce a youth to make a later statement — for example, they may try to confront the youth with "evidence" of his or her guilt that may

be inaccurate or that may not be admissible at a trial, such as a statement from an alleged accomplice[57];

- advise the youth of the right to have a lawyer present if a statement should later be made to the police;
- warn of the possibility, if the circumstances appear to warrant, of transfer to adult court;
- discuss the possibility of pre-trial detention and begin to prepare for release hearing (it will be helpful for the lawyer to ascertain what the position of the police and Crown will be about pre-trial detention);
- obtain information about the youth and parents, such as addresses and phone numbers, and discuss with the youth what level of parental involvement is desired in such issues as pre-trial detention and communication with counsel;
- ascertain what has happened since the arrest (has a statement been made to the police already?);
- ascertain the youth's present emotional and physical state (is medical attention needed?); and
- if a statement has been made, advise the youth against offering any further explanations to the police at this time.[58]

It will also be important to explain how the youth can contact the lawyer, emphasizing that the police are obliged to facilitate contact. Assuming that the youth accepts the lawyer's advice about not talking to the police at this time, the lawyer should obtain the youth's instructions to inform the police that a statement will not be made.

If the youth insists on making a statement to the police at this time, the lawyer should offer to be present, with a view to ensuring that there is no coercion and that questions are clear and fair.

H. PARENTS AND THE POLICE: SECTION 56(5) AND (6)

Section 56(2) requires the police to advise a youth of the right to consult a parent before being questioned. The youth is entitled to decide

---

57   The issue of the admissibility of a confession of an accomplice is complex and depends at least in part on whether the youths are charged jointly, and have one proceeding, or are charged separately. Counsel will not be able to advise the youth fully about this issue at such an early stage. See, e.g., *R. v. B.(K.G.)*, [1993] 1 S.C.R. 740; and *R. v. S.(R.J.)*, [1995] 1 S.C.R. 451.

58   For a more detailed discussion, see S. Scott, M. Wong, & B. Weagant, *Defending Young Offender Cases*, 2d ed. (Toronto: Carswell, 1997), chs. 1 and 2.

whether to consult a parent, or, if a parent is not available, another adult relative or an adult known to the youth. Some youths will want to see their parents to obtain emotional support and advice, though many who are arrested feel too embarrassed or frightened to have their parents immediately involved or are estranged from their families. The police are also obliged under section 9(1) of the YOA to inform a parent "as soon as possible" whenever a young person has been "arrested and detained in custody pending his appearance in court." This will apply in situations where a youth is being detained, regardless of the wishes of the youth.

It has been held that, if a youth whom the police want to question expresses a desire to see a parent, the police have an obligation to permit a meeting as soon as the parent is available. In R. v. P.(S.) a fourteen-year-old youth went to the police station with his parents and was arrested in their presence on a charge of sexual assault. He was taken to an interview room alone while his parents waited in the public area of the station. The police advised him of his rights and read him a waiver form. The youth said he wanted his father present during the interview. The officers then left him alone for forty minutes, without telling the parents anything. The officers returned and again explained his rights, at which point the youth said that he would make a statement without his father being present, and signed a waiver. The youth's statement was largely exculpatory, though he admitted that he hugged the complainant. While the trial judge admitted the statement and convicted the youth, the Ontario Court of Appeal ruled that the statement was not admissible and set aside the conviction:

> It is obvious . . . that the police failed to observe both the letter and spirit of this section. Once the [youth] . . . had stated unequivocally that he wanted his father present during the interview, he was entitled to have that right implemented immediately, where, as here, the father was already at the police station.[59]

Courts have also ruled statements inadmissible when youths have in some way been "misled" about the availability of a parent, or when they have not been informed about the arrival of a parent at the police station during questioning of the youth, even if the right of consultation has been previously waived.[60] This is consistent with the recognition of the important role of parents in section 3(1)(h) of the YOA and the fact that a waiver of section 56(2) rights must be a "knowing" waiver. That

59   R. v. P.(S.) (1991), 44 O.A.C. 316 at 317 (C.A.).
60   R. v. S.(J.L.) (1995), 162 A.R. 388 (C.A.); R. v. M.(M.), [1995] M.J. No. 654 (Prov. Ct.) (QL) [M.(M.)].

is, a youth who believes that a parent is not readily available may want to "get things over with" and decide to waive the right of consultation; if the youth had known that a parent was available for immediate consultation, he or she might have wanted to exercise that right.

While it is clear that the *YOA* and *Charter* are premised on the expectation that a lawyer whom the youth might choose to consult will provide legal advice and protect the youth's legal rights, the role of parents at the point of police investigation is less clear. Some parents will feel that their role is similar to a lawyer's and take steps to protect their child's rights, advising the youth to remain silent until legal assistance is obtained. Other parents, however, may be more inclined to try to "establish the truth" and advise their child to "come clean." While some parents may be supportive of their children, others may feel anger or embarrassment and think that "the kid had it coming."

An American study that involved the actual observation of parents meeting with their children after arrest revealed that most parents do not offer any advice about legal rights such as the right to silence or the right to obtain legal representation.[61] British research indicates that the presence of parents during a police interview with a youth has little effect on police tactics; the parents usually remained silent during the police questioning, and if they did intervene they were as likely to be helpful to the police as to their child.[62]

The ambiguity about the role of the parent at this stage is reflected in the conflict in the case law over the nature of the consultation that is to occur. In *R. v. M. (M.)* Garfinkle Prov. J. emphasized the supportive and advisory nature of the parental role, excluding a youth's statement because the Crown failed to show that there had been full compliance with the provisions of section 56, including those requiring that a youth should have a "reasonable opportunity" to consult meaningfully with a parent:

> Satisfactory consultation contemplated by section 56 means the child and the adult speaking confidently to each other with an aura of confidentiality. The adult should have sufficient facts to enable a proper consideration of the issues to be undertaken.[63]

---

61 T. Grisso, *Juvenile Waiver of Rights: Legal and Psychological Competence* (New York: Plenum Press, 1981).

62 National Association for the Care and Resettlement of Offenders, "The Police and Criminal Evidence Act of 1984 and Young Offenders: The Role of an Appropriate Adult" in *National Association for the Care and Resettlement of Offenders Briefing* (London: The Association, 1996), at 6.

63 Above note 60.

The judge ruled the youth's statement inadmissible since, before the father consulted the youth, the police had not informed the father of the charges or the nature of their investigation and the use they intended to make of the youth's statement. The judge felt that without this information the father could not have a meaningful consultation with his child. The judge also suggested that the statement was inadmissible because the officer remained close to where the consultation between the father and son occurred and could have overheard it, a fact that raised concerns about lack of confidentiality.

The approach of *R. v. M.(M.)* may be contrasted with that of Hardman Prov. J. in *R. v. B.(C.)* where a statement was admitted despite the failure of the police to give the parent an opportunity for a private consultation:

> There are clearly many reasons to view the role of counsel as different from that of parent. Lawyers are a specifically trained group of professionals who are governed by a stringent set of rules regarding their conduct. . . . As such their consultation with a client is protected by a special privilege. While parents have a special role under the Act, it is clearly a different role that would in a very practical way speak against making consultations always private with parents. There are situations where a young person may not want to be alone with a parent, particularly one who is angry. . . . What is reasonable will no doubt depend on the circumstances including the wishes of the young person and the parent. There may be security issues in some situations which would speak against private consultation with a parent.[64]

Related to the issue of the privacy of any consultation between the parent and child is the question of the legal characterization of a statement from the youth confessing guilt to a parent. Parents will normally not be considered "persons in authority," and statements made to them by their children will usually be admissible, despite the absence of any form of caution.[65] This common law position is reinforced by section 56(6), which provides that a person consulted by a youth "pursuant to s.56(2)(c) shall, in the absence of evidence to the contrary, be deemed not to be a person in authority."

In *R. v. B.(A.)*, where the Ontario Court of Appeal ruled that parents are not ordinarily in law "persons in authority," Cory J.A. discussed the role of parents in their children's lives and the significance of a discussion in which a child might admit responsibility for a wrong act.:

---

64 [1995] O.J. No. 2303 (Prov. Div.) (QL).
65 *R. v. B.(A.)*, above note 44, leave to appeal refused (1986), 50 C.R. (3d) xxv (note) (S.C.C.); see also *YOA*, above note 3, s. 56(6).

> From the point of view of the family, conversations such as this one are of great importance. . . . Whether it be directed to tracing a lost hockey stick, discovering who was . . . bullying a younger child, or investigating a broken window . . . the parental goals of discovering the truth and counselling, guiding and assisting the child will remain the same. . . . [F]amily discussions leading to the identification of problems and the provision of assistance without judicial intervention are encouraged by the Act.[66]

One could argue that, because parents are so important in the lives of their children, the law should give special protection to conversations between a parent and child, and regard them as "privileged" and not admissible in court against the interest of the child, in the same way as communications between spouses or between a lawyer and client are privileged. Some American courts have accepted this argument and recognized a parent-child privilege,[67] but this has not been the Canadian approach.

While the effect of these decisions is ordinarily to render a statement made by a youth to a parent admissible, section 56(5) allows a youth court judge to rule inadmissible any statement given by the young person if the youth satisfies the judge that "the statement was given under duress imposed by any person who is not, in law, a person in authority." In R. v. L.(S.),[68] the judge felt that a father who became actively involved with the police in the questioning of his son about a suspected homicide became a "member of the investigation team." The court ruled the youth's confession inadmissible, saying:

> There is no doubt that most well-thinking parents in a situation involving the death of a youngster would be anxious to co-operate in finding the truth, but when that involves co-operating with the police and obtaining some incriminating evidence against their own child, and without being made aware of all the information that the police had against the child, it is, I feel, not a rightful situation and can constitute an abuse of the very special relationship of authority and influence that a parent has on his child.

The definition of "parent" in section 2(1) of the YOA is broad enough to include any person or legal body "under a legal duty to provide" for a youth, or in fact or law having "custody or control" of a child. Accordingly, when a youth has been a ward of a child-welfare agency —

---

66   Ibid. at 258–59.
67   See, e.g., Re A. & M., 403 N.Y.S. 2d 375 (S.C. App. Div. 1978).
68   R. v. L.(S.) (Ont. Prov. Ct. (Fam. Div.)) [summarized (1984), Y.O.S. 84–020].

for example, because of abuse or neglect at home — the agency becomes a "parent" for the purposes of section 56. When the child is a ward and an agency worker is playing the role of "parent," concerns about duress and confidentiality may be heightened. If there is an allegation of an offence against another ward of the agency — in a group home, for example — there may also be concerns about a potential conflict of interest for the agency worker.

In *R. v. C.(D.E.)* the judge ruled that a statement which a sixteen-year-old ward of a child-welfare agency made to the police confessing to a sexual assault on a younger child was inadmissible because it was involuntary and section 56(2)(b) was not satisfied. Morrison Prov. J. remarked that a significant factor in determining that the statement was inadmissible was the role played by the agency worker who, though accompanying the youth to the police station where the statement was made, cooperated fully with the police and took no steps to advise or assist the youth:

> I am not suggesting that whenever a ward is under criminal investigation . . . there is an . . . obligation [on the agency] to automatically and immediately retain counsel. I am suggesting, particularly when a charge is a serious one, that the statutory guardian ought to offer the ward the same advice and direction one would expect to be forthcoming from a reasonable parent. A reasonable parent when informed or aware of the child's apparent complicity in an offence would . . . make a conscious and serious attempt to speak to their child in a private and meaningful way in a manner consistent with child and community interest and then determine the course of action to be adopted, including the appointment of counsel.[69]

While it may not be easy to define the role of agency workers when a ward is charged with a criminal offence, at the very least they have an obligation to take steps to ensure that a youth has adequate information to make an informed decision. Given the complexity of the position of the workers, obtaining the services of a lawyer for the youth will often be the best way to help fulfil the obligations to the ward.

---

69   *(C.(D. E.)*, above note 13.

1. NOTIFICATION OF PARENTS: SECTIONS 9 AND 10

Section 9(1) of the *YOA* provides that, if a young person is "arrested and detained in custody pending his appearance" in youth court for a pre-trial detention hearing, a "parent" must be notified "as soon as possible," orally or in writing, so that the parent knows where the child is and can provide assistance. Under section 9(2), if a youth is not detained pending trial, "a parent" must be notified in writing of the date of the youth court hearing, though if a youth is only arrested and then released, there is no need for immediate notification of the arrest. This notice[70] will allow parents to facilitate the attendance of their child in court, as well as to attend themselves.

The notice provisions in the *YOA* require notice to be given only to *a parent,* indicating that notice to one parent is sufficient, on the assumption that one parent will usually inform the other. As noted above, the definition of "parent" in section 2(1) of the *YOA* is broad and includes any person or organization with an obligation to provide for the youth, or with custody or control of the youth.

Section 9(4) specifies that, when a young person is married, notice may be given to a spouse instead of a parent. If a parent is not available, section 9(3) allows notice of detention and of the court hearing to be given to an adult relative or other appropriate adult who is known to the young person and likely to assist the youth. If there is doubt about whom should be given notice, an application can be made under section 9(5) for directions from a youth court judge or a justice of the peace concerning "parental" notice.

Under the *JDA* the failure of the Crown to prove that a parent was served with notice of a delinquency proceeding would take away jurisdiction of the juvenile court to deal with the case, even if the parent actually attended court.[71] If the Crown was careless and forgot to prove compliance with the *JDA* notice provision, charges could be dismissed. Section 9(10) of the *YOA* provides that, if a youth is detained in custody and parents are not served with notice of detention under section 9(1), the proceedings may be adjourned until notice is given, or the court

---

70   S. 9(6) provides that the notice shall identify the youth, the charge, the date and place of the court appearance, and include a statement that the youth has the right to be represented by counsel. There is, however, no requirement to specify that legal assistance may be obtained without payment pursuant to a court direction made under s. 11(4) of the *YOA*, above note 3.

71   *R. v. Cote* (1976), 31 C.C.C. (2d) 414 (Sask. Q.B.).

may dispense with notice or direct notice to be given to some person other than a parent, but the proceedings are *not* "invalid" owing to the failure to give notice.[72] If the youth is not detained in custody and no notice is given to a parent of the youth court proceeding, any finding of guilt may be "invalid" if the parent fails to attend the proceedings; however, section 9(9) gives the youth court a broad power to take steps before adjudication to remedy the failure to give notice by dispensing with notice or ordering service on some other person than a "parent."

Section 10 allows a youth court to order that a parent attend any proceedings if such attendance is considered "necessary or in the best interest of the young person." While parents are not parties to youth court proceedings, they have a statutory right to address the court prior to disposition, disposition review, or possible transfer to adult court. Parents will often attend proceedings voluntarily, but sometimes, especially with older youths, relations between the parent and child may be strained. Ordering the attendance of parents who are unwilling or unable to attend youth court with their child will rarely be desirable. One of the few reported cases where a judge made such an order involved a ward of the child-welfare authorities, who appeared to be abandoning the youth to the justice system.[73]

J.   FINGERPRINTS AND PHOTOGRAPHS: SECTION 44

Section 44 of the *YOA* allows the police to fingerprint and photograph a young person charged with an indictable offence, which includes any hybrid offence.[74] It is common police practice to have fingerprints and photographs taken, even if not necessary for the investigation of the offence charged, in order to assist in possible future investigations. In serious cases, the fingerprinting and photographing may be done as

---

72   See also *YOA*, above note 3, ss. 9(7) to (9) and *R. v. M.(L.J.)* (1995), 128 Sask. R. 134 (C.A.).

73   *R. v. H.(R.)* (26 November 1984), (Alta. Prov. Ct.) [unreported] [summarized (1984), 13 W.C.B. 170]. However, the Canada, House of Commons, *Thirteenth Report of the Standing Committee on Justice and Legal Affairs: Renewing Youth Justice* (Ottawa: Supply & Services, 1997) recommends, without explanation, that parents should be required to attend youth court except in "exceptional circumstances" (at 68).

74   *Lunney v. H.(M.)* (1984), 56 A.R. 250 (Q.B.), aff'd. (1985), 21 C.C.C. (3d) 384 (Alta. C.A.).

soon as charges are laid, while in less serious cases the youth is likely to be released and given a notice requiring attendance at the police station a few days after the charges are laid so that this may occur.[75]

Unlike the situation with an adult, a young person cannot "consent" to a police request for fingerprints for "investigative" purposes in circumstances where he or she has not been charged, since the provisions of the YOA specify that fingerprinting is to be done only if a youth has been "accused" (or convicted) of committing an offence. This affords special protections to youths who may be vulnerable to manipulation by the police and who might not appreciate the significance of "consenting" to have their fingerprints taken.[76]

If the young person is found guilty, the police force that took the fingerprints and photographs sends a record of them to the "Central Repository" kept by the Royal Canadian Mounted Police, where they may be accessed by any force in Canada for investigative purposes as part of the computerized Canadian Police Information Centre (CPIC).[77] The Central Repository cannot keep fingerprints and photographs if there is no finding of guilt, and it is generally required under section 45(1) to destroy those records three years after the completion of the disposition for a summary offence and five years after the completion of the disposition for an indictable offence, provided there are no further offences committed. The destruction provisions are consistent with the principle of limited accountability in the YOA, but 1995 amendments to the YOA were intended to increase protection to society and allow for longer retention by the Central Repository when the convictions involve the most serious offences, such as homicide and aggravated sexual assault.[78]

Failure to attend for required fingerprinting is a punishable offence under s. 145 of the *Code*, above note 1. In R. v. K.(P.A.) (4 June 1997), (Ont. Prov. Ct.) [unreported] [summarized *Lawyers Weekly*, 15 Aug. 1997, no. 1713–008] Scott J. held that a youth could be convicted under this provision only if a parent was also notified of the requirements to attend; although the YOA does not explicitly refer to such notice, the judge interpreted s. 9(6) to require this so that parents "can provide guidance and assistance to ensure those obligations are understood and complied with."

76 R. v. D.(F.D.) (11 May 1984), (Ont. Prov. Ct.) [unreported] [summarized (1984), 12 W.C.B. 152].

77 YOA, above note 3, s. 42.

78 YOA, *ibid.*, s. 45(2.1), enacted by YOA 1995, above note 11, s. 31(3).

K. FIRST APPEARANCE IN COURT AND PRE-TRIAL DETENTION: SECTIONS 7 & 8

If a youth has been arrested, the arresting police officer or the officer in charge at the police station may decide to release him or her, either with or without questioning. The provisions of the *Criminal Code* that govern the arrest of both adults and youths, sections 494–502, require the police to release a person who has been arrested unless it is in the "public interest" to detain that person, having regard to:

- the need to establish the identity of the person;
- the need to secure or preserve evidence;
- the need to prevent further offending by the person; and
- the concern that the person will fail to attend court.[79]

The police may release a youth with a document such as an Appearance Notice, or a Promise to Appear, or a Recognizance, requiring the youth to appear in youth court on a specified date. If the youth is released on a Recognizance or Promise to Appear, there may be conditions imposed, such as abstaining from communicating with potential witnesses or the complainant.

Youths who are arrested for relatively minor charges are normally released pending a hearing, but those charged with more serious offences, or who have records of prior convictions, or who might not appear for court, may be detained pending trial. The detention process is controlled by the courts, pursuant to Part XVI of the *Criminal Code* and the *YOA*. Section 7 of the *YOA* requires that, following arrest, youths must be detained "separate and apart" from adults, though section 7(4) allows the police to "temporarily restrain" a young person with adults after arrest, provided that the youth is under the "supervision and control" of an officer and the youth is transferred "as soon as is reasonably practicable" to a youth detention facility or brought before a judge. In general, the *YOA* seeks to protect youths from exploitation or abuse by adults and requires separate detention, though section 7(4) gives police some flexibility at the time of arrest and when taking a youth to the police station. It is not, for example, necessary to transport youths separate from adults when taking them from the scene of arrest to the police station, provided that an officer is supervising the youth and can prevent any exploitation by adults. In general, however, once detained, the conveyance of youth to court and detention facilities is to be separate from adults.

---

79   See, e.g., *Code*, above note 1, ss. 495(2)(d) and (e) and 498(1)(i) and (j).

Ordinarily, youths are to be detained in separate facilities from adults, but section 7(2) of the *YOA* allows a youth court to order a young person detained with adults if this is necessary for "his own safety or the safety of others," or if there is no youth detention facility available within a "reasonable distance." This provision is occasionally invoked, for example, if an older youth appears to be a security risk and is threatening other youths or staff in a youth detention facility.[80] While pre-trial detention is usually separate from adults, youths who are waiting for trial are often kept in the same facilities as young offenders who have been convicted or are serving sentences in custody. In some provinces adolescents who have been taken into the care of a child-welfare agency may also be placed with young persons awaiting trial under the *YOA*. Although young offenders sometimes have problems similar to those adolescents in need of protection, there are concerns about the appropriateness of this type of arrangement for adolescents in the care of child-welfare agencies.[81]

If the police decide to detain a youth, the youth should be brought to court within twenty-four hours, or, if a judge or justice of the peace is not available within that time, "as soon as possible" thereafter.[82] In theory most "bail hearings" (known technically as "judicial interim release hearings" and also called "show cause hearings") should ordinarily be held within twenty-four hours of arrest, but in practice some youths may be detained for a few days before being brought before the court.[83]

In the case of youth not represented by counsel, the judge is obliged under sections 11(3) and 12(1) of the *YOA*, on the youth's first appearance in court, to inform him or her about the right to counsel and the process to be followed to obtain same (more fully discussed in chapter 6). For youths who appear without having obtained the services of a lawyer, there may be a "duty counsel" (a lawyer paid by the government) to provide some assistance with the bail hearing and to

---

80   See, e.g., *R. v. P.* (1978), 8 R.F.L. (2d) 277 (Man. Q.B.), which was decided under a similar provision of the *Juvenile Delinquents Act*, R.S.C. 1970, c. J-3.

81   See, e.g., *Re B. (J.A.)*, (12 October 1984), (Ont. Prov. Ct. (Fam. Div.)) [unreported] [summarized [1984] W.D.F.L. 1522].

82   *Code*, above note 1, s. 503(1).

83   See, e.g., J. Gandy, *Judicial Interim Release (Bail) Hearings* (Toronto: Policy Research Centre for Children, Youth and Families, 1992). This study of three Ontario cities found that some youths had to wait in detention for up to a week before appearing in court. Youths with a lawyer can take steps to prevent such abuses from occurring. In theory a lawyer could bring an application for a writ of *habeas corpus* to a superior court, but in practice a call from a lawyer to the police or Crown prosecutor will invariably suffice.

help the youth begin the process of obtaining a lawyer to deal with the charges. The charge is also read at the first appearance, unless counsel for the youth waives this.[84]

While a pre-trial detention hearing for young persons is often dealt with by youth court judges, section 8 of the *YOA* also allows a justice of the peace to deal with this issue (except for murder cases) since a youth court judge may not be readily available. Under section 8(2), if a justice of the peace makes an initial order concerning pre-trial detention, a new detention hearing may be held before a youth court judge who will deal with the issue as an "original application," not as a "review" or appeal. There is also a right to have a review or appeal of the decision of a youth court judge by a higher court.[85] Pursuant to the *Criminal Code,* section 525, there must be a periodic rehearing of the detention decision, every thirty days for a summary offence and every ninety days if the offence is hybrid or indictable. If a youth is not released and is held in detention, a case will generally receive some priority in scheduling of a trial date, though it is not uncommon for a youth to spend weeks, or even months, in detention without having been found guilty of any offence.

At least in theory, the decision to order that a youth should be detained pending trial is to be made on the same legal basis as that applicable to adults. In general, the onus will be on the Crown to "show cause" why the accused should be detained pending trial, although, where the person is charged with murder or a serious drug offence, or is charged with a serious offence while on release for other serious charges, it will be a "reverse onus" situation, with the accused required to "show cause" why he or she should be released.[86]

The grounds for detention are set out in section 515(10) of the *Criminal Code* which provides that detention is justified only

    (*a*) where the detention is necessary to ensure . . . attendance in court
        . . .

    (*b*) where the detention is necessary . . . for the protection or safety of the public, having regard to all the circumstances including any substantial likelihood that the accused will, if released from custody, commit a criminal offence or interfere with the administration of justice [for example by threatening a witness] . . . and

    (*c*) . . . where the detention is necessary in order to maintain confidence in the administration of justice, having regard to all the cir-

84   *YOA*, above note 3, ss. 12(1) and (2).
85   *Code*, above note 1, ss. 520 and 521; *YOA, ibid.*, s. 8(6).
86   *Code, ibid.*, ss. 515(5) and 522.

cumstances, including the apparent strength of the prosecution's case, the gravity of the nature of the offence, the circumstances surrounding its commission and the potential for a lengthy term of imprisonment.

The courts have accepted that, if a youth has no previous record, in light of the provisions of the *Criminal Code* and the *YOA* and "in particular the principles set out in s. 3 . . . it is only in exceptional cases that pre-disposition custody of a young offender would be justified."[87] Detention is more likely to be considered when the youth has a significant record of prior offending, thereby raising a concern that there may be a "substantial likelihood" of further offending, or, if there is a history of failing to comply with court orders, non-attendance at court.

At a bail hearing the court can admit evidence considered "credible or trustworthy," which permits the Crown to rely on evidence that may not be admissible at trial.[88] A summary of the circumstances of the alleged offence, including any statement from the youth and the youth's previous record, if any, will normally be presented to the court, either by a police officer testifying or, with the consent of the accused, by having the prosecutor read this evidence from a report or file.[89] There may also be evidence about any prior releases and about any history of failing to attend court, and possibly some background information about the youth and family situation, if this is known from the investigation or prior court involvement. The youth has an opportunity to present evidence and, if appropriate, a plan for supervision in the community pending trial. If supervision by a parent or other person is contemplated, that person will normally testify. If the youth testifies, the prosecutor cannot ask questions about the alleged offence, unless the youth raises this issue.[90]

---

87 *R. v. G.(C.)*(1993), 79 C.C.C. (3d) 446 (Ont. C.A.), Labrosse J.A. Even when a youth faces a murder charge and hence has the onus of justifying release, if there is no prior record and parents can provide adequate supervision, the "court must lean against institutional confinement . . . in favour of parental custody" and release the youth: *R. v. L.(D.C.)* (15 February 1991), (B.C.C.A.) [unreported] [summarized (1991), 16 W.C.B. (2d) 137]. See also *R. v. L.(D. B.)* (1994), 155 A.R. 64 (C.A.), where the court appeared to accept this approach but was not satisfied by the youth's evidence of the adequacy of parental supervision.

88 *Code*, above note 1, s. 518(1)(e).

89 In theory the Crown may introduce evidence only through witnesses, but it is common at a bail hearing for the accused to consent to the prosecutor "reading in evidence" from the file without calling witnesses. *R. v. Hajdu* (1984), 14 C.C.C. (3d) 563 (Ont. H.C.J.).

90 *Code*, above note 1, s. 518(1)(b).

At a bail hearing, a judge may order detention or release the youth. There is a broad authority under section 515 to impose "reasonable conditions" on a youth who is being released, either to ensure attendance in court or to reduce the likelihood of reoffending. These conditions might include a requirement that the youth reside under the supervision of parents or some other person, maintain a curfew, and refrain from contacting co-accuseds or victims of the alleged offence. A judge may also require that the accused provide some form of financial security, or that some other person act as a surety or guarantor that the accused will attend court, with the possibility of a financial penalty if the accused fails to attend. With youths, imposing financial stipulations on release from custody pending trial is generally inappropriate.

Section 7.1 of the *YOA* allows a court to release a young person whose detention would otherwise be justified under section 515(10) of the *Code* into the care and control of a "responsible person," such as a parent or other adult who is respected by the youth. This will be done only if the "responsible person" undertakes in writing to exercise control over the youth and satisfy such other conditions as may be imposed, for example, ensuring that the youth maintain a curfew and refrain from consuming alcohol pending trial. An adult who "wilfully fails" to comply with an undertaking made under section 7.1 commits an offence under section 7.2 of the *YOA*. Section 7.1 is not used frequently, since, if the court feels that detention is appropriate, it is reluctant to permit an adult in the community to supervise a youth pending trial, particularly if the individuals coming forward offering supervision have previously failed in their efforts to supervise the youth.[91] Courts are also reluctant to accept supervision by parents who have criminal records, which may disadvantage youths from families with a criminal history.[92] In some localities, innovative programs have been established to allow supervision by professionals in the community of youths released pending trial, and these have had some success in keeping youths out of unnecessary periods in detention.

Despite the focus in section 515(10) of the *Code* on concerns about court attendance and reoffending, some youth court judges and other justice system personnel may be taking a range of "social factors" into account in deciding whether to detain a youth. It is also possible that some judges may be misusing detention, by in effect imposing it as a form of punishment.

---

91   *R. v. S.(K.)*, [1996] O.J. No. 2346 (Prov. Div.) (QL).
92   *Ibid.*

While a swift response to crime is desirable, the *YOA* and *Code* do not permit a judge to impose a sanction before the youth is found guilty and sentenced, even if the judge is certain that the youth is guilty. In one Saskatchewan case a sixteen-year-old Aboriginal youth with a prior record of two property offences pled guilty to three more non-violent offences. The youth court judge ordered the youth remanded in custody (detained in custody) pending sentencing, stating:

> This has got to stop, and if no one is around who cares about this young person — his parents didn't come with him — then I think what else am I to think about the guidance that's necessary to prevent young people from developing this way to do these things.

This pre-adjudication detention decision was reversed by an appeal judge who remarked that the youth court judge did not remand the youth

> for either of the purposes referred to in section 515(10); namely, to ensure his attendance in court, or for the purpose of protecting the public. . . . in remanding [the youth] . . . in custody . . . without sentencing him . . . did so because he was not certain what sentence he wished to impose, and he apparently wished to provide . . . a "wake up" call. Neither of these "purposes" would qualify a person for detention under s. 515(10).[93]

It is likely not uncommon for a youth court judge to be satisfied that a youth with a prior record is probably guilty of the new charges and to be influenced by a desire to give this individual an immediate "short, sharp shock" by ordering detention following arrest. It may be difficult to establish definitively or refute whether such a sanctioning motive alone is a factor at this stage, since concerns about sanctioning and possible reoffending pending sentencing inevitably overlap. While in theory sanctioning must not be a factor at this stage, judges are entitled to take account of a prior record at a bail hearing for the purpose of determining whether there is a "substantial likelihood" of reoffending pending resolution of the case. Indeed, this is an important, relevant factor at the bail hearing.

---

93   *R. v. Y.(D.H.)* (1995), 132 Sask. R. 107 at 111 (Q.B.). In 1997, s. 515(10) of the *Code*, above note 1, was amended by *Criminal Law Improvement Act, 1996*, S.C. 1997, c. 18, s. 59(2) to allow a court to consider the gravity of the offence and the effect of release on "maintain[ing] [public] confidence in the administration of justice." While this amendment may result in more youths (and adults) facing serious charges to be detained, it should not be used to allow "punishment before disposition," especially for non-violent offences.

The late Ontario youth court judge A.P. Nasmith expressed concern that youths are more likely to be subject to pre-adjudication detention than adults facing the same charges, and that detention may be misused, thereby contributing to the "excessive criminalization of children." The judge cited the disturbing finding of American researchers that a large portion of juveniles who were detained before trial were released after trial, indicating that detention was not justified. The judge quoted the researchers' conclusion: "Detention is used more to punish youngsters than to protect them, or society. The ease with which juveniles can be detained provides an enormous temptation to judges . . . to lock youngsters up for a few days, or longer, to 'teach them a lesson.'"[94] Judge Nasmith expressed similar concerns about the situation in Canada.

It is apparent that a host of "sociolegal" factors related to a youth's family situation and personal background can also affect detention decisions.[95] It is, to some extent, legitimate for youth court judges to take account of these factors, since they may affect the youth's likelihood of reoffending or not appearing in court, but caution should be exercised so that a judge is not detaining a youth as a means of providing social supports or in an effort to try to assist parents or child-welfare workers in dealing with a troublesome youth or a "runner." It should also be appreciated that the kind of social and family problems which can affect detention decisions are also correlated to race, Aboriginal status, and low income, and there are concerns that pre-trial detention laws may be operating in a discriminatory fashion in Canada.[96]

Some judges may, for example, be influenced into ordering pre-trial detention because the youth is "living on the street" or the parent or guardian is reluctant to provide accommodation. This problem may be most acute with wards of child-welfare agencies, a group that accounts for a substantial portion of all youths who are placed in detention. While in

---

94   A.P. Nasmith, *Judicial Interim Release for Youths: The Law and Other Exigencies*: (Canadian Association of Provincial Court Judges, New Judges' Program, 1993), quoting C.E. Silberman, *Criminal Violence, Criminal Justice* (New York: Random House, 1978) at 321–22.

95   See, e.g., P.J. Carrington, S. Moyer, & F. Kopelman, "Factors Affecting Pre-Dispositional Detention and Release in Canadian Juvenile Courts" (1988) 16 J. Crim Justice 463; S.A. Fortugno & M. Rogstad, *A Socio-Legal Analysis of Youth Justice in Saskatoon* (Saskatoon: John Howard Society of Saskatchewan, 1994).

96   Fortugno & Rogstad, *ibid.* There are substantial variations in the rates of pre-trial detention use, with Manitoba and Alberta having three times as many youths (per 10,000 youth population) in detention as Quebec and Newfoundland; S. Moyer, *A Profile of the Juvenile Justice System in Canada* (Ottawa: Federal-Provincial-Territorial Task Force on Youth Justice, 1996) at 65.

theory child-welfare or mental-health laws should be invoked to deal with such "social problems," the reality is that overburdened child-welfare agencies and mental-health facilities often seem reluctant to deal with troubled adolescents who have been charged under the *YOA*. Not infrequently, the charges are actually laid as a result of agency or group-home staff seeking police assistance in situations where a parent might not call the police, and then informing the judge at a detention hearing that the adolescent is "non-compliant" and not suitable for agency care. Although a concern about a youth's welfare should not be a justification to remand the youth in custody, this may be a factor in some cases, contributing to a rising rate of pre-adjudication detention in Canada as child-protection agencies "dump" cases into the youth justice system.

Pre-trial detention has the potential of being highly disruptive and stressful to a young person, since it may result in sudden removal from familiar surroundings and placement in an often intimidating, institutional environment. While some localities have quite good youth-detention facilities with social supports and programs to meet the needs of youths at this stressful time,[97] there is great variation; many of the facilities have inadequate programs and resources and may just be jails for adolescents. There are concerns that youths placed in detention may be subjected to harassment or abuse from other young offenders and to the negative influences of this environment.

The inadequacies of some youth-detention facilities was graphically demonstrated in a 1991 Ontario decision, *R. v. M.(T.)*, where Judge King found that the conditions in which youths were detained pending court appearance in downtown Toronto constituted "cruel and unusual" treatment, in violation of section 12 of the *Charter of Rights*. The "holding cells" where youths under sixteen were detained were hot, smelly, overcrowded, and dirty; there was nothing for them to do for hours at a time; the staff had no training in dealing with youths; and all youths were handcuffed when outside the cells. While the conditions at this particular facility have improved since this case was decided, it is illustrative of the problems that arise with pre-trial detention.[98]

---

97   See, e.g., A.W. Leschied, G.W. Austin, & E. Riley, "Description and Assessment of a Crisis Consultation Program in a Youth Detention Centre" (1989) 31 Can. J. Crim. 145.

98   *R. v. M.(T.)* (1991), 4 O.R. (3d) 203 (Prov. Div.). As another Ontario youth court judge, Bean Prov. J., emphatically stated: "[I]n most detention facilities . . . [t]he programs are terrible. The physical facilities usually stink. There's nothing for them to do. They just sit there and rot." Quoted in "Ont. Judge stresses importance of bail in young offender system" *Lawyers Weekly* (30 June 1989) 22.

Pre-trial detention will usually interfere with schooling or employment and with familial and peer relationships. It is also difficult to establish a meaningful educational or rehabilitative program for youth whose detention begins abruptly and is of an indeterminate and, often relatively short, duration. Further, it is highly intrusive since it occurs without any finding of guilt; pre-trial detention is in certain respects inconsistent with the presumption of innocence. It is, therefore, important for counsel to make a serious effort to obtain the release of a young client at this stage, though bail hearings are often a challenging proceeding for a lawyer since there may be little time to meet the client and, if needed, to prepare an adequate plan for supervision in the community.[99]

If a youth is detained pending adjudication and is found guilty, the usual practice for the sentencing judge is to take account of the pre-disposition period in detention to reduce any custodial sentence that would otherwise be imposed, though this is a discretionary matter.[100]

If a youth is released into the community, it is important that any conditions imposed are realistic and necessary to ensure attendance in court or to prevent offending. Sometimes parents or social workers will want a judge dealing with pre-trial release to impose detailed behavioural conditions on youth, for example, in regard to curfews, school attendance, or behaviour. Even if the youth is originally charged with a relatively minor offence, there may be strict limits placed on his or her behaviour for potentially lengthy periods of time until final resolution of a case. Given the circumstances and temperament of some youths, complying with strict behavioural conditions may be unrealistic. While a failure to comply with the conditions may not pose any threat to the safety of society, if there is a breach of a condition of release and a charge laid for this, the judge may be more likely to view the youth's conduct as a serious offence since it shows "disrespect" for the justice system and impose a custodial sentence. Thus, a relatively minor initial charge can result in a spiralling series of "administration of justice" charges and serious involvement with the youth justice system.

---

99   Under s. 516 of the *Code*, above note 1, it is possible to have a three-day adjournment (or longer with the consent of the accused) in a pre-trial release hearing, and counsel for a youth will sometimes want to seek an adjournment to have time to prepare a plan. Plans might involve parents, relatives, or other adults, or a child-welfare agency, a youth shelter, or some other social agency. Sometimes non-profit agencies outside the child-welfare system are willing to provide assistance; if the youth is a ward of a child-welfare agency, the agency may be willing, or obliged, to provide financial support during the release period.

100   *R. v. K.(M.)* (1996), 28 O.R. (3d) 593 (C.A.).

L. RELEASE OF CHARGED YOUTHS AND THE SCHOOLS

Special concerns may arise in the school system when youths are released pending trial, especially if the alleged offences involve serious violence or occurred on school property. There is growing concern about violence in schools, and research indicates that many students are afraid of violence, extortion, and bullying,[101] though, as with other questions related to youth violence, there is debate about how "unsafe" Canadian schools really are; some argue that, although some concern is appropriate, the media, politicians, and school boards may be overreacting.[102]

Responding to media reports and growing pressure from teachers and parents, most Canadian school boards have adopted "zero tolerance" policies for incidents of violence and weapons in schools, but a policy that requires automatic suspension or expulsion for even minor incidents of violence may not be appropriate.[103] It can be argued that summary removal of a youth from the school pending trial may seem inconsistent with the presumption of innocence, as well as depriving youths in need of educational and social supports, yet it is clear that schools have a responsibility to provide a safe learning environment and that some students may pose a threat to the safety of others.

In *Peel Board of Education* v. *B.*,[104] Reid J. of the Ontario High Court held that several male students facing serious charges involving alleged sexual assaults on a female student at another school could not be suspended or expelled pending judicial resolution of the *YOA* charges. The 1987 decision rested on the judge's interpretation of section 38 of the *YOA*, which prohibits "publication" of identifying information about a young person appearing in youth court, since the judge ruled that the effect of expulsion of the students would inevitably be to identify the students within their school. The judge observed: "Rumour and gossip to the effect that the students have been expelled and must therefore be guilty of the offences with which they have been charged are . . . the almost inevitable consequences of an expulsion." The judge also said

---

101   L. Sarick, "School violence worse than expected Ontario survey says," *[Toronto] Globe and Mail* (28 September 1993) A20; C. Ryan, F. Matthews, and J. Banner, *Student Perceptions of Violence* (Toronto: Central Toronto Youth Services, 1993); "Shakedowns in the schoolyard," *[Toronto] Globe and Mail*, 4 Oct. 1997, A1.

102   See, e.g., W.R. Dolmage, "One Less Brick in the Wall: The Myths of Youth Violence and Unsafe Schools" (1996) 7 E.L.J. 185.

103   See, e.g., "The downside of zero tolerance," *Toronto Star* (5 December 1993) E1.

104   (1987), 59 O.R. (2d) 654 (H.C.J.).

that the expulsion of the students prior to resolution of the charges "comes distressingly close to expulsion without trial. . . . That is wholly contrary to the fundamental principle of our system of justice." Justice Reid further suggested that, even if the youths were convicted of these offences, it might not, in itself, be grounds for expulsion.

Justice Reid's approach to section 38 was overruled in 1994 by the Ontario Divisional Court in *G.(F.)* v. *Scarborough (City) Board of Education*, where Montgomery J. concluded that the *YOA* was[105] "never intended to deprive principals and school boards of the ability to enforce order and discipline in their schools." The court accepted that school officials have the authority under legislation like section 23 of the Ontario *Education Act* to suspend or expel a student who has engaged in "conduct . . . so refractory that the pupil's presence is injurious to other pupils." The school officials do not need to wait until the completion of any youth court proceedings but may exercise their civil jurisdiction as soon as the charges come to their attention, as long as the requirements of education law are followed.[106] Many school boards now have "Safe School" policies that allow for expulsion, suspension, or transfer of students charged with violent offences that occur at school or victimize fellow students. This can create problems for youths who often have significant social and educational needs, though most boards have some programs for alternate education for students who have been suspended or expelled.[107] It should also be noted that the *Peel* case involved allegations that students at one school sexually assaulted a student at another school; this type of situation should generally call for different treatment in terms of school-board response than one involving a victim in the school.

The 1995 amendments to section 38(1.13) of the *YOA* allow the police to share information with school officials about the involvement of a young person in youth court if this is necessary to ensure compliance with bail conditions or to ensure the safety of staff or other students. School officials are required to keep information received from the police or youth justice system separate from other information about their students, to restrict access to the information to necessary staff, and to destroy any records of this information when it is no longer

---

105   (1994), 68 O.A.C. 308 at 312 (Div. Ct.).

106   See, e.g., A.F. Brown & M.A. Zuker, *Education Law* (Toronto: Carswell, 1994) at 151–58; and J. Wilson, *Wilson on Children and the Law* (Toronto: Butterworths, 1994) at 8.35 to 8.47.

107   See, e.g., J. Lewington, "Expelled students to get new chance," *[Toronto] Globe and Mail* (13 September 1994) A6.

required. These restrictions are intended to prevent the "labelling" of the youth within the school system, though such regulations may not do much to prevent the inappropriate dissemination of information regarding accused youths.

In some cases school authorities will expect the youth court to impose restrictions on youths who are released pending adjudication. When an offence under investigation appears to relate to a youth's school, it is desirable for police officers to consult with school authorities prior to a bail hearing. Where, for example, the alleged offence involved students in the same school, an order precluding attendance at that school might be sought as an appropriate condition of release; such an order could be coordinated with a plan by educational officials to transfer the youth to another school.

Some judges will make school attendance or employment a condition of pre-adjudication release (or probation) in the belief that the absence of structured activity may have contributed to the offending behaviour; for a youth who cannot find work, this becomes an order to attend school, which may make the school officials uneasy. If such a condition is imposed (or better, before it is imposed), the police or prosecutor should be in contact with school officials to make appropriate educational and safety plans and to ensure that compliance is monitored.

Educators and police are increasingly aware of the role that schools can play in dealing with youthful offending. Many adolescents with serious offending problems also have learning disabilities or difficulties with school, and dealing effectively with educational problems can also help resolve offending behaviour. Schools are also establishing programs to deal with aggression and bullying in schools in a positive manner, at the same time as police are becoming involved in working more closely with teachers and schools and in having more of a "presence" in schools.[108]

M. MENTAL STATUS ASSESSMENTS

If there is a question about a young person's mental capacity to stand trial (for example, to understand the nature of the proceedings or instruct counsel), if an issue of lack of criminal responsibility on account of mental disorder arises, or if there is an application for transfer of the case to adult court, the youth court may order a medical, psychological,

---

108   See, e.g., V. Galt, "Stemming the tide of school violence," [Toronto] Globe and Mail (2 February 1996) A1.

or psychiatric assessment at the pre-adjudication stage. If an assessment is ordered, the youth court may order that the youth should be detained for the purposes of assessment by medical personnel.[109] In other situations, there is no jurisdiction for a court-ordered pre-trial assessment of a young person.

FURTHER READINGS

BALA, N. & H. LILLES, eds., *Young Offenders Service* (Toronto: Butterworths, 1984) (looseleaf), s. 56

CANADA, FEDERAL-PROVINCIAL-TERRITORIAL TASK FORCE ON YOUTH JUSTICE: *A Review of the Young Offenders Act and the Youth Justice System in Canada* (Ottawa: Supply & Services, 1996), chs. 5, 10, and 11

DELISLE, R.J. & D. STUART, *Learning Canadian Criminal Procedure,* 4th ed. (Toronto: Carswell, 1996), ch. 2

FRIEDLAND, M.L. & K. ROACH, *Criminal Law and Procedure : Cases and Materials,* 7th ed. (Toronto: Emond Montgomery, 1994)

HARRIS, P.J., *Young Offenders Act Manual* (Aurora: Canada Law Book, 1984) (looseleaf)

PLATT, P., *Young Offenders Law in Canada,* 2d ed. (Toronto: Butterworths, 1995), chs.4, 5, 6, 9 and 18

SCOTT, S., M. WONG, & B. WEAGANT, *Defending Young Offender Cases,* 2d ed. (Toronto: Carswell, 1997), chs. 1, 2, 3 and 4

ROHER, ERIC M., *An Educator's Guide to Violence in Schools* (Aurora, Ont: Canada Law Book, 1997)

---

109   *Code,* above note 1, ss. 672.11 to 672.19; *YOA,* above note 3, ss. 13(3), 13.2(1) & (11). See ch. 7.

CHAPTER 5

DIVERSION AND ALTERNATIVE MEASURES

A. THE CONCEPT OF DIVERSION

While the primary legal response to youthful offending is through the court system, there are also many youths who are "diverted" from the formal justice system and dealt with in a less intrusive and more informal, expeditious fashion. The value of alternatives to the traditional judicial response was, for example, recognized in the 1993 Martin Committee Report:

> [T]he criminal law is a blunt instrument of social policy that ought to be used with restraint. The criminal law aims to achieve rehabilitation, specific deterrence, general deterrence, and the protection of society. However, there is no reason to think that the criminal law is the only method of achieving these socially desirable goals. Accordingly, it is clearly in the public interest to consider the . . . alternatives to any given prosecution, and their efficacy, remembering that these alternatives may be able to deal more sensitively and comprehensively with the particular problem at hand, while at the same time meeting the goals of the criminal justice system.[1]

---

1   Ontario, Ministry of the Attorney General, *Report of the Attorney General's Advisory Committee on Charge Screening, Disclosure and Resolution Discussion* (Toronto: Queen's Printer, 1993) at 96 (Chair: G.A. Martin).

The desirability of considering alternatives to the formal criminal response is especially strong when the violation of the law is perpetrated by an adolescent, whose act may reflect youthful immaturity.

Under the *Juvenile Delinquents Act,* alternatives to formal charging were frequently employed, most commonly informal diversion by police officers instead of charging in juvenile court. Although the *JDA* had no express provisions dealing with diversion, by the 1970s diversion programs were being established in Canada and other countries to deal with some juvenile offenders outside the courts. The drafters of the *YOA* wanted to encourage diversion, as well as to regulate certain aspects of it. The Declaration of Principle in section 3 (1)(d) expressly recognizes that "where it is not inconsistent with the protection of society, taking no measures or taking measures other than judicial proceedings" under the *YOA* "should be considered for dealing with young persons who have committed offences." Section 4 of the *YOA* creates a legislative framework for "alternative measures," that is, for the establishment of "measures other than judicial proceedings" for dealing with young persons who are believed to have committed criminal offences.

Alternative measures are a form of diversion from the court process and are generally used for youths who have committed less serious offences and who do not have a history of offending, though there is substantial variation and some provinces allow youths facing more serious charges and with a prior record of offending to be considered for alternative measures. An alternative measures program allows a youth to be dealt with in a relatively expeditious, informal fashion and enables a youth to avoid a formal youth court record.

One of the theoretical rationales offered for the first juvenile diversion programs in the early 1970s was a sociological doctrine known as "labelling theory," namely, that youths who are "labelled" as "delinquents" or "offenders" may come to see themselves as "offenders," as well as being "labelled" by parents, teachers, and others as "deviant," and that this may contribute to future offending or "secondary deviance."[2] Proponents of this theory argued that some youths may be unnecessarily harmed by being "labelled" as "young offenders" through the formal court process, and that they may be less likely to reoffend if they are "diverted" and dealt with in a relatively informal fashion. "Labelling theory" is, however, just a theory, and the empirical research is at best equivocal about whether merely identifying and describing a

---

2   See, e.g., S. Moyer, *Diversion from the Juvenile Justice System and Its Impact on Children: A Review of the Literature* (Ottawa: Department of Justice, 1980) at 67–74.

youth as an "offender" increases the likelihood of reoffending. That is, it has not been conclusively proven that use of formal diversion programs as opposed to youth court charging *reduces* recidivism, though it is clear that, in most situations where it is employed, the use of diversion does not increase the likelihood of a youth reoffending and that most youths who are sent to these programs do not reoffend.

The fact that diversion does not, in itself, *reduce* reoffending does not mean that alternative measures programs are without value. Many different models of alternative measures are being tried in Canada at present, and some may actually have the potential to reduce recidivism. Some alternative measures programs are offering responses to offending that are not available through the traditional youth court system, though others provide responses that are the same as those used by the courts, albeit without being imposed after a judicial process. Alternative measures programs have the potential to resolve a case in a way that is more expeditious and generally less expensive than youth court. Further, in comparison to the formality and adversarial youth court — a forum that tends to preclude open discussion by individuals — a properly designed alternative measures program can offer youths, parents, and victims an opportunity to be actively engaged in achieving a satisfactory resolution for the situation caused by the offending. There may also be a role for members of the community, an approach that may, for example, be especially appropriate for Aboriginal communities.

Youths can be sent to alternative measures only with their consent; further, they can be dealt with in this informal fashion only if they accept responsibility for the offence that they are charged with and waive their right to a trial in youth court. While diversion is an important potential response to youthful offending, there are also legitimate concerns about its potential misuse. There is the possibility of diversion jeopardizing the rights of young persons or victims or of failing to take adequate account of the interests of society.

B. POLICE SCREENING

The police have the responsibility for deciding whether to commence formal legal proceedings. For adolescents who are apprehended for relatively minor offences, a police officer may decide not to invoke the formal processes (either court or even an alternative measures program), but may deal with a case informally, usually by warning the youth about not committing further offences, and perhaps taking the youth home and discussing the situation with the parents.

This practice, known as "police screening" or "police cautioning," was widely employed when the *Juvenile Delinquents Act* was in force, at a time when there were few operational programs for alternative measures or diversion from the juvenile court.[3] Police cautioning was especially common with younger delinquents, those under twelve. Some police forces kept records of "cautions" so that they could determine when a youth had "run out of chances." The practice of police cautioning reflects the belief that some cases do not warrant the time and effort of formal charging, and a "discussion" with a police officer can have significant deterrent impact with some youths.

The *YOA* recognized the importance of this police practice, with section 3(1)(d) acknowledging that "where it is not inconsistent with the protection of society, taking no measures . . . should be considered for dealing with young persons." Indeed, when the *YOA* was enacted, there was a concern that the introduction of formal alternative measures programs should not result in "net widening." That is, alternative measures programs are intended to be an *alternative to youth court*, not a means of dealing formally, but outside court, with youths who in the past would have been dealt with informally by police screening. It is difficult to determine whether "net widening" occurred as a result of the enactment of the *YOA*, but there is evidence that in some localities the introduction of the *YOA* and the establishment of alternative measures programs, combined with pressures from schools and others in the community, resulted in police charging youths who previously would have been screened out and dealt with informally by the police.[4] The police decision to charge under the *YOA* rather than simply caution may, at least in part, be influenced by the expectation that the youth who has been charged with a less serious offence is still likely to be diverted to alternative measures and not dealt with by the youth court.

Police cautioning for minor offences remains an important informal response to youth crime. Often it represents the most effective, most humane, and least expensive way of dealing with an adolescent who has made a mistake. The informal, immediate response of a police officer,

---

3   See, e.g., J.M. Gandy, "The Exercise of Discretion by the Police as a Decision-Making Process in the Disposition of Juvenile Offenders"(1970) 8 Osgoode Hall L. Rev. 329; and Moyer, *ibid.*

4   See, e.g., J. Kenewell, N. Bala, & P. Colfer, "Young Offenders" in R. Barnhorst & L.C. Johnson, eds., *The State of the Child in Ontario* (Toronto: Oxford University Press, 1991) 160 at 165; and J. Hackler & D. Cousins, *Police Screening Patterns in Five Western Canadian Cities* (Edmonton: Centre for Criminological Research, University of Alberta, 1989).

especially one with sensitivity and experience in dealing with youths, can have as much or more impact in terms of deterrence and accountability than a much delayed, often perfunctory appearance in youth court.

Many countries make substantially more use of police cautioning of youthful offenders than Canada,[5] with, for example, efforts to ensure that parents are involved. In Australia, there are policies to encourage officers to caution youths at their home and to allow the administration of a caution in the presence of the parents at a police station by a senior officer. More extensive use of police screening would also be appropriate in Canada, though subject to some important qualifications. The decision not to charge involves a significant exercise of "low visibility" police discretion, and there is a concern that it may sometimes be exercised in a discriminatory fashion. Beyond the issue of racial or other bias, there may be a tendency for officers to "give a break" to youths who have "good families," thereby prejudicing youths from disadvantaged backgrounds. Any increase in police-screening practices should be accompanied by appropriate police force policies and training to guarantee fair and effective application, as well as adequate record keeping to ensure that youths are not taking advantage of police discretion not to charge.

C. ALTERNATIVE MEASURES PROGRAMS

While there is some controversy over the efficacy of alternative measures as opposed to court in terms of reducing the likelihood of the commission of future offences,[6] every province except Ontario implemented section 4 of the YOA soon after the Act came into force in 1984. It was generally felt that alternative measures represented a socially useful experiment for dealing with less serious young offenders in a humane, expeditious, and inexpensive fashion.

Ontario, however, decided not to implement section 4 after the YOA came into force; it provided no new funding for the establishment of these programs. Further, section 4(1)(a) provides that "[a]lternative measures may be used . . . *only if* . . . the measures are part of a program authorized by the [provincial or territorial] Attorney General" [emphasis added] or another person designated by the provincial government,

---

5   J.P. Hornick & S. Rodal, *The Use of Alternatives to Traditional Youth Court: An International Comparison* (Calgary: Canadian Research Institute for Law and the Family, 1995).

6   See, e.g., S. Moyer, *A Profile of the Juvenile Justice System in Canada* (Ottawa: Federal-Provincial-Territorial Task Force on Youth Justice, 1996) at 61–62.

and the Ontario government decided not to authorize any programs.[7] At
least in part, Ontario's opposition to alternative measures may have
reflected a general political resistance by the provincial government to
the federally enacted *YOA*, an attitude that critics referred to as a provincial failure to comply with the "spirit" of the new law.[8] The Ontario
government also emphasized that the research into the effectiveness of
diversion in terms of reducing recidivism was "ambiguous and conflicting," and it expressed concerns about the potential for the abuse of the
rights of youths in these programs as well as about "net widening."[9]

Since adolescents in all the other provinces and territories had access
to alternative measures, it is not surprising that the decision of Ontario
not to implement section 4 of the *YOA* was challenged as a violation of
the principle of "equality under the law" guaranteed by section 15 of the
Charter of Rights. In 1988, in R. v. S.(S.),[10] the Ontario Court of Appeal
held that the absence of such programs in Ontario constituted a "denial
of equal benefit and protection of the law" on the basis of province of residence and hence was in violation of section 15 of the *Charter*. The government of Ontario responded to the Court of Appeal decision by establishing alternative measures programs across the province, albeit on an
"interim basis," but it also appealed to the Supreme Court of Canada.

In June 1990 the Supreme Court of Canada reversed the Ontario
Court of Appeal decision in R. v. S.(S.). The Supreme Court observed that
section 4(1) of the *YOA* provides that "[a]lternative measures *may* be
used," indicating that there was a discretion granted the provincial government as to whether to establish these programs. The delegation of
authority to the provinces under section 4(1)(a) to decide whether or not
to establish alternative measures was constitutionally valid. Under Canada's federal system it is not a violation of the *Charter of Rights* to have
youths in one province denied access to alternative measures, though the
Supreme Court accepted that a "case-by-case" assessment is required to

---

7   In practice, some of the pre-*Young Offenders Act*, R.S.C. 1985, c. Y-1 [*YOA*[diversion
    programs in Ontario continued to operate with the cooperation of local police and
    prosecutors, and even with some funding from the Ministry of Community and
    Social Services. The opposition to alternative measures in the Ontario government in
    the 1984–90 period was largely centred in the Ministry of the Attorney General.

8   See K. Makin, "Ontario move on young offenders backed," [*Toronto*] *Globe and
    Mail* (29 June 1990) A7. Another example of Ontario's resistance to the *YOA*, *ibid.*
    was the "two tier" age implementation, with older adolescents dealt with in the
    criminal courts and by the adult Ministry of Corrections. See discussion in ch. 3.

9   I. Scott, in Ontario Social Development Council, *Young Offenders Act Dispositions:
    Challenges and Choices* (Toronto: The Council, 1988) at 16.

10 (1988), 63 C.R. (3d) 64 (Ont. C.A.).

determine whether interprovincial differences in the application of the criminal law are constitutionally valid. Chief Justice Dickson observed:

> [D]iversity in the criminal law, in terms of provincial application, has been recognized . . . as a means of furthering the values of federalism. . . . the question of how young people found to have committed criminal offences should be dealt with is one upon which it is legitimate for Parliament to allow for province-based distinctions. . . . benefits . . . derive from the adaptability of a program of alternative measures to the needs of different regions and communities.[11]

In a decision rendered at the same time as *R. v. S.(S.)*, the Supreme Court also accepted that if provinces choose to establish alternative measures programs, they may have different criteria for eligibility.[12]

Despite the Supreme Court of Canada decisions, the Ontario government continued and expanded its "interim" alternative measures programs. Shortly after *S.(S.)* the Supreme Court gave its decision in *R. v. Askov*,[13] ruling that delays in the Ontario courts were denying accused persons — both youths and adults — their constitutionally guaranteed right to a trial within a reasonable time. The *Askov* decision placed great pressure on the government to deal with the problem of overcrowding in the court system, and provided a strong impetus for moving less serious cases out of the courts by making use of alternative measures programs.

D. HOW THE PROGRAMS OPERATE: ROLES OF POLICE, PROSECUTOR, AND SERVICE PROVIDERS

The process for referring a youth to alternative measures varies substantially from one jurisdiction to another, and in some cases between programs within the same province. In some provinces a youth may be referred to alternative measures without charges being laid (pre-charge), but in others charges must be laid (post-charge); some provinces use both pre- and post-charge alternative measures. In a pre-charge program, the police refer youths directly to the program, generally after some form of consultation with the Crown prosecutor's office, without even commencing a youth court proceeding. In post-charge programs, a youth court proceeding is commenced, and the youth will usually have a first

---

11   [1990] 2 S.C.R. 254 at 290–91.
12   *R. v. S.(G.)*, [1990] 2 S.C.R. 294.
13   [1990] 2 S.C.R. 1199.

appearance in youth court before the Crown prosecutor decides whether the youth should be referred to the program, with the court case being adjourned pending alternative measures and the charges being dismissed once the youth satisfactorily completes the alternative measures.

Section 4(1)(b) of the YOA specifies that a person "who is considering whether to use [alternative] . . . measures . . . [should be] satisfied that they would be appropriate, having regard to the needs of the young person and the interests of society." Further, in accordance with section 3(1)(d), the use of alternative measures must not be "inconsistent" with the protection of society. These are vague criteria that require some assessment of the threat posed to society by the youth's behaviour, as well as consideration of the youth's circumstances. All jurisdictions have policies that govern the exercise of discretion by the prosecutor or police when deciding whether a youth is eligible for alternative measures.

Quebec has the broadest criteria for the use of alternative measures, with the prosecutor having a discretion to send any youth to alternative measures and a requirement that all less serious cases be referred, usually on a pre-charge basis.[14] For youths who are twelve or thirteen, the prosecutor must consult with the director of youth protection (who is responsible for both child protection and alternative measures) before a prosecution is commenced, and as a result very few youths under fourteen are dealt with in youth court in Quebec. Cases can be sent to alternative measures even if there is a prior record of offending. Because of its extensive use of alternative measures, Quebec has the lowest rate of youth court charging in Canada.

Ontario has one of the most restrictive alternative measures policies in Canada, generally operating on a post-charge basis, with the initial decision about alternative measures being made by the Crown prosecutor, usually acting on the advice of police. Before a referral can be made, it is generally necessary for the youth to appear in youth court where the case is adjourned. This process is more cumbersome and intrusive for the youth and parents, though it has the advantage of having a proceeding commenced in the event that alternative measures should not be completed. The case is sent to alternative measures only with the consent of the youth; the attendance at court will generally facilitate the youth having some access to a lawyer before deciding whether to participate, since a duty counsel is usually present. In Ontario there are offence criteria established by the provincial attorney general that help determine eligibility for alternative measures:

---

14   See P. Platt, *Young Offenders Law in Canada*, 2d ed. (Toronto: Butterworths, 1995) at 162; and N. Bala & H. Lilles, eds., *Young Offenders Service*, vol. 1 (Toronto: Butterworths, 1984) (looseleaf).

- For a youth charged with a property offence where the value is under $1000 and without a prior record of offending, there is a presumption that the youth is eligible unless there are "exceptional circumstances" (for example, vandalism that is motivated by racial hatred). If there is a record of offending in the previous year, the youth should ordinarily be sent to court, though there is still a discretion to send the youth to alternative measures.
- For a youth charged with: a property offence where the value is over $1000, a minor assault, giving a false name when arrested, or a credit card offence, the prosecutor has a discretion to refer a youth to alternative measures (consideration should be given to the views of the victim, the seriousness of the allegations, any prior record of the youth, and any other information relevant to the youth's background or circumstances); and
- More serious offences, such as any sex offence, assaults causing injury, alcohol related driving offences, and failure to comply with terms of a probation order or to attend court, are ineligible for alternative measures.[15]

The official Ontario criteria thus exclude some quite common non-violent offences, in particular break and enter. In most other provinces a youth charged with this offence may be considered for alternative measures.

In practice, there is some variation in how provincial eligibility policies are applied. In most jurisdictions the initial decision about diverting a youth to alternative measures, as opposed to having a case processed through the courts, is made by the Crown prosecutor, generally acting with the advice of the police. In some provinces, like British Columbia and Newfoundland, the Crown prosecutor may have a report prepared by a juvenile probation officer to assist in deciding whether a youth is suitable for alternative measures, and, as noted above, in Quebec the director of youth protection may be involved in consulting with the prosecutor. In some places, a pre-charge alternative measures program may accept referrals directly from the police, without the involvement of the Crown prosecutor's office.[16]

There is a duty imposed under section 4(1)(f) on the Crown prosecutor, or an agent of the Crown (such as a designated police officer), to form the "opinion" that there is "sufficient evidence to proceed with the prosecution of the offence." Section 4(1)(g) also specifies that alternative measures cannot be used where the "prosecution of the offence is . . . in any way barred at law," for example, by the passage of the six-month limitation period for a strictly summary offence. These provisions are intended to prevent "net widening" and ensure that alternative measures are not used as a way of

---

15 Ontario, Ministry of the Attorney General, *Alternative Measures Program: Policy & Procedures Manual* (Toronto: Queen's Printer, 1995). [*Alternative Measures Program*].
16 For example, the pre-charge program operated by Royal Canadian Mounted Police at Sparwood, British Columbia involving "Resolution Conferences."

responding informally to a case that is "too weak" to take to court; those cases should simply not be dealt with by the justice system, though it may sometimes be appropriate for an officer to caution a youth in such a situation.

After the YOA came into force in 1984, there were some youth court judges who argued that they had a right to refer to alternative measures cases which they did not consider suitable for prosecution in the courts.[17] However, in a number of decisions it has been held that it is the prosecutor (or police) who have the *discretion* to refer cases to alternative measures, and it is a discretion that is not reviewable by the courts. In *R. v. T.(V.)* the Supreme Court of Canada considered a case in which a fourteen-year-old girl who was living in a group home, apparently pursuant to child-welfare legislation, was charged with mischief, assault, and uttering threats as a result of a dinner-time altercation; this was a situation that a parent might well have resolved without calling the police. It appears that charges were laid only because a police officer happened to come to the group home that evening on an unrelated matter. The British Columbia Court of Appeal felt that under section 3(1)(d) of the YOA the prosecuting authorities are required to "consider" whether to use measures other than court, and if they have failed to do so, a youth court judge has "ultimate responsibility" for a case and could dismiss the charges. The British Columbia Court of Appeal suggested that a youth court judge could dismiss a charge for a relatively minor offence if it involved a person in a "parent-like role" (such as a group-home staff member) making use of the court system for "minor disciplinary infractions" for which a parent would not ordinarily resort to the courts. However, the Supreme Court of Canada reversed the decision of the Court of Appeal. It ruled that, except in cases of a clear "abuse of process,"[18] a judge has no discretion as to whether charges should be laid.[19]

---

17   See, e.g., *R. v. B.(J.)* (1985), 20 C.C.C. (3d) 67 (B.C. Prov. Ct.).

18   While a youth court judge cannot refer a case to alternative measures, there is a narrow residual discretion in any case for a judge to stay proceedings where compelling the accused to stand trial would contravene "the community's basic sense of decency and fair play and thereby . . . call into question the integrity of the [justice] system." *R. v. O'Connor*, [1995] 4 S.C.R. 441 at 457. The abuse of process power is to be exercised only in the "clearest of cases" and might, for example, be invoked if there was a lengthy delay in laying charges after a police investigation, or a person were tried several times resulting in hung juries and a further prosecution seemed "oppressive." There is also a doctrine known as *de minimis non curat lex* — Latin for "about trifling things do not go the law." This has occasionally been invoked by Canadian judges to dismiss charges, as, for example, in drug cases where a small quantity of drugs are discovered, but it would appear that this doctrine cannot be used in youth court since *R. v. T.(V.)*, [1992] 1 S.C.R 749 [*T.(V.)*]. See D. Stuart, *Canadian Criminal Law*, 3d ed. (Toronto: Carswell, 1995) at 524–46.

19   *T.(V.)*, *ibid.*

The Supreme Court held that Crown prosecutors and the police are the appropriate officials to exercise authority under section 3(1)(d) of the *YOA*, and refer a case to alternative measures. While a young person's advocate (whether a lawyer, a parent, or a social worker) can sometimes play a useful role in informally communicating with the prosecutor or police about why a youth should be dealt with by alternative measures, the exercise of discretion by the police and prosecutor is not reviewable by a court; there is no obligation to give a youth any sort of notice that consideration is being given to whether to refer a case to alternative measures or to conduct any sort of a "hearing" to decide whether a youth will be diverted from court.[20] If a judge feels that a youth has been charged for a relatively minor offence that should have been dealt with outside the courts, the appropriate response is at the sentencing stage, where an absolute discharge might be appropriate if a judge felt the youth should have been referred to alternative measures.[21]

In some localities, responsibility for meeting with the youth and arranging for the supervision of alterative measures is given to a community agency with paid staff or volunteers, while in other places government social workers or juvenile probation staff are responsible.[22] If a youth is referred to alternative measures, the person or agency responsible for the program meets with the youth to ascertain what response is appropriate and available, and to ensure that the response is acceptable to the youth. In some localities, the meeting is informal, with just the youth and a youth worker present. Increasingly, however, programs are being established in Canada that involve victims, parents, and possibly members of the community meeting with the youth and a facilitator to attempt to achieve some form of reconciliation and develop a suitable plan.

Aboriginal communities, in particular, are establishing alternative measures programs that involve meetings with victims, elders, and community members. This is consistent with Aboriginal notions of healing justice, which emphasize the importance of restoring relationships within the community. In some provinces, the offence criteria for referral of Aboriginal youth to alternative measures are broader than for non-Aboriginal youth, in recognition that there are social, political, and constitutional reasons for dealing with Aboriginal youths outside of the traditional justice system, a system that has far too clearly failed

---

20   W.(T.) v. *Smith* (1986), 45 Sask. R. 191 (Q.B.); *R.* v. *B.(G.)* (December 1994), (Y.S.C.) [unreported] [summarized (1994), 26 W.C.B. (2d) 48].

21   *R.* v. *T.(G.)* (1987), 57 C.R. (3d) 388 (Alta. Youth Ct.).

22   Statistics Canada, Canadian Centre for Justice Statistics, *A Review of the Alternative Measures Survey 1991-92* (Ottawa: Statistics Canada, 1994).

to have an impact on Aboriginal offending.[23] Alternative measures programs that give Aboriginal communities greater responsibility for their troubled adolescents have the potential to permit more effective healing-based non-adversarial responses to youthful offending.[24]

In some cases, it may be desirable to give the youth an opportunity to think about the offence by asking him or her to write an essay or prepare a poster on the subject, though account should be taken of the youth's abilities in imposing any requirements for written work. Or it may be appropriate for the youth to do some community-service work or make a donation to a charity, to make clear to the youth that offending behaviour affects the whole community. In some cases, especially if there has already been a suitable parental response to the offending behaviour or some form of reparation has been made to the victim, it may be that no further response is required after a meeting with the program operator. The decision to make no further response may also be influenced by the attitudes of the victim and the youth, as well as by the youth's reactions at the meeting.

Increasingly, alternative measures programs in Canada are trying to involve victims, to give them an opportunity to have a sense that justice has been done, and in appropriate cases to provide some form of compensation for the harm that they have suffered.[25] These programs generally notify the victim and often invite the victim to a meeting with the youth, at which the offence is discussed and an appropriate response developed. While these meetings can provide an important opportunity for victims to feel vindicated, and for offenders to gain an appreciation of the effects of their conduct, the meetings must be conducted with sensitivity (for example, to ensure that neither the victim nor youth feel intimidated by the experience). If appropriate, there may be some form of restitution, apology, or personal service by the youth to a victim. Though this may be an important restorative act for some victims, others want nothing further to do with the offender.

---

23 The courts have accepted that it does not violate s. 15 of the *Canadian Charter of Rights and Freedoms*, Part I of the *Constitution Act, 1982*, being Schedule B to the *Canada Act 1982* (U.K.), 1982, c. 11 to offer alternative measures to Aboriginals in circumstances where others do not have the same opportunity: *R. v. Willcocks* (1995), 22 O.R. (3d) 552 (Gen. Div.).

24 See, e.g., R. Ross, *Returning to the Teachings: Exploring Aboriginal Justice* (Toronto: Penguin, 1996) [*Returning*].

25 See, e.g., K.J. Pate & D.E. Peachey, "Face-to-Face: Victim-Offender Mediation under the Young Offenders Act" in J. Hudson, J. Hornick, & B. Burrows, eds., *Justice and the Young Offender in Canada* (Toronto: Wall & Thompson, 1988) 105.

In some alternative measures programs, one option is to require a youth to attend counselling or participate in some form of therapeutic intervention. Such counselling might be provided by a therapist, doctor, or community agency, or in an Aboriginal community it might involve the development of a relationship with a respected elder. This type of response is premised on the belief that some offending behaviour is a symptom of an emotional, social, behavioural, or substance-abuse problem; responding to the problem is most likely to prevent further offending, as well as being generally beneficial to the youth. Other alternative measures programs, however, are unwilling to make a referral to counselling a requirement of participation; these programs take a "non-interventionist" approach, believing that a referral to counselling is too intrusive a response to the relatively minor charges that they deal with.[26]

While most youths who are sent to alternative measures programs in Canada have not committed serious offences and are not likely to reoffend, there is a minority who pose a significant threat to society. If such youth do not have their needs addressed at this early stage, they will likely commit subsequent, more serious offences. Alternative measures programs that respond to the problems of youths at risk are consistent with section 3(1)(c. 1)of the YOA, which recognizes the importance of "addressing the needs and circumstances of a young person that are relevant to the . . . offending behaviour." This suggests that counselling or treatment conditions are appropriate options for some cases referred to alternative measures programs.

E. ROLE AND RIGHTS OF YOUNG PERSONS

An alternative measures program can offer a youth the opportunity for an expeditious, informal response to an apprehended violation of the law. The youth and parents will generally feel less intimidated than if the case goes to court, and they are likely to participate more fully in any discussions. So it is not surprising that research reveals that parents and youth may be more likely to perceive themselves as having been treated fairly in a diversion program than in the more formal, adversarial court setting.[27]

---

26   This is, for example, the official policy in Ontario. Treatment is not considered "an appropriate measure" though program workers provide "information about counselling and a referral might be appropriate as part of the negotiation process." Ontario, Ministry of the Attorney General, *Alternative Measures Program*, above note 15 at 15.

27   See, e.g., M.E. Morton & W.G. West, "An Experiment in Diversion by a Citizen Committee" in R.R. Corrado, M. LeBlanc & J. Trépanier, eds., *Current Issues in Juvenile Justice* (Toronto: Butterworths, 1983) 203 at 211.

For the youth and parents, diversion avoids the stigma of having a "youth court record." Parents may also be keen about participation since there is less likelihood of incurring the expense of having a lawyer, and there may be less need to take time away from work or other activities to attend court. As a result, there may be considerable pressure on the youth to participate, even though the alternative "measures" may actually be more onerous or intrusive than a court would impose. While the *YOA* has provisions that are intended to minimize the risk of an abuse of the rights of a youth, there are fewer protections if a youth goes to alternative measures than if the youth goes to court, and there is the potential for a fairly intrusive response to a quite minor offence, or even for participation in alternative measures by a youth who is not guilty of an offence.

Alternative measures programs are not designed to be "informal courts." Under section 4(1)(e) a youth is to participate only if he (or she) "accepts responsibility for the act . . . that forms the basis of the offence that he is alleged to have committed." A youth can explain the nature of his or her participation in the offence alleged, and section 4(1)(e) does not necessarily require that the youth accept full legal guilt for the specific offence alleged, but this provision at least requires a recognition of involvement and an acceptance of moral responsibility.

Whether or not there is successful completion of the alternatives measures plan, section 4(3) specifies that no statement or confession made by the youth "accepting responsibility" for the offence as a condition for being eligible for alternative measures may be used in any later civil or criminal court proceedings. Section 4(3) is intended to reassure youths and their advisers, as well as to encourage youths to accept responsibility and participate in alternative measures. The provision may also reflect a concern that there may be cases in which there is the potential for a youth to feel coerced into "accepting responsibility" in order to gain access to alternative measures. Even without section 4(3), in many cases there would be an argument that a statement made by a youth as a condition of participation in alternative measures was induced by a "hope of advantage" (the dismissal or staying of charges) and hence would be "involuntary" and inadmissible in any subsequent prosecution.[28]

A youth who "denies his participation or involvement" or who expresses the wish to be dealt with in youth court cannot be dealt with by an alternative measures program [section 4(2)]. A trial to determine whether or not a youth is guilty can be conducted only in youth court. Section 4(1)(d) requires that a youth must advised of the right to legal

---

28   See discussion in ch. 4, on "involuntariness."

representation and given a reasonable opportunity to consult with counsel before consenting to participation in alternative measures.

Most programs ensure that, at an early stage of the alternative measures process, the youth accepts responsibility for the offence alleged, agrees to participate, and is aware of the right to consult a lawyer. However, unlike the situation for youths who are dealt with in youth court, there are no statutory requirements for the provision of legal services to a youth who is unable to obtain representation. Some youths do consult a lawyer before agreeing to participation, if the program is post-charge, perhaps through a brief meeting with duty counsel at youth court before the case is referred to alternative measures. A few programs arrange for duty-counsel assistance at their meetings, but in times of increasing fiscal restraint it is difficult to obtain a commitment for legal aid authorities to fund this. There are concerns that some youths may in effect waive their legal rights, perhaps because of a "desire to get things over with" or because of parental pressure, without fully appreciating their position. This may happen even when they have a valid defence to the allegations.

Under section 4(1)(c) the youth must agree to the specific alternative measures plan that is developed; if the youth objects that the plan is too onerous and the matter is not resolved by discussion, he or she has the right to take the matter to court. In some cases, the plan may be more onerous or intrusive than the sentence which a youth court judge would impose, though a youth without legal assistance may not be aware of the discrepancy and may erroneously believe that any alternative measures plan is "softer" than what a court would impose. One Crown prosecutor, John Pearson, commented on the problems that can arise from the lack of access to legal assistance in connection with alternative measures:

> If parents and young persons have difficulty appreciating the need for counsel when they are going through the court system, how likely is it that they will recognize the need when a "non-judicial" resolution is being proposed? Once alternative measures are invoked, the young person is dealt with by a system that has none of the mechanisms required in order for legal representation to be effective. A well-meaning diversion committee, from which there is no appeal, determines society's response to the young person's criminal conduct. The philosophy behind the juvenile-court movement is played out on another stage.[29]

---

29   J.C. Pearson, "Legal Representation under the Young Offenders Act" in A.W. Leschied, P.G. Jaffe, & W. Willis, eds., *The Young Offenders Act: A Revolution in Canadian Juvenile Justice* (Toronto: University of Toronto Press, 1991) 114 at 118.

Pearson is concerned that in some respects the "alternative measures movement" is similar to the informal paternalistic court of the *JDA*, where actions that were intended to promote the "best interests" of the juvenile could result in a much more intrusive response than the offence itself warranted. It would be desirable to ensure that all youths who are referred to alternative measures have actually had access to legal advice before waiving their right to go to court, especially since the fact of participation may be "held against" the youth if there is a later prosecution for another offence.

Those who administer alternative measures programs should be aware of the potential for violations of rights, and in particular of the potential that a youth may feel coerced by parents or others into accepting responsibility for an offence that he or she did not actually commit, as well as for the possibility that an unduly harsh plan may be imposed on a youth. However, the possibilities for excessive intervention in an alternative measures program are generally limited, and certainly narrower than was the case under the *JDA*.

F. CONSEQUENCES OF PARTICIPATION

If a young person agrees to participate and successfully completes the alternative measures plan agreed to, the case cannot proceed to court; section 4(4)(a) specifies that, if the case is brought to youth court, the judge shall dismiss the charges. If an alternative measures plan is developed and agreed to, but the youth does not fully complete it, the case may still be brought to court by the prosecutor or police, provided they are informed that the youth has not fully completed the plan. Under section 4(4)(b) the judge has a discretion where there is only partial completion of alternative measures; he may dismiss the charge if the prosecution is considered unfair, or he may take account of the partially completed plan when sentencing the youth. The judge should consider how much of the plan was completed, the reason that the plan was not fully carried out, and whether the alternative measures experience has had an effect on the youth.

Section 45(1)(d) of the *YOA* provides that, if a youth is referred to alternative measures, the records of the program operators as well as police records, including fingerprints and photographs that might have been taken in the case of a post-charge program, may be kept for two years from the time that the youth consents to participation. After two years, if there are no further youth court convictions, no use may be made of any records kept in regard to an offence sent to alternative measures. Many alternative measures programs have a policy of record destruction two years after the youth has begun the program, and the Canadian Police Information Centre is obliged to destroy any fingerprint or photographs of the youth if there are no further charges during the two years [section 45(2)].

However, if within the two-year period the youth is charged with and convicted of another offence, then section 14(2)(c)(iv) of the *YOA* specifies that a pre-disposition report prepared to assist the judge in sentencing the youth shall include "the history of alternative measures used to deal with the young person and the response of the young person thereto." In theory, prior participation in alternative measures should not be weighed as heavily against a youth as a prior formal youth court finding, since there has been no judicial finding of guilt, but the prior involvement is a "part of the history of the person being sentenced" and may demonstrate that a less punitive response may not serve as an effective deterrent for that individual.[30] Prior participation in alternative measures is generally a negative factor at any subsequent sentencing, even if the participation arose out of a pre-charge program. The possibility of later use of a record of alternative measures participation emphasizes the need to ensure that those youths who waive their right to go to youth court are truly accepting responsibility for their acts and are aware of the consequences of participation.

G. THE FUTURE ROLE OF ALTERNATIVE MEASURES

It is difficult to get an accurate picture of the extent to which alternative measures and police screening are being used in Canada, though it is apparent that the *YOA* has encouraged the establishment of programs to divert youths from court. Available data reveal that there is substantial variation in use of diversionary measures in different provinces; it would appear that less than one case in five in Canada is diverted to pre- or post-charge alternative measures programs.[31] Canada makes far more use of the formal youth court processes to respond to adolescent offending than other countries, and has less use of various diversionary practices.[32] In the United States, which has higher rates of violent youth offending than Canada, the rate of use of a court-based response to

---

30   *R. v. Drew* (1978), 7 C.R. (3d) S-21 (B.C.C.A.).

31   Statistics Canada, Canadian Centre for Justice Statistics, above note 22.

32   J.P. Hornick & S. Rodal, *The Use of Alternatives to Traditional Youth Court: An International Comparison* (Calgary: Canadian Research Institute for Law and the Family, 1995) at 50.

youth offending is less than half that in Canada.[33] Canada's extensive reliance on a court-based response to youth offending is both expensive and associated with a high rate of youth-custody use.

Various types of diversionary schemes represent a socially useful and cost-effective response to many situations of youth offending, and Canadian governments are now slowly extending alternative measures to adults.[34] It is apparent that, for many adolescents, parents, and victims, an expeditious, informal response may be preferable to a delayed, formal adversarial court experience. There is surprisingly little research, especially in Canada, on whether alternative measures can reduce the risk of reoffending, and clearly this question merits study. One would expect that the effectiveness of alternative measures in terms of reducing recidivism would depend on the nature of the program and the types of cases dealt with, as well as on whether the program has good linkages to counselling and community supports that can assist youths at serious risk of reoffending in dealing with their problems.

Experience in other countries clearly indicates that Canada could extend the use of various diversionary programs, including making more extensive use of police screening and cautioning, as well as other community-based programs, without increasing the risk of reoffending. Indeed, some of the international experience suggests that diversionary programs based on such models as the New Zealand family-group conference may result in reductions in youth crime,[35] especially in Aboriginal communities where the traditional court-based approaches employed in Canada have proven notably unsuccessful in preventing reoffending.

There will always be a role for a formal court-based response for those adolescents who commit more serious offences or who are not responsive to informal intervention. There is also an important role for the court system in protecting legal rights, and alternative measures and other forms of diversion must be structured and monitored to ensure that the rights of youths are not abused. But there would appear to be substantial scope for the extension of various diversionary schemes in Canada. The 1997 House of Commons Justice Committee report recommended making more use of alternatives to the youth justice system such as police cautioning and family-group conferencing.[36]

---

33   S.A. Hinshaw, "Juvenile Diversion: An Alternative to Juvenile Court" [1993] J. Dispute Resolution 305.

34   *An Act to amend the Criminal Code (sentencing) and other Acts in consequence thereof*, S.C. 1995, c. 22, s. 717.

35   See, e.g., R. Ross, *Returning*, above note 24 at 19. See discussion in ch. 2.

36   Canada, House of Commons, *Thirteenth Report of the Standing Committee on Justice and Legal Affairs: Renewing Youth Justice* (Ottawa: Supply & Services, 1997) 45–57.

FURTHER READINGS

BALA, N. & H. LILLES, eds., *Young Offenders Service* (Toronto: Butterworths, 1984) (looseleaf), s. 4

CANADA, FEDERAL-PROVINCIAL-TERRITORIAL TASK FORCE ON YOUTH JUSTICE, *A Review of the Young Offenders Act and the Youth Justice System in Canada* (Ottawa: Supply & Services, 1996), ch. 4

CANADIAN CENTRE FOR JUSTICE STATISTICS, *A Review of the Alternative Measures Survey 1991–92* (Ottawa: Statistics Canada, 1994)

HARRIS, P.J., ed., *Young Offenders Act Manual* (Aurora: Canada Law Book, 1984) (looseleaf) s. 4

HORNICK, J.P. & S. RODAL, *The Use of Alternatives to Traditional Youth Court: An International Comparison* (Calgary: Canadian Research Institute for Law and the Family, 1995)

HUDSON, J., J.P. HORNICK, & B.A. BURROWS, eds., *Justice and the Young Offender in Canada* (Toronto: Wall & Thompson, 1988), chs. 7 and 8

PLATT, P., *Young Offenders Law in Canada*, 2d ed. (Toronto: Butterworths, 1995), ch.7

SCOTT, S., M. WONG, & B. WEAGANT, *Defending Young Offender Cases*, 2d ed. (Toronto: Carswell, 1997), ch.4

TOMBS, J. & S. MOODY, "Alternatives to Prosecution: The Public Interest Redefined" [1993] Crim. L. Rev. 356

CHAPTER 6

LAWYERS IN THE YOUTH COURT PROCESS

A. THE IMPORTANCE OF LAWYERS IN A DUE-PROCESS MODEL OF JUSTICE

The *Canadian Charter of Rights and Freedoms* and the *Young Offenders Act* are premised on a "due process" model of justice, with section 3(1) (e) of the *YOA*'s Declaration of Principle affirming that youths are to have all of the legal rights afforded adults, as well as recognizing that because of their immaturity they require "special guarantees of their rights and freedoms." In the due-process model of justice, legally trained professionals inevitably play a key role. The *YOA* has provisions which are intended to ensure that youths can have access to legal assistance at every stage of the youth court process. Lawyers are responsible for deciding how the case for the prosecution and defence will be presented to the judge (another legally trained professional). They also resolve a large number of cases without significant judicial involvement; in practice, many of the cases dealt with in youth court are actually resolved by means of a "plea bargain" negotiated by the lawyers and only formally ratified by a judge. As discussed in chapter 5, Crown prosecutors also generally have primary responsibility for deciding whether a young person will even go to youth court or will be diverted to alternative measures.

While legally trained professionals now play a crucial role in society's response to adolescents who are alleged to have violated the law, this is a relatively recent development and there continues to be controversy about the role of lawyers in the youth court process, as well as questioning of whether the youth justice system has become excessively legalized. At the same time, there are concerns that while the YOA in theory appears to ensure that youths whose cases are dealt with in court will have access to legal assistance, in practice many youths are either inadequately represented or not represented at all.

This chapter describes how young persons are provided access to legal services and considers some of the contentious issues related to the role and effectiveness of both defence counsel and Crown prosecutors.

B. LAWYERS UNDER THE *JUVENILE DELINQUENTS ACT*

Although the *Young Offenders Act* has provisions intended to ensure that young persons have access to legal representation, the drafters of the *Juvenile Delinquents Act, 1908* contemplated an explicit prohibition on the appearance of lawyers in juvenile court. In the end the drafters of the 1908 law settled for an Act that made no mention of the issue of legal representation but created a statutory regime that explicitly allowed for "informality" and precluded the reversal of a judicial decision on the grounds of any "irregularity" when it was felt that the disposition of the case was in the "best interests of the child."[1] The emphasis under the *JDA* was on having judges and the juvenile court system making expeditious decisions to allow interventions that would promote the "best interests" of delinquent youth. In the first part of this century, few juvenile court judges had legal training and lawyers rarely appeared in that court.

In one 1958 Manitoba case, a lawyer appeared in juvenile court with a fourteen-year-old youth charged with indecent assault and requested an adjournment before entering a plea in order to have time to investigate the circumstances of the alleged offence. The juvenile court judge noted that the lawyer had not asked him for "permission" to represent the youth; he suggested that the lawyer's presence was "gumming the works up and [would] . . . make it considerably more difficult" for the juvenile, threatening that if there was going to be a not guilty plea and trial, the juvenile might be transferred to adult court, which, under the *JDA*, the juvenile court judge could do on his own motion without the request of the Crown. The lawyer withdrew from the proceeding, and

---

1   *The Juvenile Delinquents Act, 1908,* S.C. 1908, c. 40, later *Juvenile Delinquents Act,* R.S.C. 1970, c. J-3, s. 17 [*JDA*].

the juvenile was convicted. Although the conviction was eventually overturned by the Supreme Court of Canada on procedural grounds, the comments of the juvenile court judge reflected an attitude held by many at that time, namely, that lawyers were expected to play a limited role in juvenile courts.[2]

By the 1960s and 1970s many of the judges in juvenile court were legally trained, and, as a result of provincial legal aid schemes being established, more lawyers began appearing in juvenile court. In the United States there was a growing recognition of the need to afford juveniles "due process" of law. The 1966 Supreme Court decision in *Kent* v. *United States* inaugurated the process of the "constitutionalization" of American juvenile courts, with Fortas J. observing:

> While there can be no doubt of the original laudable purpose of juvenile courts, studies and critiques in recent years raise serious questions as to whether actual performance measures well enough against theoretical purpose to make tolerable the immunity of the process from the reach of constitutional guarantees applicable to adults. . . . there may be grounds for concern that the child receives the worst of both worlds: that he gets neither the protections accorded to adults nor the solicitous care and regenerative treatment postulated for children.[3]

In 1967 the United States Supreme Court ruled in *Re Gault* that, like an adult facing a term of imprisonment, a juvenile facing a custodial disposition is entitled to the assistance of counsel, and if the parents are unable to afford counsel, the state must provide access to representation. Justice Fortas wrote:

> Ultimately . . . we confront the reality . . . of the Juvenile Court process. . . . The boy is committed to an institution where he may be restrained of liberty for years. It is of no constitutional consequence — and of limited practical meaning — that the institution to which he is committed is called an Industrial School. . . . however euphemistic the title . . .[it] is an institution of confinement in which the child is incarcerated. . . .
>
> The juvenile needs the assistance of counsel to cope with problems of law, to make skilled inquiry into the facts, to insist upon the regularity of the proceedings, and to ascertain whether he has a

---

2   *R. v. S.(G.)*, [1959] S.C.R. 638, rev'g (1958), 28 C.R. 100 (Man. C.A.). Although Locke J. in the Supreme Court and Adamson J.A. in the Manitoba Court of Appeal remarked on the "astonishing" attitude of the juvenile court judge towards defence counsel, the majority of appellate judges declined to comment or were actually supportive of the approach of the trial judge to the presence of defence counsel.

3   383 U.S. 541 at 555–56 (1966).

defense and to prepare and submit it. The child "requires the guiding hand of counsel at every step in the proceedings against him."[4]

While the American constitution, as interpreted by the Supreme Court, in theory gives juveniles the right to legal representation, in practice juveniles in the United States sometimes feel pressured by judges or parents to waive their right to counsel in order to have an expeditious and relatively inexpensive resolution of their cases.[5]

In Canada, juvenile court judges and probation officers became increasingly accustomed to the presence of defence lawyers in the 1970s, but juvenile justice professionals continued to express the view that many, if not most, juveniles did not require legal representation.[6] Further, it was clear that most professionals involved in the juvenile courts, including many defence lawyers, saw the role of the lawyer as quite different from that in adult court.

Writing in 1972, one Ontario juvenile judge questioned the role of a privately retained lawyer for an accused child, if the lawyer sees his "primary objective . . . [as] to free his client from the jurisdiction of the court." The judge felt that a "much better job" was done by "legal aid or duty counsel lawyers [who] are committed to the proposition that they are paid by the State to protect the legal rights of children while at the same time taking advantage of all of the potential powers of the Court to promote the best interests of the child."[7]

A study of thirty lawyers who appeared in juvenile court in Toronto in 1970 revealed that, while some of them saw themselves in a "traditional" advocate's role, most of them did not think that they had the same adversarial role as in adult court. One of them, for example, emphasized that a defence lawyer "shouldn't twist evidence or the juvenile would get the wrong idea of the system."[8] Many lawyers felt that part of their role was to work with other professionals in the court and promote the "best interests" of the juvenile. While some lawyers for youths charged under the *YOA* continue to have this "paternalistic" attitude, it was clearly much more prevalent among lawyers acting under the *JDA*.

---

4   387 U.S. 1 at 27 and 36 (1967).
5   B.C. Feld, *Justice for Children: The Rights to Counsel and the Juvenile Courts* (Boston: Northeastern University Press, 1993).
6   R.S. Stubbs, "The Role of the Lawyer in Juvenile Court" (1974) 6 Man. L.J. 65 at 76.
7   W.T. Little, "The Need for Reform in the Juvenile Courts" (1972) 10 Osgoode Hall L.J. 224 at 227.
8   I. Dootjes, P. Erickson, & R.G. Fox, "Defence Counsel in Juvenile Court: A Variety of Roles" (1972) 14 Can J. Crim. 132 at 137. See also P.G. Erickson, "The Defence Lawyer's Role in Juvenile Court: An Empirical Investigation into Judges' and Social Workers' Points of View" (1974) 24 U.T.L.J. 126.

C. ACCESS TO LEGAL SERVICES FOR YOUTHS: *YOA*, SECTION 11

The *YOA* has a number of provisions that are intended to ensure that youths are aware of their legal rights, and in particular of the right to have access to legal assistance. As discussed in chapter 4, under section 56 of the *YOA*, if the police want to question a youth suspected of having committed an offence, they must advise the youth of the right to counsel and obtain a signed or videotaped waiver if the youth chooses not to consult counsel. Even if the police do not want to question a youth, section 11(2) of the *YOA* as well as section 10(b) of the *Charter of Rights* require that, upon arrest or detention by the police, a youth shall be informed of the right to representation by counsel and given an opportunity to contact a lawyer. A youth who is taken to a police station for a breathalyzer test to determine the level of alcohol consumption must be given a reasonable opportunity to consult counsel before taking the test. However, despite the fact that section 11(1) of the *YOA* gives a youth the right to retain counsel "without delay," police officers who have stopped a youth who is driving for a preliminary screening with a roadside device can do so without first giving the youth an opportunity to consult a lawyer.[9] The breathalyzer result is normally admissible as evidence of intoxication in court; however, the roadside screening is used to determine only if an individual should be taken to the station for the more accurate breathalyzer test, a fact that justifies not requiring access to counsel before the roadside test is taken.

Though the police regularly provide these cautions, most youths who are arrested do not appear to appreciate the value of obtaining legal advice, or feel too intimidated by the situation they find themselves in, and will come to court on their first appearance without having consulted a lawyer. Section 11(3) of the *YOA* requires that, if a youth appears in court without a lawyer, whether at a bail hearing, a trial, or a transfer or disposition review hearing, the presiding judge shall inform the youth of the right to be represented by counsel and give him or her a reasonable opportunity to obtain a lawyer.[10]

---

9   *R. v. Frohman* (1987), 60 O.R. (2d) 125 (C.A.).

10   *Young Offenders Act*, R.S.C. 1985, c. Y-1, s. 11 [*YOA*], gives a youth who is "unable" to obtain counsel to have counsel provided at each stage of the youth court process, including transfer, trial, disposition, and disposition review, but it does not give any right to counsel in regard to an appeal. A youth who wishes to appeal a youth court decision can apply for legal aid, which may be granted depending on the seriousness of the issue and whether there is a reasonable prospect for success. If an appeal is made to the provincial Court of Appeal, there is authority in s. 684 of the *Criminal Code*, R.S.C. 1985, c. C-46 [*Code*], for a judge of that court to "assign" counsel for the accused, to be paid by the government; while the appeal court has a discretion, it is more likely to make an order for representation in cases involving youths than for appeals by adults: see *R. v. M.(A.)* (1996), 30 O.R. (3d) 313 (C.A.).

Further, and most significantly, section 11(4)(b) requires that, if a youth "wishes to obtain legal counsel but is unable to do so," the judge shall refer the youth to the local legal aid program; if the young person is "unable to obtain counsel through such program . . . [the judge] shall direct that the young person be represented by counsel." If an order is made for representation under section 11(4)(b), then the lawyer is paid by the government.

Initially, there were some judges who interpreted section 11(4) as giving a court the authority to conduct an inquiry as to whether youths or their parents had the resources to contribute to the cost of retaining a lawyer, or whether, for example, a youth might obtain employment to pay for counsel. However, in *R. v. C.(S.T.)* Russell J. of the Alberta Court of Queen's Bench ruled that there is no statutory basis for having such a hearing:

> [T]he court has no discretion to decline to direct the appointment of counsel where the young person has been unable to obtain legal aid. The Youth Court need only be satisfied that the young person wishes to obtain counsel but has been unable to do so because legal aid is not available for any reason. An affidavit to that effect, or in the alternative [a] simple inquiry into those facts alone should suffice. The court has no discretion to determine whether a young person should be provided with a lawyer out of public funds.[11]

Generally, legal aid will decline to provide representation if the case is not considered sufficiently serious, or if the youth or parents have sufficient financial means to pay for a lawyer. But a section 11(4)(b) order is to be made without reference to parental ability to pay. Since few youths have the financial means to retain a lawyer, the effect of *R. v. C.(S.T.)* is that virtually all youths have the right to have a lawyer paid by the government, regardless of their parents' financial status. This gives youths a significantly broader right than the adult right to "retain counsel." Adults who are unable to privately pay for a lawyer will generally only have a government-paid lawyer if they meet financial eligibility criteria *and* have a case considered sufficiently complex or serious to meet legal aid criteria; with government funding constraints for legal aid, the financial and case-seriousness criteria for adults are becoming increasingly narrow.[12] Youths

---

11   (1993), 140 A.R. 259 at 267 (Q.B.).

12   There is no obligation under the *Canadian Charter of Rights and Freedoms*, Part I of the *Constitution Act, 1982*, being Schedule B to the *Canada Act 1982* (U.K.), 1982, c. 11 [*Charter*], or *Code*, above note 10, for governments to provide legal representation to those who are arrested or accused in court; *R. v. Prosper*, [1994] 3 S.C.R. 236. However, there is a residual judicial discretion under the *Charter*, ss. 7 and 11(d), to order that proceedings should be stayed if an indigent accused adult does not receive legal representation; this power has not been widely exercised, though, with the cuts to legal aid, judges have been increasingly prepared to make such orders regarding adult accused.

can obtain a government-paid lawyer for even the most minor criminal charges, a fact reflective of the belief that without representation an adolescent may lack the ability to understand and participate fully in the often complex and intimidating court environment.

In this era of growing fiscal restraint, provincial governments have been expressing concern about section 11(4)(b) of the YOA. While these governments[13] have an obligation to pay for a lawyer if an order is made under section 11(4)(b), in Alberta the government has begun to demand that youths and parents with financial means repay the government for any costs incurred as the result of the provision of legal services, with parental liability based on the legal obligation of parents to provide minor children with "support." The legality of this type of civil claim under existing statutory provisions has not yet been fully tested in the courts, but governments are considering enacting legislation to make clear that such reimbursement is valid.[14]

The relationship of parents to the lawyer representing their child raises some difficult questions. Some judges have ruled that, since young persons are minors, they lack the legal capacity to retain counsel without the involvement of a parent or guardian.[15] However, the YOA was amended in 1986 so that section 11(1) now explicity states that young persons can "exercise . . . personally" the right to retain counsel or choose to waive that right.

Before the enactment of the YOA it was common for a parent with financial resources to hire a lawyer to represent a child charged under the JDA. Even under the YOA some parents will pay for a lawyer for their child, either because of a sense of moral obligation or because they are not satisfied with the lawyer provided under the government-representation plan. At least in theory the client in a YOA proceeding is the youth who is charged with the offence, regardless of who is paying the lawyer, and only the youth should be instructing the lawyer. But in practice, if parents are paying for a lawyer there may be some confusion as to who is instructing the lawyer. Section 11(8) provides that a judge shall ensure that a youth is "represented by counsel independent of his parents" if it appears that the interests of the youth and parents "conflict" or the "best interest" of the youth require representation by "his own counsel."

---

13   The federal government contributes to some of the legal aid and YOA, above note 10, s. 11(4)(b) expenses of provincial governments.

14   Canada, Federal-Provincial-Territorial Task Force on Youth Justice, A Review of the Young Offenders Act and the Youth Justice System in Canada (Ottawa: Supply & Services, 1996) at 530.

15   See, e.g., R. v. W.(W.W.) (1985), 34 Man. R. (2d) 134 (C.A.).

Even in the usual case where lawyers for youths are paid by the government, some lawyers appear uncertain of their role and relationship with parents. This is most obviously illustrated by the failure of some lawyers, especially when acting as duty counsel at court, to interview the youth alone. A youth may choose to have parents present during an interview with a lawyer; however, there should always be some time for a private interview, at least to get permission for the parents to be present for the rest of the interview. Parents can provide important support, information, and advice to their child, but their presence can also be intimidating or embarrassing to a child and may cause a youth to be less candid with counsel. Indeed, a lawyer should communicate with the parents only with the consent of the youth, and he or she must refrain from sharing any confidential information provided by the youth with the parents. It is sometimes difficult for parents to accept that an unknown professional will be playing an important role in their child's life, especially if the youth is relatively young or the lawyer appears to be offering advice that differs from the parents' views about the case.

In this era of limited fiscal resources, it is understandable that governments are looking to parents to provide financial support for youths involved in the justice system. It should, however, be appreciated that many youths come from impoverished backgrounds and no money will be available. Further, given the tensions around the court process and the problems that arise when parents pay for lawyers for their children, it may be preferable for the state not to look for reimbursement for this expense. It might make more policy sense for governments to look for parental financial contributions for youths taken into state care, provided parents have the means.

D. DELIVERY OF LEGAL SERVICES

Under section 11(5) of the *YOA*, if a judge "directs" that representation is to be provided, it is the responsibility of the provincial attorney general to establish a scheme to provide representation, and a number of different models for delivery of legal services to youths have evolved.

A common element in legal aid schemes in Canada is the provision of duty counsel. Duty counsel are lawyers who are available at the court to provide summary assistance to any person lacking a lawyer, though they are not available at all courts, or are only available at certain times, for example, when first appearances are scheduled. Some duty counsel are staff lawyers hired by legal aid plans, but many are lawyers in private practice hired at an hourly rate. Duty counsel are often available to assist unrepresented individuals at bail hearings; to assist with obtaining an adjournment to give time to apply for legal aid or to retain a lawyer privately; in entering a plea; and at the time of sentencing. Duty counsel can generally meet individuals only for a brief time before court. They often have difficulty in properly assisting with matters like bail hearings or sentencing, and they certainly lack the time or resources to assist with a trial.

A duty-counsel scheme is preferable to having individuals appear in court without any legal representation, not only in terms of protecting legal rights and advising individuals, but also for court efficiency. However, many adolescents have difficulty in communicating effectively with unfamiliar adults, especially in the context of a rushed interview in an intimidating setting, and Canadian research indicates that adolescents often do not understand the role of duty counsel and may not appreciate the advice being provided in this setting.[16] These concerns are heightened if the duty counsel lacks familiarity with youth court and is inexperienced in dealing with adolescents.

Duty counsel can help a youth apply for legal aid or may make a request to a judge for a direction under section 11(4)(b) for representation by counsel. If a direction is made under section 11(4)(b) for the provision of counsel, duty counsel will not suffice, since a lawyer must have adequate time to meet with a youth and prepare for court.

The most common method for provision of legal services to youths is by lawyers in private practice, paid by the government. In most provinces, a youth can choose any lawyer who is willing to accept the relatively low fees paid pursuant to the legal aid plan scheme or the section 11(4)(b) representation plan. Because the fees are limited, some more experienced lawyers are unwilling to do much (or any) work under the government schemes, though some junior members of the bar may have practices based exclusively on this type of work.

In Manitoba, in an effort to reduce costs, the government has established a "block fee" scheme under which law firms bid on providing representation for fifty young offenders cases, and youths are directed exclusively to firms that have the "franchise." This block fee scheme only covers the less serious cases that do not qualify for legal aid and are the subject of a section 11(4)(b) order. While this scheme has reduced costs, it has been heavily criticized for its potential to reduce the quality

---

16   K. Catton & P. Erickson, *The Juvenile's Perception of the Role of Defence Counsel in Juvenile Court* (Working Paper) (Toronto: University of Toronto, Centre of Criminology, 1975), in N. Bala, H. Lilles, & G. Thomson, eds., *Canadian Children's Law* (Toronto: Butterworths, 1982) at 711.

of representation.[17] Perhaps not surprisingly, in Canada's current fiscal environment, other jurisdictions are studying the Manitoba scheme.

In some provinces, most notably Alberta, Saskatchewan, Nova Scotia, and Quebec, legal aid clinics have been established in larger cities that deal exclusively with youths. These clinics have staff lawyers and in some cases have access to clinic social workers to assist in dealing with cases. While youths charged with the most serious offences can choose to have government-paid counsel from private practice, the clinics deal with the majority of youth court cases in the cities where they have been established. A major motivation for having youth legal aid clinics is that they can be less expensive than other models of service delivery; youth clinics allow lawyers to specialize and establish a sufficiently large case-load in the area that they can operate more efficiently than lawyers in private practice.[18] It is also possible to recruit a relatively small group of lawyers with personalities and background that suit them to this type of work, and to ensure that they have knowledge of the law, facilities, and programs that affect youth. There are, however, concerns that the existence of clinics reduces the opportunity for youths to choose a lawyer, and that staff lawyers might come to see themselves more as "civil servants" than as advocates for often disadvantaged youths. There may also be some stigma attached to the clients of legal aid clinics, since they may be more readily identified as disadvantaged youths.

Given the importance of legal representation in the justice system and the financial implications for lawyers in private practice of any extension of legal aid clinics, it is scarcely surprising that the subject of clinics — their costs, independence, and effectiveness — remain controversial.[19] There is Canadian research which indicates that clinic lawyers

---

17   See L. Keller, "Legal Aid Manitoba to seek bids from lawyers for blocks of YOA s. 11 cases" *Lawyers Weekly* (23 April 1993) 2; and T. Onyshko, "LSUC committees will study proposals to reduce fees paid by Legal Aid Plan" *Lawyers Weekly* (18 February 1994) 1.

18   J. Mahony, "Province's public defender pilot project could lead to dismantling of legal aid, Alta. lawyers fear" *Lawyers Weekly* (25 February 1994) 2; and "Alberta may keep youth court public defenders" *Law Times* (10–16 February 1997). A recently completed study in Ontario has recommended more extensive use of specialized youth clinics in that province, along with some continuing representation by lawyers in private practice: Ontario Legal Aid Review, *Report of the Ontario Legal Review: A Blueprint for Publicly Funded Legal Services* (Toronto: Government of Ontario, 1997) [known as the *McCamus Report*, after the chair], 158.

19   See, e.g., C. Schmitz, "Welfare council slams legal aid system," *Lawyers Weekly* (27 January 1995) 1; M. Zapf, "B.C. Bar raps discussion paper on public defended feasibility" *Lawyers Weekly* (28 February 1992) 14.

can provide less costly service and equally or more effective service (as measured by findings of guilt and length of sentence) for adult clients.[20] While none of the research relates directly to adolescent clients, there may be special reasons for clinics for adolescents, since they often lack the ability to make a meaningful selection of a lawyer and have special needs that support staff and lawyers in a clinic may be able to address better than lawyers in private practice. It is, however, apparent that if the clinics are not adequately funded, staff lawyers may become over-burdened and unable to provide adequate representation.

At least in theory, section 11 of the *YOA* assures every youth who wants representation the right to have a lawyer, whether from a clinic or private practice. However, in reality many youths have their cases resolved without legal representation. The process for obtaining counsel under the *YOA* can be long and frustrating, often requiring several court appearances and a rejection by legal aid before a court will "direct" that representation should be provided. Even if parents are not required to contribute to the cost of a lawyer, they may well feel humiliated by the whole experience and encourage a youth to "get things over with" without having a lawyer.

A disturbing recent study of the Saskatoon Youth Court revealed that more than one-third of all youths entered a plea and were sentenced without having a lawyer present. Although many of those youths were charged with less serious property offences, some were charged with violent offences or were being dealt with in situations where pre-trial detention or a custodial sentence were imposed. There is an indication in this study that Aboriginal youth, who were more likely to appear without a parent or guardian, were also more likely not to have a lawyer. Further, Aboriginal male youths who appeared without counsel were more likely to be detained at a bail hearing than those who had representation at the bail hearing. The researchers conclude:

> Youths who plead guilty without counsel may do so out of ignorance, apathy or the belief that a lawyer will make no difference in the outcome — especially if they have a prior conviction. . . . a lack of familiarity with procedure and available dispositions may compound the decision not to elect counsel. . . . youth often plead guilty to avoid prolonging proceedings by seeking an adjournment to obtain legal counsel. . . . Given that a youth is most likely to plead guilty, to be held for [pre-trial detention at a] show cause [hearing] and to be sentenced to

---

20   National Council on Welfare, *Legal Aid and the Poor* (Ottawa: The Council, 1995) at 50.

custody when appearing without a lawyer, it is imperative that efforts be made to have youth represented by counsel on first appearance and throughout court proceedings.[21]

Section 11(7) of the *YOA* allows a judge to permit a youth who is not represented by a lawyer to be "assisted" by an adult whom the judge considers "suitable," such as a parent or relative. While such assistance may be preferable to having a youth appear in court without any help, judges are reluctant to use this provision. As noted by one Ontario judge:

> The court may be sensitive to the fact that a young person may prefer to be assisted by a known and trusted adult rather than professional counsel, but also alert to the dangers of an overbearing adult imposing upon the young person in a possibly well-intentioned but misguided manner. . . .
>
> Even on a relatively minor charge where the young person wishes to plead guilty, I would find it difficult to be satisfied that a parent, for instance, has the required expertise and objectivity to properly advise the young person. . . . Parents may be guided by many motives, including the seeking of help for a troubled young person and encourage a totally inappropriate guilty plea, or on the other hand be so unaware of the legal issues as to believe that a defence exists [that] is not valid. I would expect that very few lay advisors will be accepted by the courts as appreciating the complexity or seriousness of the matters . . . and courts may refuse to permit the adult to assist the youth and might well, at that time, remind the youth of the right to retain counsel . . . although . . . there is no authority, aside from the issue of insanity at the time of trial, to force counsel upon a young person who does not wish to be represented.[22]

These judicial concerns about allowing non-lawyers to assist youths also reflect on the problem of youths being totally unrepresented in court. If governments make efforts to have parents or youths pay for counsel, this may well result in more youths appearing without lawyers and may also produce more cases where youths request the assistance of parents in court. Given the complexity and potential consequences of youth court proceedings, this would be unfortunate.

---

21 S.A. Fortugno & M. Rogstad, *A Socio-Legal Analysis of Youth Justice in Saskatoon: The Behaviour of the System Toward Aboriginal and Non-Aboriginal Youth* (Saskatoon: John Howard Society of Saskatchewan, 1994) at 61.
22 *R. v. A.(H.E.)* (13 June 1984), (Ont. Prov. Ct.) [unreported] [summarized [1984] W.D.F.L. 1024], Pedlar Prov. J.

E. CONTROVERSY OVER THE ROLE OF DEFENCE COUNSEL IN YOUTH COURT

There is considerable disagreement among lawyers about the role that they should adopt in representing youths charged pursuant to the *YOA*. The governing body for the legal profession in Ontario, the Law Society of Upper Canada, issued a report in 1981 advising lawyers about the role that they should adopt in representing juveniles charged under the *JDA*.:

> Even where a child may lack the capacity to properly instruct counsel, there is no place . . . for counsel representing a child [charged under the *JDA*] to argue what is in his opinion in the best interests of the child. Counsel should not be deciding whether training school would be "good" for the child . . . it is advice with respect to the legal rights of the child which is being provided to the child, not to the parents, not to the court, and not to society, but to the child.[23]

A 1986 Manitoba study indicates that many lawyers who represent youths charged pursuant to the *YOA* are adopting this approach, often known as the "advocate" role, which involves taking instructions from an adolescent client and treating that client similar to an adult.[24] The coming into force of the *YOA* in 1984, with its clearly criminal orientation replacing the welfare approach of the *Juvenile Delinquents Act,* has probably caused more lawyers to adopt the "advocate" role. Lawyers taking this approach generally emphasize the right to remain silent and advise against cooperation with the police at their initial meeting with a youth. At trial, they will raise any legal defence or challenge (provided that the client does not instruct counsel to plead guilty), for example, seeking to exclude inadmissible evidence, even if the youth is in fact guilty. While the advocate may sometimes advise the youth that the Crown's case appears strong and suggest that a guilty plea may be appropriate, especially if the prosecutor is prepared to drop some charges or offer a recommendation for a reduction as part of a plea bargain, the decision about how to plead is the client's. At the sentencing stage, the advocate will again follow the client's instructions, which will often involve seeking the least severe or intrusive disposition.

---

23   Law Society of Upper Canada, *Report of the Subcommittee on Legal Representation of Children* (Toronto: The Society, 1981).

24   H.A. Milne, R. Linden, & R. Kueneman, "Advocate or Guardian: The Role of Defence Counsel in Youth Justice" in R.R. Corrado *et al.*, eds., *Juvenile Justice in Canada: A Theoretical and Analytical Assessment* (Toronto: Butterworths, 1992) 313.

While many defence lawyers see their role as solely that of an "advocate" for the youth, others still adopt more of a "guardian" role, preferring to take into account the views of probation officers, social workers, and parents as well as those of the youth, in formulating a position that is based on the lawyer's assessment of the "best interests" of the young person. As one Manitoba lawyer with experience in representing youths commented: "My attitude to the practice of law is not adversarial. I am aware of the legal issues and the fact that I am a lawyer, but I am concerned with rehabilitation. I do take the role of a stern parent."[25] An American lawyer who favours this approach commented:

> In juvenile court cases "beating the rap" is . . . not only detrimental to the public safety but is likely to prove harmful to the juvenile offender himself. To assume that it is best for juveniles who have committed serious violations of the law to be exonerated on technical legal grounds is tantamount to endorsing the notion that juveniles should be free to steal, commit burglary, or engage in other serious offences with complete immunity.[26]

Lawyers adopting a guardian role will attempt to achieve an acquittal if the youth denies guilt, but they may not be as aggressive in pursuing more "technical" defences (for example, by raising evidentiary issues). The guardian role may be especially significant at the dispositional stage, with the lawyer seeking a sentence that promotes rehabilitation, even if it is not the least restrictive alternative and the youth does not want it; the lawyer taking this approach may aim to persuade the client that the disposition is in the youth's "best interests."

Many lawyers are not purely "advocates" or "guardians" but adopt an approach that may have elements of both and vary with the nature of the case, the age and attitude of the young person, and the stage of the proceedings. These lawyers may be more inclined to take an advocate's stance prior to a finding of guilt, strictly protecting the youth's legal rights, but more of a guardian's approach at the sentencing stage, attempting to persuade a young client to accept a "rehabilitative" disposition.

It is apparent that members of the defence bar have differing views about their role in youth court, and sometimes individual lawyers will vary their approach from one case to another, depending on the circumstances of the case and of the youth. In some measure, the uncertainty

---

25   *Ibid.* at 333.
26   D. Bogen, "Beating the Rap in Juvenile Court" (1980) 31:3 Juv. & Fam. Ct. J. 19 at 21.

of some defence lawyers towards their role in youth court may reflect the "ambivalence" of the YOA and society as a whole about the question of how to balance concerns with due process against the special needs and vulnerability of youth. Although the YOA generally places much more emphasis on due process than the JDA, supporting the adoption by lawyers of an advocate's role, some provisions of the YOA might suggest that a guardian role is sometimes appropriate. In particular, section 13(7) provides that a judge may order that a medical or psychological assessment, prepared for such purposes as a transfer hearing or sentencing, not be disclosed to the youth whom it concerns if the judge is "satisfied . . . that disclosure of . . . the report would seriously impair the treatment or recovery of the young person or would be likely to endanger the life or safety of, or result in serious psychological harm to, another person." While the youth may be denied access to the report, in whole or part, counsel for the youth will have access to the complete report but is not permitted to discuss it with the client. This provision is intended to promote the youth's well-being (or protect the safety of others) but compromises the youth's ability to instruct counsel fully and effectively in the proceedings. Counsel may have considerable difficulty in knowing how to respond to the report without having information and instructions from the client. Such reports may be influential in the proceedings, and, as one Crown prosecutor pointed out, this provision "places counsel for the young person in the impossible position of having access to information that cannot be divulged to the client."[27]

Lawyers inevitably make many decisions about the handling of a case without seeking specific instructions from their clients — for example, about tactics relating to evidentiary and advocacy issues — but major decisions, in particular about whether to plead guilty or not guilty, should be made by the client. One issue that sometimes causes lawyers for children and adolescents some difficulty is obtaining "instructions" from their young clients. In some situations, a youth may not want to decide about an issue on which the lawyer is seeking instructions, or the youth may be ambivalent or inconsistent. A lawyer may also be concerned about the intellectual or emotional "capacity" of an adolescent to appreciate fully the consequences of a decision.

The American Bar Association (ABA) has developed a detailed set of professional standards for lawyers who are representing "children" (that is, those under eighteen) in delinquency and protection proceed-

---

27   J.C. Pearson, "Legal Representation under the Young Offenders Act" in A.W. Leschied, P.G. Jaffe, & W. Willis, eds., The Young Offenders Act: A Revolution in Canadian Juvenile Justice (Toronto: University of Toronto Press, 1991) 114 at 123.

ings.[28] The ABA recognizes that a child's capacity to give instructions to a lawyer is in significant measure affected by the child's relationship with the lawyer and the information received from the lawyer. The lawyer should provide a clear explanation of the child's position and the choices that the child has, as well as giving an indication of the possible consequences of different choices. All communication should take account of the individual child's age, level of education, cultural context, and degree of language skill. An apparent lack of capacity should be viewed as "contextual, incremental and may be intermittent." That is, the child's capacity to provide instructions may increase over time, and, even if a child fails to give clear instructions at one point, the lawyer should attempt to seek instructions later. The ABA also suggests that in some cases a lawyer may need the assistance of a social worker or other professional to communicate effectively with a child. Ultimately, if a child is unable to give instructions, the lawyer should advocate for the "least restrictive intervention."[29]

None of the governing bodies of the legal profession in Canada has provided the kind of detailed direction for lawyers that has been provided by the ABA in the United States. However, a Quebec bar committee issued a lengthy consultation paper dealing with a range of issues related to the legal representation of children. This committee suggests that a lawyer must adopt an "adviser and attorney" (or "advocate") role and follow the directions of a youth with the capacity to give instructions, and that, consistent with the YOA, there should be a presumption that a youth who is twelve or older has the capacity to instruct a lawyer. The Quebec committee did not deal explicitly with the question of the role that a lawyer for a youth charged under the YOA should adopt if a youth lacks the capacity to give instructions, though it indicated that a lawyer should always ensure that the "rights and procedural guarantees of the child are respected."[30] The committee noted that the general code of ethics for lawyers applies to those representing children and youth, but it urged the adoption of special provisions for lawyers involved in these cases. The need for special ethical guidelines is greatest when

---

28 American Bar Association, Council for Family Law Section, "Proposed Standards of Practice for Lawyers Who Represent Children in Abuse and Neglect Cases" (1995) 29 Fam. L. Q. 375; and IJA-ABA Joint Commission on Juvenile Justice Standards, *Juvenile Justice Standards Relating to Counsel for Private Parties* (New York: The Commission, 1990) [*Juvenile Justice*].

29 *Juvenile Justice, ibid.* at 82.

30 Quebec Bar Committee, "The Legal Representation of Children" (1996) 13 Can J. Fam. L. 49 at 105.

younger children are involved and proceedings are civil and focusing on the "best interests" of the child.

For lawyers representing youths charged under criminal legislation like the *YOA*, the professional-conduct rules governing those who represent adults charged with criminal offences offer significant direction. The Ontario and Quebec bar committees make clear that lawyers owe the same duties of advocacy and confidentiality to youths as they do to adult clients. The lawyer's role is to present the youth's views and protect the youth's rights in court; no other professional involved in the process has this role. Despite the importance of this general guidance, it would be helpful to provide lawyers with some specific direction on such issues as a child's capacity to instruct a lawyer and the relationship between the lawyer for a youth and the parents.

F. CONCERNS ABOUT THE EFFECTIVENESS OF COUNSEL IN YOUTH COURT

While most youths who are charged under the *YOA* are represented by lawyers, there are concerns that some of these lawyers may not be communicating adequately with their young clients and may not be providing them with as effective representation as these youths should receive. These concerns about effectiveness, as well as about the costs of due process, both in financial and human terms, have led some observers to argue that there should be fewer lawyers involved in the youth court process. Others, however, advocate for the continued involvement of lawyers for youths, though suggesting that there should be better training and supervision for this type of sensitive, important work.

While there is not enough research to get a clear picture of how effectively lawyers in Canada are representing youths charged under the *YOA*, there are indications that some lawyers may not be as effective as they should be. One study of duty counsel from the 1970s revealed many lawyers did not provide juveniles with an adequate explanation of their role, and as a result the youths did not really understand the function of defence counsel.[31] Effective communication with adolescents generally requires more skill and patience than communication with an adult. Some lawyers may, for example, not be taking the time to interview their young clients properly before court.

---

31   Catton & Erickson, above note 16.

In one reported 1996 Ontario case, the mother of a youth charged with sexual assault approached a lawyer to represent the youth.[32] The youth was in pre-trial detention. The lawyer agreed to represent the youth, but he failed to attend at several bail hearings and adjournments, and the youth remained in detention pending trial. The lawyer only spoke to the youth by phone, explaining: "I don't do jails." The lawyer apparently felt that the fee received from legal aid for representation did not make a personal visit economically justifiable. The lawyer first met the youth in person on the day of the trial. The youth was convicted of sexual assault and appealed. While the Ontario Court of Appeal was critical of defence counsel's "somewhat casual approach," the Court ruled that this did not affect the outcome in the particular case. This may well have been a correct legal decision, but one can also appreciate why the youth was not satisfied with the representation provided.

Various researchers have carried out studies to determine the effect that the presence of counsel has on the outcomes of cases. This type of research is difficult to do in a methodologically sound fashion, since youths who have more serious or complicated cases are more likely to have lawyers, and merely comparing the outcomes of cases where youths had a lawyer with those where they were unrepresented does not offer a proper basis for comparison. Some researchers attempt to "control" for the nature and seriousness of the case, but such controls are not easy to devise and apply. Another complicating factor is that the effect of representation may depend on the attitude of the judges, with judges who are more "due process" oriented giving greater effect to the type of representation and argument that a lawyer is likely to bring to the court.[33]

A major research project conducted in several Canadian cities in 1981–82, when the *JDA* was still in effect, revealed that juveniles with legal representation were more likely to enter not guilty pleas and had fewer convictions than unrepresented juveniles.[34] Once a juvenile was convicted, the presence of a lawyer seemed to have limited impact on the sentence. In some localities the presence of counsel was associated

---

32   See, e.g., *R. v. B.(L.C.)*(1996), 27 O.R. (3d) 686 (C.A.).

33   See, e.g., S.H. Clarke & G.G. Koch, "Juvenile Court: Therapy or Crime Control, and Do Lawyers Make a Difference?" (1980) 14 Law & Soc. Rev. 263.

34   P. J. Carrington & S. Moyer, "The Effect of Defence Counsel on Plea and Outcome in Juvenile Court" (1990) 32 Can J. Crim 621; P. J. Carrington & S. Moyer, "Legal Representation in Canadian Juvenile Courts: Its Nature, Extent and Determinants" (1992) 34 Can J. Crim. 51; and P. J. Carrington & S. Moyer, "The Impact of Legal Representation on Juvenile Court Dispositions" (1990) Canadian Sociology and Anthropology Annual Meeting.

with more severe sentences, while in other locales representation was associated with less severe sentences or appeared to have no impact. It is difficult to draw conclusions about the effect of counsel from these studies, since youths are more likely to seek legal representation if their case is serious or they intend to plead not guilty. As noted above, a 1994 Saskatchewan study found that Aboriginal male youth who appeared without representation were more likely to be detained at a bail hearing and to be sentenced to custody than those represented by a lawyer.[35]

A 1988 study of youth court judges in Ontario suggested that lawyers were generally effective in dealing with legal issues at the trial stage of proceedings but often failed to be involved actively in the disposition process. The researcher concluded:

> Both Crown and defence counsel are failing to provide effective assistance to the court with respect to appropriate dispositions. The comments of the judges amount to an indictment of the performance of counsel, particularly defence counsel. Judges report that most defence counsel failed to call character witnesses on behalf of the offender, failed to offer any statement by the offender to explain the offence, failed to produce independent evidence about the offender's special needs, and failed to provide detailed disposition recommendations suited to the offender.[36]

Beyond concerns about the effectiveness of legal representation in terms of securing more acquittals and less severe sentences, some observers question the effect of lawyers on the adolescents who appear in youth court. The lawyer will speak for the youth, often giving the youth a sense of "being spectator" in court. It is not uncommon to see adolescents in youth court who appear bored and disinterested in the proceedings. It may be argued that the increased involvement of lawyers as a result of the *YOA* results in youths sometimes feeling less responsible for their acts, first because they may be advised by their lawyer that they have a chance of "getting off" even though they are guilty, and secondly because they may feel disengaged from the court process, even when being sentenced.[37]

---

35 Fortugno & Rogstad, above note 21 at 61.
36 D.K. Hanscom, *The Dynamics of Disposition in Youth Court*, (LL.M. Thesis, University of Toronto, 1988), commenting on "Lawyers knock report suggesting counsel to blame for increase in YOA custody rate" *Law Times* (9–15 April 1990).
37 See, e.g., P. Gabor, I. Greene, & P. McCormick, "The Young Offenders Act: The Alberta Youth Court Experience in the First Year" (1986) 5 Can. J. Fam. L. 301; and J. Hackler, "The Impact of the Young Offenders Act" (1987) 29 Can. J. Crim. 205.

These types of concerns have led some to argue that there are too many lawyers involved in the youth court process: their presence is often ineffective and unnecessary, contributes to delay, and diverts resources from badly needed treatment for youths. In one widely reported speech in 1985, James Felstiner, a youth court judge in Ontario who had worked as a social worker before going to law school and being appointed as a judge, aroused controversy when he suggested that there was an excessive use of lawyers in youth court. The judge was concerned that the lawyers' "criminal court games" were causing delays and resulting in youths pleading not guilty even if they were admitting guilt. "[A] very great majority of children are guilty of their offence, or something close to it," he said, "I think a great majority don't need a lawyer."[38] These comments would not appear to reflect the views of most judges, and Judge Felstiner was criticized for making these remarks by the Ontario Judicial Council.[39]

Most judges recognize that the formal model of criminal justice contemplated by the *YOA*, with an emphasis on accountability and due process, requires the active involvement of lawyers. The proceedings in youth court are unlikely to be comprehensible to a youth without representation. A youth without representation is unlikely to understand the proceedings or their consequences and cannot meaningfully participate in the process.

While many youths who are charged are in fact guilty, the police sometimes charge the innocent, whether because of incompetence, bias, or excessive zeal. The consequence of having a criminal justice that respects individual liberty is that some who are in fact guilty are acquitted; a system that ensured that all of the truly guilty are convicted would inevitably also convict some who are in fact innocent. Defence counsel has an important role in ensuring that the justice system functions properly and that the rights of citizens, even young ones, are not violated. Defence counsel can also have a significant role at the dispositional stage, not only in calling evidence on behalf of the youth, but also in challenging the views of various professionals who are proposing to "help" the youths. Sometimes the good intentions of these professionals outstrip their expertise and intrusive dispositional plans are proposed

---

38 K. Makin, "Use of criminal lawyers in youth courts assailed," *[Toronto] Globe and Mail* (5 November 1985) A1 at A2.

39 M. Strauss, "Judge receives 'slap on wrist' for comments," *[Toronto] Globe and Mail* (15 February 1986) A16. Judge Felstiner claimed that his remarks were taken "out of context" but acknowledged that some of them were "badly expressed." See also (1986) *Criminal Lawyers Association Newsletter*, 1–3.

that may be unrealistic or unlikely to help the youth. There is, for example, a tendency for some "helping" professionals to minimize the harmful effects of a custodial placement in terms of peer abuse and transmission of negative values from other young offenders. Defence counsel needs to be aware of the availability and benefits of community-based dispositions, and should be prepared to challenge professionals who are recommending custody.

One of the most creative and satisfying roles that defence counsel can play is to help the youth to formulate plans that can be put before the youth court, in regard to pre-trial release, or at the time of disposition or disposition review. In order to be acceptable to the court, a plan should generally have a realistic chance of meeting the youth's needs, and this will usually require consultation with the parents and family as well as professionals and agencies. Even a lawyer who adopts a strong advocate stance at disposition — following a young client's instructions to seek the least intrusive sentence possible — is most likely to be effective if the judge is persuaded that a proposed disposition meets the needs of the youth that are related to the offending behaviour.

A Nova Scotia youth court judge remarked at a disposition review hearing:

> Counsel for an accused must take an active role in assisting the client, not a passive one. That is one of the purposes of ensuring counsel be available . . . under the *Young Offenders Act*. It is not simply the traditional criminal law role, and lawyers who work in Youth Court must be aware of this difference.[40]

The reason for having different expectations of counsel in youth court at the disposition stage rests, in part at least, on the difficulty that a youth will have in formulating a realistic plan without an experienced, knowledgable adviser and facilitator. Defence counsel, however, too rarely play this demanding role, lacking the interest, time, or knowledge and tending to rely on plans put forward by agents of the state, such as probation officers or correctional staff.

Defence counsel should have an important role in the youth justice system, but measures may be needed to improve the quality of representation that youths actually receive. Some lawyers who represent youth are excellent — sensitive, dedicated, and knowledgeable — but others may not be so satisfactory. One of the difficulties with the present system is that except where there are clinics, there are no screening, super-

---

40   *R. v. R.(K.)* (1987), 80 N.S.R. (2d) 61 at 64 (Youth Ct.), per Niedermayer J.Y.C.

vision, educational, or training requirements for lawyers who do this type of work. Adolescents are, in general, vulnerable and unsophisticated consumers of legal services; they may not be able to make an appropriate selection of a lawyer for their cases, and they may not be in a good position to assess the quality of services they are receiving or know how to complain if they are not receiving adequate representation.

These types of concerns led the Quebec bar committee to recommend a process for "accreditation" of lawyers who represent children and adolescents, as well as the creation of an "Ombudsman" office to supervise the provision of legal services to minors.[41] To be accredited, a lawyer would have to meet educational and training requirements. The 1997 Ontario Legal Aid Review made a similar recommendation: that those lawyers who do youth court work should be part of a "specialized defence panel . . . trained and evaluated in relation to this idea of expertise."[42] Lawyers who do this type of work should be aware of relevant services and facilities in their communities, as well as of applicable laws. They should also be familiar with the problems and developmental stages of adolescence and have an understanding of the role of the different professionals who work with young offenders. Finally, they should be able to communicate and work effectively with parents, bearing in mind the duty of confidentiality to their clients and the need to act only on the youth's instructions.

G. THE ROLE OF THE PROSECUTOR IN YOUTH COURT

Under the *Juvenile Delinquents Act* it was common for probation or police officers to appear for the Crown, with a lawyer appearing for the prosecution only in the most serious cases. The lack of legal representation generally did not seriously hinder the prosecution since the proceedings tended to be relatively informal and juveniles were often unrepresented. Further, judges under the *JDA* often tended to take on some of the prosecutorial functions,[43] and, for example, had the authority under section 9 of that Act to commence and decide an application

---

41   Quebec Bar Committee, above note 30 at 126.

42   Ontario Legal Aid Review, *Report of the Ontario Legal Aid Review: A Blueprint for Publicly Funded Legal Services* (Toronto: Government of Ontario), 158.

43   P.G. Erickson, "The Defence Lawyer's Role in Juvenile Court: An Empirical Investigation into Judges' and Social Workers' Points of View" (1974) 24 U.T.L.J. 126 at 138.

for transfer to adult court without a request coming from the Crown. With the enactment of the *YOA*, defence counsel began to appear regularly in youth court, and Crown prosecutors' offices felt that the Crown should also be represented by legally trained personnel, both to respond to the more legalistic demands of the Act and to be able to reply to arguments of defence lawyers.

There are now experienced, knowledgeable Crown prosecutors in some youth courts, but too often youth court (or "Kiddie's Court," as it is sometimes derisively called by justice system professionals) is given a low priority or viewed as a "training ground" in the Crown's office. Representation is often provided by articling students, junior lawyers, or part-time prosecutors. In some locales, less serious cases are still prosecuted by police officers.

While there may be some controversy over the role of defence counsel in youth court, there is agreement, at least in theory, about the role of the Crown prosecutor, whether in adult or youth court. As explained in *Boucher* v. *R.* by Rand J:

> It cannot be over-emphasized that the purpose of a criminal prosecution is not to obtain a conviction, it is to lay before a jury [or judge] what the Crown considers to be credible evidence relevant to what is alleged to be a crime. . . . The role of the prosecutor excludes any notion of winning or losing; his function is a matter of public duty . . . in public life there can be none charged with greater personal responsibility.[44]

Prosecutors play a dual role as both administrators of justice and advocates. While as advocates they have a responsibility to present the prosecution's case in "forcible and direct language," they must avoid being inflammatory or unfair.[45] As administrators of justice, Crown prosecutors have a responsibility to see that the innocent are not prosecuted or convicted, and they have a duty to discontinue a prosecution if there is not a reasonable likelihood that a conviction will be obtained. Sections 3(1)(d) and 4 of the *YOA* add the requirement that the prosecutor must give consideration to whether alternative measures should be used for a youth.

An important example of the difference between the prosecutor and the defence counsel is in regard to pre-trial disclosure. The courts, relying on the *Charter's* guarantees for a fair trial and the role of the prosecution in a criminal case, have held that there is an obligation on the Crown to

---

44   [1955] S.C.R. 16 at 23–24.
45   G. Mackenzie, *Lawyers and Ethics: Professional Responsibility and Discipline* (Toronto: Carswell, 1993) at 6–4.

disclose to the accused information obtained by the Crown in the course of investigating the offence, whether or not the Crown intends to put the evidence before the court.[46] Defence counsel has no corresponding duty and may decide not to reveal any information before trial.[47]

While Crown prosecutors work with the police and other agents of the state like probation officers, it is said that the prosecutor's only client is the "public." That is, unlike a defence counsel, who takes instructions from the accused, or a lawyer in a civil case who receives direction from the client, the Crown prosecutor generally decides what to do based on his or her own sense of justice, not on the basis of instructions from a client. If anything, it is the Crown prosecutor who gives directions, or at least advice, to the police about what evidence to obtain or whether to lay charges in a particular case. Local Crown prosecutors are not, however, independent in the way that judges are; they are accountable to the attorney general or minister of justice[48] and are subject to government policies, though they should not be subject to political interference.

The Crown prosecutor is not the lawyer for the complainant (or victim). Yet, while the Crown prosecutor should not be taking directions from victims and their families about how to handle a case, there have been concerns that too often these individuals have been left uninformed and unsupported in the criminal process. Recently there have been increased efforts to provide support and information for victims, in particular in cases involving violence or abuse, and especially for children (for example, to prepare them adequately for testifying in court and to reduce the trauma of the court experience).

At the disposition stage in youth court, the Crown prosecutor should be working with a number of different professionals, including police, mental-health professionals, social workers, and teachers, as well as the "provincial director" (probation and corrections staff), to ensure that all necessary evidence is before the court, and he or she should be advocating a disposition that meets the principles of the

---

46 *R. v. Stinchcombe*, [1991] 3 S.C.R. 326. The Crown may decline to disclose certain limited types of "privileged" information, such as the identity of an informer.

47 While in general in Canada there is no duty on the accused to provide any form of pre-trial disclosure, in limited circumstances, such as when the accused seeks to rely on alibi evidence to establish a defence, the failure to provide notice of this to allow the Crown to investigate before trial may affect the credibility of this type of evidence.

48 The primary responsibility for the prosecution of *YOA*, above note 10, cases rests with the provincial and territorial governments. Some offences, in particular those involving violations of drug laws, are the responsibility of federally appointed prosecutors.

YOA.[49] While much of the coordinating and planning for disposition, at least on the "government" side, will usually be done by the provincial director, at least in theory the Crown prosecutor has an important role in ensuring that appropriate information is before the court. The prosecutor should also offer submissions about an appropriate sentence, and, according to the principles of the YOA, this requires consideration of both the interests of society and the needs of youth.

In practice, however, many Crown prosecutors have heavy case loads and may not have the time to prepare adequately for court. These problems are compounded if the prosecutor is not familiar with the relevant laws, facilities, and programs. There is relatively little research about the effectiveness of prosecutors in youth court; however, research available indicates that, as with the concerns about the lack of involvement of defence lawyers in the disposition process, judges have expressed concern that some Crown prosecutors are "winging it" and contributing little to the sentencing process. This type of concern has led to calls for better training for Crown prosecutors who appear in youth court.[50]

FURTHER READINGS

BALA, N. et al., *State Responses to Youth Crime: A Consideration of Principles* (Ottawa: Canadian Research Institute for Law and the Family, 1993)

BALA, N. & H. LILLES, eds., *Young Offenders Service* (Toronto: Butterworths, 1984) (looseleaf), ss. 9:1:1 to 9:4:4

CORRADO, R. et al., eds., *Juvenile Justice in Canada: A Theoretical and Analytical Assessment* (Toronto: Butterworths, 1992), ch. 7

HARRIS, P.J., ed., *Young Offenders Act Manual* (Aurora: Canada Law Book, 1984) (looseleaf), ss. 11.1 to 11.15

IJA-ABA JOINT COMMISSION ON JUVENILE JUSTICE STANDARDS, *Juvenile Justice Standards Relating to Counsel for Private Parties* (New York: The Commission, 1990)

---

49   See, e.g., R. S. Stubbs, "The Role of the Lawyer in Juvenile Court" (1974) 6 Man. L.J. 65 at 82; and *Juvenile Justice*, above note 28.

50   Hanscom, above note 36; Ontario Social Development Council, *Young Offenders Act Dispositions: Challenges and Choices* (Toronto: The Council, 1988) at 129.

LESCHIED, A.W., P.G. JAFFE, & W. WILLIS, eds., *The Young Offenders Act: A Revolution in Canadian Juvenile Justice* (Toronto: University of Toronto Press, 1991), ch. 5

MACKENZIE, G., *Lawyers and Ethics: Professional Responsibility and Discipline* (Toronto: Carswell, 1993), chs. 6 and 7

MARTIN, G.A., & J.W. IRVING, *Essays on Aspects of Criminal Practice* (Toronto: Carswell, 1997), chs. 6 and 7

ONTARIO LEGAL AID REVIEW, *Report of the Ontario Legal Aid Review: A Blueprint for Publicly Funded Legal Services* (Toronto: Government of Ontario, 1997), vol. 1, c. 9 and vol. 3, c. 11

PLATT, P., *Young Offenders Law in Canada,* 2d ed. (Toronto: Butterworths, 1995), ch. 15

CHAPTER 7

THE YOUTH COURT PROCESS

A. YOUTH COURT PROCEEDINGS SUMMARY

Section 52 of the *Young Offenders Act* stipulates that proceedings in youth court are governed by the provisions of the *Criminal Code* that are applicable to "summary conviction offence[s]" in adult court, except to the extent that these provisions are "inconsistent" with the *YOA*. This means that youth court proceedings are in general less complex and more expeditious than those which are applicable to "indictable offence[s]" in adult court. More specifically, there are no preliminary inquiries, and trials in youth court are conducted by a judge alone, without a jury.

The drafters of the *YOA* felt that it is important for young persons to have the more expeditious resolution of their cases available through summary procedures, as opposed to the more complex procedures that apply to indictable offences. The courts have held that the failure to provide young persons with the right to trial by jury does not violate the provisions of the *Charter of Rights* which guarantee equality and the right to a jury trial to persons facing imprisonment of five years or more. In *R. v. L.(R.)*, the Ontario Court of Appeal upheld the provisions of the *YOA* which deny a youth the right to a jury trial, emphasizing that the maximum penalties are much less severe than those an adult may face for the same offences. Justice Morden wrote:

> . . . the Young Offenders Act is intended to provide a comprehensive system for dealing with young persons who are alleged to be in conflict with the law which is separate and distinct from the adult criminal jus-

tice system. While the new system is more like the adult system than was that under the Juvenile Delinquents Act, it nonetheless is a different system. As far as the aftermath of a finding of guilt is concerned, the general thrust of the Young Offenders Act is to provide for less severe consequences than those relating to an adult offender. . . . the establishment of the legal regime . . . for dealing with young persons, which is separate and distinct from the adult criminal justice system, is of sufficient importance to warrant the overriding of the equality right alleged to be infringed in this proceeding. . . .[1]

There is an important exception to the rule that there are no preliminary inquiries and no jury trials in youth court in cases where a youth is charged with murder. In 1995 the maximum sentence that a youth court could impose for murder was increased from five years less a day in custody to ten years.[2] The *Canadian Charter of Rights and Freedoms*, section 11(f), guarantees a person facing a maximum possible sentence of five years or longer the right to "the benefit of trial by jury." Accordingly, the *YOA* was amended, with section 19(4) to (6) added to allow a youth charged with murder in youth court to have the right to choose to have a preliminary inquiry and a trial by jury. Because of section 96 of the *Constitution Act, 1867*, a jury trial must be conducted by a federally appointed "superior court" judge (for example, Queen's Bench, or Superior or Supreme Court), albeit sitting as a "youth court judge" and subject to the provisions of the *YOA* governing such matters as the right to counsel and protection of privacy. As discussed in chapter 9, it is also possible for a youth facing a murder charge to be transferred to adult court pursuant to section 16 of the *YOA*; if this occurs there is also the right to a preliminary inquiry and a jury trial, but the superior court judge will be acting in the same capacity as in dealing with adults, and adult rules about such matters as publication of the name of the accused will apply.[3]

---

1 (1986), 52 C.R. (3d) 209 at 219 & 225 (Ont. C.A.); to the same effect, see *R. v. B. (S.)* (1989), 76 Sask. R. 308 (C.A.).

2 The *Young Offenders Act*, R.S.C. 1985, c. Y-1 [*YOA*], as originally enacted had a maximum sentence of three years in custody for murder, which was increased to five years less a day in 1992 and ten years in 1995 [s. 20(1)(k.1)].

3 One of the "youth" rules that continue to apply after transfer concerns the admission of statements under *ibid.*, s. 56. There are also special provisions governing the place of detention or custody, and the length of sentence for young persons who are transferred to adult court. These and other related issues are discussed in ch. 9.

B. SUMMARY AND INDICTABLE OFFENCES: CROWN ELECTION FOR HYBRID OFFENCES

Legislation that creates offences, like the *Criminal Code,* generally specifies whether an offence is indictable or summary, with a more severe maximum penalty if the offence is indictable. Some offences are "hybrid," generally with a maximum sentence of six to eighteen months' imprisonment if the case is proceeded with summarily, and a longer maximum penalty if the case is proceeded with by indictment. In cases involving adults charged with "hybrid" offences, the Crown prosecutor will usually "elect" (inform the court about the decision) whether to proceed summarily or by indictment before the accused enters a plea. If the Crown elects to proceed by indictment, there is a more severe maximum penalty, but the accused generally has the right to a preliminary inquiry and jury trial.

Although the *YOA* specifies that proceedings in youth court are to be "summary," offences in youth court retain their character as summary, hybrid, or indictable for such purposes as: the possibility of transfer to adult court; the maximum length of a custodial sentence[4]; the length of time that records concerning the offence may be kept; and the limitation period for commencing a prosecution.[5] Accordingly, it is common practice for the Crown prosecutor dealing with a hybrid charge to indicate to the judge and the accused, prior to the youth entering a plea, how the Crown "elects" to treat the charge.[6] If the Crown prosecutor fails to elect in regard to a hybrid charge in youth court, the charge will generally be treated as summary,[7] unless it is clear from the

---

4   The maximum penalty for an adult charged under a summary procedure is generally six months in prison, though with some hybrid offences like sexual assault the maximum sentence under a summary proceeding is eighteen months. The *YOA, ibid.,* s. 20(7) specifies that the maximum custodial sentence that may be imposed on a youth shall be no longer than that which could be imposed on an adult for the same offence.

5   The limitation period for a summary offence is generally six months [*Criminal Code,* R.S.C. 1985, c. C-46 [*Code*], s.786(2)], whereas if an offence is proceeded with by indictment there is generally no limitation period; see, e.g., *R. v. C.(F.),* [1995] O.J. No. 3832 (Prov. Div.) (QL).

6   If the Crown has no reasonable opportunity to elect prior to plea, a Crown election after plea may be accepted: *R. v. J.(H.W.)* (1992), 71 C.C.C. (3d) 516 (B.C.C.A.).

7   See *YOA,* above note 2, s. 27(2) [for appeal purposes hybrid offence treated as summary unless election]; *YOA,* s. 45(5) [for records purposes hybrid offence treated as summary unless election]; *R. v. M.(F.H.)* (1984), 30 Man. R. (2d) (Q.B.) [for maximum-sentence purposes, hybrid offence treated as summary unless election]; but see *Interpretation Act,* R.S.C. 1985, c. I–21, s. 34(2).

expiry of the six-month summary limitation period that the charge must be treated as indictable.[8]

C. ADJOURNMENTS AND DELAY

A youth court proceeding is generally commenced with an "information" being sworn before a justice of the peace and the youth being served with a summons, appearance notice, or other document requiring him or her to attend court on a specific date. As discussed in chapter 4, in cases involving more serious charges or a youth with a history of failing to attend court, the youth may be detained in custody pending trial, subject to the right to seek bail (or judicial interim release).

Some cases are resolved with a single court appearance by the youth, but only if the charge is less serious and referred to alternative measures or if the youth is prepared to plead guilty at first appearance in court. A guilty plea on a first appearance is likely only in less serious cases, since the youth is unlikely to have had an opportunity to consult fully with a lawyer before a first appearance, though there may be a brief meeting with duty counsel. If the case is more serious or the youth wants to obtain legal advice, the court will adjourn the proceedings to allow the youth time to consult a lawyer. Often several brief court appearances and adjournments are needed while a youth applies for legal aid and then finds a lawyer, or, if necessary, returns to court to obtain a direction for representation under section 11(4) of the *YOA*. There may be further adjournments while defence counsel obtains disclosure from the Crown, does research into the case, and decides how to advise the client. If a not guilty plea is entered, there must be a court appearance to set a trial date. The judge setting the trial date will try to ensure that there is sufficient court time available to complete the trial. With government funding constraints, courts are frequently very busy and trial dates are sometimes set months away, or a trial has to be conducted on several different dates spread over a period of weeks or even months.

The adjournments and delays common in the Canadian justice system are a concern in dealing with adults, and even more so for adolescents whose lives develop and change and who have a greater sense of immediacy than adults. A slow judicial response in youth court is highly problematic, both in terms of delaying any rehabilitative treatment through the youth justice system and for weakening any deterrent impact from involvement in the youth justice system.

---

8   *R. v. B.(I.)* (1994), 20 O.R. (3d) 341 (C.A.).

In *R. v. M.(G.C.)* the Ontario Court of Appeal indicated that the right of an accused person to a trial "within a reasonable time," guaranteed by section 11(b) of the *Charter of Rights*, has special significance for young persons when judges are considering so-called "*Askov* applications"[9] to determine whether proceedings should be stayed because of an unreasonable delay in having a case brought to trial. While the Ontario Court of Appeal in *M.(G.C.)* declined to impose a fixed judicial "limitation period" within which youth court proceedings need to be completed, Justice Osborne remarked:

> There is a particular need to conclude youth court proceedings without unreasonable delay, consistent with the goals of the *Young Offenders Act.* . . . it seems to me that, as a general proposition, youth court proceedings should proceed to a conclusion more quickly than those in the adult criminal justice system. Delay, which may be reasonable in the adult criminal justice system, may not be reasonable in the youth court. There are sound reasons for this. They include the well established fact that the ability of a young person to appreciate the connection between behaviour and its consequences is less developed than an adult's. For young persons, the effect of time may be distorted. If treatment is required and is to be made part of the *Young Offenders Act* disposition process, it is best begun with as little delay as is possible.
>
> From a conceptual standpoint, the basis of the need to try young persons with reasonable dispatch is best analyzed and understood if it is viewed as a part of the consideration of prejudice, one of the four factors referred to in *Askov*. These four factors have to be balanced in each case to determine if an accused, young or old, has been brought to trial within a reasonable time.[10]

---

9   The term "*Askov* application" refers to the Supreme Court of Canada decision in *R. v. Askov*, [1990] 2 S.C.R. 1199, where the Supreme Court invoked s. 11(b) of the *Canadian Charter of Rights and Freedoms*, Part 1 of the *Constitution Act, 1982*, being Schedule B to the *Canada Act 1982* (U.K.), 1982, c. 11 [*Charter*], to issue a stay of proceedings where there had been an "unreasonable delay" in having a trial. In determining whether a delay was unreasonable, the court should consider: the duration of the delay; the explanation for the delay; waiver of delay by the accused; and any prejudice to the accused arising from the delay. *R. v. Morin*, [1992] 1 S.C.R. 771, has increased the percent emphasis placed on the prejudice to the accused, though it is clearly not the only factor.

10   (1991), 3 O.R. (3d) 223 at 230–31 (C.A.). D. Hendrick, "Processing Time in Youth Courts, 1986–87 to 1989–90" (1991) 11:4 Juristat 1, reported that, in 1989–90, 33 percent of young offenders cases were resolved on first appearance (80 percent were guilty pleas); 70 percent of cases were resolved in two months or less, with a median time resolution of twenty-three days, an increase of two days from 1986–87. Ontario is not included in these Statistics Canada data.

Justice Osborne went on to suggest, as an "administrative guide-line," that "in general, youth court cases should be brought to trial within five to six months, after the neutral period required to retain and instruct counsel, obtain disclosure, *etc.*" However, it is interesting to observe that in *R. v. M.(G.C.)* the Court of Appeal refused to stay pro-ceedings in which there was a delay of over ten months from the setting of the trial date until the commencement of the trial.

In its brief 1992 decision in *R. v. D.(S.)*, the Supreme Court of Can-ada noted that "account [must] be taken of the fact that charges against young offenders [should] be proceeded with promptly, [but] it [the youthfulness of the accused] is merely one of the factors to be balanced with others."[11] In that case the Supreme Court refused to grant a stay despite the fact that it took two and a half years for the youths to be brought to trial, but the delay was largely due to a transfer hearing and two subsequent appeals of the original transfer decision. The Supreme Court accepted that this type of delay was inherent in cases where the Crown seeks transfer and there are appeals. However, a delay of that length would not be acceptable in an ordinary youth court case.

The issue of "*Askov* applications" in youth court remains conten-tious.[12] Efforts have been made by judges and governments since the early 1990s to reduce delays in courts, and in recent years judges have not been quick to invoke the *Charter* to stay a proceeding because of delay. However, there continue to be cases where there are long delays and the courts accept that "prejudice more strongly must apply when young people are involved."[13] But it is still clear that a delay which may be constitutionally acceptable is far longer than one that is optimum in terms of adolescent development and needs.

---

11   *R. v. D.(S.)*, [1992] 2 S.C.R. 161 at 162, rev'g (1991), 4 O.R. (3d) 225 (C.A.).

12   In *R. v. S.(M.T.)*, (1991), (N.S. Youth Ct.) [unreported] [summarized *Lawyers Weekly* (7 June 1991) 24] Niedermayer Prov. J. held that s. 11(b) of the *Charter*, above note 9, should be invoked when the police waited almost a year to execute an arrest warrant issued in connection with a young person's failure to appear on theft charges. In staying the charges, the judge observed that this was a case where the police failed to make "reasonable, concerted efforts" to locate the youth and compel his attendance.

13   *R. v. B.(J.)*, [1995] O.J. No. 3113 (Prov. Div.) (QL), Sheppard Prov. J. The judge invoked s. 11(b) of the *Charter, ibid.*, to stay youth court proceedings that took nineteen months from the alleged offence to come to trial; the first trial that was scheduled resulted in a mistrial due to the failure of the Crown to provide adequate disclosure.

D. PREPARING FOR PLEA: DISCLOSURE OF INFORMATION

A lawyer consulted by a youth who is charged with an offence will generally be reluctant to give much advice about how to plead until he or she has had an opportunity to obtain "disclosure" from the Crown prosecutor. The courts have held that, as an aspect of the *Charter of Rights* guarantee to make a "full answer and defence," all accused persons, including youths, have a right to disclosure of information obtained by the police in the course of their investigation.[14] The right of the accused is quite broad and includes all information that the Crown intends to introduce in court as well as material in the possession of the Crown that will not be used as part of its case, whether the information is helpful to the accused or the prosecution.

Generally, disclosure of the Crown's information will be given to a youth's lawyer under the supervision of a Crown prosecutor. There are a few narrow exceptions to the rule about disclosure. For example, some information is "privileged," like the name of a police informer — one who provides a "tip" and who will not be called as a witness in court. If the defence counsel and prosecutor disagree about whether there has been satisfactory disclosure or whether some information is privileged, a judge may be required to resolve their disagreement. If the police discover new information as a result of an investigation continuing, the defence lawyer must be informed of this after the initial disclosure session. A failure by the Crown adequately to disclose may result in a case being adjourned to allow disclosure to occur, or, if the failure is more serious and cannot be fairly remedied by an adjournment, a mistrial may be declared or the prosecution may be stayed by a judge.[15]

A defence lawyer who has had disclosure will be in a better position to advise a client about the strength of the Crown's case and about whether the client should consider pleading guilty, though the ultimate decision about how to plead should be made by the client, even if the client is an adolescent. Sometimes the defence lawyer will need to do some legal research or make some inquiries before advising a client about how to plead.

---

14   *R. v. Stinchcombe*, [1991] 3 S.C.R. 326.

15   In *R. v. B.(S.)* (1990), 75 O.R. (2d) 646 (Fam. Ct.) a mistrial was declared when it was discovered that the Crown had inadvertently failed to give complete disclosure; the case provides a description of disclosure practices and policies in a youth case.

In certain types of cases, especially those involving sexual offences, in order to prepare for trial, defence counsel will want to have access to information in the records of third parties, like the therapist for a victim of an alleged offence. Or defence counsel may want disclosure of school records or child-protection files about an alleged victim or witness, in the hope that there may be information that will impeach that person's credibility. This type of information is often very personal, particularly if it is material that was shared with a therapist or other counsellor; as a result, those affected may feel threatened if such information is disclosed, especially to the lawyer for the accused in a criminal case. Nevertheless, there may be cases in which this type of information could be significant for a criminal trial.

In *R. v. O'Connor*[16] the Supreme Court of Canada held that an accused can get a pre-trial court order allowing access to records in the possession of third parties, but the court has to be satisfied that the information in the records is likely to be "relevant" — that is, that there is a reasonable possibility that the information is logically probative to an issue at trial or to the competence of a witness to testify. If considered "relevant," the judge should examine the records and determine whether they should be disclosed, weighing the privacy interests of the person to whom they relate against the right of the accused to a fair trial. Before the court makes an initial decision, the person to whom the records relate as well as the professional or agency that made the records should have notice that a court will consider this issue; they should also have the right to contest the application for disclosure.[17] The court may impose conditions on the disclosure to a lawyer for the accused to ensure that it is used only for the court proceedings and not further disseminated.

E. PLEAS AND PLEA BARGAINING: *YOA*, SECTION 19

Most youth court charges do not in fact result in trials but rather are resolved by guilty pleas, or the charges are dropped by the Crown before the case comes to trial. Frequently the youth recognizes that an offence has occurred and wishes to plead guilty. The youth's decision must be

---

16 [1995] 4 S.C.R. 441.
17 *A.(L.L.) v. B.(A.)*, [1995] 4 S.C.R. 536. *An Act to Amend the Criminal Code (Production of Records in Sexual Offence Proceedings)*, S.C. 1997, c. 30, in force 12 May 1997, clarifies some of the issues related to disclosure of records concerning a complainant or witness that are in the possession of third parties.

respected by defence counsel, even if the lawyer feels that some of the Crown's evidence is weak or that there may be some basis for achieving an acquittal. However, counsel has a duty to ensure that a youth understands the consequences of a guilty plea and is not, for example, merely giving in to parental pressure to plead guilty.

If a guilty plea is entered in court, the Crown prosecutor will read a summary of the evidence against the youth. The youth and defence counsel will be asked if they agree with the facts as alleged by the Crown. If there is a substantial disagreement about a significant fact, there may have to be a trial, though typically minor disagreements are resolved by the Crown amending its statement.

Section 19 of the *YOA* has a special provision requiring a judge in youth court to be satisfied that the facts read by the Crown at the time of a guilty plea support the charge. If the facts do not reveal that all material elements of the offence have been committed, the judge must enter a plea of not guilty and conduct a trial. Judges in adult court do not have the obligation to make this type of inquiry. This provision recognizes that youths may not understand the charges that they face or appreciate the significance of a guilty plea as fully as an adult.

It is not uncommon for a guilty plea to be the product of a "plea bargain" (or "resolution discussions"). A "plea bargain" is typically the result of informal discussions between the Crown prosecutor and the lawyer representing the accused about how to resolve a case. These discussions may occur at a session at which the Crown is disclosing information, or informally at the courthouse. Sometimes a plea bargain will be made partway through a trial. Increasingly, there are more formal "pre-trial conferences" where the lawyers meet with a judge to narrow the issues in dispute and discuss a possible resolution. A judge may help focus the discussion, and, if counsel reach an agreement, the judge may impose a sentence in accordance with their resolution, though if the case is not settled the judge from the pre-trial conference ordinarily cannot preside at the trial.

Before entering into a plea bargain, the Crown prosecutor may consult the investigating officer, and perhaps even the victim, but the prosecutor is entitled to make a decision about a plea bargain without consulting anyone. The discussions between the Crown prosecutor and the lawyer for the youth may produce an agreement to plead guilty to certain charges in exchange for dropping of other charges or an agreement that there will be a "joint submission" or request by the Crown to the court for a particular disposition. If there is a plea bargain resulting in a "joint submission" concerning disposition, the judge is not bound to impose the disposition agreed to by counsel, though the court usually accepts it. In some cases the two lawyers will meet privately with the judge for an "off-the-record" conversation to ascertain whether the judge is likely to accept the joint submission as regarding disposition.

Sometimes the Crown offers the accused some advantage (such as dropping some charges or offering a joint submission as to disposition) in exchange for the accused testifying against a co-accused or producing some evidence (such as the gun used in a killing). At least in theory it is only the Crown prosecutor and not the police who can enter into a plea bargain with the accused, since it is the prosecutor who is responsible for the case in court. The Supreme Court of Canada has made clear that the prosecutor and police have a duty to ensure that the accused has a full opportunity to have legal advice before accepting a plea bargain; they should not attempt to have the accused accept an offer for a plea bargain when defence counsel is not available: "[T]o the extent that the plea bargain is an integral element of the Canadian criminal process, the Crown and its officers engaged in the plea bargaining process must act honourably and forthrightly."[18] If there is a clear agreement and the accused has carried out his or her side of the bargain, the courts will not allow the Crown to renege on the deal.[19]

Plea bargaining remains controversial in Canada,[20] but it is a common practice. From the perspective of the Crown prosecutor, plea bargaining reflects the need to try to resolve a significant number of cases without trials. There is not enough court time for every accused person to have a trial, and a guilty plea can spare victims from having to testify. From the Crown perspective, plea bargaining also offers the assurance of a finding of guilt for at least some charges while a trial has the possibility of resulting in a total acquittal. There are also advantages to accused persons from having more certainty about the likely outcome and often a less severe sentence than might occur if there is a trial.

There is, however, a need for some controls over plea bargaining, as illustrated by R. v. K.(S.), a 1995 Ontario case where a youth was facing ten charges of sexual assault.[21] The Crown prosecutor offered to drop six of them and support a recommendation for a non-custodial disposition if the youth would plead guilty to the four least serious charges. The defence lawyer met with the youth and his parents; while stressing that the

---

18 R. v. Burlingham,[1995] 2 S.C.R. 206 at 230–31, Iacobucci J.
19 R. v. Agozzino, [1970] 1 O.R. 480 (C.A.); see also R. v. D.(E.) (1990), 73 O.R. (2d) 758 (C.A.).
20 See, e.g., "Plea bargain slammed" Southam Newspapers (30 November 1996) concerning criticism of a plea bargain for a seventeen-year-old youth initially charged with second degree murder in the shooting death of his girlfriend. The Crown accepted a guilty plea to a manslaughter charge with a Crown recommendation for two years in youth custody.
21 (1995), 24 O.R. (3d) 199 (C.A.).

decision about how to plead rested with the youth, the lawyer outlined the "dangers of seeking to defend the more serious counts and the likelihood of a significant custodial sentence" if the youth were convicted of those offences. The youth told the lawyer that the allegations were not "the truth." The lawyer explained that "criminal courts do not necessarily deal in truth, but they deal in evidence and explained . . . what the difference was." The youth then instructed his counsel to enter a plea of guilty to the four charges, and the Crown dropped the other six. The case was adjourned for sentencing, and the youth told the worker preparing the pre-disposition report that he was innocent. The youth court judge imposed a sentence of sixty days in open custody followed by twenty-two months' probation with a number of conditions, including treatment in the community. In rejecting the joint submission for a non-custodial disposition, the judge emphasized that the youth (and his parents) were not just displaying a lack of remorse but were "adamantly declaring innocence."

The youth actually served his custodial sentence but decided to appeal after his probation officer told him that unless he admitted guilt he could not receive treatment and that he would be charged with breach of probation for failure to undergo treatment. The Ontario Court of Appeal set aside the guilty pleas and ordered a new trial. Unlike the situation in the United States where it is a common aspect of plea bargaining for an accused to plead guilty while maintaining his innocence, in Canada a plea of guilty should not be accepted if the accused denies guilt. The Court of Appeal noted that the *Rules of Professional Conduct of the Law Society of Upper Canada* require a defence lawyer to be satisfied that a client is prepared to admit the necessary factual and mental elements of an offence before entering a plea of guilty. It concluded:

> The court should not be in the position of convicting and sentencing individuals, who fall short of admitting the facts to support the conviction unless guilt is proved beyond a reasonable doubt. Nor should sentencing proceed on the false assumption of contrition. . . . [p]lea bargaining is an accepted and integral part of our criminal justice system but must be conducted with sensitivity to its vulnerabilities.

It seems highly likely that plea bargaining will remain a part of our justice system, both for adults and youths, but some reforms would be desirable. The 1993 Martin Committee[22] recommended the continuation of the practice of plea bargaining, but with provisions to ensure a more

---

22 Ontario, Ministry of the Attorney General, *Report of the Attorney General's Advisory Committee on Charge Screening, Disclosure and Resolution Discussions* (Toronto: Queen's Printer, 1993) at 291–348 (Chair: G.A. Martin).

open and accountable process by involving victims in the process and by ordinarily requiring the Crown prosecutor to indicate in court that plea bargaining has occurred. The committee also suggested that judges should decline to accept "joint submissions" about sentence only in narrow circumstances, namely to avoid bringing the administration of justice into disrepute.[23] It recommended that judges should always ensure that a person pleading guilty is doing so voluntarily and knowingly, and with an understanding that an agreement between defence counsel and the Crown prosecutor does not necessarily bind the court. This type of judicial inquiry is particularly appropriate in youth court, since adolescents may have less comprehension of their situation than adults.

F. THE TRIAL: THE ONUS ON THE CROWN

Young persons facing trial have a constitutionally guaranteed right to the presumption of innocence,[24] with the onus upon the prosecution to prove its case. If the youth pleads not guilty, the Crown must call witnesses to establish its case and each witness may be subject to cross-examination. The youth is entitled to call witnesses and to testify, subject to the Crown's right of cross-examination, but there is no obligation on the accused to adduce any evidence or testify. After all the witnesses are called, there will be submissions (or arguments) by the lawyers and the judge then renders a verdict. If the case is relatively simple, the trial and verdict may be over in a few hours. If it is complex, the trial may last for several days and the judge may "reserve judgment" — adjourning the case to consider whether to convict the youth.

If, after hearing all the evidence and submissions, the judge is satisfied beyond a reasonable doubt that all elements of the offence charged have been proven, a "finding of guilt" is made and the case proceeds to disposition under the YOA.[25] Otherwise, the charge is generally dismissed

---

23 In law, a judge is not bound by a joint submissions arising out of a plea bargain, though joint submissions are entitled to "great weight" and there must be good reasons for rejecting them: *R. v. Rubenstein* (1987), 41 C.C.C. (3d) 91 (Ont. C.A.). In practice, some judges will allow an accused to withdraw a guilty plea and have a trial before another judge if they are not prepared to uphold the agreement, though this is a matter of discretion.

24 *Charter*, above note 9, s. 11(d).

25 Technically there is no "conviction" in youth court, but only a finding of guilt. These two concepts are similar but the technical difference between a "finding of guilt" for a youth and a "conviction" for an adult is significant in terms of some of the employment and civic disqualifications that accompany a conviction for certain offences.

206 YOUNG OFFENDERS LAW

and this ends the youth court prosecution, though occasionally the youth might still be referred to an agency to be dealt with under provincial child-welfare or mental-health legislation.

G. THE YOUTH COURT TRIAL: THE ROLE OF THE JUDGE

The criminal trial process in Canada, including the youth court process, is based on an adversarial model of justice. It is the responsibility of the parties, the Crown and the youth, usually acting through counsel, to decide what witnesses to call and what questions to ask those witnesses. The judge is expected to control the trial process and be an impartial arbiter, resolving disputes that the lawyers may present about the admissibility of evidence, for example, whether the police failed to comply adequately with section 56 of the *YOA* and thereby rendered a youth's statement inadmissible. At the end of the case the judge must decide whether the Crown has proven, beyond a reasonable doubt, that the youth is guilty of the offence charged. If the youth is found guilty, the judge is responsible for imposing a sentence.

After the lawyers have finished questioning each witness, a judge may sometimes ask a few questions by way of clarification, but judges must be cautious about this. If a judge is seen to "descend into the arena" by asking questions too often, or too aggressively, or too supportively, an appeal court may overturn the verdict. Judges may be in a particularly difficult position in sexual assault cases, since the judiciary has been criticized for insensitivity to victims, especially young ones. But if a judge responds by being too supportive of a victim, or too aggressive in questioning an accused, a new trial may be ordered, as occurred in a 1996 Newfoundland case involving a teacher accused of sexually assaulting a pupil where the Court of Appeal wrote:

> It is clear that while a trial judge has the right to intervene, the judge must not do so [in such a fashion] as to give the impression that he or she is aligned with one side or the other. . . . Indeed it is the duty of the trial judge to intervene to ensure the element of fairness and, in particular, to ensure that the accused person gets a fair trial.[26]

---

26 *R. v. Riche*, [1996] N.J. No. 293 (C.A.) (QL). See also *R. v. A.(J.F.)* (1993), 82 C.C.C. (3d) 295 (Ont. C.A.), where a trial judge was criticized for telling an eight-year-old girl, after she testified: "Thank you. I think you were a terrific witness, one of the best I have ever seen." The appeal court was concerned that this statement might lead an observer to conclude that the judge believed the child, which would be unfair since the accused had not yet presented any evidence.

The concern about the appearance of impartiality is greatest at the trial stage, in determining whether or not the accused is guilty of the offence charged. There is a somewhat broader scope for judicial questioning of witnesses at the disposition stage, particularly in youth court where the judge is concerned not only with the interests of society but also with the needs of the youth. There is also more scope for a judge to take an active role in the proceedings if an issue of mental disorder arises, especially if the lawyers have chosen not to raise the matter. In this situation, a judge may even decide to call a witness, usually a psychiatrist who has examined the accused, if neither lawyer will call the witness[27]; usually a suggestion by a judge that this type of evidence is of concern to the court will prompt the Crown to call the necessary witnesses.

There is also a broader scope for judges to intervene in the proceedings when the accused is unrepresented; for example, a judge may raise issues about the inadmissibility of prosecution evidence and take an active role in the questioning of witnesses. This modification of the judicial role is necessary to serve the interests of justice, especially if the unrepresented accused is an adolescent, but it places the judge in a difficult position. Fortunately, with the provisions of section 11 of the *YOA*, it is relatively rare for a youth to have a trial without a lawyer; judges have enough difficulty with unrepresented youths at pre-trial and disposition hearings.

In larger communities where there may be a large number of youth court judges, it is possible that several different judges will deal with a youth in a single case (for example, one at a bail hearing, others through several adjournments, and yet another at trial). If a judge starts to hear evidence in a trial, that judge must adjudicate on the issue of guilt; if that judge should die or be unable to render a decision, section 64 of the *YOA* allows another youth court judge to deal with the case, but that judge must "recommence the trial as if no evidence had been taken." The judge who finds a youth guilty should normally also render the disposition, since that judge will know the most about the circumstances of that case, though section 64 allows another judge to make a disposition decision after adjudication if the trial judge is incapacitated.

---

27   Justice Hartt in "Panel Discussion: Problems in Ethics and Advocacy" [1969] Spec. Lect. L.S.U.C. 279 at 314.

H. ASSAULTS: THE CONSENT DEFENCE FOR YOUTHS IN "SCHOOLYARD SCUFFLES"

In general, the same laws that govern the admissibility of evidence in adult court apply in youth court, and the substantive offences found in the *Criminal Code* and other legislation as well as the statutory and common law defences are also applicable to youths. There are, however, some offences to which a youth may have a defence which an adult may not have. One obvious statutory example is that an adult who has sexual relations with a person under fourteen commits the offence of sexual assault even if the younger person consents (the Canadian equivalent of "statutory rape").[28] However, a youth who is no more than two years older than the younger party can rely on the defence of consent.

Another example of a defence that has sometimes been more broadly applied to youths than to adults is that of "consent" for an assault charge. Assault is defined as the intentional application of force to another person without their consent.[29] Those who engage in a sport, like hockey, impliedly consent to the bodily contact that is inherent in the game, a fact that gives players a degree of legal immunity for conduct that would otherwise be criminal. Yet even in the context of a hockey game there is no implied consent to an overtly violent attack made with the intent to injure.[30]

It is not uncommon, especially for adolescents, to engage in consensual fights. In 1991 the Supreme Court of Canada in R. v. *Jobidon* accepted that consent could be a defence to an assault charge arising out of consensual fight, but it also articulated a policy-based limitation. The limitation to the consent defence is that, if a fight involves adults, there can be no consent (implicit or explicit) to an assault causing bodily harm or death. Justice Gonthier indicated that the Supreme Court ruling was

> restricted to cases involving adults[;] the phenomena of the "ordinary" schoolyard scuffle, where boys or girls immaturely seek to resolve with their hands, will not [necessarily] come within the scope of this limitation [that consent is no defence if there is an *intent* to kill or cause *serious bodily harm*]. . . . I would leave open the question as to whether boys or girls under the age of 18 who . . . ultimately cause more than trivial bodily harm, would be afforded the protection of a defence of consent.[31]

---

28   *Code*, above note 5, s. 150.1.
29   *Ibid.*, s. 265(1).
30   R. v. *Le Clerc* (1991), 4 O.R. (3d) 788 (C.A.).
31   [1991] 2 S.C.R. 714 at 768.

As the Supreme Court noted, there have been cases in which youths have been able to rely on the consent defence; one was *R. v. Barron*, where the accused was a student who pushed a classmate, an action that resulted in the classmate falling down a flight of stairs in a school and hitting his head and being killed. The Court accepted that the victim had implicitly consented to the "roughhousing" that led to his death, and that there had been no intent by the accused to injure (let alone cause death).[32] It acquitted the accused of a manslaughter charge.

In its 1994 decision in *R. v. W.(G.)* the Ontario Court of Appeal articulated limitations to the consent defence for adolescents. The case arose out of a fight between two sixteen-year-old high school students. For reasons that were never explained in court, the two were both "spoiling for a fight." In front of a number of other students, they exchanged words, which led to pushes, followed by blows. The fight was brief. The accused, who was the larger of the two, landed three blows in the other's face. The fight ended when the smaller youth's nose began to bleed profusely; he required medical assistance and missed several days of school as a result of his injuries. The trial judge found that the accused had intended to cause serious harm and convicted him of assault causing bodily harm. The Ontario Court of Appeal upheld the conviction, rejecting the argument that the accused could rely on his victim's consent to fight. Justice Doherty wrote:

> It may be that, where a young person engages in a consensual fight, not intending to cause harm, the other person's consent to the fight could negate liability even if serious bodily harm occurs. . . . Where . . . an accused intends to cause serious harm to his or her opponent, the adolescence of the accused provides no policy reason for recognizing consent as a "defence" to a charge of assault causing bodily harm.
>
> . . . . the fight occurred between two students at a school, during school hours, and in the presence of a number of students. Those facts . . . make my conclusions all the more compelling. Violence involving young persons within the school system is an ever-growing concern. . . . Schools must foster mutual tolerance and respect for the physical integrity of others. Students must realize that acts of violence intended to cause serious harm, which in fact do bodily harm, will not be countenanced.[33]

These cases indicate that there may be consensual fights between adolescents which do not result in serious injury and criminal convictions

---

32 (1985), 48 C.R. (3d) 334 (Ont. C.A.).
33 (1994), 18 O.R. (3d) 321 at 324–25 (C.A.).

but which clearly violate school-discipline policies. As a matter of social reality, if not law, there will be more situations in which adolescents as opposed to adults can rely on the defence of consent. However, if there is an intent to injure and injury does occur, adolescents will be not be able to invoke the consent defence and will be criminally liable.

I. FITNESS TO STAND TRIAL AND MENTAL DISORDER: *YOA*, SECTION 13.2

In relatively rare cases a youth is suffering from a "mental disorder" (or "disease of the mind") that affects the youth court process. Because of the potentially serious legal consequences and the relative narrowness of the legal concept, issues related to "mental disorder" are not frequently raised prior to adjudication. Most typically the emotional and psychological problems of a youth are raised at the sentencing stage.[34]

There are essentially two issues related to mental disorders that can arise prior to sentencing. One issue is whether the accused has sufficient mental capacity to participate meaningfully in the court process — the issue of "fitness to stand trial." The other issue is whether, at the time of the commission of the offence, the accused suffered from a mental disorder of such a nature that he or she should be relieved of criminal responsibility. Though both of these issues may arise in a single case, it is also possible for only one of them to be a concern. The legal issues that arise can be complex; the mental-health issues are also complex. As one judge dealing with conflicting evidence of mental disorder noted, "psychiatry is an inexact science."[35] Assessments of mental capacity and prognosis for treatment and future dangerousness are inherently uncertain for adults, and even more so for adolescents; mental-health research and concepts developed for adults may be difficult to apply to younger, developing age groups, and besides, there is less research available related to adolescents. Also, issues of cognitive development and learning disability may overlap with emotional and mental problems.

Section 13.2 of the *YOA* was enacted in 1992 as part of a major reform of the laws governing mental disorder and the criminal justice system. It provides that in general the provisions of Part XX.1 of the *Criminal Code* that govern mental disorder apply to youth court pro-

---

34 Issues related to emotional, psychological and mental disorders also arise in transfer applications, which are discussed in ch. 9.
35 *R. v. C.(S.A.T.)*, [1996] S.J. No. 492 (Q.B.) (QL) [*C.(S.A.T.)*].

ceedings, except for the provisions of the *Code* governing dangerous mentally disordered offenders and the adult mental-hospital treatment orders. Sections 13.2 (2)–(4) of the *YOA* provide that parents of youths who are involved in the justice system must receive notice of hearings that raise mental disorder issues, so that the parents can attend and support their children and, if appropriate, participate in the proceedings.

The concept of being "unfit to stand trial" refers to a situation in which an accused person lacks the capacity to meaningfully participate in the court process. The issue of fitness may arise at any stage of the process. It is sometimes apparent when a youth is arrested or first appears in court that he or she is "out of touch with reality" or mentally handicapped; in these circumstances a hearing about fitness to stand trial is required. In other cases, the issue of lack of capacity may not become apparent until the youth meets with defence counsel.

If the issue of fitness to stand trial is raised, the court will hold a hearing to determine fitness. Under section 2 of the *Code* a person is considered "unfit to stand trial" if the person is

> unable on account of mental disorder to conduct a defence . . . or to instruct counsel . . . and, in particular, unable . . . to
>
> (*a*) understand the nature or object of the proceedings,
> (*b*) understand the possible consequences of the proceedings, or
> (*c*) communicate with counsel.

If the issue of fitness arises, a youth court judge will generally order a psychiatric assessment under section 672.11 of the *Code,* with a presumption that the accused will remain in the community during the assessment process, though the youth may be detained for a total of up to sixty days to allow an assessment to be carried out. A person may be "unfit" at one point in time but may later be regarded as fit to stand trial if their condition improves; a court may order up to sixty days in detention in a mental-health facility to allow treatment of a person found unfit to stand trial, in the hope that this may result in the person becoming fit for trial.

A person found unfit to stand trial may be discharged with conditions or detained indefinitely in a mental-health facility, subject to periodic review of their mental status and trial when and if they are fit. For a youth, the consequences of being found unfit to stand trial can be much more serious than a finding of guilt in youth court since, unlike the limited custodial disposition for those found guilty in youth court, there may be indefinite committal; however, a youth found unfit may also be released on conditions that are similar to a youth court sentence in terms of control and support in the community.

In *R. v. D.(C.L.)* an Aboriginal youth facing a sexual assault charge was found unfit to stand trial. Although he had "limited cognitive ability" and some idea of the nature of the proceedings, a psychiatric assessment confirmed that his understanding was not sufficient to enable him to give proper instructions to counsel. The initial judicial finding was confirmed by a review board hearing, which made a restrictive community-based disposition placing him under virtual "house arrest" with "responsible members of [his] reserve looking after him and protecting the community against him."[36]

It is often difficult to find community members willing to supervise those found unfit to stand trial. A court may postpone the hearing into the issue of fitness until the conclusion of the prosecution's case, since, if there is insufficient evidence to convict the accused, it would be unfair to detain the accused under criminal legislation. In some cases, a person who is released under the *Criminal Code* may still be detained in a mental-health facility under provincial mental-health law if there is clear evidence that they suffer from a mental illness and pose a serious risk to their own safety or the safety of others.

In addition to issues of fitness for participation in the court process, there may be a question of whether the accused suffered from a mental disorder at the time of the offence. Since our legal system is premised on notions of moral accountability, it is considered unfair to punish people who on account of mental disorder were unable to appreciate the consequences of what they were doing,[37] though there may be a justification for detaining them in a mental-health facility if they continue to suffer from a mental disorder and pose a danger to the public. Section 16 of the *Criminal Code* provides that a person may be found "guilty but not criminally responsible by reason of mental disorder" if their condition rendered them "incapable of appreciating the nature and quality of the

---

36   [1995] B.C.J. No. 2863 (Prov. Ct.) (QL). Review boards conduct hearings to determine when to release those found unfit to stand trial or not criminally responsible by reason of mental disorder. They generally have a chair who is a lawyer, a psychiatrist, and one other member. Release may be subject to conditions. Review boards deal with both youths and adults.

37   In addition to cases where the accused may have suffered from a mental disorder such as to relieve from criminal liability, the accused may raise defences based on "automatism" or "intoxication," which both reflect some form of lack of mental capacity at the time of commission of the offence. If successful, these defences will result in an acquittal. The scope of the intoxication defence was tightly restricted by the enactment of s. 33.1 of the *Code*, above note 5, in 1995 by *An Act to amend the Criminal Code (self-induced intoxication)*, S.C. 1995, c. 32, s. 1. See K. Roach, *Essentials of Canadian Law: Criminal Law* (Toronto: Irwin, 1996), chs. 6 and 7.

act [charged] or of knowing that it was wrong." In some cases involving adolescents, issues of immaturity and mental handicap, emotional disturbance, and mental disorder may all be operative, as occurred in a 1977 Ontario case where a twelve-year-old boy killed his stepmother. Psychiatric evidence established that the youth was suffering from a personality disorder and did not appreciate that his act was wrong or even that the woman was no longer alive.[38]

If the issue of mental disorder arises, a court will invariably order an assessment under section 672.11 of the *Code;* the court may require the detention of the accused for a total of up to 60 days to allow an assessment to be carried out.

Statements made by an accused for the purpose of an assessment to determine fitness to stand trial or a mental disorder are directly admissible only in regard to these issues and cannot be used as part of the Crown's evidence to convict the accused; however, the statements may be used at a later hearing to "challenge the credibility" of the accused if the accused testifies in an inconsistent fashion.[39] In addition to a court-directed assessment, counsel for the accused will often retain a psychiatrist to do an assessment.

A court that finds a person guilty but not criminally responsible by reason of mental disorder will have a "disposition hearing," which may result in a discharge into the community, often on conditions, or an indefinite committal to a mental-health facility. Review boards conduct periodic reviews of those who are detained to determine whether the person poses a risk to society or may be safely released. For youths, parents must be notified of the review board hearings, which must be held at least once a year.[40]

Amendments to the *Criminal Code* enacted in 1992 are intended to "cap" the period of indefinite detention of a person found unfit to stand trial or not responsible for an offence by reason of mental disorder. The "cap" will be the maximum sentence that a person could face if convicted. For a young person who has not been transferred, the "cap" will be the maximum sentence under the *YOA* unless the youth has been found unfit to stand trial after a transfer application has been commenced, in which case the youth court may increase the "cap."[41] The "cap" provisions were not proclaimed in force at the time of writing. There is some question as to whether the government will ever proclaim

---

38   *R. v. C.(B.)* (1977), 39 C.C.C. (2d) 469 (Ont. Prov. Div.).
39   *Code,* above note 5, s. 672.21(3).
40   *YOA,* above note 2, ss. 13.2(2) and (10).
41   *Ibid.,* ss. 13.2(7)–(9).

the cap provisions in force, although, if this occurs, the cap provisions will be retroactive. As a result, to the present time, youths found to have a mental disorder affecting their fitness to stand trial or criminal responsibility may face indefinite committal, a potentially more severe consequence than a sentence imposed under the *YOA*, and counsel for a youth will often resist seeking a finding of mental disorder unless a youth has been transferred and faces a murder charge.[42]

Cases where issues of fitness to stand trial or mental disorder arise pose special tactical and ethical problems for lawyers, problems that may be especially acute when the client is an adolescent. A lawyer may, for example, have concerns about taking instructions from a client who appears to lack the capacity to understand the nature of the proceedings or their consequences. Sometimes a client who appears mentally disordered will instruct their counsel to resist raising issues related to the their condition. This might be due to fears of stigmatization or because the consequences of a finding of mental disorder may be more severe than a conviction, but the resistance to being labelled mentally disordered can also be a symptom of being mentally ill.

While the ethical rules governing lawyers do not explicitly deal with these complex situations, it would appear that if a lawyer doubts the capacity of a client to provide instructions, the lawyer should consult parents, mental-health professionals, and others who know the client to help form an opinion about the client's capacity. Ultimately, if the lawyer believes that a client lacks capacity, it is not unethical for the lawyer to raise the questions of fitness to stand trial or mental disorder, despite the client instructing the lawyer not to do so.[43] Even if the defence does not raise the issue, the Crown prosecutor or judge may raise the issue

---

42 *C.(S.A.T.)*, above note 35. Transferred fourteen-year-old youth facing murder charge found guilty but not criminally responsible by reason of mental disorder.

43 See A.S. Manson, "Observations from an Ethical Perspective on Fitness, Insanity and Confidentiality" (1982) 27 McGill L. J. 196. This can be very problematic, however, as illustrated in the celebrated Morin case. Morin was charged with murdering a nine-year-old girl and denied guilt although the Crown had some evidence of guilt. His lawyer at trial, despite Morin's concern, introduced psychiatric evidence that Morin was a schizophrenic capable of committing the murder and suppressing the memory. Although Morin was acquitted at the first trial, this psychiatric evidence convinced police and prosecutors of Morin's guilt, and after a Crown appeal, he was retried and convicted, serving several years in jail before DNA evidence established his innocence. Morin was profoundly critical of his lawyer at the first trial, maintaining (rightly as it turned out) that he was both innocent and sane. See K. Makin, "Hostility erupts at Morin probe," *[Toronto] Globe and Mail* (14 February 1997) A1.

of fitness to stand trial; if necessary, a judge may even call witnesses to resolve an issue of fitness to stand trial. The Crown prosecutor may also raise the issue of an accused not being criminally responsible owing to mental disorder, even if the accused (invariably acting through counsel) fails to do so, though only after the accused has been found guilty.[44]

J. PRIVACY AND PUBLICITY: SECTION 38

Consistent with the principles of section 3 of the YOA that emphasize limited accountability, special needs, and rehabilitation of young offenders, the YOA has a number of provisions intended to protect the privacy of young persons involved in the youth court process and thereby minimize the stigmatization they face. Section 12 of the old JDA, while less detailed than the provisions of the YOA, required that juvenile court hearings were to be held "without publicity" and without the public in attendance.[45] Because of the history of protection of privacy, there is little Canadian experience with publication of identifying information about youths. However, available research from the United States, where some states have a more open juvenile court process and allow publication of the identity of adolescents before the courts, indicates that rehabilitation of young offenders can be significantly hindered if their identities are publicized.[46] Publication increases a youth's self-perception as an offender, disrupts the family's abilities to provide support, and negatively affects interaction with peers, teachers, and the surrounding community.

Since their original enactment in 1984, the privacy provisions of the YOA have been controversial with the public and justice system professionals as well as with the media, which has viewed them as an unwelcome restraint on freedom of the press. There have been a number of amendments to these provisions of the YOA. These amendments have decreased the privacy protections afforded youths, though there remain very significant differences between the treatment afforded adults and that afforded young persons.

---

44   R. v. Swain, [1991] 1 S.C.R. 933.
45   See C.B. v. R., [1981] 2 S.C.R. 480.
46   D.C. Howard, J.T. Grisso, & R. Neems, "Publicity and Juvenile Court Proceedings", (1977) 11 Clearinghouse Review 203; and K.M. Laubenstein, "Media Access to Juvenile Justice: Should Freedom of the Press Be Limited to Promote Rehabilitation of Young Offenders?" (1995) 68 Temple L. Rev. 1897.

Section 38 provides that the media cannot "publish . . . any information serving to identify" a person under eighteen involved in youth court proceedings, whether as the accused, a victim, or a witness. Any individual or corporation that violates this provision commits an offence and may be prosecuted, and a youth whose identity has been wrongfully revealed may also civilly sue the media outlet for monetary damages for invasion of privacy.[47] Section 38 has been broadly interpreted to prohibit publication of not only the name of the youth but also such identifying material as a photograph,[48] and it covers publication by the press as well as broadcast via television or radio. This provision does not, however, go so far as to prevent publication of the identity of a deceased youth, since there is no longer any concern about stigmatization.[49] Section 38 explicitly allows the publication of identifying information if a youth has been transferred to adult court under section 16 of the *YOA*.[50]

Soon after it was enacted, the constitutionality of the privacy provisions of the *YOA* was challenged as a violation of freedom of the press by a major Canadian newspaper chain. In *Southam Inc.* v. *R.* the Ontario Court of Appeal upheld the validity of sections 38 and 39, noting that these provisions do not constitute a complete ban on media reporting but only restrict it in a limited fashion. There was expert testimony presented about the desirability of a ban on the publication of identifying information in terms of protection and rehabilitation of youths, and the Court of Appeal accepted that this was an objective of "superordinate importance" which justified a restraint on freedom of the media.[51] The importance of the media as "representatives of the community" has, however, been recognized. The media can give the public significant information about the courts, and accordingly, if a reporter learns of a youth court proceeding but has not attended, the reporter should ordinarily be viewed as a person with a "valid interest" in the proceedings and given access to the transcript pursuant to section 44.1(1)(k) of the *YOA*[52] in order to permit reporting of the proceedings, albeit without identifying the youth.

---

47   *F.(P.)* v. *Ontario* (2 February 1989), (Ont. Dist. Ct.) [unreported] [summarized (1989), 6 W.C.B. (2d) 350].

48   *Ibid.*

49   *R.* v. *Les Publications Photo-Police* (1986), 52 C.R. (3d) 301 (Que. C.A.)

50   *R.* v. *P.(M.G.)* (7 November 1996), (B.C.S.C.) [unreported], Davies J. held that s. 15 of the *Charter*, above note 9, requires that the same privacy protections should be given to sixteen- and seventeen- year-olds charged with very serious offences who bear the onus of seeking to "transfer down" from adult court, unless it has been determined in accordance with *YOA*, above note 2, s. 16 (1.01), that their case will be dealt with in adult court.

51   (1984), 48 O.R. (2d) 678 (H.C.J.), aff'd (1986), 53 O.R. (2d) 663 (C.A.) [*Southam*].

52   *R.* v. *S.(R.D.)* (1995), 145 N.S.R. (2d) 284 (C.A.).

In 1986 an amendment was added to the *YOA* to allow a youth court judge to permit publication of identifying information in order to assist the police in the apprehension of youths who are not in custody and who pose a serious risk to the public.[53] Section 38(1.2) of the Act now provides that, if a youth is at large, the police may seek an order from a youth court judge allowing publication of identifying information; the judge must be satisfied that there is reason to believe that the youth is "dangerous to others" and that publication is necessary to assist in the youth's apprehension. In *R. v. N.(K.)* Kimelman A.C.J.M. held that to obtain an order under section 38(1.2) the police must satisfy the court that all "reasonable and continuing efforts" to locate the youth without publication have been exhausted, and there is a "necessity" to publicize the youth's identity.[54]

A judge may also permit publication of identifying information at the request of a youth, if satisfied that doing so "would not be contrary to the best interests" of the youth.

K. 1995 AMENDMENTS — EXPANDING DISCLOSURE: SECTIONS 38(1.13) & (1.15)

A 1995 amendment, section 38(1.13), allows for administrative disclosure of identifying information about young offenders without a court order. Police and probation officers can disclose information about young offenders to school officials (such as a principal or vice-principal), or other professionals, such as child-welfare workers, if disclosure is "necessary" to monitor compliance with a court order or to protect "safety" in the school or other settings. The professionals to whom information is disclosed may share it with other professionals in their institutions, but only if this is "necessary" for their work. This information about offending and the court process is not to be more widely disseminated. Information disclosed to school officials under section 38(1.13) is to be kept separately from other records about the youth and must be destroyed when no longer required.[55] This amendment has resulted in significantly more access to information about offending

---

53   *An Act to amend the Young Offenders Act, the Criminal Code, the Penitentiary Act and the Prisons and Reformatories Act*, R.S.C. 1985 (2d Supp.), c. 24, s. 29, adding *YOA*, above note 2, s. 38(1.2).

54   (1989), 51 C.C.C. (3d) 404 (Man. Prov. Ct.).

55   *YOA*, above note 2, s. 38(1.15), enacted by *An Act to amend the Young Offenders Act and the Criminal Code*, S.C. 1995, c. 19, s. 27(1) [*YOA 1995*].

behaviour within schools. While there are legitimate concerns about safety in the schools, there is also evidence that a youth's relationships with teachers and peers may be negatively affected if they are known within their schools as "delinquents."[56]

Another 1995 amendment, section 38(1.5), allows a youth court judge, after a hearing, to permit disclosure of identifying information about a young offender to members of the public where the youth is thought to pose a "risk of serious harm" and the disclosure of information is "necessary" to avoid risk. Such an application will usually be brought by the police and may be contested by the youth. If an order is made under section 38(1.5), the media is still prohibited from publicizing the identity of the youth, but it seems likely that information about the youth will circulate widely in the community nonetheless. While section 38(1.5) does not specify whether the court should consider the potential harm to the youth from disclosure, section 13(2)(f) provides that the court may order a psychological or psychiatric assessment for a disclosure hearing. This suggests that the court should take account of the effect of disclosure on the youth.

Section 38(1.5) was enacted as a result of widespread demands that the public has a "right to know" of offenders released into their community. In particular, it was a response to one highly publicized case in British Columbia involving a young sex offender who was released into the community where he later assaulted and killed a neighbourhood child.[57] Subsection 38(1.5) could in theory permit neighbours of a young offender in such situations to be informed and neighbourhood children warned of the potential danger. There were many problems with how the British Columbia case was handled under the then existing law in terms of lack of communication between police and probation services, but this type of statutory change was not necessary to improve coordination and communication between professionals.

One can appreciate the motivation behind the enactment of section 38(1.5), especially the desire to protect children, but its ultimate effects may be problematic. Unless all children in the community are warned, the protection afforded by this provision disclosing the identity of a young offender may be slight, since an offender can seek out children who may not be aware of the danger. Further, once neighbours and fellow students are "warned" about a particular youth, meaningful reintegration into the community may be impossible, and offenders may be

---

56   D.H. Kelly, "Labeling and the Consequences of Wearing a Delinquent Label in a School Setting" (1977) 97 Educ. 371.

57   See, e.g., "Tracking young sex predators" *Vancouver Province* (31 March 1994).

likely to move away from community and family supports and seek anonymity in large urban centres, making rehabilitation much more difficult to achieve. The American experience with these types of "public warning" provisions suggests that they may often be counterproductive.[58]

The 1995 amendments that provide for broader disclosure of information were intended to address the criticisms of media, politicians, professionals, and members of the public that more needs to be known about young offenders so that appropriate protective steps can be taken. While professionals who are treating and counselling youths should have adequate access to information about them, one has to wonder whether public safety will actually be increased if more information is made available in the community. One can expect more negative stereotyping and labelling of young offenders by their communities because of these changes, and rehabilitation will be made more difficult as a result.

L. PUBLIC ACCESS TO YOUTH COURT: SECTION 39

Section 39(1)(a) provides that, while youth court proceedings are generally open to the public, the judge may make an order excluding some or all members of the public if their presence "would be seriously injurious or seriously prejudicial" to a young person accused of an offence or to a child or youth who is a witness. There is a presumption in favour of having proceedings open to the public, and there is an onus on the person seeking exclusion to demonstrate some likelihood of harm, perhaps by calling expert evidence. Youth court judges will not, for example, exclude the public merely because a youth is facing serious charges in a relatively small community, even though open proceedings may make it likely that his identity will become known within the community.[59]

---

58 See, e.g., P. Davis, "The Sex Offender Next Door," *New York Times Magazine* (28 July 1996) 20 and "Whitman Latest to Urge Laws on Notices of Sex Offenders," *New York Times* (6 August 1994) 24, reporting on the Washington State notification scheme for adult sex offenders, which has three levels of community notification depending on the offender's record and the likelihood of recurrence of an offence, and the judgment of experts. In one case in Washington the home of a sex offender was set on fire after the community was notified. There are concerns that the Washington scheme is "just creating a class of people that are moving from community to community".

59 *R. v. S.(M.)* (26 November 1984), (Ont. Prov. Ct. (Fam. Div.)) [unreported] [summarized (1984), 13 W.C.B. 192].

The youth court also has the power under section 39(1)(b) to exclude members of the public and potential witnesses, other than the accused youth and a parent, from all or part of the proceedings where this "would be in the interest of . . . [the] administration of justice." This provision is generally invoked to exclude persons who will be witnesses prior to their testifying, so that they will not be influenced by what other witnesses may say. It may also exclude members of the media during a *voir dire* into the admissibility of a confession, since the evidence in such a hearing should not be reported even without identifying the youth.[60]

If the accused youth is disrupting the proceedings, the judge may exclude that person from the court under section 650 of the *Code*. A person who disrupts court proceedings may also be charged with contempt of court.

M. YOUTH COURT RECORDS: SECTIONS 40–46

Sections 40 to 46 of the *YOA* govern the records relating to young offenders kept by the police, youth courts, probation offices, and correctional services, as well as records of other agencies to the extent that they are administering dispositions or related to the youth court process. These provisions restrict access to records and are intended to reflect the principle of "limited accountability" in section 3(1)(a. 1) of the *YOA* and to minimize the stigmatization of youths. These provisions do not, however, totally preclude use of a "youth record," and amendments to the *YOA* as well as court decisions have tended to increase the scope for later use of a finding of guilt in youth court.

Police officers have significant authority to release information in the course of their duties. For example, section 44.1(3) allows disclosure of information to victims, while section 38(1.1) of the *YOA* allows for the disclosure of information by police concerning a young person before the courts "in the course of the administration of justice where it is not the purpose of the disclosure to make the information known in the community." Section 38(1.1), for example, permits disclosure of information by police for the purpose of arranging for pre-trial release; however, those receiving information should be cautioned about not disseminating this information beyond the purposes required by the Act. Section 44.2 specifically allows a police officer to disclose informa-

---

60   *Southam*, above note 51.

tion to an insurance company to permit investigation of a claim, and to disclose any information that is necessary to "conduct . . . [an] investigation" of an alleged offence. If there is uncertainty about the appropriateness of the disclosure of information, an application can be made to a youth court under section 44.1(1)(k) for an order permitting the release of information.

While police may fingerprint and photograph youths charged with indictable offences, the records of the Canadian Police Information Centre must be destroyed after a statutorily specified period. Local police forces and others who have records related to young offenders are not obliged to destroy their records, but their use is restricted after the statutorily specified period has passed.

The statutory periods related to use and destruction of various *YOA* records were amended in 1995 to allow longer retention of records, especially where violent offences are involved.[61] For murder, attempted murder, or aggravated sexual assault, records may be kept indefinitely in a special centralized CPIC data bank; for a longer list of less serious violent and sexual offences, the period of retention was increased to ten years from the former five, and, if further offences are committed, these periods are extended. For other indictable offences, the period is five years. For summary conviction offences, records are only to be kept for three years from the completion of a disposition, provided that there are no further offences. For a youth sent to alternative measures, the period of record use is two years.

Once the statutory period has expired, pursuant to section 45(4) the young person "shall be deemed not to have committed" the offence to which the record relates, though, other than for the centralized records kept by CPIC, there is no obligation to destroy the records. This raises a controversial question as to whether any use may be made of such records after the expiration of the statutory period. Many judges have held that, once the statutory crime free period has elapsed, no use should be made of the record and it is improper for a judge at a sentencing hearing to take any account of such a record.[62] However, in 1996 in *R. v. McKay,* a majority of the British Columbia Court of Appeal ruled that it was permissible for a judge sentencing an offender in adult court to take account of a prior youth court record that was more than five years old (then the relevant statutory period), and it upheld a ruling of a youth court judge to permit disclosure of the record under section

61 *YOA*, above note 2, s. 45(1) and ss. 45.01 to 45.03, as am. by *YOA 1995*, above note 55, s. 31(2).
62 See, e.g., *R. v. R.(B.F.)* (1995), 139 N.S.R. (2d) 215 (C.A.).

45.1(1) of the *YOA*, which permits disclosure where it is in the "interest of the proper administration of justice." The majority of the Court of Appeal was concerned that the prior record, which related to a serious offence, should not be ignored, and it noted that the 1995 amendments to the record provisions "reflected Parliament's intention to readjust the balance between the rights and interests of young persons and the interests of society by favouring more disclosure, albeit in limited circumstances."[63] The decision produced a vigorous dissent from Justice Southin who argued that allowing disclosure after the expiry of the statutory period rendered section 45(4) virtually meaningless; this approach seems more consistent with the principles of the *YOA*.

Section 36(3) of the *YOA* provides that employers governed by federal law are prohibited from asking a potential employee whether they have ever been charged or found guilty of an offence prosecuted pursuant to the *YOA*, unless that person is still subject to a *YOA* disposition. This provision recognizes the "limited accountability" of young persons and is intended to afford a "second chance" to those adolescents found guilty under the *YOA*. However, a youth who is applying for a position with an employer that is not under federal employment law,[64] like a private employer or a municipality or provincial agency, may be required to submit to a "security clearance" that may include a check of youth court records kept by the police.[65]

N. APPEALS: SECTION 27

Under the *Juvenile Delinquents Act* appeals were discouraged: in each instance, special leave (or permission) was required to establish that the appeal was "essential in the public interest or for the due administration of justice."[66] Section 27 of the *YOA* changed this and grants the same rights of appeal as those applicable to adults.

---

63 *R. v. McKay*, [1996] B.C.J. No. 1019 (C.A.) (QL) Prowse J.A.

64 Federal employment law governs about 10 percent of the labour force and includes direct employees of the federal government, including the RCMP and the armed forces, as well as those enterprises that are subject to federal regulation, like banks and air lines.

65 *O.(Y.) v. Belleville (City) Chief of Police* (1993), 12 O.R. (3d) 618 (Div. Ct.), rev'g (1991), 3 O.R. (3d) 261 (Gen. Div.).

66 *Juvenile Delinquents Act*, R.S.C. 1970, c. J-3, s. 37.

If the offence was summary, or a hybrid offence for which the Crown made no election, there will generally be a right of appeal from a final adjudication or disposition[67] of a provincially appointed youth court to a judge of the superior trial court, and then to the provincial Court of Appeal.[68] If the offence is indictable, or hybrid where the Crown has elected to treat it as indictable, the appeal is directly to the Court of Appeal.

There is a right of appeal to the Supreme Court of Canada, but only with leave of that Court or if the case involves an indictable offence and there is a dissenting judgment in the Court of Appeal.[69] Because of the desire to promote early resolution of cases involving young offenders and the relatively short sentences compared to adults, there are few YOA appeals that go through the time-consuming and expensive process of appeal to the Supreme Court of Canada.[70]

Appeals do not involve a full rehearing of the evidence in a case, but only a review of the transcript to find if there has been an error of law. However, in regard to sentence appeals, especially those related to young offenders who are in custody, appellate courts are generally willing to receive information concerning the progress of the youth in custody and they may take account of this to reduce a sentence.[71]

---

67   The YOA, above note 2, s. 27(6) provides that there is no appeal from a disposition review under ss. 28–32. The appeal (or "review") of a judicial interim release decision or a transfer decision is governed by ss. 8(6)–(9) and s. 16(9) of the YOA respectively.

68   Ibid., s. 27(3) specifies that, where a youth court judge is a superior court judge, as occurs in provinces where Unified Family Court judges deal with YOA cases, all appeals are directly to the Court of Appeal. See discussion in ch. 3 concerning jurisdiction, levels of court, and classification of offences.

69   Code, above note 5, s. 691, YOA, ibid., s. 27(5).

70   See comments of Supreme Court discouraging the granting of leave in such cases: R. v. C.(T.L.), [1994] 2 S.C.R. 1012.

71   See, e.g., R. v. D.(S.) (7 December 1992), (Ont. C.A.) [unreported] [summarized (1992), 18 W.C.B. (2d) 167].

FURTHER READINGS

ARNUP, C. J. "The Mental Disorder Amendments: Impact on Young Persons" in *The Young Offenders Act: Significant Trends for the 90s* (Toronto: Canadian Bar Association – Ontario, 1992)

BALA, N. & H. LILLES, eds., *Young Offenders Service* (Toronto: Butterworths, 1984) (looseleaf)

DELISLE, R.J. & D. STUART, *Learning Canadian Criminal Procedure,* 4th ed. (Toronto: Carswell, 1996), ch. 3

HARRIS, P.J., ed., *Young Offenders Act Manual* (Aurora: Canada Law Book, 1984) (looseleaf)

PLATT, P. *Young Offenders Law in Canada,* 2d ed. (Toronto: Butterworths, 1995), chs. 12, 13, 16, 17, 18, 21 and 22

SCOTT, S., M. WONG, & B. WEAGANT, *Defending Young Offender Cases,* 2d ed. (Toronto: Carswell, 1997), chs. 5, 6 and 7

CHAPTER 8

SENTENCING UNDER THE YOA

A. DISPOSITIONS: LEGISLATION AND DISCRETION

The *Young Offenders Act* has extensive provisions governing sentencing, or "disposition" as it is euphemistically referred to in the Act. Sections 20 to 35 govern the process of sentencing and regulate various dispositions as well as the process of "disposition review," which occurs after a young offender has served a portion of a sentence and may result in release from custody before the full sentence is served.

However, the *YOA* regulates only some aspects of sentencing. The Act and appellate judgments give merely general guidance to youth court judges about what dispositions to impose in an individual case and leave judges with significant discretion in sentencing. As well, differences in police-charging practices and in the use of alternative measures result in youth courts in some provinces dealing with a much larger portion of the adolescent population than in others. The *YOA* also gives the provincial governments discretion as to the types of community dispositions and custodial facilities that they will provide.

As a result of the broad discretion given to judges, police, Crown prosecutors, and provincial governments, there are significant variations in how youths in different provinces who have committed the same offences are treated, though some national trends are apparent. In particular, while there is very significant variation between provinces,[1]

---

1   See, e.g., A.N. Doob & J.B. Sprott, "Interprovincial Variation in the Use of the Youth Court" (1996) 38 Can. J. Crim. 401.

there has been a substantial increase in the use of custody in Canada since the *YOA* came into force in 1984, and, as noted earlier, Canada now has one of the highest rates of custody use for adolescent offenders in the world.[2] Some of the 1995 amendments to the *YOA* were intended to reverse this trend of rising custody use by increasing the use of community-based dispositions for youths who do not pose a serious risk of harm.

B. THE DISPOSITION PROCESS: REPORTS AND HEARINGS

For relatively minor offences, a youth court may make a disposition immediately after a finding of guilt. In more serious situations, however, the court will normally adjourn to allow for the preparation of reports to assist the court, as well as to give counsel time to prepare for a disposition hearing.

If there has been a finding of guilt, the court may order the youth to be detained pending sentencing. This should not be done as a form of "advanced punishment," but only if there are grounds for detention under section 515 of the *Criminal Code*. Since section 24(2) of the *YOA* requires that a youth court judge must ordinarily consider a pre-disposition report before removing a youth from the community by placing the youth in custody, it is wrong for a judge who has just found a youth guilty to order the youth detained pending sentencing as a means of giving the youth a "short, sharp shock."

In one Saskatchewan case an appeal court reversed a youth court judge's decision to detain the youth immediately after making a finding of guilt. The appellate judge observed that prior to sentencing, a youth court judge can order detention of the youth only

> for either of the purposes referred to in section 515(10): namely, to ensure his attendance in court, or for the purpose of protecting the public. . . . [The trial judge] in remanding [the youth] . . . in custody . . . without sentencing him . . . did so because he was not certain what sentence he wished to impose, and he also apparently wished to provide . . . a "wake up" call. Neither of these "purposes" would qualify a person for detention under s. 515(10).[3]

---

2   See, e.g., H. Lilles, "The Young Offenders Act: Some International Perspectives for Reform" (1995) 5 (1) J. Law & Social Work. For adult offenders, Canada also has one of the highest rates of incarceration, but it is less than half that in the United States.

3   *R. v. Y.(D.H.)* (1995), 132 Sask. R. 107 at 111 (Q.B.). See also *R. v. G.(C.)*(1993), 79 C.C.C. (3d) 446 (Ont. C.A.). For a fuller discussion of s. 515(10) of the *Criminal Code,* and pre-sentence detention, see ch. 4.

Youth courts usually take account of any period of pre-disposition detention to reduce any sentence that would otherwise be imposed, "crediting" the youth with this time against the appropriate sentence, though sentencing judges are not obliged to do so.[4]

Before a youth is sentenced, section 14 of the *YOA* allows a youth court judge to order that a "provincial director" (usually represented by a professional known as a probation officer or youth court worker) should prepare a "pre-disposition" report (sometimes called a "p.d.r." or "social history"). Section 24(2) provides that a judge must order the preparation of such a report before placing a youth in custody; the only exception is when the prosecutor and counsel for the youth waive this requirement and when the judge considers that the preparation of the report is "unnecessary" and that the "best interests" of the youth do not require a report. A judge should be reluctant to dispense with preparation of a report before making a custodial disposition unless there is a relatively recent report about the youth that had been prepared for use in previous sentencing hearings.[5] In some cases, if the lawyers have entered into a pre-trial plea bargain and are making a joint submission as to sentence, the court may also dispense with preparation of a report before imposing a custodial disposition.

The person preparing the pre-disposition report will generally interview the youth, the youth's parents, the victim, and any other significant individuals, and will summarize the youth's background and provide information about the offence. The report will generally also include the youth's prior record of offending and participation in alternative measures. In 1995 section 14 was amended to specify that the author of a pre-disposition report may include a "recommendation" as to disposition. Before the enactment of that provision, it was a common, but not universal, practice for reports to provide recommendations, and the new section 14(2)(d) clarifies that this is an acceptable practice, though giving the author of the report discretion as to whether to include such a recommendation. Some authors are still reluctant to include a recommendation if the judge for whom it is prepared has expressed a concern that providing such a recommendation is "usurping the role of the court."

---

4   *R. v. W.(S.B.)*, [1995] A.J. No. 686 (C.A.) R.S.C. 1985, c. C-46 [*Code*], (QL). Adults usually get "extra credit" for pre-sentencing detention since they do not get statutory sentence remission for this pre-trial detention time. Since there is no statutory sentence remission for young offenders, there is no "greater credit" for pre-disposition detention; *R. v. O.(S.J.)* (1992), 83 Alta. L.R. (2d) 413 (C.A.).

5   See, e.g., *R. v. R.(R.A.)* (1987), 64 Sask. R. 31 (C.A.).

The report is also likely to include a description of the type of community-based programs and services that are available, and, if a custodial disposition is likely, some information about the custodial facilities that are suitable and have space available. The person preparing the report is also expected to contact, "where appropriate and reasonably possible," members of the youth's "extended family" to determine whether they can exert "control and influence" on the youth.[6] This type of information is especially relevant for Aboriginal youth, and it may allow for more community-based dispositions involving members of the extended family.

The 1995 amendments were intended to ensure that youth courts have more information before sentencing, in particular for cases involving serious violence. Together with amendments discussed below, they are also intended to ensure a more "efficient" [that is, limited] use of custody facilities and more use of non-custodial dispositions for youths who do not pose a significant risk to the community.

In more serious cases, or cases where there is particular concern about a young person, the court may make an order under section 13 of the YOA for a psychiatric, medical, or psychological assessment to assist in arriving at an appropriate disposition. A section 13 report may be appropriate when the circumstances of the youth or of the offence suggest that more information is needed to enable the court to make a disposition which is responsive to the youth's "special needs." Some commentators express concern that youth courts order section 13 reports too rarely, arguing that the orientation of the YOA has caused the lawyers involved to focus on the offence and disregard the needs and condition of the specific youth. It is apparent that some defence counsel are reluctant to have such reports prepared since information about the background of a troubled youth can result in a more intrusive disposition being imposed. The section 13 reports generally take longer to prepare than a section 14 pre-disposition report, and the delay that this may cause for a youth, especially one in detention, may also make defence lawyers reluctant to request such a report.

These section 13 reports are prepared by professionals in private practice or clinics and are paid for by government.[7] The 1995 amendments to the YOA appear to encourage more use of these reports and

6   *An Act to amend the Young Offenders Act and the Criminal Code*, S.C. 1995, c.19 [*YOA, 1995*], amending Young Offenders Act, R.S.C. 1985, c. Y-1, ss. 14(2)(c) (v)–(vi) [*YOA*].

7   A.W. Leschied & P.G. Jaffe, "Impact of the Young Offenders Act on Court Dispositions: A Comparative Analysis" (1987) 29 Can. J. Crim. 421.

allow the court to order a section 13 report even when it is not requested by the prosecution or defence, if there is a "pattern of repeated findings of guilt" or a "serious personal injury" offence, or if the youth appears to be suffering from a psychological disorder, emotional disturbance, or learning disability.[8]

A disturbingly large number of persistent young offenders have learning disabilities or suffer from such conditions as fetal-alcohol syndrome; appropriate diagnosis and treatment could do much to reduce offending, but too often these conditions are undiagnosed or ignored by the legal system. Use of section 13 reports, as well as greater awareness by youth justice professionals about these conditions, is essential for developing appropriate intervention strategies, though governments must also ensure that there are suitable programs and facilities for dealing with young offenders suffering from these conditions.[9]

To encourage the youth to cooperate with the author of a section 13 or 14 report, there are provisions in the *YOA* to ensure that any statements made by the youth in the course of preparation of such a report are to be used only for the purpose of a disposition or transfer hearing and are not otherwise admissible against the youth.[10] Youths generally are willing to participate and often try to put themselves in the best possible light with the person preparing a report, but if they are unwilling to assist in the process they may find it difficult to object to any recommendations.[11]

Although the recommendations in a pre-disposition report or section 13 assessment are not binding on the court, these recommendations are often influential. If there are no objections, a report may simply be filed with the court. Crown prosecutors rarely challenge a recommendation in a report. More frequently, if there is disagreement it will be by counsel for the youth. Either lawyer has the right to challenge the report and may cross-examine the author, as well as introducing independent evidence at the disposition hearing. Defence counsel sometimes introduce character evidence about the youth or other evidence about an appropriate disposition.

---

8 *YOA*, above note 6, s. 13(1)(b), enacted by *YOA 1995*, above note 6, s. 4(1).

9 As many as three-quarters of young offenders in custody have some form of learning disability, a rate five times higher than in the general school-age population. See Y. Henteleff, *Position Paper on the Proposed Amendments to the Young Offenders Act* (Ottawa: Learning Disabilities Association of Canada, 1996); and Canada, Federal-Provincial Territorial Task Force on Youth Justice, *A Review of the Young Offenders Act* (Ottawa: Supply & Services, 1996) at 625.

10 *YOA*, above note 6, ss. 13.1 and 14(10).

11 *R. v. R.(A.L.)* (1987), 77 N.S.R. (2d) 338 (C.A.).

The rules of evidence that apply to trials are relaxed at a sentencing hearing. Hearsay and opinion evidence about the character of a youth which would be inadmissible at a trial may be introduced through letters or other documents,[12] though, if the defence challenges a factual assertion made by the Crown or in a report, it must be proven beyond a doubt or it will be disregarded by the sentencing judge.[13] Parents also have the right to make submissions prior to disposition. In practice, however, the pre-disposition is often the only significant information given the youth court judge at the sentencing hearing. Although counsel have the right to introduce evidence and cross-examine witnesses, in practice lawyers often play a limited role in youth court disposition hearings and have been criticized for their relatively passive role at this critical stage of the youth court process.[14] A common judicial response to the low level of involvement of lawyers in the dispositional process is for judges to adopt more of an inquisitorial role than they do at the trial stage, relying on their understanding of adolescent development and the knowledge of community and correctional resources as much as on any evidence adduced at the hearing.[15] There is, however, an important role for defence counsel to play in challenging the plans put forward by agents of the state and in putting forward independent dispositional alternatives. Defence counsel may also contact the authors of any reports before they are prepared, to ensure that the youth's position is adequately understood.

The YOA was amended in 1995 to allow youth courts to receive victim-impact statements,[16] though some judges were already using them. The preparation of these statements, which describe the harm or loss caused by the offence, is usually arranged by the police or a probation officer, but the statements themselves are actually written by victims or sometimes by family members of victims. The 1995 amendments are intended to increase the use of these statements in order to give youth

---

12 Procedural and evidentiary rules for an adult sentencing hearing are in s. 723 of the *Code*, above note 3, though technically this provision does not apply because of s. 20(8) of the *YOA*, above note 6. In practice s. 723 is largely followed in youth court and codifies the case law that was applicable in cases like *R. v. Gardiner*, [1982] 2 S.C.R. 368.

13 *R. v. E.(R.K.)* (1996), 107 Man. R. (2d) 200 (C.A.).

14 See ch. 6.

15 For a discussion of some of the dilemmas faced by judges, see S.K. MacAskill & H.T.G. Andrews, "The Role of the Judge at the Dispositional Hearing" (1985) 47 C.R. (3d) 60.

16 *YOA*, above note 6, s. 20(8), enacted by *YOA 1995*, above note 6, s. 13(6), adopting *Code*, above note 3, s. 722.

courts more information at the time of sentencing, as well as affording victims a greater degree of involvement with the justice system and providing young offenders a greater appreciation of the injury that they have caused.

C. DISPOSITIONAL ALTERNATIVES: SECTION 20

If a youth court judge finds a young person guilty of an offence, the judge shall make one or more of the dispositions provided for in section 20 of the *YOA*:

- absolute discharge, section 20(1)(a);
- conditional discharge, section 20(1)(a.1);
- fine of up to $1000, section 20(1)(b);
- restitution or compensation to a victim, section 20(1)(c), (d), (e), or (f);
- community service of up to 240 hours, section 20(1)(g);
- probation for up to two years, section 20(1)(j);
- an order of prohibition, (for example, in regard to driving or possession of a firearm[17]), section 20(1)(h); and
- custody for two years for most offences (if the maximum sentence for an adult is life imprisonment, the maximum youth sentence is three years, and for first degree murder the maximum youth court sentence is ten years), section 20(1)(k) and (k.1).

An absolute discharge involves the youth being "discharged" without any official sanction other than having a "record of a discharge." An absolute discharge may be imposed if the court considers "it to be in the best interests of the young person and not contrary to the public interest." This disposition is usually reserved for minor first offenders and results in no sanction being imposed and the court record indicating that the youth has received an absolute discharge. Under section 45(1)(d.1) no use can be made of a record of an absolute discharge after

---

17 Some judgments specifically limit firearm-prohibition orders to the maximum for *YOA, ibid.,* custodial dispositions, three years for most serious offences except murder: *R. v. R.(C.N.B.),* [1995] O.J. No. 3042 (Prov. Ct.) (QL). However, the *YOA* does not specifically mention the maximum duration for such prohibition orders. In *R. v. K.(M.)* (1996), 28 O.R. (3d) 593 (C.A.) the Ontario Court of Appeal upheld a ten-year firearm prohibition for a young offender convicted of murder, even though the maximum youth court custody disposition at the time was five years less a day.

one year. When imposing this disposition, the judge is likely to caution the youth that reoffending will result in a more severe sanction and that this is a "last warning." Since most youths have been sent to alternative measures at least once before being sentenced by a youth court judge, this type of "last warning" is relatively rarely used by youth courts, being imposed in only 3 percent of cases.[18]

The *conditional discharge* provision was added to the YOA in 1995. As originally enacted in 1984, the YOA had no provision for conditional discharges, premised on the view that the various non-disclosure provisions meant that all youths who do not reoffend are in effect conditionally discharged. Judges and other youth court professionals, however, expressed a desire to have an explicit conditional-discharge option. This allows a youth court judge to give a youth receiving a sanction a clear message that, if the terms of the disposition are carried out, the youth will have the "record wiped clean" and then not be viewed as "an offender," though the record of the discharge can be used for three years after the finding of guilt in the event that there is a subsequent offence.[19] Section 20(1)(a.1) allows a court to order that a "young person be discharged on such conditions as the court considers appropriate." Conditions might include making a donation to a charity, undergoing counselling, or doing community-service work.

Youth court judges are reluctant to impose a fine on a youth, since this is a purely punitive sanction; while serving accountability and deterrent functions, the imposition of a fine has no rehabilitative function. Further, many youths have little or no income, and a fine may create a substantial burden for the youth or family or even cause a youth to commit another offence to raise funds to pay the fine. Fines are used in about 9 percent of cases, either alone or in combination with another disposition, with the portion of cases ranging from a high of 22 percent in Alberta to 4 percent in the Yukon.

Section 21 requires a judge to "have regard to the . . . means of the young person to pay" before imposing a fine or a monetary compensation order, but in some cases, a parent may end up paying a fine, an outcome that sends a bad message to a young offender.

---

18   Figures from Statistics Canada, Canadian Centre for Justice Statistics, *Youth Court Statistics 1994–95* (Ottawa: Statistics Canada, 1996), Table 2; and S. Moyer, *A Profile of the Juvenile Justice System in Canada* (Ottawa: Federal-Provincial-Territorial Task Force on Youth Justice, 1996). Note that the figures in the text add up to more than 100 percent, since some youths received more than one disposition, such as probation in combination with community service.

19   YOA, above note 6, s. 45(1)(d.2).

Under section 21(2) a provincial government may establish a "fine option" program to allow youths to "work off" their fines by performing some form of community-service work instead of making monetary payments; not many such programs have been established, and, if it seems unlikely that a youth will be able to pay a fine, it is more common for judges to impose directly a community-service order, which requires a youth to work a specific number of hours. With a community-service order, the court orders a number of hours of work to be performed; under section 21(7) the maximum community-service order is 240 hours. Specific types of community-service work are generally arranged by youth probation officers or through a community agency. These orders are intended to remind youths that they have done an act that has harmed the whole community, which is entitled to some form of compensation through a youth's service. Sometimes the community-service work can be related to the offence, so that a youth who vandalizes public property might be required to do some maintenance work for the municipality.

A judge may also order that a young offender provide some form of monetary compensation or do some type of work for a victim. This type of compensatory sanction has the advantage of bringing home to the youth the damage caused by an offence, though some victims want nothing further to do with an offender. With both community-service orders and orders that work should be done for a victim, there is a potential for problems in supervision of the work; some young offenders require substantial supervision to ensure that work is properly done.

Because of its restorative and symbolic value for youths and their communities, judges often impose a "reparative sanction" — restitution, compensation, or community service. Such a disposition is imposed in 36 percent of youth court cases, with the most frequently imposed sentence being community service, generally in combination with probation. Over half of the young offenders in Quebec and Prince Edward Island received some type of reparative sanction, but it was imposed in less than 30 percent of the cases in Ontario and New Brunswick.

The most frequently imposed disposition is probation, with 65 percent of youths receiving this sentence, often in combination with some other disposition, such as a requirement for community service or a fine. A term of probation may also be imposed to follow after a period in custody, though the maximum cumulative period of custody and probation is normally two years.[20]

---

20   *Ibid.*, s. 20(3). If a youth receives a custodial sentence of longer than two years, a court reviewing the disposition may order release on probation so that the total sentence exceeds two years.

The nature of a probation order depends on the circumstances, and judges have a wide power to impose "appropriate conditions." While some orders require that a youth meet regularly with a probation officer for counselling or supervision, this is not an essential part of a probation order. A probation order may include conditions that a youth keep a curfew, attend school, or reside with parents, or even complete a wilderness program (such as a canoe trip).[21]

Sometimes a judge will set out the "nature" of the terms of probation but allow another person to specify the "details." For example, a judge may order that a youth shall keep a curfew set by a parent or attend counselling as directed by a probation officer. These orders are quite commonly made and allow for flexibility. Some judges, however, have ruled that it is not permissible for a judge to "delegate" dispositional powers in this way, and they have held that a youth who fails to abide by specific terms imposed by a parent or probation officer cannot be convicted of breach of probation. Given the need for flexibility to meet changing circumstances and the lack of information available to a court at the time of disposition, there are good reasons to take a broad interpretation of section 23(2) and grant probation officers significant authority to set specific terms within perimeters set by a judge. However, giving parents this type of authority can be problematic and may place parents in a difficult position in the event of breach.[22]

Section 23(2)(f) specifically allows a probation order to include a term that a youth "reside in such place as the provincial director may specify." These orders are quite frequently made and allow a judge to provide that young offenders may be placed outside their homes if parental care is inadequate or unavailable, without requiring a youth to receive a custodial disposition. A "residency term" may result in a youth residing with a relative, or being required to complete a wilderness program, or being placed in a child-welfare facility or group home.[23] Some judges have even gone so far as to hold that the provincial director (youth corrections or probation officers) may direct a youth to reside in an open-custody facility pursuant to a section 23(2)(f) probation

---

21   R. v. B.(J.P.) (1993), 31 B.C.A.C. 81 (C.A.).
22   See, e.g., R. v. F.(P.D.) (1987), 57 C.R. (3d) 22 (Ont. Prov. Ct.), Nasmith Prov. J.
     (probation term: "Live with mother and obey rules and curfew" unenforceable),
     but see contra R. v. G.(J.) (26 October 1993), (Ont. Prov. Ct.) [unreported]
     [summarized 23 W.C.B. (2d) 49] R. v. R.(B.J.) (13 January 1986), (Ont. C.A.)
     [unreported] [summarized Y.O.S. 86–026].
23   R. v. M.(A.D.) (30 October 1984), (Man. C.A.) [unreported] [summarized [1985]
     W.D.F.L. 130].

order[24]; however, the better interpretation of the *YOA* is that, in light of the statutory restrictions on the use of custody by judges, it would be inappropriate to allow the provincial director to be able in effect to impose a custodial disposition on a youth who has been sentenced to probation.[25]

When a probation order is made, the judge or a probation officer is obliged to explain the significance of the order to the youth, and the youth is expected to sign a copy of the order acknowledging that an explanation has been provided; copies of the order are to be given to the youth and any parent who is in court with the youth.[26]

All probation orders include terms that the youth must "keep the peace and be of good behaviour" and "appear before the youth court when required by the court." A few judges exercise the power to have a youth return to the court so that his or her progress can be monitored. However, these terms generally have little practical significance, since youth on probation are usually required to return to court only if they are charged with a completely new offence, if they are charged with an offence under section 26 of the *YOA* as a result of breach of a specific term of the order, such as a failure to attend school if required by the probation order, or if there is an application under section 31 to review the order to make the terms less restrictive.

Under the *Juvenile Delinquents Act* judges could "commit" a delinquent youth to an "industrial school" for an indefinite period, with release occurring only when correctional officials felt that the youth was ready for release or the youth reached the age of twenty-one.[27] Since the philosophy of the *JDA* was (at least in theory) exclusively rehabilitation-oriented, the juvenile was to be returned to the community only if it was believed that rehabilitation had occurred. With more emphasis on accountability and due process, the *YOA* eliminated indefinite committals to custody. Under section 20(1)(k) of the *YOA* judges may place a youth in "custody" for a determinate period, with a process for a youth court "disposition review" and the possibility for early release. For most offences the maximum custodial sentence is two years,[28] though, for an

---

24 *R. v. J.(M.K.)* (1994), 137 N.S.R. (2d) 260 (C.A.).
25 *R. v. E.(S.M.)* (7 July 1989), (Ont. C.A.) [unreported] [summarized (1989), 7 W.C.B. (2d) 317].
26 *YOA*, above note 6, ss. 20(3)–(6).
27 *Juvenile Deliquents Act*, R.S.C. 1970, c. J-3, ss. 20(1)(g) and 21 [*JDA*].
28 Under s. 20(7) of the *YOA*, above note 6, no disposition imposed on a young offender shall exceed the statutory maximum that is applicable to an adult for the same offence. For summary offences, the maximum custodial sentence for youth or adult is six to eighteen months.

offence for which an adult can be punished by life imprisonment, a youth may receive a sentence of up to three years in custody. For first-degree murder, the maximum youth court sentence is ten years, with the possibility of longer sentences if the youth is transferred under section 16 of the *YOA* to adult court for trial and sentencing. Under the *YOA* judges decide the "level" of custody — "open" or " secure" — but youth correctional officials determine the specific facility in which the youth will be placed within that level after the sentence has been imposed.

In comparison to the *JDA*, judges are making many more custodial dispositions under the *YOA*, though the average length of time that youths spend in a custodial facility has declined since the *JDA* was in force. About 17 percent of youths sentenced in youth court receive an open-custody disposition, that is, placement in a group home, wilderness camp, or similar facility, with an average sentence of 84 days. About 14 percent of youths receive a sentence in secure custody, with an average sentence of 107 days.

As with other *YOA* dispositions, there is substantial variation between jurisdictions in the use of custody, ranging from 39 percent of the cases in the Yukon to 21 percent of the cases in Manitoba. The fact that some provinces divert more cases from court affects custody rates. In particular, youth court judges in Quebec impose a custodial disposition in about the same percentage of cases as that in the court system elsewhere in Canada; however, since that province has by far the highest diversion rate, there is a much lower rate of custody use as a percentage of the adolescent population in Quebec than elsewhere in Canada.[29]

Custody is by far the most expensive and intrusive disposition. Although some youths may receive appropriate treatment in custodial facilities, for too many youths the experience has a negative effect on behaviour. Being removed from their community and placed with other offenders often results in further offending. The negative environment created by other offenders can frequently make a correctional facility a "school for crime," and there is also the possibility of peer abuse increasing feelings of aggression. As will be more fully discussed later in this chapter, there are many legal and correctional issues related to custody, and there have been efforts in recent years to try to reduce the rate of custody use for young offenders in Canada.

One of the restrictions facing youth court judges in making a disposition is that they do not have the direct authority to order the government to provide services to a youth in the community or in custody. Nor are

---

29   See, e.g., Doob & Sprott, above note 1.

judges able to place a youth in a particular custody facility; rather they are limited to specifying a level of custody — open or secure — and at most to making a "recommendation" about a particular custodial placement.

In many places in Canada, judges face a situation in which there is a lack of community-based alternatives for youth sentencing, and the available custodial facilities may not be appropriate for a youth being sentenced. Although there are some excellent programs and facilities with good records for rehabilitating young offenders, in many places justice system professionals often deal with cases where there is a lack of real options: perhaps little or no appropriate treatment obtainable in the youth's community, and the only available custody facilities offering little more than security, accommodation, and access to some educational services.[30]

In a 1996 Alberta decision, already discussed in chapter 2, a judge invoked section 3(1)(c.1) of the *YOA*, the principle that the "protection of society . . . is best served by rehabilitation, whenever possible," as the basis for an order requiring the provincial government to pay for community-based treatment services needed by a youth who was placed on probation by the court. The judge felt that custodial sentence was not warranted for the offence, particularly because the youth had already been in detention for a significant period of time pending sentencing, and defence counsel requested probation with the requirement that the youth be admitted to treatment at a community drug-addiction program, with a judicial direction that the provincial Ministry of Justice should pay the costs of treatment in the community, to the extent not otherwise covered by other government funding arrangements. The Crown prosecutor argued that there was no authority in the *YOA* for a judge to require the government to pay for needed services. The judge acknowledged that there was no specific statutory authority to allow a judge to direct that a government provide or pay for services, but Judge Cook-Stanhope concluded that the 1995 amendments to section 3 create:

> a positive duty on this youth court to assess and then to address, appropriately, the needs and circumstances of every individual young person . . . with a view to ameliorating those risks which are likely to cause the individual to continue to exhibit offending behaviours. . . .
> If the principles enunciated in s. 3 are to be more than just hollow-sounding rhetoric, youth courts must be equipped with the authority to ensure that their orders will take effect. Failing that, this statute will not operate effectively as a special code for young persons. . . . If the

---

30   See, e.g., "Myths, Facts and the Potential of the Treatment Option" in Ontario Social Development Council, *Youth Justice in Crisis* (Toronto: The Council, 1994) 114.

youth courts are not possessed of such powers to attend to the rehabilitative requirements of young persons, public clamour for more and
harsher punitive measures instead of more effective rehabilitative ones
will continue to build and eventually completely overtake other
informed debate concerning appropriate . . . measures to deal with our
young people who come into conflict with the law.[31]

It is doubtful whether a youth court judge has the authority to order the
government to pay for or provide particular services in the absence of a
clear statutory power or a violation of the *Charter,* indeed, the making
of such an order seems inconsistent with the generally accepted role of
judges in Canada.[32] However, one can easily understand this judge's
frustration in the face of provincial reluctance to provide appropriate
rehabilitative services. The decision reflects an ongoing tension
between youth court judges and the youth corrections officials about
who will control resource decisions that profoundly affect how the
youth justice system operates.

D. REPEAL OF THE TREATMENT-ORDER PROVISION: SECTIONS 20(1)(i) AND 22

Perhaps the most controversial dispositional provision of the *YOA* as
originally enacted was section 20(1)(i), which allowed a youth court
judge to make a "treatment order" to have a young offender "detained
for treatment" in a psychiatric hospital or other "treatment facility"
instead of being placed in a custodial facility. These orders could be
made only if recommended in a medical, psychiatric, or psychological
report, prepared pursuant to section 13 of the *YOA*, and only if the
youth and the facility consented. These orders were very rarely made,
with only eight reported for all of Canada in 1994–95, and the provision
was repealed in 1995.[33]

This provision was controversial for a number of reasons. Mental-
health professionals criticized the requirement in section 22 that a youth

---

31   *R. v. A.(L.),* [1996] A.J. No. 957 (Prov. Ct.) (QL) [*A.(L.)*].

32   The Crown did not appeal; however, see, e.g., *Peel (Regional Municipality) v.
MacKenzie,* [1982] 2 S.C.R. 9 [no jurisdiction under *JDA*, above note 27, for court
to order municipality to pay for services]; *R. v. B.(K.)* (5 November 1992), (Alta.
Q.B.) [unreported], Deyell J. [no jurisdiction to order government to pay for *YOA*,
above note 6, s. 22 treatment order — provision now repealed].

33   *YOA 1995,* above note 6, ss. 13(2) & 14.

had to consent to the making of a treatment order, arguing that "youth, especially those involved in offending, may not be in the best position to make ultimate decisions regarding the value of mental health intervention."[34] Indeed, for many young offenders, their mental or emotional disturbance both causes their criminal behaviour and affects their capacity to appreciate their problems. As a result, some mental-health professionals advocated removal of the statutory requirement for a youth's consent to a treatment order. Although these mental-health advocates acknowledge that "the efficacy of compulsory treatment for young offenders is an area laden with considerable debate," they believe that once emotionally disturbed adolescents are placed in a treatment facility, they are willing to participate in treatment, even though they are unwilling to consent to it formally when asked in a courtroom.

In considering the issue of treatment orders, it should be appreciated that rehabilitative services can be provided in custody facilities without a court order for treatment, though provincial laws generally require that young persons in custody, like adults, consent or at least acquiesce to the provision of mental-health or other medical services. Further, without their consent, young offenders are sometimes placed on probation with a requirement that they attend counselling or participate in a treatment program (for example, for drug or alcohol abuse, or for adolescent sexual offenders). The *YOA* required only that a youth consent to being "*detained* for treatment," when such an order was made, *instead of* placing a youth in custody [emphasis added].

The statutory requirement for a youth's consent to being detained for treatment was premised on a belief that, except for those who are legally found mentally disordered, individuals should have the right to decide whether or not to have treatment. Offenders may be held accountable and punished by society, but they should not be subject to involuntary treatment, especially in light of the history of involuntary mental-health treatment, which sometimes involved such intrusive procedures as drug treatment and even electroshock therapy. There may be a temptation simply to sedate young offenders who are not willing to engage in therapy. There are also real questions about the rehabilitative value of involuntary treatment.

Section 20(1)(i) was repealed because so few orders were being made. This reflected both difficulties in securing the consent of young offenders to the making of such orders, as well as the concerns of mental-

34 See, e.g., A.W. Leschied & P. Gendreau, "Doing Justice in Canada: YOA Policies That Can Promote Community Safety" (1994) 36 Can. J. Crim. 291 at 293.

health facilities about their legal position if a youth consented to the making of an order but withdrew the consent upon arrival at the facility.[35]

Despite the repeal of section 20(1)(i), in cases involving severely disturbed youths, the mental-disorder provisions of the *Criminal Code* or provincial mental legislation (discussed in chapter 7) may still be invoked to require a youth suffering from a mental disorder to be involuntarily confined in a mental-health facility. Some youths who commit relatively minor offences are diverted in order to receive assistance in the community for their "special needs" through the mental-health, education, or child-protection systems.

The most effective means of successfully engaging a young offender who is in custody in therapy or counselling will usually involve offering the possibility of early review and release from custody as an incentive to participation. This type of inducement can serve to secure the youth's cooperation, and it makes sense to offer early release to a youth who has successfully undergone treatment. The biggest difficulties in providing rehabilitative services and counselling to young offenders, both in custody and in the community on probation, relate to the failure of provinces to provide an adequate level of funding and service, not to any legal concerns.

E. CUSTODY: OPEN AND SECURE

The most serious disposition that can be ordered under section 20 of the *YOA* is placement in a custodial facility. For most offences the maximum custodial disposition is two years, but for offences for which an adult may receive life imprisonment the maximum is three years, and for murder ten years. The *YOA* requires a judge placing a youth in custody to specify whether the sentence will be served in "open custody" or "secure custody."[36]

Section 24.1 of the *YOA* defines an open-custody facility as a "community residential centre, group home, child care institution, or forest or wilderness camp, or . . . any other like place or facility *designated* . . . as a place of open custody" [emphasis added] by the provincial govern-

---

35   *R. v. A.(L.)*, above note 31.

36   *YOA*, above note 6, s. 24(3) allows a province or territory to have the provincial director make an initial decision about the level of custody, subject to a right to have this decision reviewed by a youth court judge under s. 28.1. Because the court retains ultimate control, no governments have implemented s. 24(3) and decisions about the level of custody are made by youth court judges.

ment. "[S]ecure custody" means a place "for the secure containment or restraint" of young persons which is *"designated"* [emphasis added] as "secure custody" by the provincial government. The courts have held that section 24.1 gives provincial governments significant discretion to determine whether a facility is "open" or "secure," since a key part of the definition is the power of "designation." In some cases a facility that might be designated "secure" at one time can be redesignated "open" without significantly changing its nature.[37] In extreme cases, however, a court can declare that a designation of a facility as "open" is invalid if the physical environment, programming, and staffing arrangements are inconsistent with the "meaning of open custody," as occurred in one case where the government of Nova Scotia designated a former adult jail as a place of both open and secure custody, with youths in "open custody" having unlocked cells.[38] The court observed: "Parliament has stated that open custody would be something other than the previous traditional form of incarceration."

There is a judicial expectation that open-custody facilities will have a rehabilitative focus, and this is taken into account when sentencing a youth. In *R. v. M.(J.J.)* the Supreme Court upheld a two-year open-custody sentence in the expectation that it would serve a rehabilitative function. Justice Cory commented on open-custody facilities:

> [T]hose facilities are not simply to be jails for young people. Rather they are facilities dedicated to the long term welfare and reformation of the young offender. Open custody facilities do not and should not resemble penitentiaries.[39]

Since the definition is broad, facilities that are "open" in one province may be similar to ones that are "secure" in another jurisdiction or even in the same province. In practice, however, secure-custody facilities tend to be larger institutions with more emphasis on security. Open-custody facilities tend to be group homes, wilderness camps, or farms, with young offenders who are more likely to be attending school in the community. In some jurisdictions open-custody facilities may have both young offenders and adolescents in the care of child-welfare authorities. Secure-custody facilities are almost all operated by the government, while some open-custody facilities are operated by private operators or non-profit organizations.

---

37 *F.(C.) v. R.* (1985), 30 Man. R. (2d) 297 (C.A.).

38 *Re B.(D.)* (1986), 72 N.S.R. (2d) 354 (T.D.).

39 *R. v. M.(J.J.)*, [1993] 2 S.C.R. 421 at 430–31.

There are great differences between youth custody facilities both within and between provinces. The *YOA* requires youth in custody to be "separate and apart from any adult . . . in custody."[40] In some places youths are merely kept in separate sections of adult facilities, though most youth custody facilities are completely separate from adult correctional facilities. In general, youth in custody have access to education; in some facilities the educational programming is quite sophisticated, with special efforts to identify and address the needs of adolescents with learning disabilities. Some custody facilities have intensive rehabilitative programs with psychological and other rehabilitation services, while in others there is little in the way of programming or rehabilitative services and youths spend much of their time watching television. Some facilities have programming to deal with certain age groups or types of offenders, such as violent offenders. Other facilities deal with all offenders in a geographical area.

In some custody facilities, there are serious problems with some young offenders being abused and intimidated by other youths.[41] In all facilities there are concerns that youths who are more vulnerable or sensitive may be subject to negative influences from more "experienced" offenders, as well as experiencing feelings of isolation in an institutional environment. While some facilities, especially open custody, have staff who have appropriate educational qualifications as well as an interest in working with youth, in other facilities, particularly secure ones, the staff has a more "custodial" orientation. There continue to be reports of abuse by staff in youth custody facilities in Canada.[42] The sad reality, however, is that for some youth in custody, the level of care and degree of comfort they experience in these facilities is better than that in the abusive, impoverished homes they have left, although even these youth miss the freedom of their previous lives.

As originally enacted, the *YOA* has statutory rules to restrict the use of secure custody, permitting its use only if a youth committed a more serious offence or had a record of not complying with *YOA* dispositions; there were tighter restrictions for use of secure custody for youths under fourteen.[43] Amendments in 1995 removed the offence, record, and age-

---

40   *YOA*, above note 6, s. 24.2(4).

41   In a tragic Ontario case, a vulnerable sixteen-year-old in custody was murdered by his cellmate; K. Toughill, "A life in pain," *Toronto Star* (22 September 1996) B1.

42   See, e.g., "Youths pinned down, beaten, report says," Canadian Press, 7 Nov. 1996; and Nova Scotia, *In Our Care — Abuse and Young Offenders in Custody: An Audit of the Shelburne Youth Centre and the Nova Scotia Youth Centre – Waterville* (1995).

43   *YOA*, above note 6, ss. 24.1(3) and (4), as am. by *An Act to amend the Young Offenders Act, the Criminal Code, the Penitentiary Act and the Prisons and Reformatories Act*, R.S.C. 1985 (2d Supp.), c. 24, s. 17.

based statutory criteria, giving judges a broader discretion to shape secure-custody dispositions that meet the needs of individual youths while still attempting to restrict the use of secure custody. Section 24.1(4) now provides that, in deciding on the level of custody, a youth court judge shall take account of the following factors:

(*a*) that a young person should be placed in a level of custody involving the least degree of containment and restraint, having regard to

  (i) the seriousness of the offence in respect of which the young person was committed to custody and the circumstances in which that offence was committed,

  (ii) the needs and circumstances of the young person, including proximity to family, school, employment and support services,

  (iii) the safety of other young persons in custody, and

  (iv) the interests of society;

(*b*) that the level of custody should allow for the best possible match of programs to the young person's needs and behaviour, having regard to the findings of any assessment in respect of the young person;

(*c*) the likelihood of escape if the young person is placed in open custody; and

(*d*) the recommendations, if any, of . . . the provincial director.

These statutory provisions emphasize the principle of the "least restrictive alternative." In general, youth courts are reluctant to impose a secure-custody sentence on a youth who has not previously been in open custody. However, the courts have held that even a first offence by a youth which involves a significant degree of violence may warrant secure custody to "act as a sufficient general deterrent and to reflect society's abhorrence of this kind of violence."[44]

While section 24.3 of the *YOA* allows youth courts to impose consecutive sentences of a period in secure custody followed by open custody if there is a disposition being imposed for more than one offence, it is not clear that a judge can impose this type of sentence if there is a finding of guilt for only one offence. There are reported cases where this type of split custodial sentence was imposed,[45] and it gives the court some flexibility, but none of them explicitly dealt with the question of whether there is a statutory basis for this type of sentence. In cases

---

44 *R. v. H.(S.R.)* (1990), 56 C.C.C. (3d) 46 at 51 (Ont. C.A.), Galligan J.A.

45 See, e.g., *R. v. M.(M.L.)* (1990), 82 Sask. R. 81 (C.A.).

where the issue has been explicitly raised, courts have ruled that section 24.1(2) requires a custodial sentence to be either "open custody *or* secure custody," and not both, ruling that any change between the levels of custody should be dealt with by way of disposition review.[46]

F. CUSTODY ALTERNATIVES: WILDERNESS CAMPS, BOOT CAMPS, AND OTHER INNOVATIONS

Most custody programs experience a recidivism rate at or above 50 percent, and professionals who work with young offenders have tried to develop various alternatives to traditional custody-based programs with the aim of reducing recidivism. Two important innovations have been wilderness camps and boot camps.

In the 1970s a number of wilderness camps and programs for young offenders were established in Canada based on an "Outward Bound" model. Adolescent offenders were removed from their urban environments and placed in a setting where cooperation and self-reliance were developed in a wilderness-based program of physical challenge. These types of programs continue to operate. Research indicates that these programs do improve self-esteem and that offending behaviour may decline immediately after release, but that these positive effects generally erode within six months after youths return to their communities.[47] This does not mean that all wilderness camps should be abandoned, but they may be more successful if they focus on certain offenders; for example, wilderness camps may have a role in working with Aboriginal youth in a culturally appropriate fashion.

A more recent innovation has been "boot camps," a concept in youth corrections that was first developed in the United States in the 1980s. While there are different types of boot camps, they are all based on some form of discipline-oriented regime that adopts some features of camps for military recruits, with youths (almost always males) in uniform and subject to a physically demanding regime and strict supervision. Some of the American boot camps actually use former military personnel as staff. This type of regime is politically popular, premised on notions that what young offenders need is "discipline," and that they are

---

46   See, e.g., *R. v. W.(F.L.)* (1986), 78 N.S.R. (2d) 225 (C.A.). [Emphasis added].

47   J. Winterdyk & R. Roesch, "A Wilderness Experiential Program as an Alternative for Probationers: An Evaluation" (1982) 24 Can. J. Crim. 39.

more likely to "feel punished" in this type of environment and hence may be deterred from committing further offences. It is also based on the somewhat romanticized idea that a quasi-military experience can "turn boys into men."

The American experience with these programs reveals that discipline during a custodial sentence, in itself, has no effect on recidivism after release. Fred Mathews, a Toronto psychologist with extensive experience in working with young offenders, comments:

> The assumption of a boot camp is that it is only the absence of strict discipline that got these kids into trouble in the first place, which is so far down the list of difficulties they've had to deal with in their lives. It's not the absence of strict discipline that got these kids into trouble. It's being beaten up and abused; it's living in poverty; it's living in neighborhoods that are under-resourced and poorly supported; it's cutting services and support for families far earlier in their lives than adolescence.[48]

American research on boot camps demonstrates that programs that are closest to the "military models," emphasizing discipline and physical activity, are no better than ordinary custody programs in reducing the recidivism of adolescent offenders. The American "boot camps" that are successful have significant educational, counselling, and life-skills programs for youth in custody and provide substantial supervision and support after release.[49] Some critics of boot camps have questioned whether the discipline and regimentation are crucial to the success of these programs, arguing that it is the rehabilitative and educational services in custody, and the community follow-up, that are key to reducing recidivism.[50]

The idea of boot camps has struck a responsive chord among members of the Canadian public and conservative politicians. Alberta, Manitoba, and Ontario have established secure-custody facilities that emphasize "strict discipline" and a controlled, busy schedule. Drawing on American experience,[51] these facilities have significant rehabilitative and educational

---

48   Quoted from J. Coyle, "Boot camps tough, but where is the love?" [Kingston] *Whig Standard* (13 February 1997).

49   D.L. MacKenzie *et al.* "Boot Camp Prisons and Recidivism in Eight States" (1995) 33 Criminology 327.

50   John Howard Society of Ontario, *Boot Camps for Young Offenders* (Toronto: The Society, 1996).

51   Ontario, Solicitor General, *Recommendations from the Task Force on Strict Discipline for Young Offenders* (Toronto: Queen's Printer, 1996); J. Rusk, "Old prison farm to be used as boot camp, Runciman says," *[Toronto] Globe and Mail* (12 February 1997) A6.

components as well as post-release community follow-up, but there is still no research on how successful the Canadian programs are.

There is no single program or type of facility that can solve the problems of all young offenders, but some types of programs will work better than others for youths with particular needs and problems. Courts and correctional officials need to assess the situation of individual young offenders and match them with programs that meet their particular circumstances. For some youth, wilderness programs or even "boot camps" may be effective, but for many youths these programs will not be effective in preventing recidivism. While secure facilities may be needed to supervise relatively small numbers of young offenders, within these institutions there should be individualized assessment and treatment for youths; otherwise their needs will not be met and they are likely to reoffend after release. For those youths who are placed in custody, community-based after-care programs to guide re-entry into the school system, family, and labour force are critical to efforts to reduce recidivism.[52]

G. DISPOSITION REVIEW AND SUPERVISION OF YOUTH IN CUSTODY

The YOA gives a youth court continuing authority to monitor and review dispositions in order to ensure that they continue to meet the changing needs and circumstances of a young offender. A youth court review cannot increase the severity of the original disposition. However, if a youth commits a new offence while subject to a prior disposition, or violates the term of the original disposition (for example, by breaching a term of a probation order) and thereby commits an offence under section 26 of the YOA, the court may impose an additional sentence for the new offence.[53]

A disposition review hearing can be conducted under section 31 in connection with a non-custodial disposition; for example, such a hearing can be held if a young person is unable to pay a fine and wants to request a reduction in the amount, or if there is a need to review the terms of a probation order because of a change in a youth's circumstances or in the availability of community-based progress. However, most of the disposition reviews arise in regard to custodial dispositions.

---

52   R.A. Silverman & J.H. Creechan, *Delinquency Treatment and Intervention* (Ottawa: Department of Justice, 1995).

53   S. 20(4.1) of the *YOA*, above note 6, provides that if a youth commits an offence while subject to a prior disposition, the court may impose a consecutive disposition so that the total disposition may exceed three years.

With longer custodial sentences, there must be a youth court review at least once a year.[54] Provincial correctional officials, the Crown prosecutor, parents, or a young offender can seek review of any custodial disposition after six months, and after the expiry of one-third of the sentence if it is less than a year long.[55]

When a youth is ordered into custody, provincial correctional officials have significant control over the youth's placement. As noted earlier, while a youth court disposition specifies the level of custody — open or secure — correctional officials determine the specific facility where the youth will reside and can move the offender from one facility in that level to another.[56]

Correctional officials may also permit the temporary absence of the youth from custody, with or without an escort, to permit a youth to seek educational, rehabilitative, or employment opportunities, or for compassionate reasons, such as to attend a funeral.[57] A temporary absence (or "T.A.") may be for a specified number of hours each day, for example, to attend school, or for a period of up to fifteen days, such as to allow a visit home to facilitate reintegration into the community after release. In practice, some correctional officials will grant "back-to-back" temporary-absence passes to allow early release from custody without seeking court review, though this was not the intent of the legislation; such a release should be the subject of a judicial decision.

While the youth court specifies the level of custody when the original disposition is made, section 24.2(11) gives correctional officials the authority to transfer a youth from an open to a secure-custody facility, having regard to such factors as the needs of the youth, available programming, and the safety of others. If such a transfer occurs, the youth and parents are to be notified of the right to have this decision reviewed at a hearing before a youth court judge.[58] Correctional officials also have the authority to transfer a youth from open to secure custody for up to fifteen days without court review if the youth has "escaped," or "attempted to escape," from open custody (which may simply involve leaving a group home without permission), or if correctional officials consider that there is a risk to the safety of the youth or others.[59] An

---

54   *Ibid.*, s. 28(1).
55   *Ibid.*, s. 28(3). A sentence must be at least thirty days to be eligible for judicial review.
56   *Ibid.*, s. 24.2.
57   *Ibid.*, s. 35.
58   *Ibid.*, ss. 24.2(13) and 28.1.
59   *Ibid.*, s. 24.2(9).

escape or an attempt to escape from custody constitutes a new offence that will normally result in further charges and an additional custodial sentence being imposed by a court.

For adult offenders, release prior to completion of a full custodial sentence is governed by legislation; in some cases, it is automatic after expiry of a portion of the sentence and in other circumstances it is controlled by a parole board — a non-judicial administrative tribunal. For young offenders, release from custody before the completion of a sentence is regulated by the youth court review process. Section 28(4) of the *YOA* provides that a youth court judge should change a custodial disposition if: the youth "has made sufficient progress" in custody; or there are new programs or facilities available; or "the opportunities for rehabilitation are now greater in the community"; or there has been some other change in circumstances.

Often youth court reviews occur without a hearing being held. Correctional officials may recommend release of a youth from custody onto probation, or may transfer a youth from secure to open custody, subject to the approval of a youth court judge.[60] Normally, the court-approval process for such a recommendation to lessen the severity of the original disposition is completed without a hearing on the basis of written documentation, including a "progress report," prepared by correctional or probation staff, describing the performance of the youth in custody. Sometimes a hearing is required, either because the judge calls for one or because the Crown prosecutor's office, which must be informed before the decision is finalized, requests a hearing.

The review provisions are intended to give youths in custody an incentive to "mend their ways" by participating in rehabilitative programs and changing their behaviour and attitude. These provisions have been referred to by a judge as a wonderfully malleable tool and a "humane" provision.[61] However, there continues to be controversy over the effectiveness of the process of youth court review of custodial dispositions, especially in cases where the correctional officials are not supporting release or movement from secure to open custody. These contested hearings usually occur under the automatic annual-review provisions, or if a youth requests a review without the support of correctional officials. If the correctional authorities are not supporting the youth's request, it is important for the youth to present a basis for a review, and counsel for the youth has a critical role to play in helping

---

60   *Ibid.*, s. 29.
61   *R. v. T.(K.)* (1994), 125 Sask. R. 260 at 266 (C.A.), Bayda C.J.S.

to develop a plan and present evidence to the court to support a change in custody.

Typically, review hearings are conducted by the judge who made the original disposition, though this is not required. In some places there are delays in conducting review hearings. Some judges have shown considerable flexibility in applying the review provisions, ruling that factors related to the offence and concerns about deterrence are less important at the review than at the original sentencing while the progress and circumstances of the youth are more important.[62] It has also been recognized that the failure to reduce the sentence of a youth who has made good progress in custody may discourage that youth and imperil efforts at rehabilitation, as well as having a negative impact on other youths in custody.[63]

Other judges, however, seem reluctant to reduce originally imposed dispositions and, in response to such concerns, amendments were added to the review provisions in 1995 to encourage release in to the community. One significant amendment allows for a youth who is released from custody to be placed on "conditional supervision,"[64] in addition to the provisions allowing release on probation. A youth on conditional supervision may be subject to similar conditions to a youth released on probation, but there is a significantly wider authority for probation staff to control the youth who has been released. A youth who is in the community on conditional supervision may be returned to custody if there are concerns that he or she may be "about to breach" a condition of release.[65] The return to custody of a youth on conditional supervision is subject to a later youth court review. The court reviewing the case of a youth on "conditional supervision" requires only "reasonable grounds" to believe that a term of the release has been or is "about to [be] breach[ed]."[66] Community probation staff and police have significantly more control over a youth on conditional supervision than one released on probation, since with a youth on probation there must be an actual breach, and proof of it beyond a reasonable doubt, to allow this individual to be sentenced for the breach and returned to custody.

The 1995 amendments that added the conditional-supervision option for review were intended to increase control over youths who are released from custody into the community, and thereby to encourage judges to be

---

62 *R. v. T.(M.)*, [1995] Y.J. No. 6 (Terr. Ct.) (QL), Lilles Terr. J.

63 *R. v. R.(R.)*, [1996] O.J. No. 1101 (Prov. Ct.) (QL), Renaud Prov. J.

64 *YOA*, above note 6, s. 28(17)(c)(ii), enacted by *YOA 1995*, above note 6, s. 21(3).

65 *YOA, ibid.*, ss. 26.3 and 26.4.

66 *Ibid.*, s. 26.6.

more flexible about approving early release. There is ample evidence that the period following release from custody is vitally important for the long-term rehabilitation of young offenders who have been placed in custody. Youths who receive support and direction, and are able to successfully reintegrate into the education system, their families, or an employment situation, are much less likely to reoffend than those released without meaningful support.[67] This makes the custody-review and conditional-supervision provisions of the YOA highly significant for the protection of society in the long run.

There is no right to appeal a youth court's disposition-review decision to a higher court, since this is intended to be an expeditious process and it is likely that a youth would have an opportunity for a further youth court review hearing before an appeal could be heard.

H. MURDER SENTENCING

Murder is the youth offence that has, perhaps understandably, most captured public attention. Relatively few youths (twenty-five to sixty per year) are charged with this offence. The majority are ultimately convicted only of manslaughter,[68] since often the Crown cannot establish the requisite mental intent for murder; these adolescent killings often seem to be unpredictable and senseless acts. The YOA as originally enacted provided for a maximum sentence for conviction for murder in youth court of three years in custody, though youths could be transferred to adult court where they would face the full adult sanction of life imprisonment. In 1992, for the offence of murder, the YOA was amended to increase the maximum custodial sentence in youth court to five years less a day,[69] while still allowing for the possibility of transfer and longer adult sentences. Under the 1995 amendments, the maximum sentence for first degree murder in youth court was further increased to ten years, with a presumption that no more than six years will be served in custody

---

67   See, e.g., Silverman & Creechan, above note 52.

68   For example, in 1992–93, forty youths were charged with murder, of whom six were transferred to adult court, sixteen were found guilty in youth court, and eighteen had the murder charges dropped but some other conviction registered.

69   Five years less a day was chosen because the *Canadian Charter of Rights and Freedoms*, Part I of the *Constitution Act, 1982*, being Schedule B to the *Canada Act 1982* (U.K.), 1982, c. 11, s. 11(f), provides that a person is entitled to a jury trial if the maximum sentence is five years or longer. Jury trials are not easily accommodated in youth court, though, as discussed in ch. 7. Youths facing murder charges in youth court are now entitled to jury trials. Such trials, however, are presided over by superior court judges, albeit in proceedings governed by the YOA, above note 6.

and the balance on "conditional supervision" in the community.[70] For second degree murder, the maximum youth court sentence is seven years, with the first four years in custody and the balance on conditional supervision. Conditional supervision involves placement in the community where a youth will be subject to supervision by a probation officer and conditions on residency and behaviour, such as participating in therapy or drug counselling, attendance at school, and restraining from use of drugs or alcohol. With conditional supervision there is the possibility of return to custody if there are "reasonable grounds" to believe that a youth has breached or is "about to breach" a condition of release.[71]

When a sentence is imposed in a murder case for custody to be followed by release on conditional supervision, at the time scheduled for release on conditional supervision a youth court has jurisdiction not to release the youth if it is satisfied that there are "compelling reasons" to do so, such as a high risk of harm to others. A court may also order a youth who has been released on conditional supervision to be returned to custody to serve the remaining portion of the original murder sentence if the terms of the release have been breached or are "about to [be] breach[ed]."[72]

Ten years is the maximum youth court sentence for first degree murder, and seven years for second degree murder, but judges may impose shorter sentences or a youth may have the custodial portion of the sentence reduced at a disposition review. Youth fourteen years of age and older facing murder charges may be transferred for trial to adult court, where a longer sentence may be imposed.

The 1995 increases in maximum youth court sentences for murder were not a response to evidence that there was a danger to the community from having a maximum of five years less a day. Rather, the increases were clearly political — an attempt to satisfy concerns that the *YOA* is "too soft" on crime. As stated by Allan Rock, the minister of justice at the time the 1995 amendments were introduced, the government believed that the maximum youth court penalty for murder of five years less a day was "simply wrong . . . as a matter of principle."[73] That is, the issue of accountability was the dominant concern in the increase in the maximum youth court sanction.

---

70 *YOA*, *ibid.*, s. 20(1)(k.1) and 20(4), enacted by *YOA 1995*, above note 6, ss. 13(3) and (4).

71 *YOA*, ss. 26.2–26.6.

72 *Ibid.*, ss. 26.1–26.5.

73 *Minutes of Proceedings and Evidence of the Standing Committee on Justice and Legal Affairs* (22 June 1994) 34:19. See similar comments by Val Meredith, Reform Party critic: "If [youth] murders are down [without changing the law], that's great. But that doesn't mean that those who commit these kinds of crimes shouldn't be dealt with in a different fashion" Canadian Press, 1 Feb. 1995.

Once a "young person" who has been convicted of an offence in youth court and placed in custody reaches eighteen, correctional officials can apply under section 24.5 of the *YOA* to a youth court judge for an order to transfer the youth to an adult provincial correctional facility[74] to serve the balance of the disposition. If this type of custodial transfer occurs, the person remains subject to the *YOA* for such purposes as disposition review. The court is to make this order only if it is considered in the "best interests of the young person or in the public interest." Many youth facilities have significant numbers of "young offenders" who are eighteen, nineteen, or even twenty years old. Applications are generally made only under section 24.5 for those serving longer sentences, in particular for murder, or if they have been disruptive in a youth facility.

The imposition of sentences for murder is related to transfer to adult court and is discussed further in chapter 9.

I. DISPOSITIONAL PRINCIPLES: *R. v. M.(J.J.)*

For a number of years after the enactment of the *YOA* there was vigorous judicial debate about the appropriate dispositional philosophy for young offenders, accompanied by significant variation in dispositional practices. In the past few years, the Supreme Court of Canada and Parliament have attempted to provide a clearer philosophy and more structure to the exercise of judicial discretion in regard to dispositions, though it seems likely that dispositional patterns will continue to vary widely across the country.

As originally enacted in 1982, the *YOA* had no explicit dispositional principles. Section 3, the Act's Declaration of Principle, offered only general guidance and resulted in judges adopting differing dispositional philosophies and practices. For example, the Alberta Court of Appeal held that general deterrence, the imposition of a punishment on one youth for the purpose of deterring — or warning — others, should have no role in the sentencing of young offenders since it was not explicitly

---

74   Adult correctional facilities for those serving sentences of less than two years are operated by the provincial and territorial governments, while adults with sentences of two years or longer are placed in prisons operated by the federal government. In general there is a more hardened group of offenders and a more brutal atmosphere in the federal prisons, though federal prisons are divided into levels of security — minimum, medium, and maximum — with the most dangerous and abusive offenders being placed in maximum security.

mentioned in section 3 of the Act.[75] On the other hand, the Quebec Court of Appeal held that general deterrence was an appropriate factor to consider, as an aspect of protection of society.[76] Despite the fact that the Alberta courts in theory took no account of general deterrence while those in Quebec should have been using this factor to impose more custodial sentences, Alberta had a much higher rate of custody than Quebec, a fact which reveals that judicial statements of principle in regard to the sentencing of young offenders may not be that significant.

Another controversial interpretative issue was the extent to which social needs should be considered in dealing with young offenders. The Nova Scotia Court of Appeal held that the special needs of youths could be taken into account to impose relatively long custodial dispositions, especially in open custody, for adolescents requiring "strict controls and constant supervision."[77] The Ontario Court of Appeal, however, rejected this approach, stating that the "sentence . . . [must be] responsive to the offence," and held that a long custody sentence should *not* be imposed on a youth who committed a minor offence but who "had a personality problem and needed a place to go."[78] Rather, such a youth should be dealt with through the child-protection or mental-health systems.

The Supreme Court of Canada dealt with some of the controversies around *YOA* dispositions in its 1993 decision in *R. v. M.(J.J.)*.[79] The Supreme Court affirmed a sentence of two years in open custody for an Aboriginal youth convicted of three counts of break and enter and one of breach of probation. He came from an abusive home environment, which the Court characterized as "intolerable," and therefore "child welfare concerns" justified the relatively long sentence. Justice Cory began by considering the Declaration of Principle of the *YOA*:

> A quick reading of that section indicates that there is a marked ambivalence in its approach to the sentencing of young offenders. Yet that ambivalence should not be surprising when it is remembered that the Act reflects a courageous attempt to balance concepts and interests that are frequently conflicting.
>
> . . . .

---

75 *R. v. G.(K.)* (1986), 73 A.R. 376 (C.A.).

76 *R. v. L.(S.)* (1990), 75 C.R. (3d) 94 (Que. C.A.).

77 *R. v. R.(R.)* (18 June 1986), (N.S.C.A.) [unreported] [summarized (1986), 17 W.C.B. 109].

78 *R. v. B.(M.)* (1987), 36 C.C.C. (3d) 573 (Ont. C.A.) [*B.(M.)*].

79 [1993] 2 S.C.R. 421.

[T]here must be some flexibility in the dispositions imposed on young offenders. It is not unreasonable to expect that in many cases carefully crafted dispositions will result in the reform and rehabilitation of the young person. That must be the ultimate aim of all dispositions. They may often achieve this goal if the disposition is carefully tailored to meet both the need to protect society and to reform the offender.

. . . .

Section 3(1) attempts to balance the need to make the young offenders responsible for their crimes while recognizing their vulnerability and special needs. It seeks to chart a course that avoids both the harshness of a pure criminal law approach applied to minors and the paternalistic welfare approach that was emphasized in the old *Juvenile Delinquents Act* . . . there should be a departure from the strict criminal justice model in imposing penalties on young offenders.

The Supreme Court specifically accepted the "proportionality principle" for sentencing young offenders but indicated that it was less important than for adults and had to be weighed against child-welfare concerns.

It is true that for both adults and minors the sentence must be proportional to the offence committed. But in the sentencing of adult offenders, the principle of proportionality will have a greater significance than it will in the disposition of young offenders. For the young, a proper disposition must take into account not only the seriousness of the crime but also all the other relevant factors.

For example, two years of closed custody could never be imposed on a young offender with no prior record who had stolen a pair of gloves, no matter how intolerable or how unsavoury the conditions were in the offender's home. Nonetheless the home situation is a factor that should always be taken into account in fashioning the appropriate disposition. It is relevant in complying with the Act's requirement that an assessment must be made of the special needs and requirements for guidance of the young offender. Intolerable conditions in the home indicate both a special need for care and the absence of any guidance within the home.

The situation in the home of a young offender should neither be ignored nor made the predominant factor in sentencing. Nonetheless, it is a factor that can properly be taken into account in fashioning the disposition.

The Supreme Court also resolved the debate about the role of general deterrence for young offenders:

[A]lthough the principle of general deterrence must be considered, it [has] . . . diminished importance in determining the appropriate disposition in the case of a youthful offender.

. . . .

I would underline that general deterrence should not, through undue emphasis, have the same importance in fashioning the disposition for a youthful offender as it would in the case of an adult. One youthful offender should not be obliged to accept the responsibility for all the young offenders of his or her generation.

The Supreme Court emphasized that the primary aim of sentencing for young offenders should be rehabilitation.

The aim must be both to protect society and at the same time to provide the young offender with the necessary guidance and assistance that he or she may not be getting at home. Those goals are not necessarily mutually exclusive. In the long run, society is best protected by the reformation and rehabilitation of a young offender. In turn, the young offenders are best served when they are provided with the necessary guidance and assistance to enable them to learn the skills required to become fully integrated, useful members of society.

While the Supreme Court judgment in *R. v. M.(J.J.)* resolved some of the relatively abstract controversies about the legitimacy of considering general deterrence and child-welfare concerns when sentencing a young offender, it gave judges little specific direction. The Court also emphasized individualized decision making and judicial discretion, and it offered youth court judges only limited direction about how to prioritize different factors, except to indicate that rehabilitation should be a primary concern.

The Supreme Court decision also recognizes that for a variety of reasons, including inadequate funding, child-welfare services may not always be available for troubled youths, and the *YOA* may be the only available avenue. However, the decision in *M.(J.J.)* is problematic in this regard since youths may perceive themselves as receiving more severe dispositions because of their difficult family backgrounds. In a dissenting opinion at the Manitoba Court of Appeal level, Madam Justice Helper felt that a sentence of one year was appropriate as a "fit sentence" for the offences that this particular youth committed, arguing that the "criminal justice system ought not to be used to supplement the lack of resources that exist in the child welfare system." In *R. v. M.(J.J.)* the youth had actually sought assistance from child-welfare workers before the offences were committed but failed to receive it.[80]

---

80 (1991), 75 Man. R. (2d) 296 (C.A.).

The provision of needed services for adolescents under the *YOA* is not as desirable as having similar services provided by the child-welfare system, a system where the focus is truly on the "best interests" of youth and punishment and welfare are not confused. However, *R. v. M. (J.J.)* may have represented an effort by judges to make the best of a situation where the only available resources for a particular troubled adolescent were in the youth corrections system. While different sources for help would clearly have been preferable, judges do not control the delivery of services. One would at least hope that, if judges use the *YOA* to impose relatively long sentences for welfare purposes, they should be satisfied that appropriate services will actually be provided, and that they will be prepared to review a sentence if the expected help is not provided in custody.

J.   FACTORS AFFECTING CUSTODIAL SENTENCES: MITIGATING AND AGGRAVATING FACTORS

While the principles articulated in the *YOA* and the case law emphasize the need for an individualized assessment of all of the circumstances and for giving rehabilitation a paramount role, in practice the two most important factors in sentencing are the offence for which a youth is being sentenced and the youth's prior record.

For a first offence, there is a reluctance to impose a custodial term on the young offender,[81] unless the offence involves serious injury or substantial property damage. On the other hand, if there is a longer record of offences and it appears that community-based dispositions like probation have not deterred the youth from offending, there is a significant probability of a custodial disposition. The first custodial sentence should ordinarily be a relatively "short, sharp shock."[82] If there is a further offence after the completion of a short custodial sentence, it is likely that there will be a longer custodial sentence, even if the later offence is not more serious. Indeed, even if repeat offences are less serious than the earlier offence and, for example, involve only a failure to fully comply with the terms of a probation order, the sanctions are likely

---

81   *R. v. C. (J.M.)* (1994), 92 Man. R. (2d) 316.
82   *R. v. F. (J.S.)* (14 June 1988), (Alta. C.A.) [unreported] [summarized 5 W.C.B. (2d) 370] (Trial sentence of twelve months open custody reduced on appeal to three months for youth with lengthy prior record but no previous custody disposition).

to become more severe based on the "step principle" — the view that each subsequent offence requires an increasingly severe sanction.[83]

While the offence and prior record are the most important factors, other factors are considered. Courts are, for example, especially reluctant to impose custodial sentences on younger adolescents.[84] If the parents of a youth appear supportive and express a willingness to work with probation authorities, this will favour a non-custodial disposition,[85] though in practice this tends to favour adolescents from middle-class families. If a young person appears to have appreciated the consequences of his or her actions, and is expressing remorse, this will tend to mitigate the sentence that would otherwise be imposed, but an expression of remorse after a long record of offending may appear insincere and not affect sentencing.

Youth courts have clearly indicated that for "gang related" offences, especially those involving violence, deterrence will be more important and more severe sentences will be imposed. The goal is to deter other gang members and reflects the fact that such offences often have a "premeditated" or "cowardly" element.[86] Similarly, offences involving violence or bullying in schools may receive a more severe sanction because of concerns about deterrence and maintaining order as well as protection of victims who may again be confronted by the young offender.[87]

In cases where an offence involves a death, such as criminal negligence causing death, a custodial disposition will be appropriate even if there was no intent to cause death and there are no concerns about reoffending.[88] In cases involving intentional killing, such as manslaughter and murder, courts are likely to impose sentences at or near the maximum allowed under the *YOA* "'even though they may not be the worst possible kinds of cases,'" and are less likely to reduce a sentence to take account of pre-disposition detention.[89]

---

83   P.J. Carrington & S. Moyer, "Factors Affecting Custodial Dispositions under the *Young Offenders Act*" (1995) 37 Can J. Crim. 127.

84   *R. v. W.(B.)* (1995), 61 B.C.A.C. 136 (C.A.) (one month in custody followed by probation for serious assault by twelve-year-old).

85   *R. v. F.(A.)*, [1995] O.J. No. 2323 (Prov. Ct.) (QL) (twenty-four months probation for several property related offences involving breach of trust and $50,000 in losses).

86   *R. v. E.(R.K.)* (1996), 107 Man. R. (2d) 200 (C.A.) (twenty-four months secure custody for robbery by youth without prior record).

87   *R. v. B.(L.)* (1993), 62 O.A.C. 112 (C.A.)(six weeks open custody for fifteen-year-old for assault causing bodily harm to a fellow student).

88   *R. v. M.(E.)* (1992), 10 O.R. (3d) 481 (C.A.) (ninety days secure custody for criminal negligence causing death arising out of a motor vehicle accident).

89   *R. v. K.(M.)* (1996), 28 O.R. (3d) 593 (C.A.).

K. RESPONDING TO THE RISE IN CUSTODY USE: SECTIONS 3(1)(c.1) AND 24(1)

The YOA as enacted in 1984 created a highly discretionary sentencing regime, with great differences in sentencing practices between provinces and even between individual judges in the same cities,[90] and resulted in a substantial increase in the use of custodial sentences. Since the YOA came into force there has been a substantial increase in the number of custodial dispositions for young persons who have violated the criminal law.[91] On average, youths sentenced to custody under the YOA are serving shorter periods of time in custody than those sent to training school under the JDA, with average sentences under the YOA of 84 days for open custody and 107 days for secure custody; more than half of sentences are less than 6 months, and less than 1 in 10 is longer than a year. However, the increased use of custodial dispositions reflects the fact that the average daily population of young offenders in custody in Canada increased by 24 percent between 1986 and 1994.[92] Unfortunately, at least half of those young offenders who are placed in custody reoffend and return to an adult or youth custody facility.[93]

The increase in the use of custody can in part be attributed to the attitudes of some youth court judges, who appear to have emphasized the protection of society and the youth's responsibility over the recognition of special needs and *limited* accountability. It would seem that there has, for example, been an increase in the use of the "short sharp shock" type of sentence (that is, under three months), which is unlikely to have therapeutic or rehabilitation value, and in some cases may be harmful to a youth's development, but is regarded by the courts as serving accountability or deterrent functions. Arguably, some of the increase in use of custody may be attributed to changing patterns of criminality (or at least police charging practices), and in particular to an increase in charges for violent crime by young persons. However, only about 20 percent of youths in custody have committed violent offences. It is disturbing to note that as many as one-quarter of all young offenders in custody are there for failing to attend court or to comply with a

---

90   A.N. Doob & L.A. Beaulieu, "Variation in the Exercise of Judicial Discretion with Young Offenders" (1992) 34 Can. J. Crim. 35.

91   See A. Markwart, "Custodial Sanctions under the Young Offenders Act" in R.R. Corrado *et al.*, eds., *Juvenile Justice in Canada: A Theoretical and Analytical Assessment* (Toronto: Butterworths, 1992) 229.

92   Moyer, above note 18.

93   *Ibid.*

prior court order, such as probation. This indicates that many youths are placed in custody because of society's failure to provide adequate community supervision, rather than because their offending behaviour represents a direct threat to society.

It is also apparent that some youth court judges have been making use of open custody as a "middle option" for some youths who have not committed serious offences but who "need some help," as was reflected in the Supreme Court in *R. v. M. (J.J.)*. Prior to the enactment of the *YOA*, youths who needed assistance were sentenced under the *JDA* and often placed in residential facilities administered by child-welfare authorities. In several provinces the enactment of the *YOA* was accompanied by a shift in resources from the child-welfare and mental-health systems towards the juvenile justice system. In most Canadian jurisdictions, the child-welfare system is now reluctant to assist adolescents who engage in offending behaviour, even though such behaviour is common among those who have been victims of parental abuse during childhood — the very adolescents whom the child-welfare system should be trying to help. Community professionals who work with youths might want to use resources outside the youth justice system, but all too often the only available programming and care for troubled adolescents is in youth custody facilities, and so these professionals become involved in recommending custody for troubled adolescents who have committed relatively minor offences.

Canada now has one of the highest rates in the world for use of custody for adolescents. This has been expensive, both in financial terms and in regard to long-term rehabilitation, which is generally more likely to be achieved in community-based programs. There is a growing body of research that indicates that treatment programs for chronic young offenders are most likely to be effective in reducing recidivism if they address the underlying problems that youths are experiencing in their families, communities, and schools and if the treatment is undertaken in the context of working with the family and community.[94] Even if use is made of custody, a crucial element of rehabilitation must be supportive

---

94 See, e.g., Silverman & Creechan, above note 52; P. Gendreau & R.R. Ross, "Revivification of Rehabilitation: Evidence from the 1980s" (1987) 4 Justice 349–408; A.N. Doob, V. Marinas, & K.N. Varma, *Youth Crime and the Youth Justice System in Canada: A Research Perspective* (Toronto: Centre of Criminology, University of Toronto, 1995) at 14 and 87; and Centre for the Study of Youth Policy, *Home-Based Services for Serious and Violent Young Offenders* (Philadelphia: University of Pennsylvania, Centre for the Study of Youth Policy, School of Social Work, 1994).

reintegration into the community at the completion of the custodial portion of the sentence.

In amending the *YOA* in 1995, the Liberal government hoped to give a clearer message to youth court judges about the principles for sentencing of young offenders. The intent was to reduce the disparity between judges in their dispositional practices, and to encourage the use of more effective and less intrusive community-based dispositions for youths who do not pose a serious risk of harm to their communities. The 1995 amendments included additions to section 3, the Act's Declaration of Principle, and the enactment of a set of sentencing principles. The government provided some clear signals about its philosophy, in particular by explicitly adding rehabilitation to the Declaration of Principle:

> (*c.1*)the protection of society, which is a primary objective of the criminal law applicable to youth, is best served by rehabilitation, wherever possible, of young persons who commit offences, and rehabilitation is best achieved by addressing the needs and circumstances of a young person that are relevant to the young person's offending behaviour.[95]

As noted above, the concept of "rehabilitation" as a decision-making philosophy for young offenders can be problematic, and it has been used by the same judges to justify more and longer custodial dispositions. The 1995 amendments to section 24(1.1) were intended to prevent an "expansive" interpretative approach to section 3(1)(c.1) and to encourage more use of more effective and less expensive community-based alternatives to custody.

In 1986 Parliament enacted some relatively minor amendments to the custody disposition provisions of the *YOA* with the objective to prevent the overuse of custody. For example, section 24(1) was amended in 1986 to provide that a judge should not make a committal to custody unless it is considered "necessary for the protection of society, having regard to the seriousness of the offence and . . . the needs and circumstances of the young person." While the 1986 amendments were intended to reduce inappropriate use of custody, they had no appreciable effect. Indeed, the 1986 amendment to section 24(1), combined with the 1993 Supreme Court judgment in *R. v. M.(J.J.)*, could be viewed as endorsing for "rehabilitative" purposes the use of longer sentences than the offence itself might merit, that is, in order to achieve the long-term protection of society.

---

95   *YOA 1995*, above note 6, s. 1(1), amending *YOA*, above note 6, s. 3.

However, an important signal was sent to the courts in 1995 with the enactment of a new sentencing provision, section 24(1.1), the obvious intent of which was to avoid the unnecessary use of custody.

24.(1.1) In making a determination under subsection (1), the youth court shall take the following into account:

(*a*) that an order of custody shall not be used as a substitute for appropriate child protection, health and other social measures;
(*b*) that a young person who commits an offence that does not involve serious personal injury should be held accountable to the victim and to society through non-custodial dispositions whenever appropriate; and
(*c*) that custody shall only be imposed when all available alternatives to custody that are reasonable in the circumstances have been considered.

The intent of section 24(1.1)(a) is to reduce the inappropriate use of custody. This provision endorses the Ontario Court of Appeal judgment in *R. v. B. (M.)*,[96] where it was held that a youth court sentence for a young offender must be "responsive to the offence" and *not* just a "sensible way of dealing with a youth who had a personality problem and needed a place to go." It should also be noted that section 3(1)(c.1) refers to addressing "needs and circumstances . . . *relevant* . . . to . . . offending behaviour," making clear that needs and circumstances not relevant to offending should not be addressed by a youth court sentence, especially not one that is custodial. While not completely overruling the 1993 Supreme Court of Canada decision in *R. v. M. (J.J.)*, the enactment of sections 24(1.1) and 3(1)(c.1) requires some modification of the approach taken in that case, since it is apparent that the Court in *M. (J.J.)* did not fully explore the alternatives to custody, especially in the child-welfare system.

Youth court judges who impose a custodial disposition are required under section 24(4), also enacted in 1995, to give reasons why a non-custodial disposition would not have been adequate. This is intended to have judges specifically address the appropriateness and availability of non-custodial dispositions. However, in significant measure, the extent to which use is made of non-custodial dispositions will depend on the extent to which provinces make resources available for community-based dispositions.

Arguably, section 24(1.1) expects youth court judges to take a more activist role in developing non-custodial dispositions for youths, though the achievement of this objective may also require giving judges

---

96 Above note 78.

more explicit powers to fashion specific non-custodial dispositions if provincial correctional officials are unwilling to arrange or finance such dispositions. At least, the *YOA* should be amended to allow judges sentencing under the *YOA* to order provision of child-welfare services in appropriate cases as an alternative to custody.

The 1995 amendments to the *YOA* will not have as much impact in reducing sentencing disparities as the measures taken in those American states which have adopted juvenile sentencing grids[97] — presumptive sentences taking account of the nature of the offence and previous record. However, given the size of Canada and the disparities between provinces in facilities available, the adoption of juvenile sentencing grids to achieve greater uniformity would not be desirable. Further, given the prevailing public sentiments, if a sentencing grid were established by parliamentary action, there would be great political pressure to have longer sentences. It is to be hoped that the 1995 amendments will produce a more restricted and effective use of custody, but amending the *YOA* without also increasing the availability of community-based dispositional alternatives is unlikely to have much effect on sentencing patterns. The importance of crime prevention and rehabilitation was recognized in reports of the Justice committee of the House of Commons in 1993 and 1997,[98] but, without the expenditure of resources, the articulation of these goals may not be significant.

---

97   See, e.g., T.C. Castellano, "The Justice Model in the Juvenile Justice System: Washington State's Experience" (1986) 8 Law & Pol'y 479.

98   Canada, House of Commons, *Twelfth Report of the Standing Committee on Justice and the Solicitor General: Crime Prevention in Canada: Toward a National Strategy* (Ottawa: Supply & Services, 1993) (Chair: Bob Horner); Canada, House of Commons, *Thirteenth Report of the Standing Committee on Justice and Legal Affairs: Renewing Youth Justice* (Ottawa: Supply & Services, 1997).

FURTHER READINGS

BALA, N. & H. LILLES, eds., *Young Offenders Service* (Toronto: Butterworths, 1984) (looseleaf)

BEGIN, P., *Boot Camps: Issues for Consideration* (Ottawa: Library of Parliament Research Branch, 1996)

CANADA, FEDERAL-PROVINCIAL-TERRITORIAL TASK FORCE ON YOUTH JUSTICE, *A Review of the Young Offenders Act and the Youth Justice System in Canada* (Ottawa: Supply & Services, 1996), chs. 6, 7, and 8

HARRIS, P.J., ed., *Young Offenders Act Manual* (Aurora: Canada Law Book, 1984) (looseleaf)

MARRON, K., *Apprenticed in Crime: Young Offenders, the Law and Crime in Canada* (Toronto: McClelland-Bantam, 1992), chs. 8 and 9

PLATT, P., *Young Offenders Law in Canada*, 2d ed. (Toronto: Butterworths, 1995), chs. 19 and 20

SCOTT, S., M. WONG, & B. WEAGANT, *Defending Young Offender Cases*, 2d ed. (Toronto: Carswell, 1997), chs. 7, 9 and 10

TRANSFER TO ADULT COURT

Although cases involving transfer occur relatively rarely, these cases are the most difficult and the most highly publicized ones in the youth justice system. A judge who makes a transfer order under section 16 of the *YOA* is in essence deciding that the *Young Offenders Act* — its principles, legal framework, and the resources established pursuant to it — represent an inadequate response to the young person and the alleged offence. The result of a transfer order is that the young person will thereafter be dealt with in the adult court (or "ordinary court" as it is referred to in the *YOA*). In the event of conviction in the adult court, the youth may face penalties imposed under the *Criminal Code* rather than the more limited dispositions found in section 20 of the *YOA*, as well as the possibility of incarceration in an adult correctional facility, though there are provisions that may result in a youth facing a less severe punishment than an adult even after transfer.

Transfer is significant for the entire juvenile justice system since it helps define the nature of that system. The transfer provisions establish an outer boundary for the juvenile justice system. They are intended to deal with those relatively rare situations where the "interest of society" requires that a youth should be denied the benefits of the *YOA*. The transfer provision has been characterized as a form of "safety valve" for those relatively rare circumstances where the provisions of the *YOA*, in particular those limiting the maximum length of sentence, are considered inadequate for dealing with the young person.

A youth court judge making a decision under section 16 of the *YOA* faces a complex task. While consideration must be given to the "circumstances of the offence," the court is not to determine the question of guilt or innocence. Rather, the judge is to consider a broad range of evidence, much of which is ordinarily inadmissible and irrelevant in a criminal trial, and determine which court and corrections system, and which legal regime, is preferable for dealing with the young person. In making a decision, the court will be guided by the specific provisions of section 16 of the *YOA*, as well as the more general Declaration of Principle in section 3 of the Act.

The application of the statutory principles of the *YOA* to specific cases is often exceedingly difficult. In one transfer the Alberta Court of Appeal commented:

> Transfer orders present a difficult adjudicative challenge. . . . The statutory imperatives that are supposed to guide the court are couched in terms of inconvenient vagueness. . . . The facts offered to the court during applications for transfer are unusually pliable. . . . Opinion, inference, evidence of character, good and bad, are all received. . . . Such an inquiry — one commencing with sentence to be followed by judgment — is no longer the private precinct of Alice and the Queen of Hearts.[1]

The difficulties facing a youth court judge seeking to apply section 16 are compounded by the conflicting jurisprudence as well as a changing statutory regime. Owing to the high public visibility of transfer issues, the transfer provisions of the *YOA* have been subjected to considerable political scrutiny and were substantially amended in 1992 and again in 1995. There has been very substantial variation in how courts in different provinces have applied the transfer provisions. Despite significant changes in the legislation, courts in Manitoba and Alberta have consistently taken interpretative approaches that have resulted in those two provinces having transfer rates that are by far the highest in the country.[2]

---

1 *R. v. M.(G.J.)* (1993), 135 A.R. 204 at 206–8 (C.A.), leave to appeal refused (1993), 154 N.R. 400n (S.C.C.) [*M.(G.J.)*].

2 There are a number of explanations for the high transfer rates in Manitoba and Alberta, but it cannot be ignored that these two provinces have a conservative political climate, and were, for example, the first two provinces to establish "strict discipline" (boot camp) custody facilities.

A. THE NATURE OF TRANSFER HEARINGS

Section 16(2) lists factors that a youth court is to consider in a transfer hearing, including the seriousness and circumstances of the alleged offence, the character and background of the youth, and the comparative suitability of adult and youth correctional resources. The focus of inquiry at a transfer hearing is not on the question of guilt or innocence, and the rules of evidence applicable to a criminal trial do not govern a transfer hearing. Opinion and hearsay evidence about the youth and alleged offence that would not be admissible in a criminal trial are accepted at a transfer hearing, but the proceedings must still be conducted in an impartial fashion and in accordance with the rules of natural justice.[3]

It is a common practice at a transfer hearing for the Crown to rely on hearsay evidence; it can do so, for example, by having the principal investigating officer provide all of the evidence about the circumstances of the alleged offence, including relating statements made by various witnesses. In *R. v. H.(C.)*,[4] Nasmith Prov. J. emphasized the need to exercise caution when considering hearsay evidence in a transfer hearing:

> There was some discussion during these hearings about the type of evidence that should be relied upon. It seems to have been the Crown's position at the outset that all kinds of documents from various sources could be "filed" without witnesses or without further scrutiny as to admissibility.
>
> This case underlines the importance of evidence at a transfer hearing being no less credible and trustworthy than for any other adjudicative purpose. . . . I think the practice at a transfer hearing of having a police officer read in allegations is deserving of further scrutiny. The addition of some colourful language and some editorializing involved in putting together a composite of allegations leads me to suggest that the defence faced with these situations at least should be able to cross-examine on the exact allegations of the victims and the complainants rather than on selective and editorialized police composites of the allegations.

A court deciding a transfer application will also receive a great deal of expert opinion evidence about such matters as the character and previous conduct of the young person, as well as about the adequacy of the facilities available in the different correctional systems to meet his or her needs.

---

3   See *R. v. H.(A.B.)* (1992), 10 O.R. (2d) 683 (Gen. Div.), Garton J., aff'd (1993), 12 O.R. (3d) 634 (C.A.) [*H.(A.B.)*].

4   (16 December 1986), (Ont. Prov. Ct.) [unreported] [summarized 1 W.C.B. (2d) 112].

B. STANDARD OF PROOF FOR THE OFFENCE

The Crown is *not* obliged at a transfer hearing to prove beyond a reasonable doubt that the offence occurred.[5] This is consistent with the basic premise that the purpose of the transfer hearing is not to determine guilt or innocence but rather to determine the appropriate forum for the trial of the charge which the young person is facing, taking account of the fact that the sentencing options are very different in adult court from youth court.

In *R. v. H.(S.R.)* counsel for the youth argued that the evidence that the Crown introduced at a transfer hearing supported only a manslaughter charge, and not the second degree murder charge that the youth faced. The Alberta Court of Appeal observed that the Crown:

> is not required to establish that evidence beyond a reasonable doubt. Even though evidence of one element [of the offence] is weak and could result in a conviction on a lesser charge, the Court *may* nonetheless consider the charge at its most serious, unless *it is clear* that the Crown has overcharged the young person. If it is clear that it has, the Court must apply the same consideration to the lesser charge.[6]

Yet a number of decisions have recognized that, although a transfer hearing is not a trial, there is still scope for some judicial weighing of evidence, as in *R. v. V.(D.)* where LeGrandeur Prov. J. stated:

> [T]he Court need not move into the realm of weighing conflicting evidence to any significant degree. Nonetheless, I believe I am entitled to consider *the frailty of the Crown evidence* in any given area of the case, not in the sense of applying it to guilt or innocence, but in the sense of the impact of the frailty of the evidence upon the factors to be considered.[7]

In *R. v. V.(D.)*, the judge transferred one of the youths charged with murder but rejected *some* of the Crown's hearsay evidence about the "degree of participation" of a second youth in the alleged offence; this second youth was not transferred.

---

5   *R. v. H.(S.J.)* (1986), 76 N.S.R. (2d) 163 (T.D.) [*H.(S.J.)*].
6   *R. v. H.(S.R.)*, [1996] A.J. No. 239 at para 22 (C.A.) (QL). [Emphasis added].
7   [1992] A.J. No. 1032 (Prov. Ct. Youth Div.) (QL). [Emphasis added].

C. REPORTS

Section 16(3) of the YOA requires a youth court that is hearing a transfer application to consider a "pre-disposition report," prepared by a youth court worker or probation officer. Given the serious nature of the decision the court is facing, reports prepared under section 16(3) are typically more thorough than those prepared for a disposition hearing and may, for example, include information relating to incidents of misbehaviour and violence by the youth that did not result in criminal charges, sometimes going back as far as junior kindergarten.[8] This type of complete behavioural history is often important, since youths with a lengthy history of escalating violence are generally considered more likely to pose a risk of future offending than those who commit a single, serious act of violence.

It is also common at a transfer hearing to have an assessment report prepared under section 13 by a psychiatrist or psychologist. In R. v. P. (P.)[9] the Crown sought an order for a section 13 assessment for use at a transfer hearing, but counsel for the youth opposed the order. Judge Auxer held that it was not necessary for the court to have evidence of "eccentric" or "bizarre" behaviour to order a report, or for the youth to exhibit behaviour "observable to a layman" as a cause for concern. The approach of P.(P.) is reflected in the 1995 amendment to section 13(1)(b), which explicitly allows a youth court to order a psychological, medical, or psychiatric report "on *its own motion*" (as well as at the request of Crown or defence counsel), if the youth's record of convictions *or* the serious personal injury nature of the alleged offence raises a belief that the report is "necessary" for the hearing (emphasis added). There is no longer the need to believe that the youth suffers from a mental, emotional, or psychological condition to order a section 13 report, though this *may* be the basis for ordering such a report.

While sections 13.1 and 14(10) restrict the subsequent use that may be made of statements made by a youth to the assessor for the purposes of preparation of a report, defence counsel may nevertheless advise clients not to cooperate with the person preparing the report or not to discuss the circumstances of the offence. Although the disclosure of information for the report should result in a more complete report being prepared,[10] and in some cases may assist the youth, there may be situations

---

8   R. v. O.(D.), [1996] O.J. No. 2703 (Prov. Ct.) (QL) [O.(D.)].
9   [1993] B.C.J. No. 1704 (QL) (Youth Ct.).
10 See, e.g., R. v. P.(L.), [1992] O.J. No. 871 (Prov. Div.) (QL), where several experts prepared reports. The judge gave greatest weight to the views of the one psychiatrist who spoke to the youth in question about the circumstances of the offence.

in which defence counsel is concerned that information disclosed could restrict the conduct of the defence at a subsequent trial.[11] A young person cannot be compelled to cooperate with the person preparing a report for the court, though, if the youth fails to do so, the report can still be used in the transfer proceeding.

The defence may also retain its own mental-health professionals to provide an independent assessment of the youth as well as expert testimony. While this frequently occurs in transfer cases involving serious offences, cuts to legal aid funding are making it more difficult for defence counsel to obtain adequate assessments.

D. CROWN DISCLOSURE

In *R. v. Stinchcombe*[12] the Supreme Court of Canada emphasized the constitutional importance of the right of an accused prior to a plea to full disclosure by the Crown of all of the evidence in its possession. This right applies to a transfer hearing, which clearly has the potential to affect the "liberty" of the accused.

In *R. v. F.(T.)*[13] the Crown disclosed expert reports and police evidence about the circumstances of the alleged offence, a murder, to counsel for the youth. The Crown prosecutor disclosed the material as soon as it came into his possession, but it was only a couple of weeks before the date scheduled for the transfer hearing. At a judicial review application, Justice Then ruled that the defence was entitled to an adjournment of the transfer hearing because the late disclosure did not give defence counsel adequate time to prepare for a complex transfer hearing.

A sixteen- or seventeen- year-old youth charged with a serious offence and having an onus under section 16(1.01) to apply for "transfer down" to youth courts has a right to disclosure from the Crown before deciding whether to make this application.

---

11   While ss. 13.1(1) and (2) of the *Young Offenders Act*, R.S.C. 1985, c. Y-1 [*YOA*], restrict the direct subsequent use of statements made to an assessor, the statements may, for example, be used to challenge the youth's credibility at a later trial under s. 13.1(2)(f). Because a youth is not "obliged" to cooperate with a person preparing a s. 13 report, it has been held that ordering such a report for a transfer hearing does not violate the prohibitions against self-incrimination under the *Canadian Charter of Rights and Freedoms*, Part I of the *Constitution Act, 1982*, being Schedule B to the *Canada Act 1982* (U.K.), 1982, c. 11. s. 11(c). *H.(A.B.)*, above note 3.

12   [1991] 3 S.C.R. 326.

13   [1992] O.J. No. 494, (Gen. Div.) (QL).

E. TIME OF APPLICATION

Unlike the *Juvenile Delinquents Act,* which allowed for an application for transfer even after sentencing,[14] section 16(1) of the *Young Offenders Act* stipulates that a transfer application must be made prior to adjudication. A youth court judge may not initiate a transfer application under the *YOA,* unlike the situation which prevailed under the *JDA.* Then, judges occasionally made transfer decisions after initiating their own applications.

In 1986 Parliament added section 19(3) to the *YOA,* requiring that prior to accepting a guilty plea a youth court judge must specifically ask the parties whether any of them wishes to make a transfer application. This provision was intended to ensure that no cases which should be considered for transfer "slip by" because of to inadvertence on the part of the Crown prosecutor.

A 1996 Ontario decision, which was affirmed by the Court of Appeal, dealt with a case in which two seventeen-year-old youths faced murder charges, a situation that under the 1995 amendments to the *YOA* required the youths to make an application for transfer to youth court if they did not want their cases tried in adult court. Their counsel wanted a preliminary inquiry in adult court *before* making an application for "transfer down" to youth court under section 16(1.01). The judge acknowledged that there was no specific legislative provision regarding the timing of an application for transfer, and she emphasized that a youth should not be expected to make an application until counsel had an opportunity to investigate the case and receive Crown disclosure.[15] Judge Hackett concluded:

> At the same time, a potential applicant, in this case the defence, can't wait forever to decide when the application will be brought, thereby delaying the course of justice . . . the youth court may be called upon to force potential applicants to make their decision.

The judge concluded that counsel who declines to apply for transfer in the face of a judicial request to decide will have waived the right to seek it later. She also suggested that, if a preliminary inquiry occurred in adult court, this would be deemed to have been a waiver of the right to seek transfer.

---

14   See, e.g., *R. v. Metz* (1977), 36 C.C.C. (2d) 22 (Man. C.A.).
15   *R. v. J.(J.),* [1996] O.J. No. 3482, at para. 31–32 (Prov. Div.) (QL); aff'd [1997] O.J. 3588 (C.A.).

F. NOTICE TO PARENTS

Section 16(1) of the *YOA* provides that the parents of a youth must be given "an opportunity to be heard" before an application for transfer is decided. Since the parents have a right to be heard, they must also be given notice of the proceedings in order to be able to make representations.[16] In section 2 of the *YOA* a "parent" is defined to include "any person who is under a legal duty to provide for that . . . [young] person or any person who has, in law or in fact, the custody or control of that . . . [young] person. . . ." While a child-welfare agency is included in the definition of "parent" if the youth is its ward, given the importance of transfer, every reasonably identifiable biological parent should also receive notice of the application, though this is not a legal requirement.

G. PUBLICATION BAN: SECTION 17

Section 17 of the *YOA* provides that an order prohibiting publication of any information revealed at a transfer hearing must be made if requested by the Crown prosecutor or by defence counsel, or, if the youth should happen to be unrepresented, the youth court is obliged to raise the issue and make an order.

A ban under section 17 precludes the publication of any information about a transfer hearing and is in addition to the prohibition in section 38 of the *YOA* on the publication of identifying information. The purpose of section 17 is to ensure that there is a fair trial, in particular if the young person is transferred to adult court. Much of the evidence revealed at a transfer hearing may be inadmissible in a later trial[17]; in a highly publicized case, the broadcast of this type of information would have the potential to prejudice severely a jury. If a youth is transferred to adult court under section 16, the media can publish identifying information, but not anything that was revealed in the transfer hearing.

In a 1996 decision the British Columbia Supreme Court held that a young person who is being proceeded against in adult court in a "reverse onus" situation because of section 16(1.01) is, by virtue of section 15 of the *Charter of Rights*, entitled to the protection of section 38

---

16   *R. v. W.* (1986), 28 C.C.C. (3d) 510 (B.C.C.A.).

17   Because a judge at a transfer hearing will receive a great deal of inadmissible and potentially prejudicial information, s. 15 of the *YOA*, above note 11, provides that if the youth is not transferred, the transfer judge ordinarily cannot preside at the trial in youth court.

of the *YOA*, until a determination has been made that the youth will *not* be tried in youth court.[18] Only if it has been decided that the youth is to be tried in adult court can the media publicize his or her identity.

Even if there is a prohibition on the publication of information from a transfer hearing, under section 39 of the *YOA* there is a presumption that the transfer hearing will be open to members of the public. In *R. v. G.(J.K.)*[19] counsel for a youth facing transfer for the first degree murder of a six-year-old child sought to have members of the public, including the victim's family, excluded. Judge O'Donnell emphasized the statutory presumption for an open hearing and concluded that there was no evidence that the community would be so influenced by any information that might be disclosed that an impartial jury could not later be selected if the case were transferred. The judge therefore permitted the public to be present, but he did order that the public should be excluded if the Crown introduced evidence of any statements made by the youth to anyone after the alleged incident, since these statements might later be ruled inadmissible.

H. AGE OF YOUNG PERSON

An application for transfer can be brought only with respect to offences alleged to have been committed by a young person "after attaining the age of fourteen years." The reference date is that of the alleged offence, not the age at time of the hearing.

I. OFFENCES SUBJECT TO TRANSFER

Transfer is in respect only of "indictable offence[s] *other than* an offence referred to in section 553 of the *Criminal Code*" [emphasis added]. Section 553 of the *Code* sets out a number of less serious offences for which a Provincial Court judge has absolute jurisdiction, including: property offences such as theft, obtaining money or property by false pretences, possession of stolen property and mischief, cases where the value of stolen or damaged or stolen property does not exceed $5,000, as well as a number of other less serious offences. In theory, a youth may be transferred for any indictable offence, other than one listed in section 553,

---

18   *R. v. P.* (7 November 1996), (B.C.S.C.) [unreported], Davies J.
19   [1993] B.C.J. No. 945 (Prov. Ct.) (QL).

though in practice most contested transfer applications involve more serious violent offences.[20]

J. THE 1984 TRANSFER TEST

Under the 1984 provisions, as soon as a transfer order was made, a youth in pre-trial detention was placed in an adult prison, and, if a youth was convicted in adult court, the ordinary adult sentencing provisions applied. There was substantial disagreement between provincial appellate courts about the appropriate interpretation of the originally enacted standard for transfer in section 16(1) of the YOA: "the interest of society . . . having regard to the needs of the young person."

Some judges held that this provision gave "primary importance" to the "interest of society." This emphasis on the "interest of society" over the "needs of the young person" was most apparent in Manitoba and Alberta and was reflected in a relatively high transfer rate in those jurisdictions. The courts taking this approach emphasized that societal interests in accountability, deterrence, and incapacitation all favoured transfer for youths facing serious charges, especially homicides. In comparison to courts in other jurisdictions, the courts in these provinces also placed less emphasis on the potentially harmful effects on youths of transfer into adult correctional facilities and on the typically better prospects for rehabilitation in the youth system.

The approach of the Manitoba and Alberta courts differed from the more restrictive approach to transfer apparent in the Quebec, Ontario, and Saskatchewan courts. While some of the variation in transfer rates between provinces may have reflected differences in judicial perceptions of the adequacy and security of the youth corrections system in different provinces, it is also apparent that there was significant disagreement about the appropriate interpretation of section 16.

Appellate judges in Ontario, Quebec, and Saskatchewan emphasized their concerns about the enormous potential harm to young persons from serving long sentences in adult correctional facilities, arguing

---

20   Statistics Canada, Canadian Centre for Justice Statistics, *Youth Court Statistics 1994–95* (Ottawa: Statistics Canada, 1996) [*1994–95*], reports that transfers were ordered for 123 cases (listed by most serious charge) including 11 murder charges (out of 25 charges); 15 sexual offences (out of 1,692 charges); 7 assaults with a weapon (out of 3,209 charges); 8 minor assaults; 2 assaults on a police officer; 22 robbery charges; 3 for possession of a weapon; 29 property offences; and 10 others, including 3 escapes from custody and two failures to appear.

that neither the youth nor society are served if the young person is irreparably harmed by a sentence in an adult facility,[21] at least if there are reasonable prospects of rehabilitation within the youth system. These courts were unwilling to transfer youths who might have been transferred if the allegations had arisen in Alberta or Manitoba.

In September 1989 the Supreme Court of Canada rendered judgments on two transfer appeals from Alberta, *R. v. M.(S.H.)* and *R. v. L.(J.E.)*. The Supreme Court affirmed the decision of the Alberta Court of Appeal to transfer the youths to the adult system; the youths were seventeen at the time of the alleged offences and were charged with the brutal murder of an unconscious man. The majority of the Supreme Court stated that it was not appropriate to say that in a transfer proceeding the Crown faced a "heavy onus" or that the Crown had to demonstrate that the circumstances were "exceptional," though the Court recognized the "utmost seriousness" of the decision facing a judge at transfer hearing. However, the ultimate effect of the Supreme Court of Canada decisions was very limited. The majority judgments of the Supreme Court failed even to mention that different provincial appellate courts had taken conflicting approaches to the interpretation of section 16, let alone try to resolve the divergent approaches. The Supreme Court also stated that its role was restricted to correcting an "error of principle," while the legislation gave the trial courts *and* provincial appeal courts a "discretion" in how to decide cases.[22] Madam Justice McLachlin emphasized the importance of the views of the individual judges dealing with a transfer application:

> It is inevitable that in the course of the review, some factors will assume greater importance than others, depending on the nature of the case and the *viewpoint of the tribunal in question*. The Act does not require that all factors be given equal weight, but only that each be considered.[23]

These 1989 Supreme Court decisions gave the lower courts no real direction about the proper interpretation of section 16, and different courts continued to have conflicting interpretations of this critical legislative provision. The lack of direction provided by the Supreme Court of Canada was remarked upon by Locke J. of the British Columbia Court of Appeal in *R. v.*

---

21 See, e.g., *R. v. S.(W.)* (1989), 69 C.R. (3d) 168 (Ont. C.A.).
22 Ss. 16(9)–(11) of the *YOA*, above note 11, provide that provincial appeal courts have the jurisdiction to "review" the decision of the youth court judge while the role of the Supreme Court of Canada is limited to dealing with an "appeal." The Supreme Court indicated that its jurisdiction is narrower than that of the provincial courts of appeal.
23 [1989] 2 S.C.R. 446 at 467–68. [*M.(S.H.)*]. [Emphasis added].

T.(E.),[24] in a case where that court refused to transfer three youths charged with first degree murder. Justice Locke quoted the passage from the judgment of McLachlin J. set out above, and he then stated: "This provides little specific guidance. It appears to leave an almost completely free hand."

The divergence in judicial approaches to the appropriate interpretation of section 16 of the *YOA* increased the need for legislative reform. Although there continued to be different approaches to interpretation of the transfer provision enacted in 1992, at least the consequences of the different judicial approaches were substantially reduced.

K. THE 1992 AMENDMENTS

By the end of the 1980s judges and correctional experts, as well as politicians and members of the public, recognized the inadequacies of the original *YOA* provisions governing transfer, especially as they applied to cases of murder. Under the original transfer provision, in a case involving first degree murder a judge was faced with the stark choice between the three-year maximum disposition under the *YOA* and the possibility of life imprisonment in the adult system with no opportunity for parole for at least twenty-five years.[25] In some cases, neither extreme was appropriate; one was too short and the other too long.

There was also an enormous amount of public and media concern expressed about the perceived inadequacy of the provisions of the *YOA* for dealing with violent offences. Much of this concern was directed at the judicial reluctance, at least in some provinces, to transfer youths and at the maximum three-year youth court sentence, which was viewed as totally inadequate for certain offences, most notably murder. As a result of these concerns, the Progressive Conservative government introduced legislation[26] in December 1989 to amend the transfer and murder-sentencing provisions of the *YOA*. After parliamentary committee hearings, these amendments came into force on 15 May 1992. (See Table 1.)

---

24 (1989), 42 B.C.L.R. (2d) 40 at 66 (C.A.).

25 Under s. 742 of the *Criminal Code*, R.S.C. 1985, c. C-46 [*Code*], for a second degree murder the parole eligibility date is set at the time of sentencing from ten to twenty-five years. S. 745 of the *Code* — the so-called "faint-hope" provision — allows for an adult inmate serving a sentence for first or second degree murder to seek a jury review after fifteen years for "early" parole eligibility. Only about a third of those eligible apply for jury review, and only about one quarter of those are eventually paroled. See H. Hess, "Early parole appeals draw diverse rulings," *[Toronto] Globe and Mail* (27 May 1997).

26 *An Act to amend the Young Offenders Act and the Criminal Code*, S.C. 1992, c.11 [*YOA 1992*].

Table 1
Summary of Evolution of Transfer and Murder Sentencing for Youths

	1984–92	1992–95	In force 1 Dec. 1995
Maximun sentence for murder in youth court	3 years	5 years less a day [3 years custody + 2 yrs. less 1 day conditional supervision]	10 years for 1st degree [6 yr. custody + 4 yr. cond. super.] 7 years for 2nd degree [4 yr. custody + 3 yr. cond. sup.] Jury trials s. 19(4)
Murder sentence after transfer — life sentence with parole eligibility	1st degree 25 years 2nd degree 10–25 years	5–10 years	10 years for 1st degree, if 16 or 17 7 years for 2nd degree, if 16 or 17 5–7 years, if 14 or 15 years, for 1st or 2nd degree murder
Post-transfer place of deten- tion & sentence	adult facility only	adult or youth: court to decide s. 16.1 and s. 16.2	adult or youth: court to decide s. 16.1 and s. 16.2
Onus	Crown (applicant)	Crown (applicant)	Crown *unless* youth 16 or 17 and charged with murder, attempted murder, manslaughter, aggravated sexual assault s. 16(1.01)
Test:	s. 16(1): "interest of society. . . . having regard to needs of young person"	s. 16(1.1): "interest of society which *includes* objectives of . . . protection to public and rehabilitation of young person . . . if these objectives cannot be reconciled in youth court, protection of public *shall* be paramount and youth transferred" NOTICE: interest of society *arguably* may *include* other factors (e.g., accountability and general deterrence) (Alta. C.A. interpretation) — not clear that youth *not* to be transferred if protection and rehabilitation *can* be satisfied in youth court. (Alta. C.A. interpretation)	s. 16(1.1) interest of society which includes protection of public and rehabilitation of youth. (a) if both can be recon- ciled in youth system do *not* transfer. (b) if both cannot be reconciled in youth system, protection of public is paramount and transfer shall be ordered. NOTICE: *apparent* restriction on meaning of interest of society; does *not* include accountabil- ity and arguably not general deterrence.

For young persons convicted in youth court of first and second degree murder, the maximum disposition was extended from three years in custody to five years less a day, to consist of not more than three years in custody plus a period of "conditional supervision." At the time scheduled for release under conditional supervision, a youth court may order that a young offender is not to be released "if it is satisfied that there are reasonable grounds to believe that the young person is likely to commit an offence causing the death or serious harm to another person prior to the expiration" of the period of the total disposition that the youth is serving.[27] Otherwise, a youth court judge sets conditions prior to the release, establishing the terms on which the youth will reside in the community.

A youth released on conditional supervision may be apprehended on order of a provincial director for a breach of a condition of release, or where there are reasonable grounds to believe that a youth is "about to breach a condition of" release. This suspension of conditional supervision by the provincial director is subject to a youth court review hearing to determine what portion of the total original disposition should be served in custody.[28]

For young persons who are charged with first or second degree murder, transferred to adult court, and convicted there, the 1992 amendments provided that the sentence — as for an adult — was to be life imprisonment. However, unlike under the original YOA, where transferred youths were required to serve the same ten to twenty-five years as adults before being eligible for parole, the sentencing judge in adult court was to set a parole eligibility date of five to ten years.[29]

The 1992 test, set out in section 16(1.1), provided that "in making the determination" whether to transfer a case

the youth court shall consider the interest of society, which includes the objectives of affording protection to the public and rehabilitation of the young person, and determine whether those objectives can be reconciled by the youth remaining under the jurisdiction of the youth

---

27 Section 26.1(1) of the *YOA*, above note 11, as am. by *YOA 1992*, *ibid.* S. 26.1(2) sets out a list of criteria that the youth court shall take into consideration when assessing the likelihood of a youth committing a further offence. These criteria are identical to those found in the "gating provision" that permits parole authorities *not* to release an inmate on mandatory supervision; *Parole Act*, R.S.C. 1985, c. P-2, as amended by *An Act to amend the Parole Act and the Penitentiary Act*, R.S.C. 1985 (2d Supp.), c. 34, s. 21.4(5).

28 *YOA*, *ibid.*, ss. 26.3–26.6.

29 *Criminal Code*, above note 25, ss. 742.1, 743, 743.1, 744 and 744.1.

court, and if the court is of the opinion that those objectives cannot be so reconciled, protection of the public shall be paramount and the court shall order that the young person be proceeded against in ordinary court in accordance with the law ordinarily applicable to an adult charged with the offence.

Another important 1992 amendment dealt with the place where youths who are transferred serve their sentences. Section 16.1 created a presumption that a youth court judge was to detain youths under eighteen in a youth facility pending trial. If there is a conviction after trial in adult court, section 16.2 gave the adult court sentencing judge flexibility to decide whether to have a custodial sentence served in the youth correctional system, in a provincial adult correctional facility, or in a federal adult penitentiary, with provisions for later review and transfer from one type of facility to another.

The 1992 amendments provided more flexibility for dealing with transfer cases. In particular, for first degree murder, judges were no longer forced to choose between three years in youth custody, which was often too short, and life imprisonment in the adult system with no parole for twenty-five years, which was often seen as too harsh. The increased flexibility was desirable, for it allowed the courts to impose a sentence more appropriate to the circumstances of the offence and offender. While there continued to be significant differences in how courts interpreted the 1992 provisions, the significance of these differences in approach was somewhat reduced since the consequences of whether or not a youth was transferred were not as dramatic as they were under the 1984 provisions.

Reducing the parole-eligibility date for youths convicted of murder in adult court reflected the principle of limited accountability of young offenders, as well as the fact that many of them may be amenable to rehabilitation even after transfer. The introduction of the concept of "conditional supervision" for those youth convicted of murder but not transferred recognizes that youths, especially those with serious problems or a propensity towards violence, often require careful supervision and support after their release from custody.

By increasing the maximum disposition that a *youth court* could impose for murder, Parliament clearly indicated that it did *not* intend all murder cases to be transferred; rather, each case was to be individually assessed. This was a recognition that some youths can be rehabilitated if they have a longer period of time in the youth system, an outcome that serves both their needs and the interests of society.

In 1991–92, the last full year under the 1984 law, a total of 71 out of 116,397 cases were transferred (0.06 percent), including 8 out of 30 murder charges.[30] In 1993–94, with the new provisions almost fully in effect, 94 out of 115,949 cases were transferred (0.08 percent), including 6 out of 30 murder charges. By 1994–95, 123 out of 109,743 charged were transferred (0.11 percent), including 11 out of 25 murder charges. While the overall transfer rate in Canada has remained relatively low,[31] it is apparent that the 1992 amendments resulted in an increase in the number of cases being transferred to adult court, but with very significant interprovincial variation continuing.

L. JUDICIAL INTERPRETATION OF THE 1992 TRANSFER PROVISIONS

Under the 1984 provision, section 16(1) stipulated that the youth court should order transfer only if the judge was of "the opinion that, in the interest of society and having regard to the needs of the young person," transfer was required. The 1992 test required the court to consider "the interest of society, which includes the objectives of affording protection to the public and rehabilitation of the young person, and determine whether those objectives can be reconciled" in the youth system; if these objectives cannot be "reconciled" in the youth system, "protection of the public shall be paramount and the court shall order" that the youth be transferred.

There were substantial differences in how the 1992 provisions were interpreted by different courts, and these resulted in substantial interprovincial variations in transfer rates. There are two, quite different, plausible interpretations of the 1992 amendments. The Alberta and Manitoba courts took a broad approach to the "interest of society" that included consideration of general deterrence, accountability, and the "public mood"; this approach resulted in higher transfer rates. Other courts focused exclusively on the youth before the court, and, if satisfied

---

30   Statistics Canada, Canadian Centre for Justice Statistics, *Youth Court Statistics 1991–92*, (Ottawa: Statistics Canada, 1993), *Youth Court Statistics 1992–93* (Ottawa: Statistics Canada, 1994), and *Youth Court Statistics 1993–94* (Ottawa: Statistics Canada, 1995).

31   In the United States, the rate of *judicial* transfer of juvenile charges into adult court is 1.6 percent compared to under 0.10 percent in Canada. Further, in the United States substantial numbers of youths under eighteen are treated as adults because of lower ages for adult court jurisdiction in many states, as well as *automatic* transfer of juveniles charged with specified violent offences to adult court. See J.P. Hornick, J. Hudson, & N. Bala, *The Response to Juvenile Crime in the United States: A Canadian Perspective* (Calgary: Canadian Research Institute for Law and the Family, 1995).

that the youth was likely to be amenable to rehabilitation within the youth system, would not transfer the youth; this approach resulted in lower transfer rates.

When the 1992 amendments were introduced some observers expressed a concern that the new provision would "lower" the test for transfer and have the effect of significantly increasing the number of cases transferred.[32] It can certainly be argued that, in enacting section 16(1.1) and placing the "protection of the public" in a "paramount" position, Parliament was signalling a desire to increase the number of cases transferred, and that it was preferring the approach to transfer that was adopted by the courts in Alberta and Manitoba in interpreting the 1984 law.

Some judges, most obviously in the Alberta Court of Appeal, took a broad approach to interpretation of the 1992 version of section 16(1.1). These judges pointed out that section 16(1.1) specified only that, if the protection of the public and the rehabilitation of the youth *cannot* be reconciled in the youth system, then the protection of the public is "paramount" and the youth "shall" be transferred. However, there was no express specification of what was to occur if these two concerns *could* be reconciled in the youth system. Further, the section established as the transfer test the "interest of society, which *includes* the objectives of affording protection to the public and rehabilitation of the young person." Use of the term "includes" was taken to indicate that these two factors do not exhaust the concept of the "interest of society," and reference to section 3 of the *YOA* and other *YOA* jurisprudence suggested that such factors as accountability, general deterrence, and public denunciation of violent behaviour may, in appropriate cases, be taken into account in a transfer case.

One of the most frequently cited decisions to adopt the broader interpretation of section 16(1.1) is *R. v. M.(G.J.)*, where the Alberta Court of Appeal reviewed two unrelated cases and ordered both youths transferred. One fifteen-year-old youth was charged with the murder of his stepfather, his mother, and his two sisters. The other, also fifteen years old, was charged with attempted murder after he shot and seriously injured an elderly man in an apparently random act of shooting. In both cases, lower courts had refused to order transfer, basing their decision largely on the assessment that after serving a sentence in the youth system, the youths were likely to be rehabili-

---

32   See, e.g., John Howard Society of Ontario, *Jailing Kids in Adult Prisons* (Toronto: The Society, 1990); and Canadian Council on Children and Youth, *A Response to Bill C-58* (Ottawa: The Council, 1990).

tated and not pose a significant risk to society. Therefore, the youth court judges concluded that the protection of the public and the rehabilitation of the youths could be reconciled in the youth system, and the cases were not transferred.

In reversing these lower court rulings, the Alberta Court of Appeal emphasized that, in cases involving serious acts of violence, society had an interest in having a public hearing that can be reported in the media with identifying information:

> Future dangerousness is always an important consideration in sentencing and will remain so, but public confidence in any medical prognosis dismissing its possibility here will not result if it should be censored by the effect of any court order. . . . [without transfer] the Youth Court's exclusion and suppression powers set forth in ss. 38 and 39 of the *Act* could be invoked. . . . This tragedy's explanation, if there is one, must be allowed to emerge. The public mood, increasingly sullen and suspicious about the *Young Offenders Act* and its application, will not be steadied by anything less than an unrestricted trial, a hearing where the causes and likelihood of a repetition of this tragedy can be openly reviewed and reported. . . . When the acts are marked by an apparent moral indifference to the fate of the victims, the incident is of even greater public concern. The concern we express is not a yielding to the hue and cry. Nor is it pandering to a sensationalist media. It is about waning confidence in the ability of this important arm of the criminal justice system to do what Parliament has asked of it.[33]

The Alberta Court of Appeal also held that the 1992 amendments, by allowing for youths to remain in the youth corrections system after transfer, place greater emphasis on accountability and deterrence as factors in transfer decisions.

> With the amendments, however, the sentencing alternatives are not as stark as before. It is no longer a choice between needed treatment being tamped into an inadequate sentence or a fit sentence being imposed but one bereft of facilities for treatment or treatment itself. Now the sentencing regime anticipates that a fit, denunciatory sentence may be imposed in ordinary court against a young person but one which can be tempered by transfers to other facilities for treatment, including those found outside the adult penal system.[34]

---

33 Above note 1 at 211.
34 *Ibid.* at 213–14.

In a later decision, *R. v. S.(D.M.)*, the Alberta Court of Appeal cited the 1993 Supreme Court of Canada in *R. v. M.(J.J.)*, which dealt not with a transfer but rather with youth court sentencing. The Supreme Court had held that general deterrence could be a factor in youth court sentencing, albeit a less important one than when adults are being sentenced and less significant than the rehabilitation of the youth being sentenced. The Court of Appeal in *R. v. S.(D.M.)* reversed a lower court ruling and ordered the transfer of a youth charged with the murder of his stepfather, writing:

> Nor is the only issue deterrence of the accused (which is very similar to the question of whether he will reoffend). It is now clear that general deterrence is also a relevant consideration: *R. v. M. (J.J.)*. Among that segment of the population who weigh what sentence should be imposed for murdering someone with advance planning, the difference between a five-year maximum and a five-year minimum is likely to seem great. And it is. And while it may well be that a sentence of three years would be sufficient to deter this accused, the same cannot necessarily be said once general deterrence is factored into the equation.[35]

The broad interpretation of the Alberta Court of Appeal resulted in cases being transferred in that province that would not be transferred in other jurisdictions, including cases of attempted murder, sexual assault, and assault causing bodily harm. This broader interpretive approach to section 16(1.1) was also adopted by the Manitoba courts,[36] as well as being influential in British Columbia.[37]

In contrast to the approach of the Alberta Court of Appeal, which focused on a range of societal concerns, several other appellate courts adopted a narrower approach and focused on the youth before the court. These judges have reasoned that the intent of the 1992 amendments was *not* to "lower" the test for transfer. If Parliament simply intended to have more cases transferred, it would have emphasized "accountability" (or punishment or even general deterrence), as opposed to seeming to indicate that the "protection of society" is to be "paramount" *only if* the pro-

---

35   [1993] A.J. No. 717 (C.A.) (QL), Fraser C.J.A., Côté and McFadyen JJ.A.

36   See, e.g., *R. v. P.(K.N.) (No. 2)*, [1996] M.J. No. 224 (Prov. Ct.) (QL) [*P. (K.N.)*]. Manitoba has the highest transfer rate in Canada.

37   In British Columbia panels of judges in the Court of Appeal adopted different interpretative approaches to the 1992 provisions; contrast *R. v. S.(A.)*(1993), 24 B.C.A.C. 18 (C.A.)(narrower youth-focused approach adopted); and *R. v. W. (C.G.)*, [1996] B.C.J. No. 598 (C.A.) (QL) (broader approach adopted, transfer of youth charged with manslaughter, "deterrent to other youths" was a factor).

tection of the public and the needs of the youth cannot be "reconciled." Kim Campbell, the minister of justice at the time of enactment of the 1992 amendments, explained:

> The test for transfer is a two-step test. Where the judge determines that both needs can be met in the youth system, *the discretion to transfer is gone*. It is *only* where both needs cannot be met that the decision to transfer becomes one available to the judge. . . . it is a clearer test, and it is one that says there will be *no transfer if both goals of rehabilitation and public safety can be met within the youth system*.[38]

Although the comments of Kim Campbell have not been cited by any appeal courts, her approach to the 1992 provisions, one that focuses on the youth and seeks to reconcile *only* rehabilitation and potential future dangerousness, received judicial support from the Courts of Appeal in Ontario, Nova Scotia, and Quebec.[39]

In *R. v. W.(A.C.)*[40] the Nova Scotia Court of Appeal refused to transfer a youth, aged seventeen and a half years, who had been charged with first degree murder. The Court noted that the alleged offence was "impetuous" and lacked "planning and deliberation." While in detention pending the transfer hearing the youth demonstrated the potential to improve, and the Crown had not satisfied the onus of establishing that the youth would pose a significant threat after completion of a youth court sentence. Justice Pugsley offered an interpretation of section 16(1.1) that focused exclusively on the two listed factors:

> In my opinion, the injunction that the protection of the public is paramount is *only* to be followed if the Youth Court judge has reached the conclusion that the twin objectives of affording protection to the public and rehabilitation of the young persons, cannot be reconciled by the youth remaining under the jurisdiction of the Youth Court. The Youth Court judge in this case concluded that the twin objectives were, in fact, reconciled on the evidence that was adduced before him. In my opinion, he was justified in so doing.

---

38   Canada, Proceedings of the Standing Senate Committee on Legal and Constitutional Affairs (7 April 1992) 13:34. [Emphasis added]. The courts have generally held that they may consider the statements of parliamentarians to help understand legislation, but will give them only "limited weight" when interpreting legislation.

39   See, e.g., *R. v. Croteau*, [1993] A.Q. No. 847 (C.A.) (QL); and *R. v. C.(T.)*, [1994] A.Q. No. 199 (C.A.) (QL).

40   (1993), 121 N.S.R. (2d) 300 at 307 (C.A.) [*W.(A.C.)*]. [Emphasis added].

The majority of the Ontario Court of Appeal cited this Nova Scotia judgment and adopted the same basic approach. In *R. v. B.(C.)* Robins J.A. of the Ontario Court of Appeal wrote:

> [T]he transfer order test set out in s. 16(1.1) limits the "interest of society" concerns to two identified objectives — the protection of the public and the rehabilitation of the young person. Other factors which may also pertain to the "interest of society", such as, general deterrence, the gravity of the offence and the circumstances surrounding its commission, and the need to maintain and promote public confidence in the administration of criminal justice, on the court's interpretation of section 16(1.1), cannot in themselves provide the basis for transferring a young offender to adult court.[41]

In *R. v. B.(C.)* the Court refused to transfer a sixteen-year-old youth who was charged with the first degree murder of his mother and the attempted murder of his father but was considered an "ideal candidate for therapeutic intervention" in the youth system.

While courts that focused on the youth had a lower transfer rate, they did not always refuse to transfer. For example, in *R. v. C.(D.)* the Ontario Court of Appeal reversed a youth court judge's decision and ordered the transfer of a youth who had just turned fifteen and was charged with the murder of a nine-year-old girl.[42] The youth had a history of violent and intimidating behaviour, and the majority of experts testified that the "*minimum treatment*" period would be three to five years, with longer periods of psychotherapy to follow (emphasis in original). It was only "possible" that such treatment would be successful in rehabilitating the youth.

Under the youth-focused approach to the 1992 provisions that was adopted by the appeal courts in Ontario, Quebec, and Nova Scotia, if a youth was charged with a serious offence which might merit a longer sentence than three years (or five years for murder) in terms of societal accountability, then transfer might be considered. If in this situation a youth court was of the opinion that a youth could not be rehabilitated by a sentence of three years in the youth system (or five years less a day for murder), the youth had to be transferred to the adult system, where he or she would be incarcerated for a longer period and society afforded

---

41   (1993), 86 C.C.C. (3d) 214 at 218 (Ont. C.A.). In a vigorous dissent, Weiler J.A. adopted the broader interpretative approach of the Alberta Court of Appeal.

42   (1993), 14 O.R. (3d) 705 (C.A.), leave to appeal refused (10 March 1994), (S.C.C.) [unreported] [*C.(D.)*].

protection, at least during the period of incarceration. On the other hand, if the youth was likely to be rehabilitated within the time and facilities provided under the *YOA*, the youth was not to be transferred since both the protection of the public and the needs of the youth could be "reconciled" under the *YOA*.

While the approach of the Alberta courts rested in part on the notion that society's protection is enhanced by giving youths convicted of violent offences longer sentences for purposes of general deterrence, there is significant evidence that increasing the severity of sentences or increasing the transfer rate has no real effect on violent young offenders. As observed by MacEachern C.J.B.C. in arguing against a transfer:

> If I thought for a moment that there was any real possibility that a four year sentence for this youth would deter some other youth from committing the same or any other offence, then I would naturally balance that against the advantages of trying to rehabilitate this offender. I believe sending this youth to prison may possibly deter some other youth from offending, but none of the scientific material I have read, including various reports of the Canadian Law Reform Commission and the Canadian Sentencing Commission persuade me that a long sentence is any more useful for this purpose than a moderate sentence.[43]

The courts in Nova Scotia, Ontario, and Quebec generally gave little or no weight to general deterrence as a factor in interpreting the 1992 version of section 16(1.1).

As noted, the words of section 16(1.1) required that the youth courts give paramountcy to the protection of society if the objectives of the "protection to the public" and "rehabilitation of the young person . . . cannot be . . . reconciled" in the youth system. In all provinces the courts accepted that under the 1992 provision there continued to be an onus on the applicant, invariably the Crown, to show that the "protection to the public" and the "rehabilitation" of the youth could not be reconciled in the youth system, and in that sense there continued to be a requirement for the applicant to satisfy the youth court of the need to transfer the case. However, in practical terms, in cases involving homicide charges or a prior history of serious violence, there was already a tactical burden on the young person to satisfy the youth court that rehabilitation was likely to occur within the sentencing provided under the

---

43   *R. v. D.(E.L.)*, [1992] B.C.J. No. 1696 (C.A.) (QL), in a dissenting opinion.

YOA, and hence that the protection of society could be secured without transferring the youth.[44]

For courts that adopted an approach that focused on the youth, expert evidence about the youth's condition, amenability to treatment, and future dangerousness was especially significant, though it was relevant in all jurisdictions.

M. A CONCLUDING COMMENT ON THE 1992 TRANSFER TEST

The judicial controversy over the interpretation of the 1992 amendments is hardly surprising given the ambiguity of section 16(1.1) and the disagreement over the interpretation of the 1984 transfer provisions. It is not easy to be certain of what was the "intent of Parliament" in enacting section 16(1.1) in 1992.

As discussed below, the 1995 amendments *seem* to be clearer than the 1992 provisions and would *appear* to specifically limit the factors to be considered in assessing the dual interests of society, namely, rehabilitation of the youth and the protection of the public. This may imply that the 1992 test was intended to be broader. It may be ironic, but the 1995 amendments, purportedly intended to "toughen" the *YOA*, actually introduce a new section 16(1.1) that appears to focus exclusively on the youth before the court and preclude consideration of broader societal concerns like accountability and general deterrence.

N. THE 1995 AMENDMENTS: MURDER SENTENCING

Relatively few youths (twenty-five to sixty per year) are charged with murder, and the majority of these are ultimately convicted only of manslaughter since the Crown cannot prove that the often unpredictable and senseless acts were deliberate homicides.

---

44 Under the provisions of *YOA*, above note 11, s. 16 as originally enacted, counsel for young persons were regularly adducing evidence about amenability to rehabilitation in transfer hearings. See *R. v. S.(G.)* (1991), 5 O.R. (3d) 97 (C.A.), leave to appeal to refused (1992), 6 O.R. xiii (note) (S.C.C.)[(S.(G.)], where Goodman J.A. stated (at 109) [emphasis added]: "It seems to me that in a case such as the one under consideration, where the facts disclose a brutal killing, *the offender should ensure that evidence* [is provided to the court] that the offender is likely to be rehabilitated in a three-year period (if such is or can be made available). . . ."

For youths *not* transferred to adult court, the maximum sentence set out in the 1995 amendments is ten years for first degree murder, with a maximum six years in custody and the balance on conditional supervision, presumptively served in the community.[45] For second degree murder the maximum sentence in youth court is seven years, with a maximum initial sentence of four years in custody and the balance on conditional supervision. (See Table 1.) These are maximum custodial sentences, and in appropriate cases youth courts can impose shorter sentences or release earlier on review. However, it seems likely that most judges will view the 1995 amendments as a signal to impose long sentences for murder.

These relatively long youth court sentences for murder will require custodial arrangements for "young offenders" who will ultimately be in their mid-twenties. Presumably, most will be released on community supervision before reaching the age of twenty, or will be transferred into adult correctional facilities by youth court order under section 24.5 of the *YOA* sometime after reaching their eighteenth birthday. This provision allows provincial correctional officials to apply to youth court for an order transferring a "young person" over eighteen into an adult provincial correctional facility; the court shall order such a correctional transfer if it is in the "best interests" of the offender or in the "public interest," but the provisions of the *YOA* concerning such issues as disposition review and records will continue to apply.

To limit the overlap between the youth system sanctions and the adult system sanctions, the minimum periods for parole eligibility for transferred youth who are sixteen or seventeen at the time of the offence and are convicted of murder in adult court were increased in the 1995 amendments to ten years for first degree murder and seven years for second degree murder.[46] Transferred youths who are under sixteen at the time of the offence and are convicted of murder will have life sentences with parole-eligibility dates set in the range of five to seven years.[47]

One might expect that the effect of the longer youth court sentences and longer periods to adult court parole eligibility, *considered alone*, should tend to *decrease* the number of youths facing murder charges who are being transferred, since these changes will tend to make youth

---

45 *YOA, ibid.,* s. 20(1)(k.1).
46 *Code*, above note 25, s. 742.1, as am. by *An Act to amend the Young Offenders Act and the Criminal Code*, S.C. 1995, c. 19, s. 38.
47 *Code, ibid.,* s. 744.1.

court sentences seem more appropriate for murder. However, any assessment of the total effect of the 1995 amendments on transfer has to also take account of other changes in the section 16 test.

O. TRANSFER TO ADULT COURT UNDER THE 1995 AMENDMENTS: SECTION 16(1.1)

The *YOA*, as originally enacted, stipulated that transfer was to occur if a youth court was satisfied that this was "in the interest of society . . . having regard to the needs of the young person." Not surprisingly, there were great differences in the judicial interpretations of this vague standard, with the result being enormous variation in how youths in different provinces were treated.

The 1992 test for transfer was *somewhat* more structured than the 1984 test. The primary test is the "interest of society," which "*includes* the objectives of affording protection to the public" and the "rehabilitation of the offender" (emphasis added). The 1992 provision specifies that, if these latter two objectives can*not* be reconciled by the youth remaining in the youth system, then the "protection of the public shall be paramount" and the youth transferred. It did not, however, specify what is to occur if both *can* be reconciled but rather left the vague concept of the "interest of the public" as the dominant factor.

The 1995 provisions that deal with transfer are complex (see Table 1). For youths under sixteen, there is an onus under the new section 16(1) for the applicant, invariably the Crown, to apply to the youth court for transfer and satisfy the court that transfer is necessary. Section 16(1.01) applies to youths sixteen and seventeen years- old and charged with:

- murder;
- attempted murder;
- manslaughter; or
- aggravated sexual assault.

For those youths, section 16(1.01) provides that prosecutions are presumptively to be dealt with in adult court, but the youth may seek "transfer down" by applying to youth court. For any other situation, the prosecution is presumptively in youth court, with the onus on the applicant, invariably the Crown, to satisfy the youth court that transfer is appropriate.

For all situations, the 1995 test for transfer is

16.(1.1) In making the determination . . . [whether to transfer] the youth court . . . shall consider the interest of society, which includes the objectives of affording protection to the public and rehabilitation of the young person, and determine whether those objectives can be reconciled by the youth being under the jurisdiction of the youth court, and

(*a*) if the court is of the opinion that those objectives can be so reconciled, the court shall

   (i) in the case of an application under subsection (1), refuse to make an order that the young person be proceeded against in ordinary court, and

   (ii) in the case of an application under subsection (1.01) [reverse onus for 16 and 17 year olds charged with listed offences], order that the young person be proceeded against in youth court; or

(*b*) if the court is of the opinion that those objectives cannot be so reconciled, protection of the public shall be paramount and the court shall

   (i) in the case of an application under subsection (1), order that the young person be proceeded against in ordinary court in accordance with the law ordinarily applicable to an adult charged with the offence, and

   (ii) in the case of an application under subsection (1.01), refuse to make an order that the young person be proceeded against in youth court.

(1.11) Where an application is made under subsection (1) or (1.01) [the provision for 16 and 17 year olds charged with murder, attempted murder, manslaughter or aggravated sexual assault], the onus of satisfying the youth court of the matters referred to in subsection (1.1) rests with the applicant.

The 1995 test for transfer *appeared* to clarify some of the issues that have arisen in the conflicting jurisprudence under the 1992 law. The 1995 version of section 16(1.1) seems to indicate that the "interest of society" includes *only* an assessment of rehabilitation of the youth and protection of the public. Arguably, factors such as accountability and the value of fully accessible public hearings, which, for example, influenced the Alberta courts in applying the 1992 test, should *not* be taken into account.

Notwithstanding the change in the words of the *YOA*, it would appear that Alberta judges are still prepared to consider these broader societal factors in transfer cases. For example, in *R.* v. *C.(R.)*, the first reported Alberta case under the 1995 law, a seventeen-year-old youth applied to be tried in youth court under section 16(1.01) for attempted murder and armed robbery. Brownlee Prov. J. ordered the charges dealt with in adult court, commenting:

> I take judicial notice that where there has been a home invasion . . . by a gang or group of youths, where a gun is used or life threatening words have been inflicted, as in the case here, the *public mood* in the City of Calgary is such that the public looks to the courts to use *general deterrence and denunciation*, amongst other principles, as criteria in determining such issues as transfer and sentencing.[48]

The 1995 amendments did not explicitly resolve the judicial controversy that arose in interpreting the 1984 and 1992 provisions about whether general deterrence should be a factor in assessing the "protection . . . [of] the public." Under the earlier provisions, some judges used general deterrence as a factor in favour of transfer in serious cases, since they believed that this would enhance the "protection . . . [of] the public." As a matter of statutory interpretation, one would expect that general deterrence should not be a factor under section 16(1.1), since otherwise the individualized assessment of the youth contemplated by that section will not occur. If accountability or general deterrence were to be factors, one might expect that all very serious charges should be transferred, but the new provisions clearly do not contemplate automatic transfer for any offence. Further, all available social-science evidence indicates that increasing the number of youths transferred does *not* have any deterrent effect on other offenders or enhance the protection of society.[49]

In interpreting section 16(1.1), consideration also should be given to the 1995 amendments to the Declaration of Principle, found in the new section 3(1)(c.1), which provides that "[t]he protection of society . . . is best achieved by rehabilitation, wherever possible . . . and rehabilitation is best achieved by addressing the needs and circumstances of a young person." This statement of parliamentary intent supports the view that the appropriate interpretation of section

---

48   [1996] A.J. No. 909 (Prov. Ct.) at (QL) para. 60 [*C.(R.)*]. [Emphasis added].
49   There is a significant amount of American research that indicates that increasing the transfer rate in a jurisdiction does not produce any reduction in youth offending. M. Frost, J. Fagan, & T.S. Vivona, "Youth in Prisons and Training Schools: Perceptions and Consequences of the Treatment — Custody Dichotomy" (1989) 40 Juv. & Fam. Ct. J. 1; S. I. Singer & D. McDowall, "Criminalizing Delinquency: The Deterrent Effects of the New York Juvenile Offender Law" (1988) 22 Law & Society Rev. 521; E.L. Jensen & L.K. Metsger, "A Test of the Deterrent Effect of Legislative Waiver on Violent Juvenile Crime" 40 (1994) Crime & Delinquency 96.

16(1.1) should focus on the youth before the court and his or her amenability to rehabilitation.[50]

This argument, that accountability and general deterrence should not be factors in interpreting section 16(1.1), has not, however, been accepted by the courts in the first few reported decisions under the 1995 provisions. As noted above, Brownlee Prov. J. clearly considered general deterrence, denunciation, and accountability in ordering a seventeen-year-old youth tried in adult court in *C.(R.)*.[51] This decision is consistent with Alberta cases decided under the 1992 law, but this interpretative approach taken to the 1995 provisions appears to ignore the significance of the change in the transfer test.

For fourteen- and fifteen- year-olds (12 out of 123 in 1995–96), even those charged with murder, the new test in section 16(1.1) combined with the longer sentences for murder in the youth system and the longer period before parole eligibility in the adult system may well result in a decrease in the number of transfers.

The first reported Ontario decision under the 1995 provisions, *R. v. O.(D.)*, involved a youth just under sixteen at the time of an alleged first degree murder. There was no clear explanation offered for the killing, but at the transfer hearing the judge accepted that the "most probable" explanation seemed to be that the youth felt that he had been "dissed" (disrespected) by the deceased. Expert evidence and testimony about the youth's background revealed a history of behavioural problems and school difficulties but no prior criminal record and no clearly identified mental-health problems or personality disorder. As a consequence of having no diagnosis of mental or psychological disorder, medical experts were unable to give clear evidence about the length of time that would be required to rehabilitate the youth. Judge Cole refused the Crown's transfer application, concluding:

> In summary, I cannot say with any certainty that the interest of society and the rehabilitation of the respondent cannot be reconciled by the respondent remaining within the youth court system. Mindful of the need for restraint in the invocation and application of the criminal law process, in the absence of clear evidence, I feel it is only right to revert to the "default" position.[52]

---

50   S. 3(1)(c.1) was cited in a 1997 transfer decision, albeit under the 1992 test, as a basis for focusing on the youth before the court and her amenability to rehabilitation; *R. v. W.(J.)*, (27 February 1997), (Ont. Prov. Ct.) [unreported], Cousineau Prov. J.

51   Above note 48.

52   *O.(D.)*, above note 8 at para. 171.

It would seem that the question of onus for this fifteen-year-old youth was crucial to the outcome in *R. v. O.(D.)*.

The shift in onus under section 16(1.01) for sixteen- and seventeen-year-olds charged with the four designated offences may result in more of these youth being transferred, though it would seem from the case law under the 1992 transfer provisions that relatively few cases will be decided differently because of the change in onus.[53] Under the 1984 and 1992 provisions in transfer cases involving violent offences and older youth, judges indicated that they would not transfer if the prospects of rehabilitation in the youth system were "sufficiently promising."[54] Conversely, in cases where an older youth facing a charge like murder was not able to satisfy the court that rehabilitation was "likely" to occur in the youth system, but only was "possible," transfer was ordered.[55] That is, in practice there was already a tactical onus on the youth to adduce evidence of amenability to rehabilitation within the youth system. Thus, the shift in onus created by the 1995 law should have only a limited impact.

YOA sections 16.1 and 16.2 (allowing transferred youths to remain in a youth custody facility by court order) and section 24.5 (allowing a youth court to transfer a convicted "young offender" from a youth facility to a provincial adult facility after the age of eighteen is reached) will continue to provide flexibility over the place where sentences are served. Those youths who are transferred under section 16(1) may nevertheless serve a significant portion of the "adult" sentences in youth facilities because of sections 16.1 and 16.2, while those who are not transferred may still serve part of their sentences in an adult correctional facility after reaching the age of eighteen because of section 24.5.

Police and prosecutors may also have a significant effect on the number of transfers. In many situations involving sixteen- and seventeen-year-old youths, like aggravated sexual assault, there will be significant police or prosecutorial discretion about whether to lay a charge with a presumption of transfer; in cases involving some lesser offence, like sexual assault causing bodily harm, the onus remains on the Crown to satisfy the court of the necessity for transfer. In the form first proposed, the 1995 amendments would have included aggravated assault in

---

53   For cases that illustrate that even under 1992 provisions there was a significant onus on the youth to adduce evidence of amenability to rehabilitation, see *R. v. B.(R.V.)*, [1994] A.J. No. 41 (C.A.) (QL), and *R. v. S.(M.)*, [1994] M.J. No. 302 (Prov. Ct.) (QL). For a case that might have had a different outcome, see *W.(A.C.)*, (1993), above note 40.

54   *R. v. P.(P.)*, [1994] B.C.J. No. 150 (C.A.) (QL).

55   *C.(D.)*, above note 42.

the section 16(1.01) list of offences for which there would be an onus on the older youth to justify not having the case in adult court. This would have resulted in many more transfer hearings (there were 212 such charges in 1992–93 for sixteen- and seventeen- year-olds, compared to only 69 for murder, manslaughter, attempted murder, and aggravated sexual assault). Aggravated assault was removed from the list in section 16(1.01) after hearings of the justice committee of the House of Commons because of concerns that there would be a huge increase in the number of transfer hearings.

The 1995 transfer provisions were evidently intended to give the *public* the *impression* of a tough new regime for violent youth, especially sixteen- and seventeen- year-olds, and they raise the corresponding spectre of relatively large numbers of adolescents serving sentences in adult correctional facilities, with their relatively brutal atmosphere and lack of appropriate services. It seems likely that the net effect of the 1995 changes to the *YOA* will be *an increase, but not* a huge increase, in the number of transfers.

P. ONUS ON THE YOUTH IN TRANSFER PROCEEDINGS: SECTION 16(1.01)

An important feature of the 1995 amendments was the introduction of situations in which a sixteen- or seventeen- year-old youth will be dealt with in adult court, unless the young person (or the Crown) successfully applies under section 16(1.01) to a youth court judge to have the case dealt with in youth court. Section 16(1.11) specifies that the onus is on the applicant to satisfy the youth court that the test of section 16(1.1) is met, namely, that protection to the public and the rehabilitation of the young person can be reconciled in the youth system. If this onus is not met, the youth will be tried in adult court. Section 16(1.01) applies only to the most serious charges: murder, attempted murder, manslaughter, and aggravated sexual assault.

Section 16(1.11) makes clear that the "onus" is on the applicant (invariably the youth) to satisfy the youth court that the case should be tried in youth court. As Brownlee Prov. J. stated, technically this should not be described as a "reverse onus" provision but rather as a provision that places a "tactical" or "procedural" burden on the applicant.[56]

---

56 *C.(R.)*, above note 48. In this case, the judge stated that, "since the onus rests upon the young person," the youth was required to call his witnesses first.

The burden in a section 16(1.01) proceeding is both "tactical," in the sense that the youth must adduce evidence to satisfy the court, and also "persuasive," in the sense that if the court is left uncertain as to whether the protection of the public and the rehabilitation of the youth can both be satisfied in the youth system, the case shall be heard in adult court. However, in regard to the conduct of the transfer hearing, a judge has the authority and "flexibility" to control the presentation of the case. It would, in particular, seem unfair to require the youth to call police and other potential Crown witnesses who could testify about the "circumstances of the offence" and lose the opportunity to cross-examine these witnesses. Consistent with *Charter* cases, where the persuasive onus is also on the applicant to exclude evidence, the judge should be able to ensure a fair process, which may sometimes require the Crown to call its evidence first,[57] even though the ultimate persuasive burden is on the youth. This may also ensure a more logical "flow of testimony." In some cases, a judge may even decide to call certain witnesses (identified by counsel) as the court's witnesses to give both counsel an opportunity of cross-examination.

Q. *CHARTER* CHALLENGES TO SECTION 16(1.01)

It has been argued by defence counsel that section 16(1.01) is unconstitutional, but these arguments have not been accepted by the courts. The arguments have been largely based on age discrimination, in violation of section 15 of the *Charter*, since sixteen- and seventeen- year-olds face a burden not placed on younger young persons, and on section 11(d) of the *Charter*, as a violation of the presumption of innocence.

In *R. v. C.(R.)*[58] the Alberta Youth Court rejected a number of *Charter* challenges to the new provisions. Brownlee Prov. J. focused on the "procedural" nature of the amendments, and he observed that the transfer provisions of 1984 and 1992 also created age-based differences (between twelve and thirteen year olds and older young persons) and had been held constitutionally valid. Similarly, in *R. v. P.(M.G.)*, Davies J. concluded that the new provisions do not affect the presumption of innocence. In rejecting a section 15 *Charter* argument, the judge noted that sixteen- and seventeen- year-olds do not constitute a "discrete and insular"

---

57   See D. Stuart, "Annotation to *Kutynec*" (1991) 12 C.R. (4th) 153.
58   Above note 48.

minority who could claim to be "historical" victims of discrimination. Even if the *Charter* were violated, Davies J. ruled that section 1 of the *Charter* could be invoked, since these provisions were justifiable to protect the public. However, Davies J. did rule that section 15 of the *Charter* required that section 38 of the *YOA*, prohibiting publication of identifying information about a young person, should apply to a youth in a section 16(1.01) situation until after resolution of any transfer proceeding.

It is true that sixteen- and seventeen- year-olds are treated differently by the 1995 amendments. However, the transfer provisions have always treated youths fourteen and over differently from those under fourteen who could not be transferred, and the courts have consistently rejected arguments that this difference in treatment violates the *Charter*.[59] If a section 15 argument were successful in regard to section 16(1.01), similar arguments could be made to challenge the entire transfer scheme on the basis that youths fourteen and over are discriminated against in comparison to those under that age.

R. FACTORS FOR THE COURT TO CONSIDER: SECTION 16(2)

Although the interpretative approach a court takes to sections 16(1.1) and 16(1.01) is important, the specific factual circumstances, reflected in the factors listed in section 16(2), will also be significant in any transfer case. While section16(1.1) adopted a new transfer test in 1992 and again in 1995, section 16(2) remains essentially unaltered since its original enactment in 1984. It reads:

> 16.(2) In making the determination referred to in subsection (1) or (1.03) in respect of a young person, a youth court shall take into account
>
> (a) the seriousness of the alleged offence and the circumstances in which it was allegedly committed;
> (b) the age, maturity, character and background of the young person and any record or summary of previous findings . . . of guilt under this Act or any other Act of Parliament . . .
> (c) the adequacy of this Act, and the adequacy of the *Criminal Code* . . . if an order were made under this section to meet the circumstances of the case;

---

59 See, e.g., *H.(A.B.)*, above note 3.

(*d*) the availability of treatment or correctional resources;

(*e*) any representations made to the court by or on behalf of the young person or by the Attorney General or his agent; and

(*f*) any other factors that the court considers relevant.

Subsection 16(2) of the *YOA* specifies that a youth court "*shall* take into account" the factors set out, but the list is intended only to serve as a guide to judges and not a mandatory "checklist" (emphasis added). The criteria in section 16(2) are *not* necessarily all significant in every case, but rather the judge is to determine which are the most relevant.[60]

S. SERIOUSNESS AND CIRCUMSTANCES OF OFFENCE: SECTION 16(2)(a)

Most of the reported transfer decisions involve the most serious offences such as murder, manslaughter, robbery, and sexual assault, though there have been cases involving less serious offences such as escaping custody or multiple charges of break and enter.[61] Some decisions appear to suggest that, for very serious offences, most notably murder, it is almost axiomatic that it is in the "interest of society" to have proceedings conducted in adult court. However, unlike the situation in some American states, it is clear from the Canadian legislation that there is no offence for which transfer is automatic. The seriousness of the offence is only one factor, albeit an important one, in assessing the "interest of society" in a transfer application.

In *R. v. H.(E.E.)* Sherstobitoff J.A. of the Saskatchewan Court of Appeal refused to order the transfer of three youths charged with second degree murder, stating: "The facts of the alleged murder in this case, given that all murders can be said to be brutal and vicious, do not by themselves require transfer to adult court."[62]

An important factor when assessing the "circumstances and seriousness" of the offence is the youth's role and "degree of participation" in the alleged offence. Thus, a court will be less likely to transfer a youth who

---

60   See, e.g., *R. v. M.(A.J.)*, (1986), 73 A.R. 52 (Q.B.).

61   Statistics Canada, *Canadian Centre for Justice Statistics, 1994–95*, above note 20, reports that 123 were transferred, of which 82 were violent offences and 29 property offences. In most or all of the cases involving less serious charges, such as break and enter (15), the "young persons" were actually 18 years or older at the time of the transfer hearing and often were also facing charges in adult court for incidents that occurred after they became adults.

62   (1987), 54 Sask. R. 304 at 309 (C.A.).

is a party to a murder as a result of having acted as a lookout but who did not have a significant role in carrying out the physical acts of violence. As observed by Goodman J.A.: "[I]t is self-evident that a young person who delivers the death blows to a victim is more likely to be a threat to the safety of the public than one who is an aider or abetter, and perhaps a somewhat reluctant one, to a murder."[63] Conversely, there is a greater tendency to transfer where a youth has a role as an instigator or principal participant, or where a homicide seems particularly brutal[64] or deliberately executed as opposed to more spontaneous.[65] A premeditated murder, especially one that appears "recreational" or to be motivated purely by greed, seems more reprehensible. Rehabilitation of such offenders is likely to be more difficult and any concerns about accountability and deterrence are weighted strongly in favour of transfer in these cases.[66]

A number of decisions have held that "gang related" offences should also be viewed more seriously as denunciation and general deterrence weigh heavily in favour of transfer, especially if the case involves the death of a victim.[67] Involvement in a gang may also support an argument that a youth has adopted a set of values and attitudes that will make rehabilitation much more difficult.

If a young person commits a serious offence while already in youth custody, this is an aggravating factor, since it indicates that the youth corrections system may not be adequate to protect society. Concern with such cases also reflects the desire to protect staff and youth in custody facilities.[68]

Judges are more likely to transfer a youth who is charged with acts of violence, especially murder, that are committed against strangers, particularly if it occurs in the course of commission of a robbery or rape.[69] Conversely, there is a more sympathetic approach in cases where a youth commits an act of violence against a family member, such as a

63 S.(G.), above note 44 at 108.
64 As noted in R. v. K.(C.J.), [1993] M.J. No. 74 (C.A.) (QL) by Helper J.A., in a case where a youth charged with second degree murder was not transferred: "All murders are violent, brutal and shocking. I make no attempt to minimize the violence involved in this offence. However, I have no hesitation in stating that some murders are more violent and more brutal and more shocking than others."
65 See, e.g., R. v. R.(S.) (1991), 1 O.R. (3d) 785 (C.A.).
66 See, e.g., R. v. P.(L.), [1992] O.J. No. 871 (Prov. Div.) (QL) where three youths were transferred on murder charges arising out of the alleged planned, "recreational" killing of a friend; and, e.g., R. v. F.(D.M.), [1992] B.C.J. No. 705 (C.A.) (QL) where two youths were transferred for involvement in an alleged "contract killing."
67 P.(K.N.), above note 36.
68 R. v. W.(R.), [1995] O.J. No. 3627 (Prov. Div.) (QL) Youth transferred for attempted murder charge based on an attack on a staff member at an open-custody facility.
69 See, e.g., R. v. I.(J.), [1993] O.J. No. 3123 (C.A.) (QL).

parent, especially if the act is reflective of an emotionally difficult family life. The familial circumstance is not a justification for the offence, but it may mitigate against full societal accountability and offer a somewhat better prognosis for rehabilitation.[70]

T. AGE, MATURITY, AND RECORD: SECTION 16(2)(b)

Some decisions consider the age of the youth and, in particular, the closeness to eighteen, as an important factor in transfer proceedings. In considering age, courts generally[71] focus on the date of the alleged offence, not the date of the hearing.[72] However, in assessments of the possible effects of transfer, some account may be taken of age as of the date of the hearing.

In *R. v. M.(C. R.)* the Manitoba Court of Appeal dealt with a young person who was one week away from the age of eighteen at the time of the alleged offence.[73] The age of the youth seemed to be an important consideration in deciding to transfer the case. The trial court noted that the youth was not "a person of tender years." Similarly, in *R. v. S.(G.)*, the Ontario Court of Appeal ordered a youth facing a murder charge transferred, noting that it was "influenced . . . by his age, as he is now nineteen years old and for all other purposes an adult."[74]

---

70   See, e.g., *R. v. C.(D.)* (1993), 14 O.R. (3d) 705 (C.A.) (youth charged with murder of mother and attempted murder of father not transferred). But contra *M.(G.J.)*, above note 1 (fifteen-year-old charged with murder of mother, stepfather, and two sisters transferred). See also J. Toupin, "Adolescent Murders — Validity of Typology and Study of Their Recidivism" in A.V. Wilson, ed., *Homicide: The Victim-Offender Connection* (Cincinnati: Anderson, 1993)

71   However, in cases where charges are not laid until the accused "youth" is well into adulthood, transfer may be more appropriate. See *R. v. J.(W.W.)*, [1992] Y.J. No. 232 (Terr. Ct.) (QL) where a twenty-six year-old was transferred for various sexual offences alleged to have occurred more than a decade earlier.

72   See *R. v. Z.(D.A.)*, [1992] 2 S.C.R. 1025 at 1048–49 where Lamer C.J. remarked: "It would be unjust to subject a person to a higher standard of accountability merely because of his or her age at the time of the trial. . . . It is the age of an accused at the time of the offence which must determine the appropriate measure of accountability and not his or her age at the time of being charged or tried."

73   (1987), 46 Man. R. (2d) 315 (C.A.), aff'g (1986), 46 Man. R. (2d) 317 (Q.B.) [*M. (C.R.)*]. See contra *R. v. C.(D.)* (1986), 43 Man. R. (2d) 246 (C.A.) where the same court refused to transfer a young person charged with second degree murder who was just a few weeks short of his eighteenth birthday at the date of the alleged offence.

74   *R. v. S.(G.)* (12 December 1989), (Ont. C.A.) [unreported] [summarized] (1989), 9 W.C.B. (2d) 222].

However, age is not always decisive, as in *R. v. H.(S.J.)* where the young person was one month short of his eighteenth birthday and was charged with the first degree murder of his mother, but was not transferred. Glube C.J.T.D. stated:

It is my view that although the current age of the person may be beyond the age of 16, the person is looked at as a young person for purposes of the transfer and for other considerations namely, the interest of society and the needs of the young person.[75]

Maturity was considered in *R. v. H.(D.P.)*, where a youth was charged with indecent assault, gross indecency, sexual assault, and buggery. The judge granted the transfer application, in part because of the youth's maturity and sophistication, stating:

The accused has been living independently at a Bible College in the State of Iowa from January to May of 1986 and he intends to return there to complete his program. He has no prior record of offences. He has a Grade 12 education, has been involved in school sports, and apparently is not involved in the consumption of alcohol and drugs. As a result of this background, I have concluded that he has a considerable degree of adult maturity.[76]

Although it may seem a little ironic that the youth's lack of record and his stable background should be considered as "maturity" for the purposes of transfer and in effect "held against" the youth, other cases have similarly suggested that "the gravity of the alleged offence is greatly increased by the young person's good background, high level of intelligence [and] lack of psychiatric or psychological illness."[77] These circumstances may render transfer more appropriate since the youth should be more accountable for his acts.

While some reported decisions seem to place little weight on the age of the young person, there is a much greater reluctance to transfer youths who are fourteen- or fifteen years of age at the time of the alleged offence.[78] The reluctance to transfer fourteen- and fifteen- year-olds will

---

75 *H.(S.J.)*, above note 5 at 170.
76 (19 January 1987), (Man. Prov. Ct.) [unreported] [summarized 2 W.C.B. (2d) 39].
77 See *R. v. M.(D.M.)*, [1992] B.C.J. No. 705 (C.A.) (QL).
78 Statistics Canada data from 1994–95 Statistics Canada, Canadian Centre for Justice Statistics, *1994–95*, reports 109,743 cases, of which 123 were transferred; 3 youths were 14 years (at date of alleged offence); 9 were 15 years; 41 were 16 years; 64 were 17 years; and 3 were over 17 (presumably facing charges relating to violation of youth court orders). For 3 the age was not known. In all, 117 were male and only 6 female.

probably be increased by the 1995 amendments, with onus placed clearly on the Crown to justify transfer and with longer maximum sentences for murder in youth court.

The prior record of convictions of a young person is an important factor in a transfer case. Although not always determinative, the longer and more serious the record of prior offences, the greater the likelihood of transfer, especially if the record involves violent offences. When assessing the character of a youth, and especially whether there has been a history of violence that may make transfer more appropriate, courts will consider not only the history of convictions but also other evidence of violence which did not result in charges being laid.[79] A longer history of violence, especially of acts of increasing seriousness, makes transfer more likely, while a shorter history of violence or misconduct that starts later in adolescence suggests a better prognosis for treatment and makes transfer less likely.

In assessing the character and amenability to rehabilitation of a youth, good conduct and response to treatment while in detention pending a transfer hearing may be important factors in convincing a court not to transfer a youth.[80] Conversely, a youth who is disruptive in a detention facility or engaging in abusive behaviour towards other youths or does not seem motivated towards rehabilitation is much more likely to be transferred.[81]

U. ADEQUACY OF LEGISLATIVE PROVISIONS: SECTION 16(2)(c)

Section 16(2)(c) requires the court to consider the "adequacy" of the *YOA* in comparison to the *Criminal Code* "to meet the circumstances of the case." If the judge feels that a sentence of longer than the three-year maximum (or ten years for first degree murder) is required, then a transfer to the adult system may be appropriate. On the other hand, if there is no need to provide for incarceration or treatment beyond the three- (or ten-) year maximum, there is little need to make the transfer.

Where the length of likely dispositions in both the young offender and adult systems is the same or similar, section 16(2)(c) may have no

---

79 See, e.g., *O.(D.)*, above note 8. Court considers conduct as far back as kindergarten.

80 *W.(A.C.)*, above note 40.

81 *M.(G.J.)*, above note 1.

application; the legislative provisions are equally adequate, and transfer is less likely.

When comparing the adequacy of a *YOA* disposition to an adult criminal sentence, it should be appreciated that a youth who is sentenced in adult court will generally be eligible for parole after serving one-third to one-half of his sentence and will normally be subject to mandatory release prior to completion of the sentence. Early release under the *YOA* is judicially controlled and occurs less frequently than the early release of adult offenders.

In most cases judges compare the "real time" likely to be served in each system, as opposed to "paper time"— the sentences courts impose.[82]

V. AVAILABILITY OF TREATMENT OR CORRECTIONAL RESOURCES: SECTION 16(2)(d)

In many transfer applications under the 1984 provisions, the relative availability and suitability of treatment and correctional resources in the adult and youth systems was a central issue in the transfer proceedings. While this type of evidence is still significant, the effect of the 1992 amendments has been to diminish its weight. Evidence is often called with regard to the resources available in the two systems, and expert witnesses, both correctional and mental-health professionals, are often called in order to help assess the amenability of the young person to treatment in each system.

Judicial perceptions of the suitability of the different correctional systems for rehabilitating young persons have varied considerably. This variation may, at least in part, be a reflection of differences between systems in different provinces. For example, in Manitoba one of the factors that seems to have encouraged transfers is the judicial perception that the security and rehabilitative services available in the youth system are not suitable for dealing with the problems of many of the most violent young offenders.

In most provinces judges have generally emphasized the potential harm to a young person placed in an adult facility and the superior rehabilitative resources of the youth system. In 1989 the Ontario Court of Appeal refused to transfer six youths charged with a brutal sexual assault, emphasizing the potential risks to young offenders in the adult system, including the risk of physical attack, of becoming involved in

---

82 See, e.g., *R. v. C.(T.P.)*, [1993] O.J. No. 719 (Prov. Ct.) (QL).

involuntary homosexual activities, and of having to accept the "codes of behaviour" of an adult facility.[83]

In most provinces, the youth corrections system has generally been regarded as having superior educational and rehabilitative resources for adolescents and young adults to either the provincial or federal adult systems. Further, placing a young person with adult offenders has been recognized as posing significant psychological and physical risks for the youth. While it may be that for some offenders, especially older adolescent sexual offenders, there may actually be better treatment programs in the adult system, judges have also recognized that even if the rehabilitative programs and services in the federal system are more suited to a particular young offender, the negative effect of the adult "environment," including the increased risk of exposure to drugs, alcohol, and inmate abuse, weigh against transfer.[84]

In some cases, the court indicates that the young person has exhausted "all the resources" in the youth system and that this is a reason for transfer. What this usually means is that the youth has been sentenced by the youth court on previous occasions and that a variety of alternatives has been tried, including secure custody, or that the youth was a detri-

---

83   See, e.g., *R. v. S.(W.)* (1989), 69 C.R. (3d) 168, 47 C.C.C. (3d) 72 (Ont. C.A.). There is relatively little rigorous empirical research on the long-term effects of imprisonment, in particular on those who are adolescents or young adults at the time that a sentence is commenced; see Bonta and Gendreau, "Reexamining the Cruel and Unusual Punishment of Prison Life" (1990), 14 Law & Human Beh. 347. However, it is believed by those who work with offenders that such sentences are psychologically destructive. See John Howard Society of Ontario, *Jailing Kids in Adult Prisons* (Toronto, March 1990), which describes many of the concerns about placing youths in adult facilities. The Society writes: "We think the admission of young people into adult institutions is absolutely abhorrent and unnecessary. Young offenders are recognized as not having the degree of maturity which would warrant that they be handled as adults. Every day we see adults in our prison system who are barely able to survive in the hostility and fear which predominates in these places. The prospect of placing a young person, who has already demonstrated his/ her immaturity and lack of responsibility, into such a damaging environment is terribly short-sighted." The Society quotes a penitentiary inmate: "Terrible crimes will always shock us, but the truth of youth in prison would shock us more than the most terrible of crimes. Young people know what it is to die each day in prison. . . . How would a child with an unformed body and undeveloped mind know better? Rather than condemn them to share the ultimate adult horror, we should help them by seeing them at the very least remain in places designed for the young. No society should allow its children to be raped, tortured and murdered as punishment. If we are to change the youthful offenders' act, then let's never confine them in adult facilities or consider punishing them as adults."

84   *R. v. L.(R.A.)*, [1995] B.C.J. No. 2459 (C.A.) (QL).

mental influence on other youths in the youth system. It is not necessary for the Crown in a transfer application to prove that all resources in the youth system have been tried and failed,[85] but the fact that such an "exhaustion" of resources has occurred clearly supports transfer.

Difficult issues arise when a judge believes that the youth system should have resources available to help a youth but does not. In *R. v. M.(C.R.)* a young person charged with first degree murder was transferred, in part because "the facilities of the youth court system are not adequate to treat the youth for his severe alcohol problems."[86] It could be argued that making transfer orders in such circumstances will only help ensure that these programs, often badly needed in the youth system, will never be developed in the future. In *Re E.(N.G.)* Kimelman A.J.C.M. commented:

> I think there is responsibility on the part of the provincial government to arrange for adequate programs for the likes of this boy and its failure to do so should not be a good reason for transferring a 15 year old boy to the adult system for the purpose of enabling him to be sent to the penitentiary.[87]

Hearing evidence with regard to the availability of resources in both systems can be time-consuming for a youth court dealing with a transfer case. Information about the two systems is sometimes provided in a predisposition report, though in contested cases corrections officials from both systems are likely to testify. Defence counsel may also call their own expert witnesses; these may be, for example, from the John Howard Society or even former inmates. Consideration of the adequacy of resources raises the question of whether a youth court judge deciding a transfer case may take "judicial notice" based on their personal knowledge of the resources and facilities available in the two systems. If the judge takes judicial notice, the demands on the court's time and the delays inherent in transfer proceedings can be reduced, but there may be concerns about whether the judge's information is accurate. It is apparent that some judges, especially those who deal regularly with transfer cases, are relying on their personal knowledge. While this may

---

85   See *R. v. M.(D.)* (1990), 61 C.C.C. (3d) 129 (Ont. C.A.) [*M.(D.)*].

86   *M.(C.R.)*, above note 73. Some American courts have accepted that juveniles should not be penalized by the "realities" of the youth correctional system. In the United States some judges have responded to this type of situation by refusing to transfer youths or ordering that adequate facilities be provided. See *J.E.C. v. Minnesota*, 225 N.W.2d 245 (1975).

87   (8 August 1986), (Man. Prov. Ct. (Fam. Div.)) [unreported] [summarized [1986] W.D.F.L. 2096].

be appropriate, it should be indicated to the parties so that they may call evidence to rebut any judicial misapprehensions.

The addition of sections 16.1 and 16.2 in 1992 has made the relative availability of treatment and correctional resources and the relative rehabilitative potential of the two systems less of a factor than it was in the past, especially in the most typical situation where the youth system is superior. These provisions now allow judges to keep an offender in the youth corrections system even after transfer, while section 24.5 of the *YOA* permits those youths who are not transferred but are eighteen or over when serving their sentences to have the benefit of any facilities and programs in the adult system.

This flexibility has made some judges less reluctant to transfer, since the youths who are transferred may not be placed in adult facilities until after reaching adulthood. In *R. v. M.(G.J.)*, the Alberta Court of Appeal discussed the 1992 amendments and commented: "[T]he statutory machinery available for the appropriate placement of a young person who has been transferred to the adult system has been usefully widened by the amending provisions."[88]

A comparison of adult and youth facilities is not, however, totally immaterial under the 1995 amendments, since a youth who is transferred is *more likely* to spend at least part of the sentence in an adult facility, while one sentenced in youth court is *more likely* to serve all of the sentence in youth custody facilities.

W. "OTHER RELEVANT FACTORS": SECTION 16(2)(f)

The treatment of co-accused individuals is a factor in transfer decisions, but it is never determinative. Courts will consider the involvement of adults who are charged with the same offence and will face trial in adult court. In *R. v. M.(D.)* a seventeen-year-old youth was transferred on nine charges, including three counts of attempted murder, where there were several adult co-accuseds. The Ontario Court of Appeal cited with approval the comment "While not determinative in and of itself, in the interests of avoiding multiplicity of proceedings as well as inconsistent verdicts and uneven sentencing the presence of adult co-accused in this case clearly weighs in favour of transfer."[89]

88   Above note 33 at 130.
89   *M.(D.)*, above note 85 at 130.

However, as the Quebec Court of Appeal noted in refusing to transfer a seventeen-year-old youth charged with attempted murder and with being a party to a first degree murder along with an adult:

> [F]or Parliament it [the involvement of an adult co-accused] did not have the same importance as the criteria that it took the trouble to enumerate [in s. 16(2)]. Nor is this rule found at the level of the principles . . . set forth in s. 3 of the Act.
>
> Strictly applied, the principle of equal treatment would fundamentally contradict the very existence of the special treatment program for young offenders.[90]

The argument for transfer based on the fact that there is an adult co-accused is especially weak if the adult was the prime instigator of the offence and the youth a follower. Indeed, there is an argument against transfer if the youth was "easily influenced, being induced or persuaded by a dominant adult person," especially if the youth was intimidated or pressured into participating in the offence.

When young persons are co-accused facing very serious charges, it is common to have a joint-transfer hearing. While a desire for fair treatment often suggests that both should be treated in the same fashion, the courts have made clear that each is to be considered as an individual. In *R. v. R.(E.S.) and R.(W.J.)* the Manitoba Court of Appeal dealt with two co-accused youths charged with attempted murder. Hall J.A. stated: "Each accused must be viewed separately. Both should be treated the same if the circumstances warrant but it does not have to be the case. . . . It is only one factor to be taken into account."[91] The court in that case emphasized that one youth was older and had a more serious previous record and worse prospects for rehabilitation; he was transferred but the other youth was not transferred.

If a "young person" is over eighteen and is also facing charges in adult court related to conduct since turning eighteen, this will strongly favour transfer. Section 16(4) of the *YOA* provides for an expeditious transfer procedure in relation to an offence alleged to have been committed "while the young person was being proceeded against in ordinary court pursuant to an order previously made" under section 16(1). Section 24.5(2) allows youth correctional officials to transfer to an adult correctional facility a "young offender" who has reached the age of eighteen and is sentenced to a concurrent adult sentence after reaching eighteen.

---

90 *R. v. D. (John Robert)* (1988), Y.O.S. 88–206 (Que. C.A.)
91 (1985), 49 C.R.(3d) 88, 36 Man. R.(2d) 276 (C.A.).

306 YOUNG OFFENDERS LAW

There are situations in which the young person does not contest transfer or may even make the application to be dealt with in adult court. One circumstance in which this might occur is when the accused is at or past his or her eighteenth birthday at the time of the application and would prefer to be sentenced in adult court. In such situations the young person may believe that, given relative sentencing and release patterns, less time may actually be spent in custody if the case is transferred. A transfer order cannot simply be made on a "consent basis"; the court must always be satisfied that transfer is "in the interest of society." However, the fact that the young person is not opposing transfer or is requesting it should be a "relevant factor" under section 16(2)(f), though it should not be determinative, and the court should assess the youth's reasons for taking this position.[92] Unopposed applications can often be dealt with quite expeditiously.

X. REVIEW: SECTION 16(9)

Section 16(9) of the *YOA* provides for the "review" by a provincial Court of Appeal of the decision of a youth court on a transfer application. The Court of Appeal may, in its discretion, confirm or reverse the decision of the youth court. There is also the possibility of seeking leave to appeal to the Supreme Court of Canada against the decision of a provincial Court of Appeal in a transfer case.

The 1989 decision of the Supreme Court of Canada in *R. v. M.(S.H.)* made clear that a "review" is broader in scope than an "appeal," with McLachlin J. concluding:

> Section 16(9) and (10), by conferring on the reviewing court the "discretion" to confirm or reverse, establish different rules for the review than normally apply on appeals, where the court is limited to correction of error. The reviewing body's function must be to "review" the decision, and then, "in its discretion", confirm or reverse it. This involves evaluation, not only of whether the court below made an error of law or jurisdiction, but of whether its conclusions are correct based on the factors set out in the Act. *In short, the reviewing tribunal can go into the merits of the application.* If this review leads to the conclusion that the decision below was wrong for any of these reasons, the reviewing court in the exercise of its discretion may substitute its own view for that of the judge below.

---

92 *Re G.(D.E.)*, [1993] A.J. No. 103 (Prov. Ct.) (QL).

There is, however, an important limit on the power of the review tribunal. Because it has not heard the evidence, it must accept the Youth Court's findings of fact and defer to it in matters involving the credibility of witnesses. . . . it is a fundamental rule that review tribunals which have not had the advantage of hearing and seeing the witnesses should defer to the trial judge who has had this advantage.

In summary, it is my conclusion that the review court *must base its review on the facts found by the Youth Court judge and give due deference to the Youth Court judge's evaluation of the evidence.* It must then proceed to apply the factors set out in s. 16(2) to that evidence. In applying these factors, the review court is *not confined to asking whether the youth court judge has erred, but should make an independent evaluation on the basis of the facts found by the Youth Court judge.*[93]

This passage is widely cited by appellate courts as giving a broad scope for "review"; however, appeal courts do not want to take too broad an approach to their powers or there may be lengthy review proceedings in every transfer case.

Y. REFORMING THE TRANSFER PROVISIONS

The 1992 reforms to the transfer provisions of the *YOA* provided a more flexible and appropriate statutory regime for dealing with youths charged with very serious offences. The reforms resulted in a relatively small increase in the number of transfers, but these transfers still remain a tiny fraction of all cases.[94] Although some might argue that the 1995 changes were necessary to increase social protection, there is no evidence that longer sentences for young offenders produce lower levels of youth crime, and there are significant concerns that placing more youths in adult correctional facilities may actually increase levels of crime in the long term.[95] Somewhat ironically, youth court data indicate that charges for the most violent youth offences dropped from 1992 to 1995, suggesting that more punitive legislation did not need to be enacted in 1995 to reduce youth offending.[96]

---

93   Above note 23 at 465–66. [Emphasis added].
94   Until 1995, transfers averaged less than 100 a year out of over 100,000 youth court charges.
95   Bishop, Frazier, Lanza-Kaduce & Lonn, "The Transfer of Juveniles to Criminal Court: Does It Make a Difference?" (1996) 42 Crime & Delinquency 171.
96   Statistics Canada, *Youth Court Statistics*. Murder charges fell from 45 in 1992–93 to 32 in 1993–94 and 25 in 1994–95; attempted murder was down from 75 charges to 52 and 36 in 1994–95; aggravated assault dropped slightly from 311 to 309 in 1993–94 and to 251 in 1994–95; manslaughter, however, went from 10 to 7 to 24 charges in this period.

Virtually every country that has a youth justice system which is separate from and less punitive than the adult system has some mechanism to have longer adult-like sentences for a relatively small number of youth offenders. The Canadian model of transfer to adult court based on individualized judicial determinations is preferable to the regimes in several American states that are based on prosecutorial discretion or automatic transfer for specified offences.

However, a better regime for Canada for the problem of very violent offences would be to abolish pre-adjudication transfer but permit individualized judicial decisions about longer sentences under the *YOA*, in certain limited circumstances.[97] In appropriate cases, before a youth enters a plea, the Crown could inform the youth and the court that a sentence of longer than five years may be sought, and then give the youth the option to have a jury trial. In the event of conviction, the issue of an unusually long sentence and possible placement in adult prison could be dealt with on a post-adjudication basis, when the circumstances of the offence are fully known. If no pre-adjudication notice were given, the youth could receive only a maximum sentence of three years.

FURTHER READINGS

BALA, N. & H. LILLES, eds., *Young Offenders Service* (Toronto: Butterworths, 1984) (looseleaf), s. 16

BALA, N. "The 1995 *Young Offenders Act* Amendments: Compromise or Confusion?" (1995) 26 Ottawa L. Rev. 643

CANADA, FEDERAL-PROVINCIAL-TERRITORIAL TASK FORCE ON YOUTH JUSTICE, *A Review of the Young Offenders Act and the Youth Justice System in Canada* (Ottawa: Supply & Services, 1996), ch. 8

HARRIS, P.J., ed., *Young Offenders Act Manual* (Aurora: Canada Law Book, 1984) (looseleaf)

PLATT, P., *Young Offenders Law in Canada,* 2d ed. (Toronto: Butterworths, 1995), ch. 14

SCOTT, S., M. WONG, & B. WEAGANT, *Defending Young Offender Cases,* 2d ed. (Toronto: Carswell, 1997), ch. 8

---

97   See Canada, House of Commons Committee on Justice and Legal Affairs, *Reviewing Youth Justice* (1997), 63–65, which endorses this recommendation except for cases within s. 16(1.01).

CHAPTER 10

CANADIAN YOUTH CRIME IN CONTEXT

A. APPROACHES TO YOUTH JUSTICE: CANADA IN AN INTERNATIONAL CONTEXT

Concerns about adolescent irresponsibility, rebellion, and offending date back through history to Roman times and are common in all modern societies.[1] This is not, however, to suggest that patterns of offending are the same in all societies. To the contrary. While some level of youthful deviance is an inevitable part of the adolescent stage of development, a host of complex, interacting social, economic, political, cultural, and legal factors all influence the nature and extent of youthful offending. Currently, Canada is going through a period of rapid and profound change, and this is influencing adolescent behaviour as well as societal perceptions and reactions to that behaviour.

Canada has a serious youth crime problem, but, contrary to public perceptions, it is not a problem that is spiralling out of control and it may well be no worse now than it was a decade ago. We are, however, experiencing increasing police charging of adolescent offenders and rising amounts of media reporting of youth offenders, as well as an unprecedented level of political attention to the issue of youth offending with accompanying demands for "tougher" laws.

---

1   K. Onstad, "What Are We Afraid of? The myth of youth crime" (1997) 112:2 Saturday Night 46.

Canada has higher rates of youthful violence than many Common-wealth and European countries, but we clearly have a much lower rate of serious youth violence than in the United States, especially if the comparison focuses on youth homicide rates. However, Canada relies on a formal youth-justice-system response and youth custody to a greater extent than other countries. This type of response is an expensive and often ineffective way to combat youth crime, but its inability to reduce levels of offending creates demands for ever more punitive responses, while its expense creates a growing justice-corrections industry that can lobby for ever more resources.

B. CRIME PREVENTION THROUGH SOCIAL DEVELOPMENT

Youth in Canada are experiencing a number of interrelated social, economic, and cultural conditions which are producing self-destructive and socially costly adolescent behaviour, such as suicide and drug and alcohol addiction, as well as offending. Youth unemployment is high by historical and international standards, while child and youth poverty is increasing. More children than ever are growing up in single-parent families, and youth are inundated with a popular culture that seems to glorify violence and instant gratification. While none of the problems faced by youth will have an easy, quick, or inexpensive solution, a social-investment strategy that focuses resources on children and adolescents at risk will have positive effects for a range of social problems. Failing to address these problems adequately will result in enormous social and economic burdens in the future.

Dr Fraser Mustard, one of Canada's most eminent scholars and social commentators, has warned of the costs of not undertaking a social-investment strategy that directs resources to children at risk, in particular those growing up in poverty:

> The higher the degree of income inequality, the harder it is to get economic growth because your society is becoming more destabilized. You just can't build an economy with an unstable society because you have to put too many people in prison and lock them up and shift too many resources into policing and all kinds of things. . . . It's probably how you were handled before the age of three and certainly before the age of six that basically sets your rhythm for adult life. . . . To build a new economy you actually need a high quantity of well-educated population. If you degrade children then they're going to be permanently

handicapped as adults and it's going to be very difficult to build a new economy and it also leads to juvenile crime and delinquency problems.[2]

The federally appointed National Crime Prevention Council has also written eloquently on the economic and human value of a "crime prevention through social development" strategy that focuses resources on children at risk, in particular at the elementary and pre-school level.[3] The Council cites a number of well-documented long-term studies of programs aimed at young children from economically and socially disadvantaged backgrounds; these are children with a high risk of experiencing social and legal difficulties later in life. Early intervention programs for children and parents which increase a child's social and educational capacities will substantially reduce later adolescent and adult offending, teen pregnancy, and welfare use as adults. Children who participate in these programs are more likely to develop the social and intellectual skills as well as the attitudes and values that will help them succeed at school and resist participation in socially destructive adolescent behaviour. These intensive early intervention programs do not eliminate such problems as youth offending, but they do reduce it significantly and produce substantial economic and social returns.[4]

The value of a crime-prevention strategy based on social development was accepted in the 1995 amendments to the Declaration of Principle of the *YOA*, with section 3(1)(a) now recognizing that

> crime prevention is essential to the long-term protection of society and requires addressing the underlying causes of crime by young persons and developing multi-disciplinary approaches to identifying and effectively responding to children and young persons at risk of committing offending behaviour in the future.

---

2   J. Hall, "Rough waters ahead," *Toronto Star* (1 September 1996) E1 at E2.

3   National Crime Prevention Council, *Money Well Spent: Investing in Crime Prevention* (Ottawa: The Council, 1996).

4   One of the most famous long-term studies is of the Perry Preschool in Ypsilanti, Michigan. An expenditure on a pre-school program of about $5,000 per child produced an average savings in criminal justice, social welfare, and other costs of $29,000 by the age of twenty-seven. L.J. Schweinhart *et al.*, *Significant Benefits: The High/Scope Perry Preschool Study Through Age 27* (Ypsilanti, MI: High/Scope Press, 1993). Research is being undertaken to replicate this type of long-term research in Canada; see, e.g., R. Peters & C. Russell, "Promoting Development and Preventing Disorder: The Better Beginnings, Better Futures Project" in R. Peters & R. McMahon, eds., *Preventing Childhood Disorders, Substance Abuse and Delinquency* (Thousand Oaks, CA: Sage, 1996) 19–47.

A social-development response to youth crime has great human and financial advantages. Unfortunately, it also is a long-term strategy. Resources invested today will produce a return over the lifetimes of the children and adolescents who are helped. While there is clearly symbolic support for this approach, too often when Canadian politicians, who face reelection every four or five years, are making resource decisions, the time horizon for a return on a social-development approach to crime prevention seems too far away to make the investment attractive. Indeed, in times of fiscal restraint, it is frequently prevention and early intervention programs that are the first to be cut, since resources are concentrated on responding to those who have already committed crimes. It is only through public education and political support that our society will adopt a preventive approach. While crime cannot be eliminated through a social-development strategy, in the long term this is the most effective way to reduce youth crime and produce a safer, healthier, and wealthier society.

C. COMMUNITY ACTION AND POLICING

While a social-development strategy premised on early intervention with children at risk can produce a social environment in which fewer adolescents are committing fewer crimes, there are more immediate steps that communities can also take which will reduce levels of youth crime. Some of these measures involve schools, families, and adolescents in programs that make it less likely that youth will commit crimes; other strategies are aimed at improved policing and other security measures that deter criminal behaviour.

Community-based preventive programs that are directed at adolescents with a high risk of offending can reduce crime. Programs that involve families and schools, and help youth deal with such issues as anger management, can have an effect on youth crime. Some of these programs may involve recreational or cultural activities and focus on developing positive social values. It must, however, be appreciated that the adolescents who are at the highest risk of serious repeat offending are often the most difficult youths to engage in voluntary school-based or recreational programs, and the more closely programs can be targeted at high-risk youth and engage them, the greater their impact is likely to be.

Concern about crime prevention should be a factor in any decisions about policies and programs for adolescents. Careful consideration should, for example, be given to the effect of a "zero tolerance" policy for violence in schools. While steps must be taken to deal with violence and to protect students and teachers in schools, the students who are engaging in offending behaviour in schools are also those with the greatest need for assistance from the education system. It may be necessary to remove such students from regular schools settings, but, if they are not placed in alternative educational settings where they will receive substantial supervision, direction, and support, they are likely to commit more serious offences in the future.

It is clear that a general deterrence-based model of youth sentencing will not increase social protection. That is, lengthening the time that youth spend in custody or increasing the number of youth transferred into the adult system does not reduce levels of offending. Adolescents who are likely to offend are not giving any thought to getting caught, let alone to the penalties that might be imposed by the justice system.

While "tougher" sentencing will not reduce youth crime, improved and more visible policing efforts in communities where there are serious youth-crime problems can have some effect. Although some adolescents will not be affected by an increased police presence, others will be deterred since increased police visibility serves as a reminder of the likelihood of apprehension. Further, an increased police presence can change the social atmosphere in high-crime areas, giving potential victims a greater sense of security and encouraging positive social values.

Commentators believe that the 15 percent decline in American youth-homicide rates between 1994 and 1995 is in part attributable to increased policing in high-crime areas.[5] Canadian police forces are moving towards "community policing" and focusing more attention on prevention of youth violence by having an increased presence and involvement with schools and community agencies.[6]

For police to be successfully engaged in prevention and response to youth crime, specialized education and training are needed. Many police forces identify officers with the personality and temperament for this type of work, and have specialized youth bureaus or designated officers to do it. Such officers need to have good working relationships with a range of social agencies and the schools.

As noted, Canada makes more use of a court-based response than other countries, but there is substantial variation between provinces in charging rates and use of custody. Most of the responsibility for initial charging and entry into the court system rests with the police. Police

---

5   C. Krauss, "New York City's Gift to Clinton: A Lower National Crime Rate," *New York Times* (1 September 1996) E5.

6   See, e.g., *Police Reference Manual on Youth & Violence* (Ottawa: Solicitor General of Canada, 1994).

need to appreciate the limitations of the traditional court-based response, and they also require training and policies that will encourage use of diversion and alternative measures.

D. RESPONDING THROUGH THE YOUTH JUSTICE SYSTEM

While efforts at prevention have great potential to reduce levels of youth crime, there will always be some role for a youth-justice response with the objectives of providing accountability and a sense of justice for victims of crime, as well as a need to provide rehabilitative services.

For most young offenders, a formal court-based response is not required and is too intrusive and expensive. We need to make more use of expeditious, informal, community-based responses to youthful offending, such as police cautioning and restorative-justice approaches that involve community members and victims, as well as offenders and their parents. Section 3(1)(d) of the *YOA* recognizes the value of making no formal response and of using diversion, and section 4 allows for alternative measures programs to be established. Section 69 provides for the establishment of community-based youth justice committees which can work with the youth justice system (for example, by providing alternative measures). But these provisions have not been adequately used. More community-justice and alternative measures programs with wider mandates need to be established. Many youth who are now dealt with by the courts pose little risk to their communities and can better be dealt with outside the formal youth court system. A response that involves the community has especially great potential for Aboriginal offenders.

Some young offenders have serious problems that relate to their offending or have committed serious offences. These youth require a more intrusive response and should be identified and targeted for intervention. In our society, if there is to be an intrusive criminally based response, this gives rise to the need for respect of legal rights and access to a formal court-based system.

There is clearly a need for research and monitoring of what types of programs, facilities, and responses are most effective for serious offenders or those who do not respond to informal intervention. While there is a need for more knowledge, much is already known. A purely custodial response based on deterrence of the individual youth or other adolescents is unlikely to provide social protection. Responses must be individualized to meet specific needs that are relevant to offending.

Most serious young offenders have problems that can be amelio-
rated by working with their family and community. Even those young
offenders who have genetic, physiological, or neurological conditions
related to their offending behaviour, like fetal-alcohol syndrome or a
learning disability, will often benefit from this type of response. There
is significant research evidence that, for most young offenders, the
interventions that are most likely to reduce the risk of reoffending have
a significant link to their community, families, and schools.[7]

For many young offenders, the most effective dispositions will be
community based. These dispositions will ordinarily have a component
of accountability, but, if a youth has serious problems that are related to
the offending, there must also be measures that will address these problems too. In order for a youth court to be able to identify and address
problems, judges must have adequate information about the youth; this
will often require an assessment prepared by a competent professional.
Judges also need to have access to appropriate resources for intervention with young offenders.

While too many youths are in custody in Canada, some youths display offending behaviour and related problems that are sufficiently
severe that removal from the community is required. Still, unless the
underlying problems of the individual young offender are identified and
addressed in custody, the custodial placement is likely to be an expensive but ineffective exercise. Custody facilities that are relatively small,
close to the offender's home, culturally appropriate, and properly
resourced are usually best. If a period in custody is required, close
supervision and support after return to the family and community are
critically important to reducing chances of recidivism.

At least symbolically, the value of rehabilitation was explicitly recognized by the 1995 amendment to the *YOA*, which added section
3(1)(c. 1) to the Act's Declaration of Principle:

> the protection of society, which is a primary objective of the criminal
> law applicable to youth, is best served by rehabilitation, wherever pos-
> sible, of young persons who commit offences, and rehabilitation is
> best achieved by addressing the needs and circumstances of a young
> person that are relevant to the young person's offending behaviour;

There were also amendments to section 24.1 which direct youth
court judges to consider community-based dispositions in all cases not

---

7   See, e.g., National Crime Prevention Council, above note 3; and R.A. Silverman &
    J.H. Creechan, *Delinquency Treatment and Intervention* (Ottawa: Department of
    Justice, 1995).

involving serious personal injury. While these are important signals from the federal government to the judiciary, there are likely to be significant reductions in custody use only if provincial and territorial governments take steps to increase the availability of community-based programs. The federal government can influence provincial and territorial decisions in this regard through its cost-sharing programs. The *YOA* could also be amended to give judges a broader power to fashion community-based dispositions that meet the needs of young offenders.

There is also a need for better education and training for lawyers and judges who work in youth courts. All professionals who work with adolescent offenders should have at least basic knowledge about adolescent behaviour and needs, as well as training to improve communication with these troubled youths.

Although not all young offenders can be rehabilitated, Canada can certainly do more to help adolescent offenders overcome their problems and become productive, law-abiding adults.

E. RECOGNIZING THE LIMITS OF THE LAW

The youth justice system and legislation like the *YOA* obviously have an important role in the societal response to youth crime, but the limitations of the legal response must be appreciated. No piece of legislation can by itself provide safer communities.

There is a substantial amount of research which demonstrates that the most effective long-term strategy for reducing levels of youth offending and producing adults who are generally mature, law-abiding, and productive members of society requires a long-term investment in social infrastructure and family support, with a particular emphasis on early childhood and pre-adolescent stages of life. For adolescents who are at high risk of serious or repeat offending, community-based programs that involve families and schools also can have an important role in diverting youth away from criminal behaviour, while for a minority of adolescent offenders custodial-based rehabilitation is necessary.

A response that emphasizes social investment in children and adolescents, without ignoring the role of the justice system for serious or repeat offenders, is dominant in countries in Western Europe which have lower youth crime rates than Canada.

Certain types of policing strategies and improvements to community-security measures can also have a role to play in reducing offending behaviour. It is, however, clear that a punitive model of juvenile justice, one that focuses on longer sentences or more transfers to adult court for young offenders, is not the answer. The United States has tried this deter-rence-based model of social protection and it has not achieved its objec-tives. A punitive response may serve the political function of appearing to "do something" about crime, but it does not lead to a safer society.

The folly of present Canadian approaches was recently recognized by the Manitoba Court of Appeal in *R. v. T.(B.).*[8] The Court upheld a decision to transfer a fifteen-year-old youth charged with armed rob-bery and attempted murder to adult court for trial. The youth, from a Laotian immigrant family, had a difficult background but was described as "very manageable" while in detention at the Manitoba Youth Centre. A psychologist testified that he was amenable to treatment and that it could be completed in two to three years. Unfortunately, there are no youth custody facilities in Manitoba that have treatment programs that last more than a few months, and the Court concluded that the youth therefore had to be transferred to adult court. Justice Monnin deeply regretted this result, and wrote:

> There is a crying need for a facility which would offer long-term inten-sive psychotherapy or psychological intervention. . . . That such a facility is not available is no doubt for the oft-cited reason of lack of funds. That is a shortsighted approach to the problems which society is facing today. . . . the authorities may wish to consider the desirability of improving the resources available for young people. This is surely the best approach to long term public protection.

Focusing on social development as a primary strategy for reducing youthful offending does not mean that there is no role for the youth jus-tice system. Social development takes a long time, and will never be fully successful in eliminating serious youth crime. The law has an important role in terms of social symbolism and support for victims.

The public rightly expects the legal system to provide "justice." Jus-tice requires fair treatment and due process for those charged with offences, but it also includes an important element of accountability to victims and society for those who are found guilty, though for adoles-cents this should be a lower level of accountability than for adults. There is as well a very small minority of adolescents who commit such serious offences and who pose such a threat to society that long-term incarceration is justifiable.

When considering issues of reform of the *YOA* and youth justice system, it is always important to assess realistically the function and

---

8   [1997] M.J. No. 97 (C.A.) (QL).

likely effect of any changes. Changes that make the youth justice system more punitive may serve political and symbolic functions for their advocates, but they will be expensive and not produce a safer society. Reforms that recognize that adolescents should be held accountable, but that also understand that such individuals are neither adults nor children and have special needs as well as capacities for personal change and development, are most likely to result in increased social protection.

FURTHER READINGS

BALA, N. et al., *State Responses to Youth Crime: A Consideration of Principles* (Ottawa: Canadian Research Institute for Law and the Family, 1993)

CANADA, HOUSE OF COMMONS, *Thirteenth Report of the Standing Committee on Justice and Legal Affairs: Renewing Youth Justice* (Ottawa: Supply & Services, 1997)

HORNICK, J.P., N. BALA, & J. HUDSON, *The Response to Juvenile Crime in the United States: A Canadian Perspective* (Calgary: Canadian Research Institute for Law and the Family, 1995)

HORNICK, J.P. & S. RODAL, *The Use of Alternatives to Traditional Youth Court: An International Comparison* (Calgary: Canadian Research Institute for Law and the Family, 1995)

NATIONAL CRIME PREVENTION COUNCIL, *Money Well Spent: Investing in Crime Prevention* (Ottawa: The Council, 1996).

PLATT, P., *Young Offenders Law in Canada,* 2d ed. (Toronto: Butterworths, 1995), chs. 2 and 23

SCHISSSEL, B., *Blaming Children: Youth Crime, Moral Panics and the Politics of Hate* (Halifax: Fernwood, 1997)

SILVERMAN, R.A. & J. CREECHAN, *Delinquency Treatment and Intervention* (Ottawa: Department of Justice, 1995)

GLOSSARY

accountability: the principle of intervention and sentencing that considers the responsibility of offenders for their acts and calls for a response that is proportional to the offence. Section 3(1)(a. 1) of the *YOA* declares that youths should be held accountable but generally not to the same extent as adults.

adult: a person eighteen years of age or older. Generally, age is established as of the date of the alleged offence.

adult court: the court that normally has jurisdiction over adult offenders. Technically referred to as "ordinary court" in the *YOA* s. 16, which provides for transfer of youth for trial and sentencing in ordinary court.

adversarial: a system of justice premised on each party having an obligation to present evidence and argument to support its position, though there are special obligations of fairness for the Crown prosecutor. A hallmark of the adversarial system is a judge who is neutral and relatively passive, whereas, in the inquisitorial model of justice that is used in some European countries, judges play a more active role in investigation and questioning witnesses.

aid and abet: an act by a "party" to assist or encourage another person in carrying out a crime; see "party."

alternative measures: a program outside the formal court system to deal with youth believed to have committed offences. Established under s. 4 of the *YOA*, some alternative measures programs operate "pre-charge" and accept police referrals of youth believed to have committed offences but who are not charged, while other alternative measures programs are "post-charge" and accept referrals of youth who have been charged.

bail hearing: a court hearing, usually held soon after the initial arrest, at which it is determined whether the accused will be detained in custody pending trial, or released, often with some conditions imposed, such as refraining from contacting the complainant. Technically referred to as a "judicial interim release" hearing in the *Criminal Code*. Also called a "show cause" hearing since the onus is generally on the Crown to "show cause" why the accused should not be released pending trial.

Canadian Charter of Rights and Freedoms: the part of the *Constitution Act, 1982*, that guarantees fundamental rights and freedoms of individuals in their relationship to the government and its agents. The *Charter* can be invoked by a judge to exclude evidence that was obtained by the police in violation of guaranteed rights if its admission in court proceedings "would bring the administration of justice into disrepute." In other cases, a *Charter* violation may result in a judicial stay of proceedings. The *Charter* is occasionally used to nullify pieces of legislation, as, for example, happened to abortion provisions of the *Criminal Code* in 1988.

child: for the purposes of the *YOA* the word "child" refers to a person under twelve who cannot be charged with a criminal offence. The term is sometimes used more broadly, for example, in the *United Nations Convention on the Rights of the Child*, it refers to anyone under eighteen, that is, not an adult.

complainant: the term used in the *Criminal Code* to refer to the alleged victim of an alleged offence. Though complainants often report to the police, sometimes allegations of an offence are made by others.

community-justice committee: a voluntary community group established to provide services, support or direction to youth involved in the justice system. Such a committee may be responsible for administering alternative measures or court-based programs or for advising judges or other officials. These committees may be sanctioned by provincial or territorial governments under s. 69 of the *YOA*.

community service: a disposition imposed by a court as a form of alternative measures. It involves the youth doing work for a community agency, municipality, or non-profit organization for a specified number of hours. If imposed by a youth court as a disposition under s. 20(1)(g) of the *YOA*, it is subject to conditions in s. 21 such as a maximum of 240 hours and the stipulation that performance is not to interfere with education.

Crown: refers to the government or prosecution team, including the police, in criminal and *YOA* cases. In some contexts, it refers to the lawyer who represents the Crown in court, who may also be referred to as the Crown attorney, prosecutor or attorney. Occasionally, if the Crown is unwilling to prosecute, cases are prosecuted "privately," typically by the victim or a lawyer acting on the victim's behalf, but this is rare in youth court.

custody: the most severe disposition that can be imposed by a youth court is to place a youth in "custody," which requires that the youth reside in a facility. Youth-custody facilities must not have any adult offenders confined with youths. They are designated as "open" and "secure," with youth court judges specifying the level of custody and correctional officials determining the specific facility within that level. There is significant variation in the size and nature of custody facilities between and within jurisdictions; some are just parts of an adult jail, while others are small treatment-oriented group homes.

delinquent: the term (juvenile) delinquent was developed in the nineteenth century to distinguish youthful offenders from adult criminals, who should be treated in a fashion that promotes their welfare, as reflected in the *Juvenile Delinquents Act,* in force from 1908 to 1984. Delinquent is sometimes used to mean a youthful offender.

determinate: for a specified period. The *YOA* has determinate custodial dispositions, while the *Juvenile Delinquents Act* allowed for indeterminate committal to training school.

deterrence: a principle of sentencing which holds that punishing offenders will cause a reduction in future offending because of a desire to avoid punishment. Courts consider both "specific deterrence," using punishment to inhibit reoffending by the person being sentenced, and "general deterrence," using the punishment of one offender as a warning to other potential offenders of the consequences of offending. Under the *YOA,* courts may consider both specific and general deterrence in sentencing a youth, but deterrence should not be considered as heavily as in the sentencing of adults.

disposition: the sentence imposed by a youth court under s. 20 of the *YOA* on a youth who has been found guilty of an offence. Technically, the term "sentence" is used for adult offenders, though in practice "disposition" and "sentence" are used synonymously for young offenders.

disposition hearing: the stage of the youth court process after a finding of guilt when the judge imposes the disposition (or sentence). In less serious cases, the disposition may be imposed immediately after a finding of guilt, but in more serious cases the proceedings will be adjourned to allow for the preparation of reports and other evidence for the disposition hearing.

disposition review: a disposition imposed under the *YOA* may be subject to "disposition review" pursuant to ss. 28 to 32 of the *YOA*, which may result in a reduction in the severity of a disposition. While the process may require a youth court hearing, if all parties agree there may be a "paper review" by a judge without a formal hearing.

diversion: refers to the idea that some youths who have committed offences should not be dealt with by formal youth court processes but rather should be "diverted" from the system and dealt with informally. Diversion includes both police screening and use of alternative measures pursuant to s. 4 of the *YOA*.

due process: a set of ideas related to the protection of legal rights in the criminal or youth justice system, in particular, providing for full participation of lawyers in that process and ensuring that important decisions are made by judges after a fair hearing. The trend towards adoption of a due-process model of justice in Canada was reflected and reinforced by the adoption of the *Canadian Charter of Rights and Freedoms* in 1982. The *Juvenile Delinquents Act* placed much less emphasis on due process than the *YOA*.

duty counsel: a lawyer paid by the provincial or territorial legal aid plan who is available to consult and assist those with an immediate need for legal assistance. Duty counsel may be at youth court or available to assist those individuals who are arrested by police. Most duty-counsel schemes involve lawyers from private practice, paid on an hourly basis, though in some places legal aid staff lawyers act as duty counsel.

expert evidence: evidence presented by a person who is accepted by the court as an "expert," based on educational qualifications and experience, and is permitted to express an opinion about technical or complex issues. In *YOA* proceedings the most commonly admitted expert evidence deals with mental-health issues and the likelihood of rehabilitation or future offending. Expert evidence may also be introduced to deal with forensic issues, like DNA evidence. Expert evidence may involve testimony by a witness, or, if not contested, it can be presented to the court by a written report.

forensic: to do with the court or investigation; for example, a forensic assessment of a youth may be conducted by a psychiatrist pursuant to s. 13 of the *YOA* to assist the court in determining whether the youth is mentally competent to stand trial. Forensic investigation by the police covers a range of scientific techniques to apprehend criminals, such as fingerprinting and DNA analysis.

hearsay evidence: a statement made by a person who is not a witness that is repeated by a witness in order to establish the truth of the statement. In general, a witness in a criminal trial cannot give "hearsay testimony" (that is, testify about something that another person — the so-called declarant — told the witness). There are a number of exceptions to the hearsay rule, and it is usually not applied at bail, disposition, or transfer hearings.

hybrid offence: see "summary offence."

indeterminate: without specified length. Under the *Juvenile Delinquents Act*, committal to training school was usually indeterminate, with a delinquent released when correctional officials believed that the youth was rehabilitated or the delinquent had reached adulthood (twenty-one). The *YOA* adopted determinate dispositions, that is, sentences of a specified length.

indictable offence: see "summary offence."

information: the sworn statement that a person (usually a police officer) makes before a justice of the peace to commence a criminal prosecution.

judicial interim release hearing: see "bail hearing."

judicial notice: a doctrine that allows a judge to make a decision based on "common knowledge" without receiving testimony or other evidence on the matter.

justice of the peace: the lowest level of judicial officer, usually not legally trained. Their responsibilities are limited in criminal proceedings, especially under the *YOA*, though they may conduct bail hearings. They have broader responsibilities, especially for adults, under provincial offence statutes (like *Motor Vehicle Acts*), including trials and sentencing.

Juvenile Delinquents Act: enacted in 1908 and in force until 1984 when replaced by the *Young Offenders Act*. The *JDA* placed much less emphasis on legal rights and had a child-welfare oriented (or *parens patriae*) philosophy.

obiter dicta   Latin for: "Thing said by the way." In an appellate court judgment, the *ratio decidendi* (the reason for the decision) is binding on lower courts, but the comments that are *obiter dicta* and not necessary for the judgment are only "persuasive" for future cases.

open custody: a place of custody designated as "open" by the provincial or territorial government, including community residential centres, group homes, child-welfare institutions, or wilderness camps.

opinion evidence: it is a general rule of law that witnesses can testify only about what they observed, but an "expert witness" can express an opinion or draw a conclusion. There are certain matters about which even a lay person can express an opinion in court, such as whether another person was intoxicated or seemed tired. See "expert evidence."

ordinary court: the technical term in the *YOA* for "adult court" (see above).

Parens patriae: Latin for "parent of the country." Refers to the child-welfare oriented philosophy reflected in the *Juvenile Delinquents Act*, with the judge acting as a "stern but wise" parent.

parent: defined in s. 2(1) of the *YOA* to include, in respect of a young person, "any person who is under a legal duty to provide for that . . . [young] person or any person who has, in law or in fact, the custody or control of that . . . [young] person, but does not include a person who has the custody or control of that . . . [young] person by reason only of proceedings under this Act." It may include a biological parent, a legal guardian, or, if the youth has been made a ward of a child-protection agency, that agency.

party: a person who helps ("aids or abets") another person (the principal offender) to commit an offence. A person is guilty as a party only if they have done some act to assist or encourage the principal, and they have a degree of knowledge or common intention related to the offence. A party is guilty of the same offence as the principal, though the court's disposition may be influenced by the degree of participation. See *Criminal Code*, s. 21.

plea: a declaration by an accused person to the court that they admit the charge (guilty) or that they require the prosecution to attempt to prove guilt (not guilty). There are other pleas that can be made, such as guilty but not criminally responsible because of mental disorder. *Autrefois acquit* or *autrefois convict* refer to pleas that can be made if the accused asserts that he or she cannot be tried for this offence since there was already a trial for the same offence that resulted in acquittal or conviction.

plea bargain: an agreement about the resolution of charges. Usually made between the Crown prosecutor and defence counsel, it specifies that the accused will plead guilty to one or more charges if the Crown drops other charges or agrees to make a "joint submission" about disposition. While the judge is not bound to follow a joint submission as to disposition, it is usually adopted by the court.

positivist philosophy: the positivist school of criminology developed in the nineteenth century premised on the notion that delinquency was a product of external forces, such as poverty, poor parenting or abandonment by parents, lack of education, and association with adult offenders.

pre-disposition report: a report on the personal and family history and present environment of a young person in accordance with s. 14. Often referred to as a "p.d.r." or "social history." Usually prepared for a disposition hearing, but also for a transfer hearing.

preliminary inquiry: a hearing held to determine whether there is sufficient evidence to require an accused person to stand trial for an alleged offence. Adults facing indictable charges generally have the right to a preliminary inquiry, but, in the case of young persons, they are held only for those who are transferred to adult court or who are facing a murder charge in youth court.

private prosecution: see "Crown."

progress report: a report on the performance of a young offender since the disposition was imposed, prepared for a youth court disposition-review hearing.

probation officer: see "youth worker."

provincial director: a person designated by the provincial or territorial government to carry out a range of duties in connection with the *YOA*, especially in regard to supervision of young offenders, such as determining which facility within the level of open or secure that a youth will be placed in. Each jurisdiction has a significant number of individuals with the designation of "provincial director."

R.: abbreviation for *Regina* (Latin for the Queen) or *Rex* (Latin for the King) in the "style of cause" (or name) of a criminal case, and refers to the prosecution, which in Canada is, in theory, brought in the name of the Sovereign, as in *Boucher* v. *R.* or *R.* v. *B.(A.)*. The v. is for versus (or against). For adults, the last name of the accused is used in the style of cause. For young persons, because of the prohibition on publication of identity in s. 38 of the *YOA*, law reports use the first initial of the last name, generally followed in brackets by the first and other initials).

recidivism: refers to repeat offending after being processed by the youth justice system for an earlier offence.

restitution: a court order or alternative measure that requires the offender to compensate the victim of the crime for the loss or injury. May be a sum of money or an order that the offender perform some services for the offender, if this is acceptable to the victim.

secure custody: a custody facility designated by a provincial or territorial government as "secure" by virtue of its physical attributes or staffing arrangements. Secure custody facilities typically are relatively large and are generally operated by the government.

show cause hearing: so called because of the onus on the Crown to "show cause" why the youth should be detained pending trial. See "bail hearing."

status offence: an offence that is a crime only for a person under a particular age, that is, having a particular status, namely being a "child" or "juvenile." There were a number of status offences when the *Juvenile Delinquents Act* was in force, such as the vaguely worded engaging in "sexual immorality." The *YOA* largely eliminated status offences, though some provinces retain truancy — the failure of a child under a specified age, usually sixteen, to attend school without lawful excuse.

stay of proceedings: to suspend court proceedings without resolution of guilt or innocence. A judge may, for example, stay proceedings if there has been an abuse of process. The Crown sometimes enters a stay: for example, if a youth is referred to alternative measures. A proceeding stayed by the Crown may be recommenced within one year (*Criminal Code* s. 579). Sometimes a violation of the *Charter* may result in a judicially ordered stay of proceedings.

summary offence: In the *Criminal Code* offences are categorized as indictable, summary, and hybrid. Indictable offences are the more serious offences, like robbery and homicide, for which adults may face longer sentences and generally have the right to a preliminary inquiry and a jury trial. A relatively small category of the least serious offences are summary offences, and adults charged with these offences must be tried by a "summary" process without a jury. Many offences, such as sexual assault and theft, are hybrid, with the Crown having an "election" (or choice) to proceed summarily or by indictment; for adults, if the Crown elects to proceed summarily, the maximum penalty is less, but the accused loses the opportunity to have a preliminary inquiry and jury trial. By virtue of s. 52 of the *YOA*, all proceedings against young persons in youth court (except murder) have a summary process (no jury or preliminary inquiry), though the offences retain their character as summary, hybrid, or indictable for such purposes as arrest. At the time of arrest, a hybrid offence, even for a young person, is regarded as indictable: *Interpretation Act* s. 34(1)(a). The

Crown will often "elect" in youth court to treat a hybrid offence as indictable, for such purposes as having a longer records-retention period [s. 45(1)] as well as the longer maximum sentence (generally six months is the maximum sentence for summary or hybrid offences treated as summary, whereas for hybrid offences treated as indictable under the YOA the maximum is two or three years in custody).

training school: the term most often used when the *Juvenile Delinquents Act* was in force to describe facilities that would today be secure custody (also called industrial school or reformatory).

voir dire: an inquiry in a trial to determine whether a particular piece of evidence, such as a confession of the accused to the police, is admissible in evidence. In a jury trial the jury will be excluded during a *voir dire,* while, if the judge is sitting alone, as is normally the case in youth court, the judge must not consider any evidence heard at the *voir dire* if it is ruled inadmissible. (The expression derived from Norman French — which was the language used in English courts in the Middle Ages — *vrai dire,* literally, to speak the truth.)

young offender: a young person (twelve through seventeen as of the date of the alleged offence) who has been found guilty of an offence.

young person: a person who is, or, in the absence of evidence to the contrary appears to be, twelve years of age or more but under eighteen. Section 2(1) of the YOA specifies that "where the context requires, [young person] includes any person who is charged . . . with having committed an offence while he was a young person or is found guilty of an offence under this Act." That is, even if a person has passed his or her eighteenth birthday, for most purposes a person alleged to have committed an offence while a "young person" will continue to be treated under the YOA for purposes for prosecution, sentencing, and disposition review.

youth court: the court designated by the provincial or territorial government as having jurisdiction over cases prosecuted pursuant to the YOA. In most jurisdictions it is at the Provincial or Territorial Court level.

youth worker: a person appointed by the provincial or territorial government to perform a range of functions in relation to the youth justice system, including preparation of s. 14 pre-disposition reports, supervision of youths on probation, and working with youths after release from custody on probation or conditional supervision. Often referred to as a probation officer ("p.o."). In some jurisdictions they have caseloads of only youths; in others they may work with both adult and youth offenders. In some places youth workers also do social work with non-offender populations.

TABLE OF CASES

INDEX

ABOUT THE AUTHOR

Nicholas Bala is Professor and Associate Dean of Law at Queen's University. He is one of Canada's most distinguished scholars in the area of youth justice. He is the author or co-author of numerous books and reports on youth justice including: *Canadian Children's Law* (1982), *The Young Offenders Act Annotated* (1983), and *Juvenile Justice in Canada* (1992). His work is frequently cited by the courts and his opinion is sought by policy makers at all levels.